THE BOOK ON

MANAGING RENTAL PROPERTIES

THE BOOK ON
MANAGING RENTAL PROPERTIES

A proven system for finding,
screening, & managing tenants with
fewer headaches and maximum profit!

By Brandon Turner

BiggerPockets PUBLISHING

The Book on Managing Rental Properties
Brandon Turner and Heather Turner

Published by BiggerPockets Publishing LLC, Denver, CO
Copyright © 2015 by BiggerPockets Inc.
All Rights Reserved.

ISBN
13 digit: 978-0-9907117-5-9 —10 digit: 0-9907117-5-7

Cataloging-in-Publication Data
Turner, Brandon, 1985—
Turner, Heather, 1985—
The Book on Managing Rental Properties: A proven system for finding, screening, & managing tenants with fewer headaches and maximum profit / Brandon and Heather Turner.
        p cm
ISBN 978-0-9907117-5-9
1. Real Estate Management 2. Real Estate Investment I. Turner, Brandon
II. Title

First printing: December, 2015   Second printing: June, 2016

Printed in the United State of America
10 9 8 7 6 5 4 3 2 1

Dedication

This book is dedicated to our parents, Rick & Lori and Shane & Rachel. Not only did you raise us to be financially wise, you also raised us to know that there are things far more important than money in this world. Thank you.

Table of Contents

Acknowledgments

Thousands of hours go into the creation of any book, and only some of those hours were our own. Therefore, we want to take a moment to thank the many individuals who helped put this book into its final form.

Thank you to Allison Leung, for your many hours spent editing our rough text.

For Mindy Jensen, for your diligent research into numerous aspects of this book, including the 50 state-specific rules/laws at the end!

For the BiggerPockets Book Launch Team who helped read this book before the launch and helped us hone in our message!

To Josh Dorkin, CEO of BiggerPockets, for your leadership in this book writing and publishing adventure and for taking a risk on us.

To the leaders in the BiggerPockets community who helped record interviews in preparation for this book's launch.

And finally, thank you to the BiggerPockets community, from who's shoulders we have long stood upon. Without your stories, lessons, guidance, and advice we would not be where we are today.

And to anyone and everyone we missed...
Thank you.

CHAPTER 1:
SO YOU WANT TO BE A LANDLORD?

This book was written for anyone who wants to make more money, work less, and have fun doing it.

For anyone who wants to build wealth while still maintaining a life.

For anyone who wants to travel more, freak out less, spend more time with family; for anyone who wants to maintain stability while rocketing their net worth into the stratosphere.

That's right, effective landlording can accomplish all these goals and can do so in powerful ways. You might be a first-time landlord, just struggling to get started with your first rental house. Or perhaps you are an experienced property owner, looking to find better ways to maximize your time so you can spend quality hours with your family and friends. Or maybe you are a property manager, looking after other people's properties for a fee and trying to improve your skills. Whatever your background is, if you want to improve your landlording skills, this book is for you.

We wrote this book for *learners*—people who don't have all the answers but are continually trying to improve their skills and pick up new tricks. It's for experimenters, those willing to hear new ideas and try them out in their own lives, willing to take the risk of trying something new to find a long-term solution to their problems. And it's for hard workers, those who don't believe success comes overnight, who are willing to get down and dirty and not give up with the first failure.

In short, this book is for you. If you want to see the power that effective management can have on your real estate investments and on your personal life, keep reading.

About the Authors

The beginning years of marriage are often the most blissful. Romantic dates, chocolate gifts—and real estate?

That's our story, anyway.

I (Brandon) first met Heather in college and instantly fell in love. That's no exaggeration: I remember seeing her across the lawn from my dorm room, and I said to myself before ever meeting her, "That's the woman I'm going to marry." Less than four years later, we tied the knot in an outside ceremony in the middle of the Quinault Rainforest, two hours from Seattle.

Instead of the traditional American story of getting solid jobs, moving to the suburbs, having 2.5 kids, and growing old, we decided to buck tradition and invest in real estate, foregoing law school to pick up a paint brush. After selling the home I had purchased before getting married, we bought a small fixer-upper duplex together in the small logging town of Hoquiam, Washington and immediately jumped into the world of landlording, knowing absolutely nothing about what that really meant—other than it *sounded* like a good idea.

(On a side note, that duplex, we soon discovered, had a very unique history. After repeated complaints from our tenants about people taking photos of the property, we learned that the duplex was the very first childhood home of Nirvana's frontman Kurt Cobain, who lived in both halves of the duplex during his first two years of life. Sadly, this factoid does nothing for our business, but it's a great conversation starter at parties and in landlording books!)

Over the next decade, we continued to acquire more and more rentals while continuing to manage them ourselves. We made every mistake in the book (which you'll hear about in the pages to come) and learned painful lessons along the way. However, we also discovered that *landlording success is NOT a mystery*. In fact, managing tenants is fairly routine once we learned how to do it correctly. We built relationships with other landlords to learn everything we could from their experiences, picked more brains than any person on earth should, read every landlording book we could get ahold of, and spent hundreds of hours learning and asking questions on the BiggerPockets Real Estate Forums.

Over time, we've gotten pretty good at this landlording thing. There is rarely a problem we haven't encountered before, and most of this has become second nature. Recently, one of our close friends purchased a duplex for themselves in the same manner we originally did. As they began to ask us questions and we noticed them making the same mistakes we did, we realized how new and foreign this whole "landlording thing" must be for them. As we tried to recommend books they should read, people they should talk to, and paths they should take, it occurred to us that no book existed that perfectly described a step-by-step process on how to be a successful landlord. There are some books with good theories, some books with good stories, and some books with good tips, but we wanted to offer our friends and fellow landlords a book that laid everything out in an easy-to-follow guide.

Hence, *The Book on Managing Rental Properties* was conceived.

What This Book Will Teach You

This book will teach you how to effectively manage tenants in your rental properties. We're going to share every trick, every tool, every system that we use to manage our rentals. You'll learn how to run a business that allows you more freedom, less drama, and higher profits. We'll share personal stories of the mistakes and successes we've had, as well as how you can succeed on this journey.

In Chapter 2 you are going to learn about the process of transitioning how you think about your landlording business. You'll learn the subtle differences that separate those who manage properties as a "hobby" and those who manage properties like a business.

Chapter 3 is all about getting your property ready to rent and what you need to have in order before getting there. You'll learn about the importance of market research in getting top dollar for your property. We'll also talk about property condition and the mistakes many landlords make when trying to get their property rent-ready.

Chapter 4 will focus on the Fair Housing Laws and making sure you stay out of legal trouble in your landlording business.

In Chapter 5 you'll learn how to market your property to get the most qualified applicants begging to rent from you. We'll share the best advertising tips, locations, and processes for making sure your property is filled quickly.

Chapter 6 is all about saving you time when trying to pick tenants by mastering the art of "pre-screening." You'll learn how to apply the 80/20 rule to your landlording to help you weed out the duds and only deal with great prospects.

In Chapter 7 we'll talk all about the application process and include a sample application and other sample forms that you can use in your own business. We'll walk you through each step of the screening process, including running background and credit checks, obtaining references and verifying income, and go over the red flags to look for from tenants. We will also go over how to accept or deny an applicant.

Chapter 8 is all about the lease, but don't worry, this isn't a bunch of legal theory! This chapter is all about how to find a good lease, what to include, and how to protect yourself as a landlord. We have also included a sample lease for your reference.

Chapter 9 will introduce you to our system for managing tenants and dealing with day-to-day interactions with tenants, including every landlord's favorite pastime: collecting rent and getting paid!

In Chapter 10 you are going to learn about handling the problems that will pop up in your landlording business—because there will be plenty of problems. It's how you handle those problems that will define your landlording career.

Chapter 11 discusses the topic of bad tenants and how to remove them from your property, both through the legal system and through some controversial yet powerful strategies.

In Chapter 12 you'll dive into the world of contractors, discovering the best way to find, harness, interact with, pay, and manage these individuals fundamental to your business.

When we get to Chapter 13, we'll look at the process of moving a tenant out of your property, focusing on the strategies that will keep the most money in your bank account.

Chapter 14 will look at the organizational structure of your business, from the office supplies you must have on hand to the bookkeeping that will not only keep you organized, but legal and profitable.

In Chapter 15 we'll wrap everything up by looking at 13 principles for being an incredible landlord. We'll pull together all the lessons gathered so far and make sure you are left feeling empowered to create a landlording business that will help you achieve your most ambitious life goals.

Finally, in the appendix of this book we have included samples of all the forms we use in our landlording business for your reference.

What This Book Won't Cover

This book is geared toward the management side of residential rentals: how to be a landlord. As such, we will focus very little on the investment strategy side of things. We're not going to teach you how to find incredible deals or how to finance those properties. We won't spend time on how to acquire rentals, build an investment strategy, set goals, or analyze the numbers. These skills are incredibly important to have, so Brandon wrote an entire comprehensive book on this one subject titled *The Book on Rental Property Investing*. We highly encourage you to pick up a copy of that book as well if you are looking to build a real estate empire.

Furthermore, this book is not going to teach you a bunch of theories that don't actually work. Everything in this book is actionable. It is designed to help give you tangible ideas for improving your landlording business based on our personal experience and the experiences of others within the BiggerPockets community.

What is BiggerPockets?

For those unfamiliar with the name, here is a quick rundown on how BiggerPockets can change your life.

Started by Josh Dorkin in the early 2000s, BiggerPockets is known as "The Real Estate Investing Social Network, Marketplace, and Information Hub." Fancy. Yes, it's a rather corporate-sounding slogan, but let us break it down a bit more for you.

Social Network: BiggerPockets is a social network, like Facebook, Twitter, and LinkedIn. But rather than sharing cat videos and photos of last night's dinner, BiggerPockets members engage with one another to help each other achieve greater wealth and financial freedom through real estate investing.

Marketplace: Secondly, because of the millions of people who come to the site each year, BiggerPockets has emerged as a major real estate marketplace where real-life deals are happening all the time. Sometimes it's in an official capacity when someone lists a property for sale in the BiggerPockets Marketplace (http://www.biggerpockets.com/marketplace), and sometimes it's just a result of people getting together on the site to work together on a project. No matter how, the truth is that business happens on BiggerPockets.

Information Hub: Finally, BiggerPockets is perhaps most well known for the sheer volume of information you can obtain for free on the site. Currently there are more than 1,500,000 forum posts, 40,000 blog articles, 140 podcast episodes, and hundreds of videos, interviews, and other content—all for free. In addition, through BiggerPockets Publishing real estate investors can purchase incredible real estate books like the very one you are reading right now.

BiggerPockets believes that real estate education should not be learned from some get-rich-quick, late-night TV guru for tens of thousands of dollars. Instead, we believe information is best learned in a community setting from those who are actively involved in real estate. You learn from me, I learn from you. Through our shared experiences, we can grow together to benefit everyone. That is the spirit of BiggerPockets.

As you read this book, you'll likely have more questions and want to dig in deeper. That's good! I would encourage you to dig into the BiggerPockets community for those answers. Search the site to see if your question has been asked (and answered) before, or start a new thread and ask for advice from thousands of experienced landlords. Build relationships, ask for help, offer guidance, and become part of this incredible community.

What is Landlording?

Perhaps before going any deeper, we should all get on the same page. What exactly are we talking about here? What IS landlording?

Landlording, also known as property management, is defined for the purpose of this book as the business of protecting and growing one's real estate investment through the careful placement and oversight of tenants. Now let's break down that definition into several distinct parts.

Notice that the definition begins with the idea that landlording is a business. Whether you are managing one small rental property that you own or managing thousands of properties for hundreds of different owners, landlording IS a business. We'll spend most of Chapter 2 talking about the concept of property management being a business versus being a hobby. You might be tempted to skip this chapter to get onto the actionable meat, but that would be a mistake. Looking back on our own lives, if there is one thing we would change, it would be to understand this fundamental concept from the start.

Next, the definition moves to that of "protecting one's investment." Most people have separated the idea of their "investment" from that of "management," but we believe the two are one and the same. Landlording is an integral part of the investment and the driving force behind success. While you can invest in a lot of things (gold, stocks, mutual funds) without much management, real estate is a different beast. Its success is not dependent upon the market, but upon the manager. That's right: Success in rental property investing is dependent upon the effective management of that asset. You could purchase an incredible real estate deal that would turn you from a mill worker to a millionaire, but without good management, you'll be back at the mill in no time.

Now, management does more than just protect wealth, as the definition explains; it also *grows* it. Good property management seeks to continually improve both the condition and financial position of the property being managed. This is done not just to preserve the condition, but to help the investment grow in value. This happens naturally through inflation or appreciation, as well as through increased rents and decreased expenses on the property. A good property manager has a pulse on the market, knowing when to squeeze more from the property to help the investment produce greater returns.

Finally, the mechanism by which property managers protect and grow wealth is "through the careful placement and oversight of tenants." In other words, managers must find the best potential occupants of the rental property and control the actions those tenants take while in the home. Landlords are the cowboys who put a corral around what the tenant must and must not do, while considering both the well-being of the tenant and the well-being of the investment.

Landlording Tasks

Now that we have a book-smart definition of landlording on the table, let's talk about the common tasks you might perform as a landlord. Of course, we're going to dive deep into every single item on the list below later in the book, but this will give you just a sample of the kind of tasks a landlord is responsible for:

- Preparing a property to rent
- Collecting forms needed for the businesses
- Placing ads in the newspaper and/or online
- Placing signs in the yard
- Determining fair market rent
- Determining the security deposit amount
- Setting minimum qualification standards
- Taking phone calls from prospective tenants
- Pre-screening tenants
- Scheduling appointments to show properties
- Meeting with prospective tenants

- Answering questions about the property
- Selling the property's features (yes, landlording is about sales!)
- Distributing and accepting applications
- Screening tenants
- Calling former landlords
- Verifying prospective tenants' income
- Running background and credit checks
- Approving great tenants
- Denying tenants who aren't great tenant material
- Ensuring compliance with Fair Housing Laws
- Accepting the deposit to hold
- Scheduling a lease signing
- Signing the lease and addendums
- Inspecting the condition of the rental before a tenant moves into the property
- Setting up the payment method for the tenant
- Accepting rent and depositing rent into the bank
- Making sure utilities were properly transferred
- Getting copies of the lease to all parties
- Creating a tenant file to house their information
- Accepting phone calls from tenants
- Dealing with maintenance requests
- Settling disputes between tenants
- Raising the rent when appropriate
- Ensuring tenants comply with their lease
- Ensuring tenants keep the property in good condition
- Scheduling regular inspections of the property
- Finding and maintaining a list of reputable, licensed contractors
- Managing contractors to make sure the work gets done
- Checking the progress on any repairs and ensuring tasks are completed
- Paying contractors and dealing with the legal paperwork
- Dealing with late rent and getting the required legal forms served
- Evicting bad tenants
- Dealing with tenants who may be on drugs
- Making sure the property is always operating up to code

- Firing tenants, if needed
- Accepting notices to vacate and overseeing the transition
- Bookkeeping to keep track of income and expenses
- Keeping a record of tenant communication
- Monitoring and paying the bills that the tenant doesn't pay
- Monitoring the lawn care and landscaping
- Balancing the checkbook and accounts each month
- Producing monthly reports on the financials of the property
- Responding to legal threats against the landlord
- Performing a move-out inspection of the property after a tenant vacates
- Handling the repairs or repainting after a tenant moves out
- Getting the tenant's security deposit returned or applied toward repairs
- Scheduling a carpet cleaner and someone to change the locks
- Maintaining property management licensing, if needed
- Staying up to date on rental-related local, state, and federal laws
- Keeping the tenants happy as much as possible
- If managing for other landlords, keeping owners happy as much as possible
- Keeping the property running at peak performance
- Starting back at the beginning of this list and doing it all over again for each property

Wow! To be honest, that was the first time we've ever sat down and tried to list every single thing a landlord does—and it's overwhelming, isn't it? Now, multiply that list for every single unit you own, and it's easy to see why so many landlords fail at this game. From the outside, most people see landlords as doing two tasks—accepting rent and fixing things when they break—but clearly they are doing a bit more than that!

We didn't include this list here to scare you, but to give you an idea of all the moving parts that are in store for you. The good news is that nearly everything on this list will become repetitious and easy for you to handle. We'll touch on every single item on this list, and by the time you finish this book, you'll be ready to tackle each step of the process. And if you are anything like us, you might even end up loving the process. If not, you could always hire a property management company to do it for you. Let's talk about that.

Should You Manage Yourself or Hire a Professional Management Company?

What if we told you that you could easily condense that HUGE list we just talked about into just a few bullet points? Actually, you can—but it's going to cost you. Professional property management companies exist to take care of most of the above list for you, everything from finding tenants and signing leases to answering phone calls, dealing with turnover, and more. When you hire a property management company, you don't even have to ever meet the tenant.

Property management fees vary by location, but typically for a single family house or small multifamily property, you'll be looking at 8–12 percent of the rent in a monthly fee and a large, one-time fee each time the unit is rented. This placement fee is often 50 percent of the first month's rent all the way up to the entire first month's rent. In other words, if your property will rent for $1,000 per month, the property manager might earn $100 per month for their management, plus an additional $500–$1,000 each time the property is rented. Some managers also charge a "renewal fee" each year, as well as "marking up" the maintenance costs. For a property owner who doesn't have a lot of cash flow, property management can quickly turn a decent investment into a negative cash-flowing investment.

Of course, the other side of the coin is that by allowing a manager to look after a property, it frees up the investor to do "higher value" tasks, like finding more properties. If a management company costs $2,000 per year, but the time saved helps an investor buy one more property per year that nets him or her $5,000 in cash flow, then the savings might be worth it. Or perhaps you are simply not interested in learning *how* to become a good landlord and you are going to be just like most other failed landlords. In this case, it would be better to pay the $2,000 per year to avoid *losing* tens of thousands on your investment.

Now, keep in mind that hiring property management is not going to be perfect. The truth is, a lot of property management companies are *terrible*. Becoming a property manager is not a difficult task, so the market abounds with managers who have no idea what they are doing. They saw property management as an "easy" way to make money and decided that managing tenants would be the way to go. At best, these managers are terrible at getting units rented, horrible at communication with the owner, slow at getting repairs completed, and allow the tenant to let the property fall into disrepair. At worst, they could steal, lie, and cheat their way into the owner's pocketbook and completely destroy an investment.

Even if you hire a great manager, your job as the owner is not completely "work-free." You must continue to manage the property manager and ensure they are doing their job correctly. Perhaps the biggest complaint from owners about property management companies is "they just don't care about my property." And with hundreds or even thousands of properties under management, it's probably the truth. Your property does not stand out to them from the others. When they have 50 vacancies at one time, yours included, they are trying to fill all of them at once. They don't have an incentive to get just yours rented, which could cause the property to sit vacant longer. On the other hand, professional property management companies have a much wider reach for finding tenants due to the marketing they run. While you might put up a Craigslist ad or sign in the yard, they may have hundreds of signs and ads all over town, with dozens or hundreds of potential tenants calling every week. They also may negotiate "bulk rates" on their services, which could bring down the cost of some maintenance.

If you do decide to hire a property manager to run your rentals, do your due diligence and find the best manager in your town. Ask other local landlords for referrals, interview dozens of companies if you have to, ask the hard questions, talk with their current clients, and don't be afraid to fire a bad manager. And keep reading this book, as it will help you build a baseline for what a good landlord should do, helping you become a much more effective manager of the manager.

But our guess is that because you are reading this book on how to be an effective, successful landlord, you are interested in managing yourself. We have managed our own properties since day one. On the couple of occasions we have attempted to hire a property manager, we leave with the realization that we do things ten times better! We don't say this to brag; we say this to inspire. It all comes down to knowing that nobody cares about your property or about your investment as much as you do. Anyone can manage, but managing *effectively* is a skill that must be learned and perfected. This book is designed to help you accomplish that.

Surprise: Everything Won't Always Apply

We know we don't need to say this for the majority of readers, but there's one person in every bunch who doesn't think outside the box and gets in trouble for it. So here you go: *Not everything in this book is going to work for you.* This is not an Ikea instruction manual that you must follow to the letter and have a perfect system when you are done. You will need to use your brain! There is just no way for us to know everything about you, your rental, your location, your skills, your situation, etc. This book is filled with hundreds of tips, tricks, and techniques that have served us well in our landlording business, but the responsibility is on you to learn what works and what doesn't for you and your business. There are few "right and wrong" questions in real estate, but a whole lot of "right for me, wrong for me" questions. So use your head, think critically, and be prepared to work.

We promise, it'll pay off well for you.

CHAPTER 2:
THE 8 BUSINESS ATTRIBUTES OF A SUCCESSFUL LANDLORD

A Tale of Two Landlords

"Landlord A" and "Landlord B" both purchased rental properties in the hopes that those properties would someday pay off big for their financial future. Both decided to manage their properties by themselves and deal with the tenants, but each landlord views landlording differently and they lead very different lives.

- Landlord A receives phone calls at all hours of the day and night. Landlord B receives a few phone calls here and there, mostly during business hours.

- Landlord A often stays up late, dreading the next day when difficult phone calls must be made. Landlord B sleeps like a baby, barely thinking of the rentals.

- Landlord A has to constantly get after his tenants, chase rent, and deal with difficult evictions and trashed units. Landlord B's tenants rarely act up, and when they do, the problems tend to take care of themselves through the systems created.

- Landlord A forgets to return phone calls, loses receipts, and easily gets overwhelmed—for good reason. Landlord B has a place for everything and a system for handling the paperwork neatly.

- Landlord A doesn't like being a landlord. Landlord B loves it.

Which landlord do YOU want to be? Landlord A or Landlord B?

I'm guessing you chose Landlord B, and you would be wise to do so. But let me fill you in on a little secret: **Landlord A and B are the same people—us!** That's right, over the past decade, we have been Landlord A and we have been Landlord B. Early on, we were Landlord A most of the time, struggling to keep up with all the headaches and drama our rentals gave us, but as we grew in our knowledge and skill with our investing, we learned that becoming Landlord B was not a difficult task.

Want to know the difference between Landlord A and Landlord B?

Landlord B learned to run the business of landlording *like a business*. Landlord A treated it like a hobby.

Now, that concept might not be incredibly clear to a lot of folks. What's the difference? What does a business owner do that a hobbyist doesn't? First, a business-minded landlord succeeds where others fail, has more free time to do the things they love, maintains more financial stability, and has an enjoyable time doing it. A hobbyist landlord struggles to find success, is always out of time, remains on the verge of going broke, and grows to hate the job of landlording.

So, which do you want to be?

Let's look at eight characteristics and processes that sets a business-minded landlord apart from the landlord who only does things half-heartedly or on the fly.

1. They Implement Systems and Repeatable Processes

Have you ever noticed how every Starbucks store you walk into looks and feels pretty much the same? The same colors, the same aprons on the employees, the same font on the chalkboard. You know that when you walk in and order your "Tall, Extra Hot, Peppermint Hot Chocolate" or "No Water, Extra Hot, With Whip, Chai Tea Latte," you're going to get the same drink taste wherever you go. This is because businesses like Starbucks are simply a collection of systems and recipes that everyone has learned to follow.

Savvy business owners seek to create procedures or systems within their business that instruct how all situations are handled. Systems are *repeatable* processes that guide how a business operates at all times. A system doesn't necessarily need to be written, though that is a good idea. It's simply a way of doing good business consistently.

Having pre-defined systems in place in a business helps in four distinct ways:

1. It simplifies decision-making. When a business has specific systems that guide how things are done, decision-making is a much easier task. To use the Starbucks example once again, because they have defined within their system what syrups to use in their Peppermint Hot Chocolate, the barista doesn't need to think too long and hard about how the drink should be made. A "Tall" would receive three pumps of chocolate, three pumps of peppermint, and one pump of vanilla. Combine this with meticulously steamed milk and whipped cream, and you've got perfection. Customers come to expect this, employees have less chance of screwing it up, and the consistency makes everyone much happier. Additionally, management can feel confident knowing that their employees (or "partners," as Starbucks calls them) are making each drink exactly to standard without the management themselves having to physically make each and every drink.

In your landlording business, the same benefit exists. When you have a system that guides how your decisions are made, there is far less chance that something could be screwed up. For example, a tenant calls and asks for an extension (more time) on the rent. If you have no system for dealing with this question, you'll be forced to make a decision on the fly, which may not be the best choice for your business. Instead, if your system has identified this potential question and determined a process for dealing with it, the stressful situation becomes just a routine answer. No big deal. (We'll talk about the specifics of this question later in the book and provide several processes for dealing with it.)

2. It frees up management's time. Because the business is operating under a strict collection of systems and repeatable processes, management needs to contribute far less to the day-to-day operation of the business. A barista doesn't need to bug the manager and ask how to make a drink, a teacher doesn't need to bug the principal to ask whether a field trip is acceptable, a construction worker doesn't need to bug the foreman to ask where the wall needs to be nailed, and the tenant doesn't need to ask the landlord if they can hang a picture on the wall. It's all part of the defined system.

3. It ensures customer satisfaction. At our core, we are all a little bit "rebellious" against systems and rules. After all, that's why we decided to get into real estate investing, right? We conjure up images of useless TPS reports from middle managers and robotic-sounding support staff that can't think outside their script on the other end of the phone when we need help. While systems and processes may be frustrating at times and tend to feel very "un-American," imagine life without them! As consumers, we come to rely on the systems and processes that businesses maintain because they lead to stability in what we are getting.

We are happy that every 2x4 piece of lumber is the same dimensions because a house would be terribly difficult to build otherwise. We are thankful the DMV has a process for getting our new photos taken and we don't have to hope that the person behind the desk is in a good enough mood to allow it. We are thankful that the US Department of Transportation has a system for signs and lines on the road, or else we'd be lost every time we got on the highway. And tenants are thankful when their landlord has systems and processes because they know what to expect and how to get what they need. And yes, you DO want your tenants to be happy. You may not be able to give them everything they want, but a happy tenant is a long-term, paying tenant, and that is music to any landlord's ears.

4. It helps maintain financial stability. When a business is guided by specific systems and processes, the business can achieve better financial stability because there are fewer unpredictable winds that could rock the boat. Of course, not everything is predictable, but systems allow a business to stay level throughout the year. When decisions are made on the fly, it's easy to go over budget and say "yes" to things that probably need a "no." For example, Starbucks charges the same $3.42 for a Tall Peppermint Hot Chocolate, and they don't change the price on a daily whim. This way, they can better predict the revenue they'll make over the next year and plan occasional price raises that maximize profit. As a landlord, because we have a system in place for handling advertising, late rent, evictions, and so on, we can maintain a fairly steady cash flow throughout the year.

A business-minded landlord builds systems and relies on those systems to make their business run like a well-oiled machine. Systems help decrease stress and improve the bottom line, no matter what business they are a part of. Throughout this book we'll discuss hundreds of systems and repeatable processes that you can implement in your business. These are repeatable processes that we use in our landlording business and that have been developed over many years. They can be as simple as knowing how tenants submit repair requests or as complicated as dealing with evictions or angry tenants. Once you master these systems, landlording becomes much easier, simpler, predictable, and more fun.

Of course, you don't need to follow each and every one of these systems to the letter. In fact, a savvy business owner seeks to continually improve their systems, streamlining processes in order to make things run even better. Let's talk about that next.

2. They Strive for Continuous Improvement

Have you ever noticed how ugly the US Government is?

Last week I (Brandon) spent a lot of time learning and writing about taxes. No, this isn't something I do in my spare time because my Netflix is down. I was working on an epic blog post for BiggerPockets about the tax benefits for real estate investors and did most of my homework for the post on various government websites. Throughout the process, I was continually reminded of how unorganized, difficult, and just plain ugly the government's websites are. The same could be said about most government buildings and processes. Why? Because the government is *not* a business, it has no incentive to continuously improve or innovate. Instead, it operates in a way that is purely functional. No one makes more money by improving a system or process.

In the private sector, however, businesses are rewarded for improvement. When Steve Jobs at Apple created the first iPhone, it was a turning point because it was better than anything that had come before. But Apple didn't stop there. They kept improving products and improving their value. Unlike in the government, thousands of hours have been poured into every aspect of the iPhone to make it the best smartphone on the market. Every curve, every line, every pixel is continually being optimized for a better user experience and to make more profit for the company.

Non-profit businesses often suffer the same fate as the government. They focus much more heavily on "need at hand" and not on the systems to help scale their operation. As a result, most non-profits remain small and are only able to reach a small number of people. They are often not treated like a business.

So, do you want to run your landlording like the government, like a non-profit, or like a business? My guess is *like a business*. But you don't need to be the next Apple in order to continuously improve. You can begin creating your systems today, right now.

We just talked at length about the need for your business to have systems and processes that guide its operations. However, most likely your systems and processes won't be perfect on day one, on day one hundred, or on day one thousand. In fact, you will likely never reach perfection with your systems. All you can really do is continuously improve, and that is one of the biggest factors that sets apart a successful business from a struggling one.

As a landlord, it's your job to continually improve your business, finding ways to make things run easier, faster, and with greater profitability. For example, when we first purchased our 24-unit apartment complex, we required all tenants to mail their rent in to our post office box. We quickly realized, however, the inefficiency of that system, being that every month someone's rent would get lost in the mail and show up days late. Occasionally this was due to the post office losing the rent, but more often tenants would simply lie, say they mailed it, and blame its MIA status on the post office.

So eventually we did away with tenants mailing in their rent and installed a rent drop-box on site. However, not only did we have to physically go to the property every day from the first of the month until all the rent was received, but we also eventually realized the compromised security of this system. Anyone could easily break into the box and steal all the rent, which would be incredibly troublesome for our business. In an effort to improve, we ended up changing our system once again.

Our tenants now have two options for paying the rent each month, online on our website with direct deposit from their bank account or via a service that allows them to pay their rent in cash at a local 7-Eleven, which then gets directly deposited into our account. (We'll talk in depth about all this later.) Eventually we will switch the system up again in an effort to streamline things even more. None of this is "easy" to do, but once the system has been changed and is in place, the work will pay off tenfold, as your business will operate with more fluidity and ease.

3. They Are Firm But Fair

Are you a nice person? Most likely, you are. Most of your family/friends would probably say great things about you. And with family and friends, there is absolutely nothing wrong with that. But if there's one trait that above all others causes landlords to fail, it's this: *being too nice.*

We are not suggesting you be a rude individual or anything like that. You must be fair and treat all people, including your tenants, with respect. But being nice can hurt you and ultimately cause you to lose your entire business. For example, let's say you rented a home to Sherry and her two kids. Then, after a few months, you discover that Sherry moved in a large German Shepherd puppy. The "nice" side of you is going to want to allow it because confrontation is never fun. And you love dogs, so what's the big deal? You'll be "nice," only to discover when Sherry moves out that the dog destroyed the carpet with urine, ate part of the trim, and caused several thousands in damage (true story!). Not to mention your increased liability for allowing an animal to dwell on the premises that is listed as a dangerous breed on many landlord insurance policies. Oops.

Rather than being "nice," we want to encourage you to be something else: *firm but fair*.

The agreement between you and Sherry included no pets being allowed, so being firm means holding up the contract for both parties. Sherry wouldn't allow you to suddenly hike up the rent mid-lease because the lease wouldn't allow it. Being firm means holding both parties to the agreements that were legally agreed upon. This helps keep the emotion out of tough situations *and* helps you run a more efficient, stress-free business. Being fair means not taking advantage of tenants or trying to sneak things into a contract just to be a jerk. Being fair means letting everyone know the terms up front, explaining the ramifications, and holding the tenant's feet to the fire.

Being firm but fair doesn't just help your bottom line, it also *helps your tenant*. Let us use an example you'll likely run across when dealing with tenants: late rent. When a tenant pays rent late, they will always have an excuse. Their check was held up, their kid was sick, they forgot what day it was. The "nice" side of you will want to forgive them and let them have more time to come up with the rent. Three days, five days, ten days later - eventually the rent might come in, probably after the next pay period two weeks later. Yes, you got the rent, but now the rent next month will be late again because the tenant gets paid every other week and now needs the next paycheck for other bills.

Furthermore, you've trained your tenant to know that rent does not need to be their number one priority, so the next time drama pops up in their life, the rent will be late again. There will always be drama in the life of a tenant. Before you know it, the tenant is four months behind in rent, and you are losing your mind on what to do. You are forced to go through an expensive eviction because there is no way the tenant can come up with all the late rent. They trash the unit because, you know, you're "such a jerk of a landlord," leaving you with thousands of dollars in clean-up fees and hindering THEIR future ability to find a good place for their family to live—all because you wanted to be nice. Had you instead been firm but fair, you would have held the tenant to their contract, and magically, the tenant would likely have found a way to pay rent. If not, you would find out a whole lot sooner than four months down the road.

The frustrating thing about this "firm but fair" policy is that, although it makes sense, this is something you will likely ignore. Yep, everything you just read and nodded your head along to will be thrown out the window the first time someone pushes your buttons. Nearly every first-time landlord will make this same mistake, and it will cost you big-time. Then you'll lose a lot of money and learn that "nice" will kill your business, but "firm" will keep everyone happy.

4. They Use Outsourcing and Delegating

The fourth aspect that defines a business over a hobby is the focus on outsourcing and delegating tasks within your business. Yes, you could probably do almost anything in your business, from plumbing to roofing to screening and more. But is this the best value of your time?

Savvy business owners learn to delegate tasks to others. And yes, this is something that must be learned. From the time we are born, we are taught to do things for ourselves, to be independent. We have a tough time trusting others to do tasks that we know we could do. This problem is compounded by the fact that, at first, no one will likely be able to do your tasks as well as you. "They're all idiots!" you say. And at first, that's true.

"But what if I don't have the money to delegate things?" is the common question people ask—and a good one at that. Especially at the beginning, you may not be able to outsource any work to others. However, over time, a business owner looking to grow must learn how to get more accomplished than a typical 40-hour week can provide. Of course, you could always just hunker down, put your nose to the grindstone, and work longer hours, but something tells us you didn't get into real estate because you wanted longer hours. Hence, the need for outsourcing.

When you don't have the money to outsource tasks, we offer two suggestions:

1. Ask yourself: "By outsourcing certain tasks, could I achieve more money doing other tasks?" In other words, if I can hire someone to do data entry at $10 per hour for three hours per week, could I take those three hours and apply them to something else in my business that I enjoy doing more and that I would have to pay someone $100 per hour to do?

A good example of this is in finding new real estate deals. If you spent

20 hours finding, analyzing, and seeking out funding for a new rental property that will make you $50,000 over the next 20 years, that's a $2,500 PER HOUR task. Now, compare that with 20 hours of accounting, which you could get a bookkeeper to do for around $20 an hour. Yes, you could save $400 by doing the bookkeeping yourself, but will you be sacrificing the $50,000 by using your skills more appropriately?

2. Cultivate an attitude of delegation even if you can't delegate yet. Mindset is so important when growing a business, and landlording is no different. If you *think* like a savvy business owner, in time you'll be able to operate like one. Maybe you can't afford to hire a bookkeeper right now, and you don't have any higher-earning tasks to fill the place. There's nothing wrong with that.

However, if you structure your business, your to-do list, and your life with an "attitude of delegation," it will be easier for you to eventually outsource certain tasks. This brings us back to the discussion we just had on creating systems and processes. Even if you'll be doing the work yourself, structure it in such a way that you could replace yourself at any point if needed. We recommend dividing your tasks up into groups that you could eventually hire a person to take over.

For example, we decided early on that we didn't like talking on the phone with tenants. So we created a system that could easily be transferred to another when desired. To do this, we created a Google Voice phone number and wrote down numerous scripts and policies to deal with 99 percent of the issues that come in. When we could finally afford to outsource that task, it was fairly painless because we had built the system with an *attitude of delegation.*

So what kind of tasks can you outsource? Anything, really. In fact, as we mentioned in the last chapter, you could outsource the entire property management process to a professional. However, if you plan to be the manager of your rentals, we'd recommend starting with the lowest "dollar per hour" tasks on your to-do list, as well as those tasks that you absolutely hate or are terrible at doing. Here are a few tasks you may want to take off your plate:

- Maintenance and repairs
- Accepting daytime phone calls
- Accepting nighttime phone calls
- Showing units

- Bookkeeping
- Advertising units
- Updating Craigslist
- Cleaning units
- Conducting tenant inspections
- Signing leases
- Doing a walk-through after a tenant moves out

As you work your way through this book, if you have an attitude of delegation, your mind will naturally begin to see ways that you can outsource certain tasks. Keep a list of those tasks and begin building systems and processes right now to make it easier to someday outsource.

5. They Keep Strict Financial Control

As your business grows, so will your responsibility to maintain incredible financial control over your business. Financial control is the management you hold over the incoming, outgoing, and organization of resources from your business. In other words, a savvy business owner knows exactly what's coming in and what's going out and can demonstrate that clearly on paper (and to the IRS). Let's break down those three parts of financial control and spend a moment on each.

Incoming: As a rental property owner, it will be your duty to know where all the income for your business is coming from. You'll need to define all the parts of income you will receive, create systems for accepting that income, and find ways to maximize that income. The most common form of income is obviously the rent, but it doesn't stop there. You may also receive security deposits, late fees, pet fees, storage fees, laundry fees, and more. We'll talk about all these throughout this book, so don't worry if you don't understand these all right now. You will!

Outgoing: Few things will sink your business as fast as overspending. As a business owner, you'll need to have a tight reign on your company's spending, knowing where every dollar is going and finding ways to decrease those expenses over time. Expenses will range from the normal (like utilities, repairs, mortgage, etc.) to one-off expenses (refunding security deposits, legal costs, etc.), but all must be cataloged and chronicled carefully.

Organization: Finally, as a business owner, you must maintain incredibly accurate records of all the financial dealings of your company. Not only should you be able to understand exactly what's going on, but you also need to be able to prove to the IRS how your business did. Bookkeeping is not the most glamorous job of a business owner, which is why it is often one of the first things outsourced, but it is one of the most crucial. Understanding how your company is running is key in helping you make better decisions for your business.

6. They Focus on Customer Service

Those who view landlording as a business focus heavily on solid customer service. They know that their nice house, their car, their vacation, it's all paid for *by* their customers. Now, most people don't think of landlording as a "customer service industry," but then again, most landlords are miserable!

An intentional focus on customer service is not just an ethical issue, it's a monetary one. Incredible customer service as a landlord will help your business increase revenue and decrease expenses in the long run. We like to ask tenants during the screening process, "Why are you moving?" In fact, this question is on the application each tenant fills out, which we'll talk about in Chapter 7. The number one reason given is because their landlord wouldn't respond to maintenance issues. How silly for a landlord to avoid fixing a $200 issue when the cost of a turnover could cost thousands!

Now, keep in mind that we are not talking about giving the tenant whatever they want. In landlording, the customer is NOT always right. However, treating tenants with respect, clarity, and promptness goes a long way. We believe customer service in the landlording business can be summed up in two general principles:

1. **Be respectful**. Your tenants are people, just like you. Treat them how you would want to be treated, no matter how you personally feel about them.

2. **Be responsive.** Don't be difficult to get in touch with, and don't make the tenant wait too long before you take action or communicate what action is being taken. Do what you say you are going to do, when you say you are going to do it, and keep them in the loop.

By simply following these two principles, you'll hold onto your tenants longer and keep your property running at maximum efficiency and profitability.

7. They Understand the Rules and Laws That Govern Their Business

Business owners may control most of the ways their business is run, but even being "the boss" doesn't mean you have 100 percent freedom. Business owners still must abide by numerous rules and laws that govern their particular industry. In the rental property management business, this means knowing the laws that govern real estate. In general, these rules fall into three categories:

1. Fair Housing Laws

2. Landlord-Tenant Laws

3. Local Laws/Codes

Let's talk about each briefly.

Fair Housing Laws

True or false: Discrimination is a bad thing.

You probably said "true," but in fact, discrimination for a landlord is NOT always bad. You probably want to discriminate against someone who was just evicted. You might want to discriminate against someone who has no income source. These are forms of discrimination that are allowed and encouraged. However, there ARE several forms of discrimination that are not allowed. Fair Housing Laws are government-enforced rules that govern what you can and cannot discriminate against as a landlord. (Technically, Fair Housing Laws extend to all areas of real estate, but we'll focus on the landlording side.)

The Fair Housing Laws were enacted to stop landlords from discriminating against tenants based on certain protected classes. There are seven federally protected classes (race, color, religion, sex, handicap, familial status, and national origin), as well as several others that are considered protected classes in certain locations, such as sexual orientation, being on Section 8, or marital status. We'll spend a significant portion of Chapter 4 talking about Fair Housing, discrimination, and the protected classes.

Landlord-Tenant Laws

In an effort to maintain stability between tenants and landlords, each state in America has enacted certain laws that govern the rules and responsibilities of each party. These laws, often called "The Landlord-Tenant Act" of the state, lay out rules for things like security deposits, the eviction process, allowable deposits and fees, due dates, grace periods, maintenance requirements, and more. In other words, the landlord-tenant laws in your state are incredibly important, so read them! That's right: As a business owner, it is your responsibility to know what you can and can't do. There are likely things within this book that, although allowed in our state (Washington), are not allowed in yours, so how are you going to know unless you read them?

Luckily, the landlord-tenant laws are not difficult to find. By simply searching Google for "Landlord-Tenant Laws" and your state's name, you'll find your state-specific laws. Although there are numerous websites that offer summaries of the laws, we recommend actually finding the official landlord-tenant laws for your state, printing them out, and reading them, highlighter in hand. Yes, they might be long—but so are lawsuits. If you want to run a serious business, then take the laws seriously and read (and follow) your landlord-tenant laws.

(In the appendix of this book, we've also included a summary, as well as links, to the landlord-tenant laws in your state.)

Local Laws/Codes

Finally, business owners must be aware of local laws and codes that guide how they run their business. After all, local municipalities can enact rules, laws, and codes that are even more strict than the state or federal guidelines. For example, a local business code might require you to have a business license to operate rentals in your area, or another law might require you to pay certain utilities for your tenant. As a business owner, it is your responsibility to research these laws and codes and make sure you are complying.

No one likes to follow the rules, but if you plan to be a successful landlord, you must take responsibility to learn what you can and can't do legally within your business. It might cost a little more money and take a little time to learn, but by operating your business legally, you give it the breathing room it needs to grow.

8. They Ask for Help

Have you ever had an itch on the middle of your back that you just couldn't reach to scratch? It happens to me (Brandon) all the time. Usually I end up making a fool of myself as I'm trying to dislocate my arm to reach that unreachable spot. After struggling for a few minutes, I usually just ask Heather for help. Ah, relief!

In much the same way, when you get into real estate, you are going to encounter a lot of itches, and many of them you won't be able to scratch yourself. You will run into problems you don't know how to solve. It might come as a shock to you, but most people don't know what they are doing when they get into business. Perhaps it's the risk and thrill of entrepreneurship that attract people to this career in the first place. However, one thing smart (and long-lasting) business owners do well is *reaching out for help and guidance on a continual basis.*

Landlording is a team sport. You need others to help you accomplish your goals and solve your problems. Whether it's ongoing educational help, decision-making help, ideas to help solve a sticky situation with a tenant, or just another person to look over your numbers—you will likely need help. So don't be shy and hide in your office, afraid to come out into the world. Emerge from your cave and start having meaningful conversations with people willing to help.

Of course, there are probably not a lot of people around you who care at all about real estate. Most of the time when we try to explain what we do, we get a lot of blank stares and glossed-over looks. If you haven't found that out yet, you will. The world just doesn't get us. They don't understand the passion we have for financial freedom. Most people fall into one of two camps:

1. Those who think you are crazy for trying.

2. Those who think you are just greedy.

Can you relate? Most of your family, friends, and almost anyone else you talk to will fall into one of these two camps, though if you're lucky, they'll simply be happy for you. They'll discourage you, try to tell you all the reasons why it won't work, and try to talk you back into the routine 9-5 life they feel comfortable in. Screw that—you don't feel comfortable there, and you shouldn't! So how can you get out there and talk with people when no one wants to talk? Easy: *You need to find the right people.*

With 28 million real estate investors walking around America, there are plenty of investors around to talk with, to ask advice from, to get referrals from, and more. But you aren't going to typically find them at your local grocery store or church picnic. You need to go to where the investors are.

Of course, we'd recommend spending a good deal of time at BiggerPockets.com, the real estate investing social network. When everyone told us that real estate investing was a crazy venture and we'd probably lose everything and go broke, we found BiggerPockets and discovered a community of individuals who were already succeeding with real estate. They didn't try to talk us out of it. They didn't try to tell us why we'd fail. BiggerPockets came to us at a pivotal moment in our lives, when we were hanging on the edge of our destiny, deciding where we would go next. BiggerPockets helped us to choose extraordinary over ordinary, freedom over job-slavery, and real estate investing over monotony. I hope it'll do the same for you.

In addition to BiggerPockets, we'd encourage you to get together with local landlords and property managers on a regular basis. Your area likely has a real estate club or landlord organization, so consider joining. If you don't have one, why not start your own? Even if you are starting with just a few local landlords meeting for Starbucks, start that today.

As famed business leader Jim Rohn says, "You are the average of the five people you associate with the most." So forget the cat videos on Facebook and the marketing on Twitter, and spend time with those who want to help you change your life and help you answer the tough questions that you will face. It's difficult—if not impossible—to be a good landlord alone. So get out there, make connections, and start growing.

Wrapping it Up

By now, we hope you see our point. Landlording can either be a business, a hobby, or something in between. The more "business" you make it, the less stress you'll have to deal with in the long run. It's our hope that this chapter has given you the motivation you need to change the way you look at landlording. Stop being "Landlord A" who struggles and become "Landlord B" who dominates. You can do it, and this book can help.

The rest of this book leaves the theory and moves on to the actual practice of running a landlording business. But don't leave behind the lessons you learned in this chapter. Remember to think in terms of "systems." Find ways to improve upon the systems you build. Be fair but firm with your tenants to avoid being taken advantage of. Develop an attitude of delegation so those systems can eventually be outsourced. Monitor your finances like a boss, treat your tenants with respect and value, and educate yourself on the laws that govern your rentals. Finally, seek out others who can help you on your journey. By putting these eight business attributes into regular practice in your landlording, you will find yourself miles ahead of the competition, with more free time, less drama, and greater profitability.

CHAPTER 3:
INITIAL STEPS

Congratulations, you've officially (almost) entered the world of sleepless nights, constant headaches, 2 a.m. (non) emergency maintenance phone calls, and stress, stress, stress—all with a newfound awareness of what's wrong with the world today. Just kidding!

Congratulations on becoming a landlord. Being a landlord can be full of all the aforementioned woes, but it's also a great way to generate extra cash flow, build equity, and grow your empire. By properly setting up your business in the beginning and continually learning and expanding your knowledge and skillset, you can avoid at least some of the hassles inexperienced landlords face. That's what this chapter is all about: setting up your business the right way so you can avoid these hassles. In many areas of your life, landlording included, the manner in which you start something has a direct correlation to the way you run something. Therefore, by taking the appropriate steps up front, you can ensure a long-lasting, successful career for many years to come.

7 Things to Do Before Signing Your First Lease

Becoming an effective landlord actually begins before you ever get your first tenant. The following is a list of seven things every landlord should do before signing a single lease.

1. Consider Asset Protection.

Before signing your first lease, you should definitely sit down and have a conversation about asset protection. When most people hear "asset protection," they immediately assume "LLC," but there are other types of asset protection (corporations, limited partnerships, etc.) that you may want to consider. Asset protection works to separate your business debts from your personal debts, helping you avoid losing your personal home or personal savings account if a tenant were to sue you and win.

Of course, you do not need to *have* asset protection in place to own rental properties, and for brand-new investors, it might be overkill. We only include it in this list of things to do before signing your first lease so you can have that conversation with your attorney. Many people think that by having an LLC or other asset protection they are protected from getting sued, but asset protection merely helps manage the fallout of being sued. Even more, if that LLC or asset protection entity was not set up with 100 percent accuracy or has not been maintained following 100 percent of the rules, a judge could "pierce through the corporate veil" and go after your personal assets anyway. So don't think that by going online and opening an LLC you are safe. It's never that easy.

One final note on LLCs: Most residential banks do not loan on properties owned by an LLC. Some investors choose to transfer the property into an LLC after purchasing the property with their own name, but that can have some serious ramifications as well involving the "due on sale" clause in a mortgage. The "due on sale" clause says that if the title is transferred, the bank has the right to call the loan due. Of course, just because the bank has the right to call it due doesn't mean they will, but in recent years, banks have been increasing their enforcement of this clause.

2. Get Insurance

Insurance is a no-brainer when it comes to owning and managing rental properties. Insurance protects you, the owner or manager, from losing everything if you get sued or if catastrophe strikes the property. Therefore, before signing your first lease, ensure you have good insurance coverage that protects you and the property.

When shopping for insurance, there are a few things to keep in mind. First is your choice of a "full replacement coverage" or an "actual cash value" policy. Full replacement coverage will cover the entire cost of rebuilding your property should something drastic happen, whereas actual cash value will likely give you just enough to cover your loan in a bad situation. Keep in mind, choosing between the two may or may not be a choice you can even make, depending on the condition of the property or even your bank. If the property is older or not in mint condition, an insurance company may not allow full replacement coverage, whereas if you have a loan on the property, your bank may require full replacement coverage. These are things you will need to talk to your insurance agent about before making a decision.

Furthermore, these insurance policies should also include liability coverage, which protects you if you were to get sued. Typically, insurance policies will cover either $300,000 of liability, $500,000 of liability, or $1,000,000 of liability. It's usually not too much more expensive to go with the higher levels of insurance, and the extra protection in case of a lawsuit is probably money well-spent.

Another option to help protect yourself from lawsuits is through the use of an umbrella insurance policy. An umbrella policy is used for liability purposes and is meant to extend above your property insurance policy limits. In other words, if you have $300,000 in liability coverage on your property but you get sued for $1,000,000 and lose, the umbrella policy will kick in on the remaining $700,000 so you don't need to pay that out-of-pocket.

3. Set Up a Bank Account

Next, you'll need to set up two bank accounts for the property: a checking account and a savings account. This will help keep all the finances separate from your personal finances and make your bookkeeping much easier. The savings account will hold the security deposit, while the checking account will of course be used to handle the income and expenses on the property. We would also recommend that those accounts be business accounts, not personal accounts. Talk with your banker, and they will likely have an ideal deposit account for you and your situation.

Although check writing has become less necessary in daily life due to the use of credit/debit cards and online payments, you'll likely want to order actual, physical checks for your checking account. Many of the contractors and other vendors you'll be paying in the future will not accept cards, and using cash is just asking for trouble.

4. Gather Forms and Documents

It's a good idea to get together all the forms and documents you'll need for the property *before* you actually need them. Below is a list of the forms and documents you'll want to gather prior to launching head first into this landlording thing. Don't worry if you don't have all these forms right now, as we've included all these documents with the purchase of this book. (You can find these documents at the end of this book or by visiting http://www. BiggerPockets.com/LandlordBookBonus, but before you use any of them, be sure to read the disclaimer in the appendix regarding the legality of the forms.)

Be sure to gather:

- **Rental Application:** Unless you plan to do online-only versions of an application, you'll want to have numerous applications on-hand at any given point.

- **Acceptance Letter:** When you've accepted a tenant, an acceptance letter simply lets the tenant know they are approved and gives them the next steps in the move-in process.

- **Deposit Receipt/Deposit to Hold:** This form is given when the tenant has paid a deposit to hold the unit until they actually move into the property.

- **Denial Letter/Adverse Action Letter:** When a tenant is denied, you must notify them and let them know why they were denied. This form provides a convenient way to do this.

- **Lease Agreement:** A lease agreement is a legal contract between the landlord and the tenant that spells out the terms, conditions, and responsibilities of both parties. This is likely the single most important document in your collection.

- **Rules and Regulations:** In addition to the lease, you will likely also have property-specific rules and regulations that the tenant must follow.

- **Pet Addendum:** If you do plan to accept pets, you'll want to make sure there is paperwork documenting the pet, its breed and description, license number, and any applicable pet fee or deposit, as well as the tenant's responsibilities regarding the pet.

- **Move-In/Move-Out Checklist:** Landlords should always document the condition of the property when the tenant moves in and moves out to accurately account for damages. This is done on the Move-In/Move-Out Checklist.

- **Lead-Based Paint Pamphlet and Disclosure & Certification:** For any US property built prior to 1978, the tenant must be given a Lead Paint Informational Pamphlet from the EPA, where the landlord must disclose in writing whether lead-based paint is known in the property and provide any reports associated with the known lead-based paint. If no lead-based paint is known to be present and the landlord doesn't have any reports, this must also be disclosed, and the tenant must also acknowledge in writing their receipt of the required information and pamphlet.

- **Other State Required Forms:** Your state will likely have several other forms that must be given to tenants. For example, in Washington State, we are required to give a Mold Handout that describes what mold is and how to deal with it.

- **Legal Notice to Pay or Vacate:** If a tenant doesn't pay rent by their due date, most states require a Notice to Pay or Vacate form be served to the tenant or be posted on the premises prior to eviction proceedings. Usually the notice gives the tenant "X" number of days to either pay the rent, vacate the premises, or be faced with an eviction.

- **Legal Notice to Comply with Lease:** When a tenant breaks a rule (such as parking on the lawn, moving in another occupant, etc.), a Notice to Comply form is usually served. Again, the timing depends on the state where you live, but in Washington State, the tenant has 10 days from the time the notice is served to remedy the problem.

- **Notice to Enter Property:** You cannot simply barge in on your tenants any time you want, even though you are the landlord. Except in cases of emergency, notice must be given ahead of time, so the Notice to Enter form will give the tenant proper notice that you plan on sending someone inside their unit. Check with your state's landlord-tenant laws on the advanced notice required before entering a unit to complete inspections, complete repairs or maintenance, or show the property to would-be renters.

- **Move-Out Instructions:** Tenants do not naturally know exactly how the move-out process will happen nor what your expectations are for them in the process. The move-out instructions guide them on exactly how to clean and vacate the property, helping to ensure minimal cost to you, the landlord.

- **Disposition of Deposit:** When the tenant moves out, their deposit must be returned to them promptly with specific documentation on what they were charged for and why. The Disposition of Deposit form is an easy way to do this.

There are two ways to accumulate and store all these documents: electronically or in a physical file cabinet. We would probably recommend both, as either could fail you, and you'll have a backup no matter what. For storing them digitally, Google Drive (drive.google.com) can be a great tool for hosting all your forms online, and it's free and easy to use. Simply upload files from your computer into organized folders on your Google Drive and access them anywhere in the world with just a few clicks.

For physical storage, we recommend getting a small file cabinet to store several copies of each document. If you are only managing one or two properties, you can get a small, portable file holder for under $20 at an office supply store or on Amazon. If you plan to manage a lot of properties, you may want to invest in a larger file cabinet system to keep in your office. Look for one that can be locked, which may come in handy in the future.

5. Create a Policy Binder

In Chapter 2, we talked about the difference between a business and a hobby. One of the points we stressed quite a bit is the idea of having systems and processes for everything you do. One of the best ways to do this —and to keep track of it—is to create a company policy binder.

A policy binder is a collection of documents that outline how you do everything. It includes checklists, instructions, and details for every aspect of your landlording business. The policy binder should be written so that if you were to suddenly be hit by a truck and a complete stranger were to come in to manage your properties, they could do so in the exact same manner you do.

We would recommend including the following sections in your policy binder at a minimum. Feel free to add more as needed.

- Company Mission and Values
- Company Managers/Owners/Employees
- Telephone Standards (Hours, Expectations, etc.)
- List of All Properties, Addresses, Mortgage Companies, and Insurance Companies
- The Application Process

- Minimum Standards for Tenant Approval
- Tenant Screening Process
- Rental Collection Practices
- Rent Extension Process and Late Fees
- Security Deposit Process
- Basic Lease Terms
- Pet Policy
- Smoking Policy
- Vacating Tenant Process
- Turnover Process

A policy binder helps in several ways. First, it helps YOU remember that this is a business, just like any other, and will help to keep you from falling into the "hobby mentality." It also helps you organize your thoughts on how you want to operate your business. Third, it allows you to make fewer "on the fly" decisions, and instead base your decisions on the policy. And fourth, a policy binder gives you a third party to blame (besides the lease) when tenants complain about issues, such as, "Sorry, but our company policy does not allow for pets." The policy becomes the bad guy, not you.

6. Get to Know the Neighbors

We recommend building a relationship with several of the neighbors around your property. Simply stop by, introduce yourself, and give them your business card. Ask them to keep an eye on the property, and if they notice anything weird, to give you a call. No one likes a dirty neighbor or a neighbor doing illegal things, so most neighbors are more than willing to report any suspicions or problems directly to you. They can be your eyes and ears on the property, at least from the outside. They can also notify you in the case of an emergency, like a fire or burglary.

7. Set Up Your Bookkeeping

It's a good idea to get your bookkeeping method down before you begin managing. We'll talk more about this in Chapter 14, but let's touch on it briefly now. You'll need to have a good system for tracking the money that comes in to your bank account, as well as the money that goes out. You can do this with a spreadsheet (like Excel or Google Sheets) if desired, or you can use a more professional accounting software like QuickBooks or Xero. There are also a few property management programs that can help you track your income and expenses as well, such as AppFolio, Buildium, or VerticalRent. You could also hire a professional bookkeeper from the start to handle this side of the business for you.

If you are just getting started with one property, a good spreadsheet will likely do the trick. To help with that, we've included a copy of the spreadsheet that we use with this book. To download it, just head to http://www.BiggerPockets.com/LandlordBookBonus.

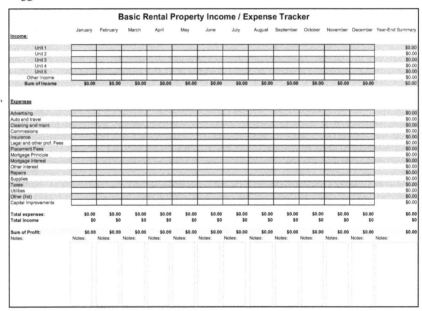

Inherited Tenants

When you purchase a rental property, it may come with tenants in place, and those tenants will suddenly become YOUR tenants. These tenants are known as "inherited tenants." Inherited tenants can be beneficial, as you will not need to immediately spend time filling the vacant unit, and you'll be receiving income from day one. However, inherited tenants can also be risky, as they were not put in place by you, and you don't have a clear indication of how well they were screened or what type of tenant they are. Furthermore, they may have been poorly trained by the last owner and will need to be re-trained to follow your rules and way of doing business. Or maybe those tenants will be absolutely perfect, and you'll be thankful to have them.

The truth is, you won't really know for sure until you begin dealing with those tenants. However, there are a few things you can do to increase the chance of a successful acquisition of inherited tenants. But before we get to that, understand that legally, the leases go with the property, which means everything about the lease stays the same when you take over. For example, if you purchased a property and the existing tenant was three months into a one-year lease, you would be required to abide by the terms of their lease for the next nine months. Again, the leases go with the property.

Review Existing Leases

Before closing on the property, you will definitely want to review the leases for each existing tenant to verify the income and what expenses are the tenant's responsibility. Do they match the financials that the seller provided? For example, let's say you purchased a triplex and the seller claimed to get $500 per month, per unit. If the lease shows just $400 per unit, you have a problem. This is actually not as rare as you might think, as sellers like to talk about their opinion of "fair market rent" (what they think it COULD rent for) rather than what they are actually receiving. This is known as the "pro forma" rental income. If this is the case, start asking questions and be sure to run your numbers with accurate data, not pro forma numbers.

Verification doesn't end with comparing the leases to the financials. Leases can easily be altered or forged. Imagine purchasing a property, only to find out (after closing) that the lease was changed by a shady landlord. This kind of thing does happen, so you must verify the terms of the lease with each tenant before purchasing the property. This is done through an Estoppel Agreement.

An Estoppel Agreement is a simple, one-page form that the tenant fills out letting you know the terms of their lease to the best of THEIR knowledge. If the seller of the property will not let you speak with the tenants and get Estoppel Agreements, you might be dealing with a seller who is trying to hide something. If you do get the Estoppel Agreements signed and discrepancies are found, you'll want to make sure they are cleared up before closing. Sometimes it could be an honest mistake, sometimes a tenant might be lying to try to get lower rent, or sometimes the seller might be a liar. You don't want to buy a property until you understand exactly what you are getting.

We've included an Estoppel Agreement with the purchase of this book, which you can get at http://www.BiggerPockets.com/LandlordBookBonus.

An Estoppel Agreement should contain at a minimum:

- The tenants' names and who resides in the unit
- The lease term (including start date)
- The rental amount due each month and the due date
- The security deposit amount
- Who pays which utilities
- Who owns the appliances
- Whether there are any pets in the property
- Whether there are any problems or repairs needed
- Whether there are any other agreements with the landlord

Make sure both you and the tenant sign this agreement, and keep it in their "tenant file." This way, if a tenant tries to tell you later on that their deposit was actually $1,000 instead of the $500, you can back up your claim with their signature on the Estoppel Agreement. It's hard to argue with that.

Put Yourself in Their Shoes

When purchasing a property that has inherited tenants, keep in mind that they are likely aware of the sale and are concerned about the unknown. They probably have a lot of questions, like "Who is this new owner," or "Are they going to kick us out," or "Is my rent going to be raised?" This uncertainty for the tenant can lead to a frustrating start to your relationship, so put yourself in their shoes and try to make the process as easy as possible on them.

We like to send a letter to the tenant on the day we take over a property, introducing ourselves and the company, letting them know we are the new owners and will be responsible for taking all phone calls, maintenance requests, lease-related questions, and anything else involving their tenancy. In this letter we like to let the tenants know about some of the improvements that will be taking place at the property in the coming months. This can help reassure the tenant that you are not a slumlord, but someone who takes pride in your work.

Raising the Rent on Inherited Tenants

Perhaps you purchase a property with existing tenants and you know that the rents are far too low. This is common, as many landlords are reluctant to raise the rent even as the market rate climbs, leaving long-term tenants with leases far below market rent. When we purchased our 24-unit apartment complex, this was the case. Most units were renting for $475 per month, when the market rent was a full $50 per month higher than that at that time. All the tenants were on month-to-month agreements, so we could raise the rent with just a 30-day notice.

But should we? Do we tear the band-aid off right at the get-go in one swoop, or do we raise the rent slowly or only on a few units? If we suddenly raised the rent on all the tenants, it's likely many of the tenants would move, and we'd be left with a lot of units that needed to be rehabbed and very little income coming in to help with those expenses. On the other hand, if we let the tenants stay at that $50 per month difference, that is thousands of dollars in potential rent we would not be receiving each year.

There isn't always a clear-cut answer on whether or not you should raise rent. We personally didn't have a lot of capital to handle that storm so we opted to keep the rent the same for most of the tenants for the first year, only raising the rent as we fixed up units and moved new tenants in. Another investor, someone with a lot more capital, may have decided to raise everyone's rent and accept the immediate loss, choosing instead to rehab multiple units and get new tenants in quickly. It's a balancing act and something only you can decide.

We'll talk a lot more about raising rent in Chapter 9, so let's move on and talk about getting a property ready to rent. First, let's start with the condition!

What Condition Should Your Property Be in?

Most importantly, your rental should be empty (unless you are offering it "furnished"), clean, free of repairs, and up to code. In addition to these items, take a look around the town and neighborhood where your rental is located and determine if there are any updates or upgrades you could do that would make your rental stand out from the rest.

Consider if it makes sense in your market to update any of the following, especially if they are reminiscent of a trend from a different era, such as 1970s bright orange countertops or gold shag carpet:

- Flooring
- Wall color
- Countertops

- Fixtures

To be perfectly clear, we have nothing against bright orange countertops and gold shag carpet, but your ultimate goal is to find the best tenant possible, and the best tenant possible isn't going to be too excited to walk into a seemingly Austin Powers-themed rental. Little things like changing out outdated light or sink fixtures with new ones can also go a long way in attracting tenants. The rental does not need to be fancy (unless, of course, your market calls for that), but it does need to be competitive. Tenants will generally not take as good of care of your property as you do, so don't spend too much time or money making unnecessary upgrades that will only be ignored or broken. The key is to find the right balance of quality and attractiveness for your rental without going overboard or breaking the bank.

How Much Can You Rent Your Property for?

Once you have a rent-ready property, your next step is to determine what to charge for rent. In a theoretical sense, the value of something is not based on what the seller wants, but what the market is willing to pay. In the world of rentals, this means that you do not necessarily set the rental amount—the market does. Your job is to discover what your market will allow for your rental and attempt to get that amount, known as "fair market rent." You will want to keep your market rent in mind when you are getting your property ready to rent so you are not over-improving, leading to an insufficient return on your investment.

Luckily, discovering what rent amount your market will bear for your property is not difficult; the best way to determine how much your property will rent for is to simply do market research. In business, market research means to get out there and find out what others in your industry are charging—and learning how much to charge for rent is no different. Pricing for rentals is usually determined by the following factors:

- Property Type: Apartment, Duplex, Single-Family Dwelling, etc.

- Number of Bedrooms

- Number of Bathrooms

- Square Footage

- Rental Quality

- Location

- Extra Amenities: Laundry, Included Utilities, Yard, etc.
- Special Features

Your property will generally rent for about the same amount as other properties that are similar in regard to the list we just mentioned. To determine this and do your market research, there are many methods you can use to look, such as:

- Craigslist.org
- Zillow.com
- Trulia.com
- PadMapper.com and Other Online Rent Services
- Driving Around, Looking for "For Rent" Signs
- Calling Local Property Management Companies
- Talking to Other Local Landlords
- Local Newspaper

For each of these sources, call and speak to the landlord and ask questions, posing as a prospective tenant if you wish. This will help you determine how similar the target property is to your own. By doing a little research, you will quickly be able to determine what the going rate is for your type of property. For example, if you are trying to rent an updated 3-bedroom, 2-bath home in good condition, it's logical to assume your property should rent for about the same amount as other updated 3-bedroom, 2-bath homes nearby in similar neighborhoods. Likewise, if you are renting an updated 3-bedroom, 2-bath home, it is logical to assume tenants will be willing to pay a little more than for the dated or dilapidated 3-bedroom, 2-bath home down the street.

You will also want to consider other concessions or amenities your competition is offering. Do they include utilities, such as water, sewer, garbage, gas or electric, covered parking or a garage, laundry facilities, such as coin-operated machines, or in-unit laundry hookups? If so—and if you don't— then your rental price might be lower. To keep your vacancy time as short as possible, you will want to make sure your rental stands out among all the others in your market. So, in addition to offering a quality product, if it's common in your market to include water, sewer, and garbage in an apartment, you will want to consider also including water, sewer, and garbage in yours—or adjusting your price to be competitive if you decide not to.

Remember, something is only worth what a person is willing to pay, so after following the above suggestions, if your unit is still sitting vacant for long periods of time, consider lowering the rent until you reach a price that people are willing to pay. If your rent is too high and no one is biting, it's better to lower your price to get it filled more quickly than let it sit for an unknown amount of time.

The Security Deposit

Of all the precautions a landlord can take, besides adequately screening tenants, requiring a security deposit is one of the most important. In addition to motivating the tenant to comply with their obligations, the security deposit can be used to cover the tenant's negligence in the event the pie hits the fan.

What is a Security Deposit?

A security deposit is money the tenant gives to the landlord when they gain tenancy to guarantee their compliance with the lease and state and local laws regarding their tenancy. It is also their guarantee that they will return the property to its original move-in condition, minus any reasonable wear and tear, when it comes time for them to move out.

Contrary to what some may think, the security deposit is the tenant's money, not the landlord's. Many dishonest landlords simply consider the security deposit extra income, never intending to give it back to the tenant when they move out. That is not only wrong, but it is also illegal. The purpose of the security deposit is not to line the landlord's pockets, but to encourage positive behavior on behalf of the tenant. If the tenant does not live up to their end of the bargain, the landlord has the security deposit to use towards the tenant's debts.

How Can the Tenant Pay the Security Deposit?

When accepting a security deposit from a new tenant, *always* get the deposit in guaranteed funds. Never allow a new tenant to write a personal check for the move-in money (this includes the first month of rent). Imagine your predicament when two weeks into your new tenant's lease, you discover that their deposit and rent have bounced. Now you're dealing with a potential eviction and absolutely **no** money to work with except your own hard-earned cash. Avoid this situation altogether by simply requiring all move-in funds be made with a money order or cashier's check.

How Much Can the Security Deposit Be?

The landlord sets the amount to be charged for the security deposit for each individual property. Since the security deposit is there as a safeguard for the landlord, it is wise to require as much as your market will allow *and* is legally permitted in your state and local jurisdiction. Some states have a statutory limit for the maximum a landlord can charge, so be sure to research the security deposit laws in your area. Most tenants are going to be accustomed to paying at least the equivalent to one month's rent for their security deposit. Never charge *less* than the equivalent of one month's rent for the security deposit; in the event that you need to use the security deposit, you'll wish you had more.

Cleaning Deposits, Pet Deposits, and Damage Deposits, Oh My!

Some landlords break the deposit up into different categories, specifying a separate cleaning deposit, pet deposit, damage deposit, etc. There is really no need to break the security deposit up into different categories, and doing so actually just adds a constraint on the landlord. For instance, if you specify a $200 cleaning deposit, a $200 damage deposit, and a $200 pet deposit, you'll be up a creek without a paddle when when your tenant's pet ruins the carpet throughout the home and you only have $200 to apply toward the damages. For this reason, simply refer to the deposit monies as the "security deposit" in general so you can apply it toward *any* debts incurred by the tenant.

When Should You Accept the Security Deposit?

Always require that the security deposit be paid **in full** along with the rent prior to the tenant obtaining occupancy. Allowing a tenant to pay their security deposit in installments after they have gained occupancy is never a good idea for a few reasons:

1. Any financially responsible person should be able to afford the move-in amount required for the property. If they can't afford the security deposit, you may want to reconsider your screening criteria.

2. It sets a bad precedent from the very beginning that you are the type of landlord who is wishy-washy and will negotiate on important matters. Don't negotiate on important matters! Have a policy and stick to it. Be firm from the beginning. You won't lose out on any good prospects because of it.

3. There is a good chance your tenant won't make the scheduled installation payments as agreed to because as stated above, any financially responsible person wouldn't have to make their payment in installments in the first place.

What is the Difference Between a "Deposit" and a "Fee"?

The difference between a deposit and a fee is simple: A deposit is refundable, and a fee is not. If the landlord charges the tenant a non-refundable fee, it must be specified in the rental agreement and cannot be referred to as the deposit. Most experienced landlords understand the value in keeping non-refundable fees to a minimum since a non-refundable fee takes away the incentive for the tenant to uphold their obligations. For example, if the tenant is being charged a $200 cleaning fee at move-out, what motivates them to clean themselves since they are being charged for it anyway?

One common fee landlords charge in addition to the security deposit is the pet fee. A pet fee is charged in addition to the security deposit and is different than a pet deposit in that the pet fee is simply an amount paid up front to the landlord for the *privilege* of having a pet on the premises. The pet fee is then the landlord's to do with as they wish. In the event the tenant's pet ends up damaging the property in any way, the expense would come out of the tenant's deposit. Or instead of a pet fee, some landlords will require a double deposit for added security if a tenant wishes to have a pet on the premises. You should require whatever you feel most comfortable with that is legally acceptable in your area.

Are There Any Specific Laws I Need to Know About the Security Deposit?

Each state has different specifics when it comes to the security deposit, so it is important that you research your state and local laws for guidance. In Washington, according to the Residential Landlord Tenant Act, in order for the landlord to collect a security deposit, they must:

- Have a *written* rental agreement.

- Specify the terms of the security deposit and which part, if any, is non-refundable (for professional carpet cleaning when the tenant moves, for example).

- Deposit the security deposit into a trust account designated specifically for security deposits by the landlord at a financial institution.

- Provide to the tenant in writing the name and address of the financial institution where the security deposit will be held during the tenancy.

- Provide to the tenant a receipt of monies paid as the security deposit.

- Detail the circumstances of how the security deposit can be withheld.

- Provide a written (detailed) description of the condition of the rental and its cleanliness at the time of move-in, including damages. The description (also called the Move-In Condition Report or Checklist) must be signed and dated by both the landlord and the tenant, with a copy provided to the tenant at the beginning of their tenancy.

- At the end of the tenant's tenancy, provide a written statement to the tenant detailing any deductions, along with the remaining refund, to the tenant's last known address within 14 days of vacating.

Wrapping it Up

Alexander Graham Bell once said, "Before anything else, preparation is the key to success." We believe this quote to be exceptionally true in regard to rental property investing. If you want to run your rental business like a business, then treat it that way from the start and prepare for the future. Not only will it help you save time as you begin managing tenants, it will also help you keep a level head and make your landlording as stress-free as possible. Don't be a retroactive landlord, simply responding to life as it is thrown at you. Be a proactive landlord and prepare for the journey you are about to take.

There is one more important area of preparation that we want to cover, but it's so important that we have decided to dedicate an entire chapter to it: Fair Housing Laws. There is no faster way for a landlord to get sued and lose it all than when he or she violates one of those laws, so let's go to Chapter 4 now to make sure you are ready to stay legal in your rental management business.

CHAPTER 4:
FAIR HOUSING

In July of 2014 the Department of Justice awarded five families in the Woodland Garden Apartments in Fremont, California a settlement from the landlord to the tune of $77,500 to the victims and an additional penalty to the government.

The five families filed claims of discrimination because the apartment complex enforced a policy that said children couldn't play in the grassy common areas of the complex. It may seem silly because after all, the landlord probably had a legitimate reason for not wanting children playing in the lawn—maybe it was a really nice lawn!

It brings to mind the little old lady who used to live down the street from me when I (Heather) was a child. She used to chase children off her perfect, beautiful lawn with a broomstick. However, whatever reasoning the landlord had for wanting to keep children off the lawn, it was an illegal policy and considered discrimination against families according to the Fair Housing Act. A landlord cannot enforce restrictions or conditions on tenants with children that they do not equally enforce with other residents. If the landlord wanted to protect the lawn and avoid a claim of discrimination, he would need to have the policy apply to all residents, meaning no one was to be allowed on the lawn—not just the children[i].

Before you put your property up for rent and go through the process of advertising, answering potential tenant's questions, screening your applicants, and eventually placing your new tenant, it is vital you become familiar with local, state, and federal Fair Housing Laws to understand exactly what illegal discrimination is so you can avoid it at all costs.

What is Fair Housing?

Fair Housing Laws were enacted with the Fair Housing Act in 1968 and amended in 1988 to protect against illegal discrimination by housing providers in regards to:

- Race

- Color

- Religion

- Sex

- National Origin

- Familial Status, Including:

  o Pregnant Women

  o Parents With One or More Children Under 18

  o Persons Obtaining or Who Have Legal Custody of Children Under 18

- Disability

The US Department of Housing and Urban Development (HUD) plays a large role in enforcing the Fair Housing Act and investigating complaints. According to HUD.gov, no person may do any of the following because of one of the protected classes:

- Refuse to rent or sell housing.

- Refuse to negotiate for housing.

- Make housing unavailable.

- Deny a dwelling.

- Set different terms, conditions, or privileges for sale or rental of a dwelling.

- Provide different housing services or facilities.

- Falsely deny that housing is available for inspection, sale, or rental.

- For profit, persuade owners to sell or rent (blockbusting), or

- Deny anyone access to or membership in a facility or service (such as a multiple listing service) related to the sale or rental of housing.

- Threaten, coerce, intimidate, or interfere with anyone exercising a Fair Housing right or assisting others who exercise that right.

- Advertise or make any statement that indicates a limitation or preference based on race, color, national origin, religion, sex, familial status, or handicap. This prohibition against discriminatory advertising applies to single-family and owner-occupied housing that is otherwise exempt from the Fair Housing Act.

Aside from the above classifications, each state and different cities have additional protected classes. If you are unsure of what additional protected classes are in your area, do an internet search of Fair Housing with your state, and you should get a plethora of helpful information. For example, a quick search in Google brings up the following additional protected classes in certain parts of Northwest Washington, in addition to the federally protected classes:

- Sexual Orientation
- Section 8
- Age
- Marital Status
- National Origin
- Creed
- Gender Identity
- Ancestry
- Use of a Service Animal
- Parental Status
- Political Ideology
- Source of Income
- Veteran/Military Status

Be sure to do some research into your local Fair Housing Laws. You don't want to find your mug on the front page of the Sunday paper for discrimination that you didn't even know you were doing. Ignorance is no excuse for discrimination.

Exceptions to the Fair Housing Rules

Of course, it wouldn't be United States law if there were not some loopholes that one could use to get around the law. Specifically, there are four common exceptions to the Fair Housing Laws, so let's touch on those now.

1. Age Discrimination and 55+ Communities

As mentioned above, Federal Fair Housing Laws prevent discrimination against familial status, and it is illegal to prohibit children. However, there is an exception to the law that exempts certain properties that are designated as a "55+ Community."

In order to qualify for the exemption, the housing community/facility must satisfy each of the following requirements:

1. At least 80 percent of the occupied units must be occupied by at least one person 55 years of age or older per unit;

2. The owner or management of the housing facility/community must publish and adhere to policies and procedures that demonstrate an intent to provide housing for persons 55 years or older; and

3. The facility/community must comply with regulation requirements issued by HUD for verification of age and occupancy.

In other words, if 80 percent of the units in a community owned by you have someone older than 55 living in them, and your visible intent is to provide housing for an older age bracket, and you abide by the laws that govern this exemption—you have the ability to exclude a familial status to include only those who are 55+ in age, thus discriminating legally against anyone younger with children.

Another note about the children issue: Simply *asking* the age of children can get you into hot water when screening for or renting out a property. Instead, we request the dates of birth for all persons living in the unit, so we can determine who needs to be on the lease and who doesn't. It may seem silly, but this distinction is important.

2. Owner-Occupied Residential Properties

If you own a single family home, duplex, triplex, or fourplex and currently live in one of the units or bedrooms (commonly known as "house hacking" on BiggerPockets), the Federal Fair Housing Laws do not apply to you. That said, it's still probably stupid to discriminate against someone, but it is not covered by the Fair Housing Laws.

3. Some Single Family Homes Without Advertising or Brokers

If you are trying to rent out a single family home and you don't use any sort of advertising or listing broker AND if you own less than four such homes at the same time, the Fair Housing Laws do not apply to your situation. Again, probably still stupid to discriminate, but the Feds won't be pounding down your door if you do.

4. Religious/Private Organizations

The fourth exception to the rule involves private organizations where allowance for certain individuals is required across the entire property. For example, a church owns a small multifamily property that they rent out to members of their congregation, or a charity buys single family homes and rents out rooms to women who are escaping domestic violence. As long as the discrimination is across the board for all tenants, the exception may apply.

While it's unlikely any of the above four are issues you'll be dealing with, it's still a good idea to know what those exceptions are in case they ever come up in your life. We still don't recommend discriminating against individuals even if you have a loophole, but that choice is yours.

Now, let's move on to talk about one of the most common and confusing discriminatory acts landlords unknowingly commit: discrimination against people with disabilities.

Dealing with Disabilities and Fair Housing

Tenants with disabilities have additional protections under the Fair Housing Act that landlords need to be aware of when renting out a unit. Like the other protected classes, a person with a disability should be treated no differently than someone without a disability. According to HUD's website, a person is disabled if they:

- Have a physical or mental disability (including hearing, mobility and visual impairments, chronic alcoholism, chronic mental illness, AIDS, AIDS Related Complex, and mental retardation) that substantially limits one or more major life activities.

- Have a record of such a disability, or

- Are regarded as having such a disability.

When you rent a unit to a person with a disability, the Fair Housing Act requires that you accommodate reasonable requests for changes in rules, policies, practices, or services and that you accommodate the tenant should they have a reasonable request to modify the dwelling or common areas—at their expense—to better suit their needs. Should the tenant choose to make modifications to the rental, they are legally obligated, when reasonable, to return the unit to it's previous condition once they have vacated. To refuse reasonable requests for adjustments in these areas is considered discrimination towards the person with the disability. However, notice that the cost of the expense rests upon the tenant, not you. We once had a tenant who requested a ramp leading to her door because she had trouble walking up the stairs. We explained to the tenant that we were not comfortable with the expense at that time; however, she did have the right to have the ramp built herself. Not paying for the ramp out of our own pockets was not discrimination, but refusing to allow the tenant the *option* to build the ramp herself would have been.

When speaking with any prospective or current tenants, never inquire as to the nature of their disability or make any comments as to why your unit would or would not accommodate their disability, even if you are just trying to be helpful. It is up to them to come to their own conclusions about whether or not your property suits them. However, according to the Washington Landlord Association, medical verification from a qualified medical professional can be requested if the applicant is seeking a reasonable accommodation. (Keep in mind, this is the legal opinion of a Washington State landlord advocacy group, not a lawyer in your city, so don't take this as legal advice—just passing on tips as we've heard them.)

For example, if a person requests accommodation for a service animal, the landlord may request verification from a medical professional that the service animal is needed. A service animal is not considered a pet and must be allowed by the landlord no matter what the pet policy is. If you would normally charge a pet fee or pet deposit for the privilege of keeping a pet on the premises, this must also be waived since a service animal is not considered a pet. That said, many tenants play the "service animal card" because they know it is a great way to get around the "no pet" policy. They will even get a doctor's note—and there is nothing you can do about it. Remember, do NOT ask them what their disability is or why they need the animal.

If you suspect that an applicant is lying about their need for a service animal ("My angry pit bull is my service animal," or "My seventeen cats are service animals!"), remember, do not reject them because of this. Instead, look at the other aspects of their application and determine if they meet ALL the other minimum qualifications. It's likely you'll find something that doesn't fit your qualifications, and only deny them based on that. (And be sure to keep a paper trail on why you denied them, which we'll cover in Chapter 7, just in case they later threaten a lawsuit.)

Marijuana and Fair Housing

With the legalization of recreational marijuana in Colorado and Washington and the use of medical marijuana in many other states, landlords are in the midst of a quandary regarding Fair Housing. Since the legalization is relatively new, and federally it's still illegal, there isn't much to go on as far as how a landlord should proceed in the case of a tenant using marijuana in their properties. However, to protect their property from smoke damage or the increased risk of a fire caused by smoking, the landlord may decide to place a ban on **all** smoking on their properties—except medical marijuana. In the case of medical marijuana, it appears the landlord cannot discriminate because of the Fair Housing requirement to allow reasonable accommodations and changes in policy in regard to disability. For the use of medical marijuana, the Washington Landlord Association currently suggests designating an outside area specifically for this purpose, but please check with a lawyer in your area if you live in a state that allows medical marijuana.

Drug Abuse, Disability, and Discrimination

This next topic might surprise you, but it's something you should be aware of: Federal law currently prohibits landlords from discriminating against prospective tenants who have had a felony conviction for drug use. Why? Because drug or alcohol abuse is considered a disability. According to the US Department of Housing and Urban Development (HUD):

"An individual with a disability is any person who has a physical or mental impairment that substantially limits one or more major life activities. The term physical or mental impairment may include, but is not limited to, conditions such as visual or hearing impairment, mobility impairment, HIV infection, mental retardation, drug addiction (except current illegal use of or addiction to drugs), or mental illness."[ii]

Notice that this concerns drug use, not drug sales or manufacturing. We would hope you would discriminate against drug dealers! But with those struggling with substance abuse, you must be careful. Obviously this is a sticky situation and one that is not 100 percent clearly defined by our government, so it would be wise to consult with an attorney on this subject.

Examples of Fair Housing Discrimination

So, now that you have some insight into protected classes under the Fair Housing Act, let's take a look at some examples of how discrimination might play out in the rental business based on what we just read.

Prospective Tenant: "This home is perfect for us and our four children!"

Landlord: "Oh, I'm sorry, but we don't allow children in our rentals. Too much liability!"

This is an example of discriminating against a person because of their familial status.

Prospective Tenant: "Would I be able to make some changes to the unit to accommodate my wheelchair?"

Landlord: "I'm not really comfortable with someone making changes to the house, so I don't think this is going to work out."

This is an example of discriminating against a person because of their disability. According to the Fair Housing Act, a tenant with a disability may make changes to the unit to accommodate their disability at their own expense; though when reasonable, they are responsible for returning the unit to its previous condition prior to vacating.

Prospective Tenant: "I was just wondering if you had a chance to go over my application?"

Landlord: "Yes, I did. You know, I'm not completely comfortable renting to a single lady in the neighborhood where the rental is located. I feel you would be safer and more comfortable in one of my other units. Why don't I show you one of those instead?"

This is an example of discriminating against a person because of their gender, as well as "steering." Steering is the act of a landlord directing a tenant to another location for a discriminatory reason: in the example above, the landlord is discriminating against the tenant by not renting to them based on their gender, as well as trying the steer them to a "safer" neighborhood, also based on their gender.

Now, let's look at some examples of words or phrases landlords use that could get them into trouble.

> **Landlord:** "Second floor unit, so individuals with wheelchairs shouldn't apply."

This is an example of using discriminatory language against people with a disability. You can mention the second floor unit, but don't tell people what they can or can't do. They can make that choice for themselves.

> **Landlord:** "For rent: Studio apartment for single female applicant."

The is an example of using discriminatory language against men.

> **Landlord:** "Because of the church next door, we're looking for a catholic applicant to rent the property."

This is an example of discrimination against a person's religion.

6 Tips for Staying Compliant with Fair Housing Laws

Of course, these are just a few examples—and fairly obvious ones at that. After reading the above list of protected classes and examples of discriminatory language, you may think you have nothing to worry about. After all, most of us would never *intentionally* discriminate against any of the above classifications. However, intentional or not, discrimination is discrimination, and even a well-meaning comment or decision made by the landlord (or anyone acting on behalf of the landlord) can be considered discriminatory, putting the landlord at risk. Therefore, it's important to review the Fair Housing Laws regularly to avoid sticking your foot in your mouth and winding up with a lawsuit on your hands. We don't want to scare you, but we also want to ensure you are prepared for your journey into landlording, so here are a few things you can do to ensure you aren't discriminating against any of the protected classes and to protect yourself from a potential lawsuit.

1. Be Knowledgeable

Know your local, state and federal Fair Housing Laws. In addition to what you'll read in this chapter, there are many resources online that you can look to for guidance, including The Department of Justice's website at www.justice.gov and The Department of Housing and Urban Development's website at www.hud.gov, to name a couple.

2. Have Your Standards in Place and Treat Everyone Equally

When advertising your unit for rent, and after you have placed your tenant, treat everyone equally and *be consistent*. You may find this hard to do when everyone who contacts you is coming from a unique position and is going to have their own unique questions, but one way to ensure you are treating everyone equally when renting out your unit is to have a predetermined list of questions and responses for every person, as well as predetermined qualification standards that you communicate clearly to all interested persons.

For anyone who contacts us about one of our advertised units, we use a form aptly titled "Potential Tenant Questionnaire" that gets completed for each person. Not only does the questionnaire make it easy to be consistent, but based on the answers we receive, we get a good idea whether or not they will meet our qualification standards, *and* we have everything in writing should they accuse us of being unfair or discriminating. We've included this form free for you in the appendix of this book, or you can download it by going to http://www.BiggerPockets.com/LandlordBookBonus.

After your tenant has moved in, stick to the lease and have a written policy for how to respond to all situations—then don't deviate from it. Deviating from your written lease or policy indicates inconsistency, which may lead to an accusation of showing partiality, also a form of discrimination. For example, if your lease states that a late fee will be charged for any rent not paid by the 5th and you enforce the late fee with one tenant (they're kind of a jerk) and not another (you like them), the tenant charged the late fee may feel they were discriminated against because of another reason. Regardless of your reasoning (one tenant was nice and the other a jerk), that situation could quickly get out of hand. It's best to simply practice consistency and stick to your written policies.

3. Don't Make Assumptions

When filling a vacancy, don't assume you know your potential tenant or know what they want. Prospective tenants who contact you are most likely contacting you about a specific property, but if not, don't make assumptions such as what type of dwelling you think they would prefer or the neighborhood you think they would be most comfortable in. "Steering" or pointing persons towards specific units or neighborhoods is also considered discriminatory and will potentially land you in hot water. One way to combat steering is by letting your prospective tenant know about *all* your available properties and letting them decide which ones they would like to see and which ones to avoid. Also, and this goes back to the Potential Tenant Questionnaire, if you have a predetermined list of questions for every caller, such as their price range, the type of housing they prefer, and the size and location they are looking for, you can quickly and legally point them towards any available rentals you have that meet those requirements.

4. Stay Consistent

When filling a vacancy, have a pre-determined set of **qualification standards** in place that you require of all applicants. Never set different requirements for different people. Your qualification standards should be based on valid business reasons. For example, you can set an income requirement of the minimum income your potential tenant must make to be accepted. By setting an income requirement, you are not discriminating against any particular class, just protecting your interest by taking precautions so they can comfortably pay the rent.

We'll talk much more in-depth about the qualification standards in Chapter 6, so we won't get into them now. Just keep in mind, the qualification standards are based solely on business reasons to ensure a responsible tenant. If an applicant falls short of any of the screening criteria, chances are they would eventually become a liability to our business. Therefore, *all* persons interested in renting one of our units must meet *all* of our qualification standards.

5. Be Careful with Your Words

When speaking with potential tenants, be very aware of what you say or how you phrase things. Even an innocent, friendly question or statement could be seen as discriminatory and a violation of Fair Housing Laws. An example would be asking a person in a wheelchair how they ended up there or even stating that they would probably prefer your downstairs unit since it's more accessible.

6. Keep Excellent Records

Keeping records of current (and former) tenants and all prospective tenants is extremely important. Not only will keeping detailed records potentially protect you in the event a discrimination charge is brought against you, but it's also a good business practice for staying organized and keeping track of things while you are filling a vacancy or during someone's tenancy.

In the case of renting out your unit and speaking with potential tenants, keep notes of each contact you had with the potential tenant, including the date and time they occurred. If they apply for your rental, you will also want to keep records of your screening results and the reason behind whether or not they were approved. If they were denied, send them an Adverse Action Notice, which you can read more about in Chapter 7, and keep all the information you collected about that applicant should the need arise to prove no wrongdoing on your part. We have a file in our file cabinet called "Prospective Applicants," where all our notes about each person get stapled together and go after our last contact with that person. We also have a file called "Denied Applicants," where all the information we collected about each applicant goes after they have been denied. It's not a fancy set-up, but it's organized and it's there if we ever need it.

The same goes for current and past tenants. Each tenant should have their own file, where all of their information is stored from beginning to end. During a tenant's tenancy, keep records of anything having to do with that tenant, such as phone calls, emails, letters, texts, complaints, notices, maintenance requests, repairs, and anything else having to do with their tenancy. After the tenant is no longer with you, don't toss the tenant's file - keep it in case you ever need it. Not only could it protect you in the event of a Fair Housing complaint, but accurate and detailed record keeping will also make your job as a landlord much easier.

When keeping records, try to think of it this way: You are telling a story from beginning to end. If someone other than you were to read it, would the story be absolutely clear?

Penalties for Violating Fair Housing

The specific penalties for a landlord who is found to be violating Fair Housing Laws vary, but assuredly they are expensive, painful, and public. If you would like to avoid attorneys fees, fines, and being made a public spectacle, avoid violating any of the protections under the Fair Housing Act. According to hud.gov, the penalties for violating any Fair Housing Laws are as follows:

- To compensate you for actual damages, including humiliation, pain, and suffering.
- To provide injunctive or other equitable relief; for example, to

make the housing available to you.

- To pay the Federal Government a civil penalty to vindicate the public interest. The maximum penalties are $16,000 for a first violation and $70,000 for a third violation within seven years.

- To pay reasonable attorney's fees and costs.[iii]

If that sounds painful and expensive, that's because it is! Don't discriminate and you'll do fine.

Wrapping it Up

If this chapter has scared you, that was not our intent. But the fact is, with great power comes great responsibility, and as a landlord you have incredible power over the housing situation of those in your community. America was built upon the principles of freedom and fairness for all, even if it's taken a few hundred years to get here (and we are still trying to improve). Fair Housing Laws are designed to keep landlords from knowingly or unknowingly committing acts that could affect the freedom of their tenants, so just be careful in what you do and say. And if you ever have any questions, don't hesitate to reach out to a lawyer who can help you make sense of a sticky situation.

Now that you have a solid grasp on how NOT to discriminate, let's use this knowledge going forward and talk about advertising your vacancy to maximize great applicants and minimize duds.

CHAPTER 5:
ADVERTISING YOUR VACANCY

What is the number one way to find tenants?

No, it's not by bribing them with free candy.

The correct answer is *marketing*.

Marketing your property is essential for reaching and appealing to the most people qualified to rent your property. In this day and age, there are many different options for advertising besides the old tried-and-true methods of simply placing a classified ad in the newspaper and a sign in the yard. When you are advertising your rental, find out what methods work in your market, then advertise the heck out of your property. After all, time is money. You'll have an awfully hard time finding tenants if no one knows about your rental! Before we get to where to advertise, though, let's talk about *how* to advertise your rental.

Defining Your Ideal Tenant

First, you need to know *who* your target audience is. Who are you marketing to? If you are renting a 4-bedroom house, you will most likely be appealing to a family (but for goodness' sake, don't say that in your marketing—remember the Fair Housing Laws!). If you are renting an apartment near a college, you are most likely appealing to a student. Knowing the audience you are marketing to will significantly affect the verbiage in your ad.

For example, you probably wouldn't include a line about the popular elementary school down the street while marketing a studio apartment, but you might when marketing your 4-bedroom house. Besides mentioning the type of property you are offering, research the area online and find out what people are saying about it. Are people drawn to the area for the schools, jobs, location, etc.? Get out in your neighborhood and talk to the neighbors. What appeals to them most about the neighborhood? Is it a transitional neighborhood or more family-oriented? Knowing if you are marketing to a family moving to the neighborhood for the great nearby elementary school or a single professional interested in nearby restaurants and jogging trails will significantly help you write an appealing ad for that person you are trying to reach.

When drafting your ad, it's important to be extremely careful to avoid any discriminating language. To conform to federal and state Fair Housing Laws, first you need to know what they are, then you can begin drafting your ad. Some things are obviously discriminatory, like refusing to rent to a person of a particular ethnic background, stating "no kids," or refusing to rent to a single mother because you believe she is "high-risk." However, not all discriminatory behavior or language is so cut and dry; this is another one of those situations where ignorance is certainly not bliss, and a well-meaning comment or remark, such as, "How old are your children?" or "I think you would prefer our downstairs unit because of your difficulty walking up stairs" might land you in the middle of a lawsuit.

When marketing your rental, you may use language that *appeals* to a certain audience you think may be interested in your property, but you cannot use language that indicates a specific preference or discriminates against any of the protected classes. According to Hud.gov[iv], "It is illegal for anyone to: Advertise or make any statement that indicates a limitation or preference based on race, color, national origin, religion, sex, familial status, or handicap. This prohibition against discriminatory advertising applies to single-family and owner-occupied housing that is otherwise exempt from the Fair Housing Act."

For example, do not include "perfect for families" in your ad; rather, if you are marketing to a family, highlight the parts of your rental or neighborhood that *makes* it perfect for a family. What do families generally gravitate towards? Perhaps the size of the rental (square footage and number of bedrooms), features like a fenced yard, the immediate location of the rental (at the end of a cul-de-sac, for example), or the approximate location of the rental and its proximity to nearby schools, parks, and other activities. Of course, your goal should be to rent to anyone who meets your legal screening criteria (see Chapter 6), and anyone should be welcome to apply to rent the home, but your marketing is really going to appeal to your target audience.

What Makes Your Property Desirable?

When advertising to your target audience, you will want to include descriptive language, not only of the *features* of your rental, but of its benefits as well. Merriam-Webster.com describes "benefit" as "a good or helpful result or effect." So, what are some good or helpful results or effects that your target audience will experience by renting your property? The point is to show your prospective tenants how your rental will be advantageous to their daily lives through the comfort, ambience, or convenience it provides. Is your property close to shopping, restaurants, coffee shops, parks, schools, walking or biking trails, a Farmers' Market, a desirable part of town, bus lines, the subway, popular attractions, or is it down a small country road, in a residential neighborhood, or at the end of a cul-de-sac? Does it have a bright, cheerful kitchen or a spacious backyard perfect for entertaining family and friends? Give your advertisement some personality and give your potential tenant the best description you can of your property.

Where to Advertise

Regardless of where you are advertising, remember to include all the pertinent information about your rental in your ad, such as location, price, deposit amount, utilities, and lease term, as well as a description listing the benefits of your property. Try and answer as many questions as you can up front in your ad to reduce unnecessary calls. Here are some of our favorite ways to let potential tenants know our rental is available.

Yard Signs

One of the oldest and most successful ways to market your rental is with a "For Rent" sign in the yard. The biggest drawback to a sign is instant notification of a vacant house to any would-be criminals. However, the benefit is that interested people walking or driving by are already familiar with the area, and neighbors can tell their friends and family.

Not any yard sign will do though. For under $20, you can create your own professional yard sign using a site like vistaprints.com to give your business a professional look right off the bat. Other signs that are helpful are directional arrow signs that you can put up around the neighborhood and literally point people right to your property. In addition to your professional yard sign, you can also leave informational flyers at the property as well, which we will talk about in more detail next.

Flyers

Flyers are a quick, easy, and almost free way to advertise your rental in places your target audience might frequent, as well as at the property itself. Common places that may have a bulletin board in the vicinity of your rental are grocery stores, schools, the post office, hospitals, coffee shops, churches, malls, restaurants, and business breakrooms. When we have a vacancy at our 2-bedroom apartment complex, we put up flyers at the grocery store, college, mall community board, and hospital cafeteria located nearby. We also provide a flyer box at each rent-ready property and keep flyers attached to our application there as well so interested parties can learn more about the property immediately.

The downside to unattended flyer boxes is that sometimes people will take ALL the flyers, either because they are interested and don't want anyone else to have a flyer or because they are just punks messing around. Regardless of the occasional empty flyer box, we still highly recommend using them since the benefits of having all of the information available to interested parties outweighs the couple of dollars we might have to spend replacing stolen ads. We like to make sure each person who schedules an appointment to view the property leaves with both the application and flyer so they have a reminder of all the details, features, and benefits of that particular place even after they leave.

Craigslist.org

Craigslist.org is one of the internet's largest classified advertising websites and one of the most effective ways to find tenants in your area. Perhaps the best part? Craigslist is free (unless you are a property manager in New York City). With Craigslist, potential tenants have the ability to search for available listings in a specific desired location using specific search criteria if they wish, and the landlord has ample room and flexibility to create an informational and appealing ad about their property. For safety purposes we choose not to put the exact address of our single-family rentals on Craigslist, but we do list the cross streets to give an approximate location on the map. One of our favorite features of Craigslist, besides its popularity, is the ability to upload up to 24 pictures, showcasing the entire property, to go along with your ad. To create your Craigslist ad, you can do so directly on their website - or read on to the next paragraph to learn how to post your Craigslist ad with Postlets.com.

Postlets.com

Postlets.com is owned by Zillow and is a great resource for landlords to create ads that will get maximum exposure. Postlets is an advertisement creation listing site; however, in addition to just creating your ad, Postlets also *distributes* your ad to numerous other sites (20+), including Zillow, Hotpads, Trulia, Yahoo! Real Estate, Military.com, and many more. You really can't beat the exposure. For the complete list of sites where your ad will appear, check out https://postlets.com/syndication-partners. Postlets is free (for landlords with buildings of less than 50 units), user-friendly, and gives you additional options of including a video or virtual tour in your ad and uploading unlimited pictures. After you have created your ad, Postlets gives you the HTML code to distribute your ad to other sites of your choosing that allow embeddable objects, such as Craigslist or your own website. The previous example is a Craiglist ad using Postlets HTML.

To create your Craigslist ad with Postlets, simply copy and paste the HTML code into the body of your Craigslist ad, confirm the location and contact information, and upload your pictures. The resulting ad appears orderly and professional with less work than simply creating a single Craigslist ad.

Zillow

Zillow is essentially the grand slam of rental marketplaces and probably a site your potential tenants are very familiar with when searching for a rental. Like Craigslist, Zillow is free for the landlord to advertise on and allows users to search for rentals based on certain criteria, including location, price, size, etc., then filters their results accordingly. To post an ad on Zillow, you simply create a Postlets ad, and it will automatically distribute your ad to Zillow and other sites.

The Local Newspaper

This may not work in every market, but advertising in the local newspaper is still a valuable tool for finding tenants in our market, though it can be spendy so it's not our very first option. Make sure to include all the pertinent information, like the general location, number of bedrooms, price, and contact information, as well as some of the features and benefits your property offers. Newspaper ads are usually fairly short and to the point, but don't be afraid to stand out a little and offer some descriptive wording.

We recommend not putting the address in the newspaper for a couple of reasons: 1) so your house isn't a sitting duck for would-be criminals, and 2) it forces anyone interested to call you so you can have a one-on-one conversation, do some pre-screening, and further "sell" the property before sending them over to check it out in person.

Sample:

(Location): Beautifully remodeled, 2-bedroom, ground-floor apartment available in nicely maintained complex in residential neighborhood. Convenient on-site laundry facilities. Walking distance to the Supermarket, College, and the Mall. Includes water, sewer, and garbage! Pet and smoke free. Rent: $535/month + Deposit. Call us today! (360) 555-5555.

Social Media/Facebook

That's right, you can (and maybe should) be using Facebook to advertise your vacancies. (Of course, you may be reading this in the future when Facebook is no longer the powerhouse it currently is. Just replace "Facebook" with whatever is popular for you.) People on Facebook love to see local topics, so by putting a link to your Craigslist ad on Facebook, you will likely find numerous local people sharing the listing on their wall, both in an effort to help you out and help their own family or friends.

There are several ways you could go about using Facebook to advertise your vacancy. First, you could simply share the link on your personal Facebook wall for your own family and friends to see. This is the free option, though you will be limited to just a small portion of your audience. Facebook currently allows you to "boost" your post so more of your Facebook friends will see the listing, which might be a good idea since just $10 will likely get you hundreds or maybe thousands of views. You'll also find that those who see the ad might not be interested in the property for themselves, but everyone knows someone who is looking for a place. They will likely "tag" people that they know, allowing even more people to see it. We've found incredible success this way—and it costs almost nothing.

Another way you could use Facebook to advertise your rentals, especially if you have more than a few properties, is by creating a Business Page for your management company. Then, you can either begin building a following for your company naturally through good engagement OR advertise your properties using Facebook Ads. Facebook typically charges per click, and as of this writing, We pay around $0.40 per click. That means if 100 people clicked on the ad, we would pay $40. Of those 100, how many will call? That will depend a lot on who you advertise to (Facebook allows you to get VERY specific) and where you are sending them. We've found that it typically costs between $30 and $40 to acquire a new tenant using Facebook Ads, which is more expensive than Craigslist but comparable to the newspaper. You may find better or worse results, depending on numerous factors.

Existing Tenants

If you own or manage multiple properties, one of the best sources for potential tenants will come from your existing tenants. Everyone has family or friends who are looking for a new place, and if you are a good landlord (which you will be after finishing this book!), then tenants will love to refer your company to everyone they know—especially if they are incentivized to do so. If you offer a referral bonus to your tenants for referrals that lead to tenancy, they have a *really* good reason to tell people they know about your vacancy. We offer our tenants a $100 referral bonus for any applicant they bring us who becomes a tenant. Don't worry about the money the referral bonus might cost you—because vacancy costs a lot more!

We market to our existing tenants in our multi-family properties by sending out postcards that say "Choose Your Neighbor!" In an apartment complex, what tenant wouldn't want to have a say in who moves in next door? Rather than leave it up to the landlord to fill the vacancy with a complete stranger, tenants have the opportunity to have their best friend, co-worker, cousin, barista, mom, nephew, or babysitter right next door. We also include information about the property and a coupon on the back of the postcard for a $100 referral bonus for any leads that result in tenancy. To track this, the applicant must give us the postcard when they apply. If they were not given the coupon, we also have a spot on our application asking where the applicant heard about our property. If they write the name of a current (or past) tenant and are later approved for tenancy, we send the referring person a thank you card with their check enclosed. However, if the applicant writes "Craigslist" on the application, then later someone tries to claim they referred them, we have a way to verify the legitimacy of their claim.

Tracking Your Advertising Results

Lastly, when advertising your property for rent, always make sure to ask interested callers where they heard about your property. Tracking your incoming calls, emails, or texts will help you discover what parts of your marketing are working—and what aren't. After all, there's no point advertising in the local newspaper if it doesn't generate any calls. Our Tracking Spreadsheet is *really* simple and broken down by the week. Whenever someone calls about our property for rent, we just make a tally next to the appropriate source.

Property: _____

Week of: ___/____/____ - ___/____/____

Source:

Source	Tally
Newspaper	1
Yard Sign	111111111111
Flyers	1
Craigslist	111111111111111
Zillow	11
HotPads	111
Facebook	111111
Referral	111111111
Other	

At the end of every week, we can see where the majority of our leads are coming from, which gives us some insight on where we can amp up our advertising or pull back. For instance, in the previous example, just one person called from the newspaper ad. If this was a regular occurrence, we would know the newspaper probably isn't a valuable source for finding tenants in our area and we should focus more on other avenues for advertising the property. Tracking where your callers are coming from is just one thing you can do to become more efficient.

Taking Quality Photos

Have you ever seen an ad for a property for rent and were immediately turned off because of the awful, quickly shot, low-quality pictures? Online ads are especially guilty of this, and in fact, the *majority* of rental ads you will find on Craigslist (for example) are full of ads that were obviously taken with a cell phone, usually at weird angles, in poorly lit rooms, or of awkward things (toilet seat up, anyone?). Your ad is usually the first time your prospective tenant is introduced to you, so it's logical to aspire to make a good impression. Taking some time and putting a little effort into your pictures will help accomplish that goal. In fact, the majority of prospective tenants won't even look at online ads without pictures. Here are some tips for using pictures in your marketing.

Lighting

Lighting plays a huge role in determining the outcome of your pictures, as it makes the space look more open, warm, and inviting. You want your prospective tenants to imagine themselves sitting at your kitchen counter, sipping a steaming cup of tea with the warm, bright sunlight shining in on them. That's going to be hard for them to imagine if you took your pictures in the evening or in the middle of a rainstorm. For this reason, consider taking your pictures on a bright, sunny day. In addition, make sure you turn on all the interior lights in the property and open all the blinds and curtains to make the property look as warm and inviting as possible.

The best time of the day to take your pictures is going to be when you have the most natural light available, most likely in the middle of the day. Avoid taking pictures when you have dark shadows to deal with or when it is dark. If you live in an area where it rains frequently (such as Northwest Washington), consider taking at least exterior pictures of your property when the sun is out, even if you aren't advertising it at that time. Those pictures will come in handy when you have a hard time getting bright pictures during the dead of winter.

A Rent-Ready Interior

Before taking the pictures for your ad, make sure the unit is orderly, clean, and rent-ready. Don't take pictures mid-rehab or before the unit is completely ready to show. Take a look around and make sure there is nothing that will stand out as "awkward" in your shots, such as your purse or cleaning supplies sitting on the counter or open toilet lids. Consider staging the interior with a few items—such as a vase of flowers or fruit on the counter, or curtains in the windows—to make it appear more "homey." If you have tenants currently in a property and you know they have nice furniture and decorating skills, offer them an incentive such as a gift card or rent credit for the opportunity to take a few "furnished" pictures for future marketing. Those will be very useful in the future for showing tenants a visual of how the unit looks furnished.

A Rent-Ready Exterior

The exterior should be free of any items that don't normally belong. If there is off-street parking, such as a driveway, make sure your car is not in it. The lawn should be freshly landscaped with nice lines and the flower beds weeded. If it is a property that has bark mulch, it's not a bad idea to freshen that up as well. Your goal here is for the property to look well-maintained and in tip-top shape.

Ready, Set, Shoot: Equipment

Now that the property is ready for its glamour shots, it's time to actually take the pictures! For high-quality pictures, you will need high-quality equipment. No 1997 flip-phone camera photos allowed!

The Camera: A normal point and shoot digital camera or even an iPhone camera will do the job; however, consider investing in a DSLR camera if you really want a professional look. A DSLR camera is going to take higher quality, crisper images, give you wider angles, and allow you control with the depth of field, creating that beautiful "blurred" background that makes the image you are focusing on really stand out. The Canon T3i is the camera we use, and it takes beautiful, high quality shots. This particular camera is currently around $550 dollars but is worth every penny. And as an added bonus, you can use it for candid shots on family vacations! If a DSLR camera is not in the budget, at the very least use a camera that takes high-quality images - the outcome will still look professional if you take the necessary steps to prepare the property ahead of time for your pictures.

Tripod: Though a tripod isn't necessary, it's just one more tool you can add to your tool belt to create professional-looking pictures. You can find a tripod for around $20 on Amazon or even a tripod adapter for your smartphone for under $10, which will give you an even angle (you don't want potential tenants thinking the walls are slanted) and steadiness.

Cheese!: Lastly, take lots of pictures! Besides being descriptive with your ad wording and including all of the pertinent information like rent, deposit, utilities, and lease specifics, your ad is going to make the biggest impression with pictures. Remember, the majority of people won't even bother with an online ad without pictures. First, you will want to include a picture of the front of the home, followed by pictures of all the main rooms, such as the kitchen, living room, dining room, recreation room, bathrooms, and bedrooms, as well as the garage, yard, landscaping, patio, garden, and all the special features of the property, both inside and out.

When creating your online ad, include as many pictures you can since you are giving your potential tenant a virtual tour of the property and you will want to show them as much as possible. Craigslist, for example, allows posters to include up to 24 photos, and Postlets allows you unlimited photos, so feel free to take advantage of that space!

Wrapping it Up

Hopefully you gleaned some useful tidbits from the information in this section that you can implement when you market your next rental property. Just remember, when advertising your property for rent:

- Know who you are advertising to.
- Include the facts—this means all of the pertinent information.
- Don't be boring—be descriptive in your wording.
- Don't do anything that could be considered discriminatory based on the Fair Housing Act.
- Advertise like crazy.
- Use lots of pictures!
- And above all, be professional.

Whether your prospective tenant learns of your property from a sign, a flyer, or an ad you created online or for the newspaper, marketing is essential to a successful rental property business. Not only is this the quickest way to attract high-quality tenants, it's also their first impression of you and the way you run your business. Make it a good one.

Now that you have a firm grasp of how you are going to get the phone ringing, what do you do next? How do you pick the best tenant and avoid the duds who will destroy your property? The next two chapters will focus on picking the right tenant, starting with the pre-screening process. Let's go there now!

CHAPTER 6:
TENANT PRE-SCREENING

Are you looking forward to phone calls at 3 a.m., consistently late rent, drug-dealing tenants, and costly evictions?

Of course not. No one wants to be the landlord with those problems. So why do so many landlords find themselves in this kind of trouble? The answer is that most of these landlords never learned the correct way to rent out their property from the beginning.

Chances are you've heard the horror stories from landlords about costly evictions, destroyed properties, professional tenants from hell, and all the reasons why you should not rent your property out. While these stories receive the most press and attention, the fact is, every day millions of landlords are renting out houses and apartments to great tenants across the world. While all hassles can't be eliminated completely, by following the tips, tricks, and techniques outlined in this chapter, you will be able to minimize those hassles and turn your rental into a profitable venture. Many look at the process of filling a vacancy like the "pregame" show - but in reality, getting your house rented IS the game. And if you learn how to rent your property intelligently from the beginning, you can avoid years of headaches later.

Screening your applicants is one of your most important tasks as a landlord. In fact, we would even go so far as to say it is your *most* important task, as the tenant you choose today is going to affect you for better or for worse for the entire length of their tenancy. We can all agree we would choose a good experience over a bad one any day. Your tenants are the lifeblood of your rental business, so it is essential you do everything you can to screen out the deadbeats and only rent to quality tenants.

A deadbeat tenant can wreck havoc on a landlord's sanity in more ways than not paying the rent on time. They will also allow the property to fall into disarray, and despite your best efforts, their drama will somehow always manage to involve you. This doesn't sound like anything a landlord would willingly volunteer for.

So what kind of tenant DO you want?

Simple: a **great** one.

What Makes a Great Tenant?

The most important decision you make that will determine the success or failure of your rental is *the person you put in the property*. A bad tenant can potentially cause years of stress, headache, and financial loss, while a great tenant can provide years of security, peace, and prosperity. Don't underestimate the importance of renting to only the best tenants. While it's not possible to know with 100 percent certainty what type of tenant your applicant will be, there are some telltale signs and traits that will give you a pretty darn good indication that they are great tenant material. Here's what you should be looking for.

Their Ability to Afford the Rent Payment

The first and foremost quality of a good tenant is their being financially responsible and their ability to afford the rent. Without proper payment, the landlord will be forced to evict *and* be faced with potentially thousands of dollars' worth of legal fees, lost rent, and damages. Most landlords require that a tenant's (documentable) income equal at least three times the monthly rent. Many tenants believe that they can afford more than they really can - so it is the job of the landlord to set the rules to protect their investment. If the tenant is already financially responsible, earning three times the monthly rent should be sufficient.

Their Willingness to Pay on Time

While some landlords look at late rent as a benefit because of the extra income from the late fee, a late-paying tenant is more likely to stop paying altogether. The stress involved when the rent doesn't come in is not a pleasant experience and can be avoided by only renting to tenants who have a solid history of paying on time.

The Long-Term Outlook for Their Job Stability

While a tenant may be able to pay the rent and pay it on time right now, their ability to do so in the future is often determined by their job situation. If they are the type to switch jobs often or have long periods of unemployment, you may find long periods of missed rent.

Their Cleanliness and Housekeeping Skills

No tenant stays forever—and when they leave, you want the property back in good condition. As such, it is important that the tenant's day-to-day living be clean and orderly. They must take good care of the property you have entrusted with them.

Their Aversion to Crime, Drugs, and Other Illegal Activities

A person who has no regard for the law will also likely have no regard for your policies. Tenants who engage in illegal activities will cause nothing but stress and expense.

The "Stress Quotient"—How Much Stress Will They Cause You?

The final quality of a great tenant is something we call their "stress quotient," or in other words, the amount of stress a tenant will cause you, the landlord. Some tenants are very high maintenance and constantly demand time and attention. Others simply ignore the terms in their lease and need constant babysitting, reprimanding, and discipline (late fees, notices, phone calls, etc.). This type of tenant will only be a thorn in your side.

Obviously, no tenant is going to be 100 percent perfect, so deciding how close to perfection you will require is a personal choice that largely depends on your desired involvement level and the community in which your property is located. If tenants are difficult to find, it may be financially advantageous for you to rent to a less-than-perfect tenant in order to fill vacancies. Notice we say "less-than-perfect tenant," not "anyone." On the other hand, if you have plenty of applicants to choose from, you can be significantly more picky. Just remember, it's much better to have your unit vacant a little longer while you wait for the right tenant than to rent to the wrong person.

So, how exactly do you weed out the bad ones and find those quality tenants? The answer involves setting strict qualifying standards and screening your applicants to verify whether or not they meet those standards. Now let's go over what tenant screening is, and then we'll move on to how to set your qualification standards.

What is Tenant Screening?

When we talk about screening tenants, what exactly are we talking about?

Screening tenants is about digging into a potential tenant's background and discovering *who* they really are. Because, like we previously discussed, who they really are is going to play a very large role in what type of tenant they will be. Most potential tenants (though not all) will attempt to put their best face forward and be on their best behavior when looking for a rental and speaking with their new potential landlord. If they don't, that's not a very good sign. If they do, that still doesn't tell you everything you need to know about whether or not they will make a great tenant. You need **verifiable proof** based on their past and present that they will be a great tenant like the ones we just talked about, without taking their word for it or simply relying on your gut.

An application (which we'll discuss in Chapter 7) can only tell you so much and can be easily manipulated or falsified by the person completing it. Never rely solely on the information the applicant has provided you. Screening your tenant means looking into the information they provided on their application and verifying its validity, as well as analyzing any additional outside information you can discover. After you have vetted your applicant, you should be able to come to a reasonable estimate on the kind of tenant they will be. We say "reasonable estimate" because there are no surefire ways to know with absolute certainty the future quality of a tenant, though based on the results of your screening, you should get a pretty good idea. As landlords it is our job to simply screen effectively and choose the best possible candidate.

So, what does screening your potential tenant look like?

Pre-Screening Potential Tenants

You've begun advertising for your property and receiving calls, emails, and texts with questions from potential tenants. Contrary to popular opinion, screening doesn't begin with a background check or an application; it begins with the initial contact. This is known as **pre-screening**.

Screening is not a flippant activity that you can do in a few seconds. It can take a considerable amount of time, time that you shouldn't spend on every person who shows interest in your property since chances are most won't work out anyway. That would be exhausting. This is why pre-screening is so important. Think of the screening process as a funnel—like the kind you would use to pour oil into your vehicle. At each step of the process, you are able to narrow down the pool of applicants until only a small few—or just one—match. Pre-screening is the widest part of that funnel and will help to keep away those who obviously won't qualify or don't fit the property, either by their own determination or yours.

Before we continue, we want to offer a bit of a disclaimer on the subject of pre-screening. We'll talk a lot in this section of pre-screening about how to identify and eliminate people early on who will take up your valuable time, only for you to realize later on that they aren't the tenant you are looking for. Just remember, at the end of the day you are simply trying to find someone who meets all of your *qualifying standards*, indicating that they will be a great tenant and take care of your property during their tenancy. To help avoid Fair Housing violations or complaints during the pre-screening and screening process, remember to treat everyone equally, have a pre-determined list of qualifying standards that each person is informed of and all applicants must meet in order to be approved, offer everyone the opportunity to apply (even if you have already told them they don't meet your minimum standards—if they know they won't qualify, they usually won't apply; it's the invitation that matters), and keep notes of each interaction. Also, as we talked about already in this book, be sure to avoid discriminating language, such as:

- "No kids."
- "Family-friendly."
- "How many kids do you have?"
- "Are you married?"
- "What country are you from?"
- "When is your baby due?"

Lastly, always respond to questions on qualification based on your screening standards, instead of a "yes" or "no" answer. This will help keep people from misinterpreting your rules or policies for the property as discriminatory. Here are a few examples:

> **Question:** "Do you accept the XYZ government assistance program?"
>
> **Answer (if you don't want to accept that program):** "One of our minimum screening standards requires a minimum income of three times the rent."
>
> **Question:** "I was evicted three years ago. Is that a problem?"
>
> **Answer:** "One of our minimum screening standards requires good references from all previous landlords for the last five years."
>
> **Question:** "Do you rent to people with bad credit?"
>
> **Answer:** "One of our minimum screening standards requires a credit score of at least 600."

None of these questions in particular are covered by Fair Housing (unless you are in an area that prevents discrimination from Section 8). However, by always referring to your qualifying standards, the person will quickly get the idea that you base your decision for qualification on whether or not they will meet the qualifying standards, not based on **them** in particular (such as being a certain gender, a certain race, familial status, etc.).

Pre-Screening Through Your Advertising

Your pre-screening efforts begin with your advertisement. Regardless of your method of advertising, the information you include in your advertisement will help to weed out time wasters. For example, stating "no pets" in your ad will significantly reduce the number of calls from people with pets. Stating "no smokers" will significantly reduce the number of calls from people who smoke. Stating your qualifying standards will significantly reduce the number of calls from people who would not qualify due to lack of income, references, previous evictions, background, etc. The point is to include as much information as possible in your advertisement to save yourself from 1) answering obvious questions over and over, and 2) spending time on someone who sounded great until you met them in person and they had a cigarette in their mouth while shaking your hand. Save yourself the trouble and include as much information as possible up front.

Pre-Screening Through the First Phone Call, Email, or Text

The initial phone call or other contact from the interested party is the next logical step in screening tenants. When someone calls, don't simply agree to show them the property. This is a common mistake nearly every rookie landlord makes, but you'll waste countless hours if you simply agree to show the unit without talking with the potential tenant first.

The first thing you hear is often an indication (though not proof) of the kind of tenant they might be. If the first words you hear after saying hello is a voice yelling into the phone, "How much do I have to have to move in," you can assume the tenant might not be a great fit. (We get these calls weekly!) After all, they are more concerned with getting in *anywhere* than even asking to look at the property.

When a tenant calls about a property we have for rent, we pull out our "Potential Tenant Questionnaire" (included in the appendix of this book or at http://www.BiggerPockets.com/LandlordBonusBook) and begin with, "What can we tell you about the property?"

This open-ended question allows the tenant to begin talking and asking questions. Many of the answers to these questions are already listed in the advertisement for the property, but that's when you just smile and answer them anyway. Chances are they are simply trying to get the conversation going, or they scribbled your contact information down on a piece of paper with multiple other available rental numbers and they simply don't remember which one you are.

The typical questions are generally:

- "How much is it?"
- "What's the address?"
- "Do you accept pets?"
- "Are the utilities included?"
- "How much is the security deposit?"
- "Will you work with me on my security deposit?" (No.)
- "When can I schedule a showing?"
- "Do you do background checks?" (Yes.)

The kinds of questions asked by the tenant are great indications of the type of tenant they are going to be. Are they concerned only with obtaining occupancy as soon as we'll let them in? Are they asking questions that would interfere with our policies, such as whether they can pay the deposit in installments or whether their significant other can be absent from the lease even though they'd be living there, too? Some of the best indicators they won't work out aren't even questions at all, but red flags you can pick up by simply letting them talk and gleaning what you can from what they say.

Are they complaining about their current landlord? They'll complain about you, too. Do they currently live with friends or family? There is a good possibility they are trying to hide their current landlord from you due to a bad reference. Are they hollering at family members on the other end of the line in between breaths? They'll holler in your apartment, too. We are not suggesting that you immediately judge a tenant on their ability to ask good questions or say the right thing—in fact, that's a bad idea—but it is important to take note of what they say and how they conduct themselves to refer back to *if and when* you have further contact with them.

In the initial contact conversation, we also make sure to tell them the minimum qualifying standards for getting accepted to rent the property. Usually this is easily worked into the conversation, beginning with, "We like to let everyone know up front the minimum standards for this property, which are…"

Many times we simply get a *click* after stating a standard they may not particularly like, or they simply tell us, "Thank you," and we never hear from them again. However, many times they will volunteer information, which we keep notes of, on each one of the standards as we go down the list. If they state something that is in conflict with one of the standards, we can easily let them know that in order to qualify, they must meet all of the qualifying standards. Even though it may be obvious to us both at this point that they won't qualify, we still let them be the one to decide if they would like to proceed with applying for the rental or not to avoid any Fair Housing complaints.

This simple, short phone call accomplishes some important time-saving tasks:

- It eliminates most of the "bad apples" right off the bat.

- It eliminates people who aren't necessarily "bad apples," but who still fall short of our qualifying standards.

- It eliminates people for whom our property or terms didn't meet their requirements.

- It informs the good prospects that we care about the property and those who rent it, and that we take the time to make sure we only rent to great tenants.

In all four cases, a win for us. This is what makes pre-screening so important. It allows you to save time, avoid nuisances, and project a good image to your future tenant. Without pre-screening, you may not have found out it wasn't a good fit until you had already invested your valuable time in showing the property and processing an application.

Pre-Screening a Tenant in Person

The next step of the pre-screening funnel happens when meeting with the potential tenants and showing them the property. This is a great opportunity to do some additional "unofficial" screening before any paperwork is filled out and processed. At this time, we also always restate our minimum requirements to the potential tenant in person, as well as give it to them in writing at the showing, just in case they didn't understand, forgot, or chose to ignore the minimum requirements when we spoke previously. We will talk more about showing your property later on in this chapter, but for now, let's just look at some things you will want to observe when pre-screening in person.

- **How are they dressed?** There is no need to dress up for a showing, but you will want to observe if they appear put-together or if they are a wrinkled, dirty mess. Showing up in pajamas is a huge red flag (yet still happens 10 percent of the time!).

- **Are they clean?** A stinky person, a stinky rental makes!

- **How do they conduct themselves?** When meeting a landlord for the first time, a potential tenant should approach it as an "interview" and behave accordingly. If they are loud, obnoxious, rude, flippant, careless, and letting their tag-alongs run wild throughout the home, that won't change if they become your tenant.

- **Do they make eye contact?** If a potential tenant can't look you in the eyes when speaking with you in person, that should be considered a red flag. What are they hiding?

- **Who did they bring along with them?** It's normal to bring the people who will be living in the home with you when looking at a potential rental—or maybe even your parents or a friend. What the landlord will want to observe, however, is who else the potential tenant brings along with them. If they indicated on the phone that they would be the only person living in the home but then bring along their thug boyfriend, you can bet that person expects to live there as well.

- **What condition is their car in?** If they showed up in an old, beat up car with fast food cups falling out the doors, landlord beware. The type of car doesn't matter so much as the *condition* the car is in—but both are something to be aware of when meeting the tenant for the first time. If they don't maintain their car, how can you expect them to maintain your home?

In addition to your observations when meeting the tenant for the first time, this is also the point where the potential tenant might be a little more honest and open with you than perhaps they were previously. Maybe they admit that they don't *quite* meet all of the requirements but are really interested in the rental. Or maybe they ask a question that we are not comfortable answering immediately, such as permission for a cat or small dog in a pet-free rental. If we need time to think about it, we always tell them that we will get back to them. If we know immediately that they will not be approved, we let them know but also still provide them with an application and an invitation to apply. Why? If they know they won't be approved, they usually won't apply, but we don't ever want to be accused of being discriminatory to any of the protected classes. For more information on the Fair Housing Act and how it relates to the landlord, refer back to Chapter 4.

These suggestions are just one small part of the screening process in your search in finding a tenant. In addition to pre-screening, you will also need your prospective tenants to fill out an application, then you will need to process that application to make sure the tenant is a good fit for your property. We have referenced multiple times the *qualification standards* you should have in place before renting out your unit. Before we get much further in discussing the screening process, let's go over those now.

Setting Your Minimum Qualification Standards

The minimum requirements you set that potential tenants need to meet in order to qualify to rent from you are extremely important and not something to take half-heartedly or deviate from if you have a momentary lapse in judgment. In fact, the qualification standards that you set now will protect you *during* that hypothetical lapse in judgment. By having qualification standards that all applicants must meet in order to be approved for tenancy, you are increasing the likelihood that the person you approve will have the traits of a "great tenant" and will be someone you can feel confident will take care of the property, pay their rent on time, be responsible, and in general meet all the other qualities landlords look for in a tenant. You are also protecting yourself from discrimination complaints since you require all applicants to meet the same requirements.

A landlord who does not require their applicants to meet certain requirements and rents to the first nice person to walk through the door is setting themselves up for major disappointment. Chances are, that "nice" person isn't who they say they are, and eventually their true colors will shine, most likely sooner rather than later. The landlord who doesn't screen their applicants has a painful learning curve in front of them.

As a landlord, you should require they at minimum meet the following requirements if you want to increase your chances of success:

1. Income Must Be Three Times the Monthly Rent

Tenants rarely know how much they can really afford for rent. We've had people interested in renting from us who make either less (yes, less) or barely more than the rent, and they expect that everything will just magically work out each month. How can they afford food, clothing, utilities, and all their other bills if their entire monthly income is going toward rent? Unfortunately for the landlord, the answer is probably by them not paying it. Requiring their income to be three times the monthly rent (or more) has been used by landlords for many years, as well as by banks and other financial institutions that supply loans. It's an important standard if you want to receive that rent check every month. By giving an exact minimum income requirement, you can keep out those who might believe they can afford to pay the rent but really can't, and you can feel comfortable knowing that your tenant should have enough money coming in each month to pay all their bills.

Besides having a current income of three times the monthly rent, the landlord also needs to be aware of where that income is coming from and how long it will last. We will discuss in the next chapter how to verify income on an applicant, but understand that income could come from a variety of sources. For example, the most common form of income is employment, but it's not the only source. Retirement benefits, government programs, child support, and more could all be counted toward income.

Additionally, you will want to know more than just the amount, so you'll need to dig into the stability of that income. For example, if the potential tenant is employed, you will want to take into account 1) how long the potential tenant has been in their current position and 2) whether the position is considered seasonal or temporary. If they are new to their position or have a history of changing jobs frequently, you may want to require a double deposit for added security if you decide to rent to them.

Social Security: In addition to your other screening criteria, if your tenant's income is from Social Security, you will need to verify that it equals three times the monthly rent. Some landlords will waiver on this policy when it comes to tenants who receive Social Security since it is guaranteed money every month. However, even though it is guaranteed, it is still extremely important to require that it equals three times the rent to be sure they can afford the rent in addition to their other bills. Just because it is guaranteed to them doesn't mean it is guaranteed to you.

Section 8: Another common source of income you will likely encounter is via a government program known as Section 8. Section 8 is not a protected class where *our* rentals are located; however, in some areas it IS. You will need to check whether or not refusing to rent to Section 8 tenants violates your local laws. Conversely, if it is not a protected class, you will need to decide if it is a program you are willing to accept or not. We'll talk about that in more detail later in this chapter.

Other Programs: There are many programs out there that help tenants with their moving expenses or with their rent each month, usually due to being low-income or while waiting to get on some other program or income assistance source. While these programs are tempting because they seem "guaranteed," there are a few problems the landlord could run into:

1. They are fairly easy to get on—and equally as easy to lose if the tenant doesn't hold up their end of the bargain by continuing to meet the program requirements. The requirements are usually fairly simply, such as attending periodic meetings or doctor's appointments or turning in periodic paperwork, but from our experience, tenants on these programs seem to have a difficult time completing them, resulting in their being dropped from the program and leaving us without a paying tenant.

2. If the tenant does manage to stay on the program, it won't last forever. Most if not all of these programs have a time limit and will run out, once again leaving the landlord without a paying tenant.

3. Since these assistance programs are for low income tenants, these applicants automatically don't meet the income requirement of bringing in at least three times the monthly rent, putting the landlord at a lot of risk when the tenant is dropped from the program or it runs out. Once again, this leaves the landlord without a paying tenant.

Income is one of the most important factors you will be looking at when deciding to rent to a tenant. However, it's not the only requirement, so let's talk about the rest now.

2. Tenant Must Have Good References

The references you receive from past landlords are the best indication of the way the tenant will behave for you. A bad reference from a past landlord is a huge red flag. People change, sure, but why take that gamble? Always get references from multiple past landlords, and do not rely solely on a reference from a current landlord since you don't know their motivation for giving a good or bad reference. A past landlord has nothing to gain or lose by being honest, whereas a current landlord may not want to lose a good tenant or may be overly excited to get rid of a bad one. Both situations may affect the legitimacy and integrity of their reference.

Negative references from family and friends are also a huge red flag. Don't put too much stock in a good reference from a friend or family member since most people close to the applicant are going are to be "on their side" and give a good reference whether or not they know the facts. We've known a lot of people over the years who were nice people, but we'd never want to rent to them! Where you'll want to pay attention is if a friend or family member gives a negative reference. That reference is most likely based on facts.

3. Tenant Can't Have Evictions

This falls under the same category as requiring good references from past landlords. Obviously, an eviction equals a bad reference. A very bad reference. An eviction on a tenant's record is the equivalent to committing murder in a landlord's eyes. An eviction means the tenant severely violated the rental agreement, usually by non-payment of rent, and rather than make it right, they buried their heads, forcing the landlord to use the law to remove them from the premises. An eviction also usually involves a trashed house,

1-3+ months of lost rent, and extensive damages. If a tenant has an eviction on their record or a judgment from a previous landlord or property manager and you accept them anyway, just know that there is high probability that you will be next. This is another situation where people can change, but it's best to let another landlord take that chance.

Early in our investing business, we accepted a tenant who had a prior eviction, charging her a double security deposit to reduce our risk. We believed that because the eviction was several years prior and her income was significantly higher now, she had turned over a new leaf. During the next three years, that tenant consistently paid rent late, threw trash out her window, broke items in her unit, and finally stopped paying rent one day, and we were forced to evict. That eviction, plus lost rent and damages, cost us nearly $5,000. Lesson learned: People seldom change. Now if a tenant has an eviction, we just say "no."

4. Tenant Must Pass Credit Requirement

A person's credit score is evidence of their willingness and ability to pay their bills. Since a landlord needs a person who is willing to consistently pay their rent and utilities, it's never a good idea to rent to someone with bad credit. For consistency, determine the lowest credit score you are comfortable accepting, and make that part of your screening criteria. Companies vary on what score exactly determines good and bad credit, but below are the determinations from credit.com[v].

- Excellent Credit: 781-850
- Good Credit: 661-780
- Fair Credit: 601-660
- Poor Credit: 501-600
- Bad Credit: Below 500

In the beginning of our landlording career, we didn't have a credit score standard since it seemed every tenant at the time claimed to have "bad credit." However, we quickly learned the importance of adding a credit standard to our qualification standards since a person's credit life is evidence of their financial responsibility and plays a large role in their "tenant life" and subsequently our "landlord life." As a recent guest on the BiggerPockets Podcast declared, "Tenants have to actually put effort into building a credit score, whereas a criminal report just shows they haven't yet been caught."

We found over time that most of our challenging tenants were also the tenants who had bad credit. When we set a standard, it automatically disqualified the majority of applicants who were not financially responsible, and our lives as landlords got that much easier. To meet our qualification standards, all applicants must have a credit score of at least 600+. This standard works for our business in our market and has produced quality tenants who pay their rent on time. We'll talk about how to run a credit check in Chapter 7.

Keep in mind, according to the Fair Credit Reporting Act, if you deny an applicant based on information received in a consumer report, you have to provide that applicant with the name and address of the reporting agency and give them the option of obtaining a copy of the report themselves. This should also be done if you accept the tenant but require additional securities or different terms due to the information contained in the consumer report. Whenever you deny an applicant or accept them conditionally, send them a Denial/Adverse Action letter, as discussed in Chapter 7 (and included in the appendix of this book and at http://www.BiggerPockets.com/Landlord-BookBonus), and simply fill in the blanks.

If a prospective tenant doesn't have any credit, you may want to consider denying the tenant, requiring a cosigner, or requiring a double deposit for added security.

What if an Applicant Has Had a Bankruptcy?

A person may file bankruptcy for a number of reasons, and although it is indicative of their financial responsibility, it may not be a 100 percent "no" from us. When dealing with bankruptcy, we just adhere to the credit score requirement. Our belief is that the credit reporting agencies have done a lot more research into the subject than we have, so we'll trust their judgment on it. If you do plan to rent to someone who has a bankruptcy, it would be wise to require a double security deposit for any applicant who has a bankruptcy in their past for added security. And of course they better meet every other one of the qualification standards.

5. Tenant Must Pass Background Check

Another important qualification requirement is to require a background check be completed on all applicants over the age of 18. Currently we use either Rentprep.com or MySmartMove.com to complete these reports, and for around $35, we will receive the applicant's background *and* credit report. A thorough background report will verify the applicant's identity (Social Security number, past/current addresses), as well as search the applicant's background for their:

- Criminal/Sex Offender History

- Judgments/Liens

- Prior Evictions

When you receive the results from the background check, you will need to verify that the applicant's Social Security number is valid and that their past (and current) addresses line up with what they listed on their application. If there are any discrepancies, the applicant has some explaining to do.

Discrimination and Felonies

As we discussed briefly in Chapter 4, federal law currently prohibits landlords from discriminating against prospective tenants who have had a felony conviction for drug use (as drug abuse is seen as a disability and is therefore covered under Fair Housing Laws), but not drug sales or manufacturing[vi]. Keep this in mind when looking at a tenant's background or holding to a blanket "no felony" policy, as technically you cannot refuse to rent based on someone's previous drug abuse-related felony. This would also apply to someone with DUIs or DWIs on their background, as they are drug and alcohol-related!

There are also some who have the opinion that a blanket "no felony" policy could be constituted as discrimination, as some demographics may have a higher rate of criminal convictions, and therefore, a "no felony" policy hurts one demographic over another. We think this is baloney, as that logic could be applied to anyone in any situation, but to avoid any issues, we simply take into account the tenant's "whole picture" in relation to ALL of our qualification standards and make our determination for qualification based on whether or not they meet or exceed our standards and exhibit a pattern of responsibility with regard to their life and background. If the applicant has a criminal history, you may want to evaluate that on a case by case basis. For example, if they have an assault felony from a bar fight nine years ago, it's probably not going to affect their tenancy, though they wouldn't be our first pick if we had better options. However, if they have had multiple run-ins with the law or have offenses with a sexual or violent nature, that's probably your cue to move on to the next applicant. They aren't great tenant material, so deny them and move on.

Note: When you deny someone tenancy based on information received in a consumer report, you must send them an Adverse Action Notice. We'll talk about this in depth and provide you the form in Chapter 7.

Additional Qualification Standards to Consider

The previous five standards are critical measures every landlord should consider implementing if they are interested in ensuring that the tenants they approve are "great tenant" material. You'll notice that all the qualification standards listed are based on the tenant's previous actions and decisions. How a tenant has lived and responded to situations in the past is an excellent indicator, good or bad, of how they will live and respond to situations in the future. In addition to the above critical qualification standards, you may also decide to require additional standards, such as:

- Establish a non-smoker requirement. (We do.)

- Establish a no pet requirement. (We do, depending on the property.)

- Establish a reasonable occupancy limit. (We limit two people per bedroom.)

Of course, just be sure that those requirements neither violate any Fair Housing Laws nor limit your prospective tenant pool to unreachable levels.

Next, let's move on and talk about something mentioned earlier that you will likely encounter in your search for the ideal tenant: Section 8.

Section 8

Section 8 is a rental subsidy program funded by The Department of Urban Housing and Development (HUD) and run by local public housing agencies. In other words, Section 8 will help pay all or some of a tenant's rent. Section 8 is available to low-income, elderly, and disabled tenants to help pay their rent and utilities. According to the HUD's website[vii], in order to qualify for Section 8, the applicant's combined total family income cannot exceed 50 percent of the average income for the area, and over 75 percent of vouchers go to applicants whose income is 30 percent below the average income for the area.

Additionally, Section 8 requires that properties be held to certain HUD-approved standards, and all Section 8 rentals must be inspected before the landlord can receive money from the Section 8 program. Most of these requirements are common sense things that you shouldn't have a problem making sure your properties have, such as windows that open, heat, ventilation in the bathroom, and more. Furthermore, Section 8 defines the maximum amount of rent they will pay based on bedroom, which can be both good and bad, depending on what they define for your area. In our area, Section 8 pays almost $100 more per month over what we can get from other non-Section 8 tenants, which provides added incentive to take the Section 8 Program.

So should you accept Section 8? Let's look at some of the pros and cons to help you decide.

Pros of Section 8:

1. You'll generally not need to worry about the Section 8 paid portion of the rent being late, as it comes directly from the local public housing agency every month.

2. Tenants must meet and adhere to certain requirements of the Section 8 program or potentially be faced with being dropped from the program. For example, one of the expectations is that the tenant complies with the terms in their lease.

3. Housing Authority will conduct annual inspections of the unit, making sure the tenant is not destroying the property.

Cons of Section 8:

1. In order for the rental to qualify for Section 8 tenants, the unit must be inspected by the local public housing agency and meet the program's standards for habitability on an annual basis. We listed this as a "con" since it requires that the landlord adhere to the government's standard of habitability, not their own. It's not necessarily a bad thing, just something to keep in mind.

2. If the landlord presents a nice, clean, habitable home that meets all Section 8 requirements, then the tenant allows the home to fall into disrepair by not caring for it properly or failing to report maintenance issues, not only is that a problem in and of itself for the landlord, but it can also lead to the tenant being dropped from the program. This means no income, no rent, and no reimbursement

for forthcoming damages.

3. Even though the tenant must meet the Section 8 program's guidelines to keep their Section 8 status, there is no guarantee they will, once again resulting in being dropped from the program and leaving the landlord with a tenant who can't afford the rent.

4. Finally, in our experience, Section 8 tenants can be more difficult to manage than their unsubsidized counterparts. We've typically found that Section 8 tenants cause more damage to the property and often allow more garbage and junk to pile up than our other tenants. Perhaps this is due to the fact that (in their mind) they aren't financially responsible for what happens, or perhaps it's simply a correlation between low-income tenants and cleanliness. But whatever the reasons, whether financial or socio-economic, Section 8 tenants are often harder on a property, which is the number one reason why we don't jump to rent to Section 8 unless a weak rental market makes it advantageous.

We have had both good and bad experiences with Section 8 tenants. One bad experience we had with Section 8 involved an inherited tenant (they were in the rental when we purchased it), and it was *really* bad. We'll spare you all the dirty details, but it went from bad to worse very quickly and ended in a long, drawn out eviction, a house full of cockroaches, a death threat, and a few thousand dollars in rehab costs—plus months of lost rent! This situation could probably have been avoided altogether had the property manager who placed the tenant screened correctly, but that's one of the risks you take when buying properties with existing tenants.

Just because a tenant is on Section 8 doesn't automatically make them a good or bad tenant. It's up to the landlord to screen every applicant correctly and thoroughly and only accept those who meet their minimum standards. If you do decide to accept Section 8 in your rentals, you will need to be sure all applicants meet all your other criteria, including rental references (do they abide by the terms of the lease, do they have good housekeeping habits, are they all-around good tenants?), credit (do they pay their bills?), background (do they obey the law?), and any other criteria you have for your rental.

Ok, enough on Section 8. Let's get back to the landlord job of pre-screening.

Showing the Property

One of the first questions prospective tenants ask when contacting a landlord about an available rental property is, "When can I schedule a showing?" Since your rental could potentially be their new home, it's a logical question. However, your response should not be, "How about today at 4:00 p.m.?" Before ever scheduling a personal tour of the property with prospective tenants, there are a couple things the landlord needs to do first.

Phone Pre-Screening

Remember when we talked about pre-screening your prospective tenants during your initial contacts with them earlier in this chapter? Most people value their time—I'm sure you do, and I'm sure your prospective tenant does as well. Because of this, it's in your best interest to do a little investigative work to determine whether the home is a good fit for both parties before taking the time and effort to show the property. You can accomplish this with a short conversation. During your first contacts with the prospective tenant, make sure you have a list of standard information you go over and ask of them, like the following four tips. Never show a property blindly not knowing that the person you're showing it to is a legitimate option—unless of course you've got a lot of time on your hands. Before scheduling a showing:

- **Ask them what they would like to know about the property.** This is always the first question we ask a tenant when they call. Usually the answer is met with a few seconds of silence or stuttering, as the tenant is not used to being asked questions. However, we think this is a valuable question, as it will help you gauge what's important to them and give you the first glimpse into the kind of tenant they'll become.

- **Make sure they are aware of all the terms for the rental.** This includes items such as rent, deposit, lease terms, pet policy, and what utilities are and are not included, as well as the general description of the home, including amenities. During this part of the conversation, you might find out they are looking for a short lease term that you can't accommodate, or they are looking for a home with a dishwasher, which yours doesn't have. Both examples result in the same outcome—they aren't going to work out. By getting that out of the way early on, you've saved yourself a trip to the property.

- **Make sure they are fully aware of the qualification standards for the home.** Usually prospective tenants are fairly open during this part of the conversation, which gives the landlord a heads up of whether or not they are worth pursuing further. If they don't meet any one of your standards, they will usually (though, not always) tell you. For example, if you tell them you have an income requirement of $2,500 per month for a particular rental and they tell you they only make $1,500, you can easily let them know that in order to qualify for the home, they must meet the income requirement. Once again, you've saved yourself a trip.

- **Finally, let them talk.** People don't like pauses or "awkward" breaks in conversation, so feel free to simply be silent and let them tell you a little bit about themselves. When prospective tenants are the ones having to fill in the conversation, you'd be surprised at what you might learn.

Have Them Drive by the Property

This step can happen before or after the pre-screening conversation, but it's important that it happens before you schedule a showing. You have no idea if the neighborhood in which the rental is located or the rental itself is what the prospective tenant is looking for, and neither do they, so always send them by the property first, and tell them to call you back after they have driven by to schedule their showing. Doing so will save you both unnecessary time lost. If they contact you after driving by and you have pre-screened them as well, you can feel more confident that they may be a legitimate option when you schedule their tour of the home.

Group Showings vs. Individual Showings

Scheduling group showings versus individual appointments are up to the landlord's personal preference, but both are options and accomplish the same task.

Pros and Cons of Individual Showings

By scheduling a separate appointment for each prospective tenant, you are able to give them your full attention to highlight the properties features and conduct further pre-screening. The downside to scheduling individual showings is you might have to do quite a few of them before you get your ideal tenant. Also, something we discovered early on when renting out units is that many times the people who are scheduled to meet fail to show up. Why? We are still trying to figure that one out! Maybe they found something else, changed their mind, slept in, forgot, or are just plain irresponsible. Pre-screening and calling ahead of time to verify the appointment significantly improve the show-up rate, but even so you will have some no-shows when meeting prospective tenants individually. To combat this, we started doing group showings.

Pros and Cons of Group Showings

Group showings are exactly how they sound: showing the available rental to a group of prospective tenants all at the same time. The obvious benefit to group showings is you can knock a whole lot of showings out at once. If you have five people scheduled all at the same time and only three show up, that's still a successful showing. Having a group showing also creates an atmosphere of competitiveness, resulting in prospective tenants applying right away rather than waiting and potentially finding something else.

Another benefit to group showings is each person gets the chance to see who their competition is and may decide to disqualify themselves. If a prospective tenant doubts their chances of beating out their competition for being the most qualified applicant, there's probably some validity to that. Some people may feel slightly uncomfortable during a group showing since they are in direct competition with their fellow attendees, though in our experience the benefits of group showings outweigh the short period of awkwardness they may feel. Keep in mind when doing a group showing, it will be impossible to be everywhere in the house at the same time, so I don't recommend group showings when another tenant still lives in the property.

Another good option for showing your rental to multiple people without wasting multiple trips is scheduling showings 15 minutes apart. This gives you the best of both worlds in a small amount of time: dedicated one-on-one time with each person, while also overlapping each appointment with the next, letting each person know there are others interested and creating that feeling of competitiveness.

Always Confirm Appointments

Before taking the time to interrupt your day, jump in your car, and drive over to your available rental to meet a prospective applicant, always call first to verify the appointment. As we discussed previously, for whatever reason the turnout rate for rental showings is far from perfect, so always confirm the appointment with each person the day of to verify that they will be there. This is especially important if you are doing individual showings. However, even after calling and confirming the appointment the **day of** with your prospective tenant and getting their assurances that they will see you there, sometimes they still don't show. Don't think about it too much—it'll drive you crazy.

To combat this problem, we have also had success with the following solution: Instruct your prospective tenant to *call you* to confirm the appointment one hour before their scheduled time. If they call, then you know they will be at the appointment, and you can plan on the showing as scheduled. Since we live and work approximately thirty minutes away from many of our rentals, we always let our prospective tenants know that if they don't call to confirm their appointment, no one will be there to meet them. If they don't call, don't waste your time going to the property. If they end up calling at the property wondering where you are, you know they aren't very good at following simple instructions.

Make Sure the Property is Rent-Ready

Before showing your available rental to prospective tenants, first make sure it's ready. On the day of your showing, always make sure to arrive early. If the unit is vacant, turn on all the lights, open all blinds and curtains, and adjust the temperature to suit the season: If it's cold outside, turn up the heat; if it's summer, open up a couple of windows or turn on the AC if you have it. You may even want to put a bowl of chocolates or a vase of flowers on the counter, depending on the unit. Your goal is to make the home appear as comfortable, welcoming, and "homey" as possible.

If you will be showing an occupied unit, make sure you are aware of the condition it is in and the tenant's housekeeping skills before scheduling any showings. It would be a waste of time to show a unit that has not been maintained by the current tenant. With that said, if you are confident of the condition and cleanliness of the unit and you will be showing the unit while it is still occupied, be sure to notify your tenant at least one day prior to make sure the showing coordinates with their schedule. Each state has specific laws regarding the amount of notice the landlord is required to give the tenant prior to showings, so be sure to become familiar with the laws in your area. As long as you have the tenant's permission, you can give less notice than what is legally required, but remember to be considerate of the fact that it is still their home. Most tenants are very cooperative with showings and will be very accommodating. Arrive to the appointment early enough to greet your current tenant and assure them you will disturb them as little as possible.

Safety

Showing vacant units to prospective tenants, while most of the time harmless, can place the landlord in a vulnerable position. After all, prospective tenants are complete strangers. You don't know their true history or their true motive for wanting to view the property. It is for these reasons that the landlord should take precautions to ensure their safety.

- Leave valuables in the car and out of sight.
- Conduct showings during the day, never at night or dusk.
- Always let someone know where you are going, who you will be meeting, and how long you will be gone.
- Consider carrying pepper spray, like the kind you can attach to your keychain.
- Be aware of your surroundings at all times.
- When scheduling the showing, in addition to collecting the usual information like name and contact information, also request their driver's license number.
- If you feel uneasy around them, let them walk through the home on their own while you wait outside.
- If you will be doing group showings or showings back to back, make sure they know that other people are on their way.
- If you are doing individual showings and feel uncomfortable showing the unit alone, have a spouse or friend ride along and wait in the car.

Don't let these suggestions make you think that every prospective tenant who comes through your property is a potential ax murderer. The point is, you simply don't know them. Maybe they are, maybe they aren't, but you have nothing to lose by being cautious.

The Tour

Now that you have met your tenant in person and are ready to show the unit, we broach the question, "Should you let the tenant walk through the unit alone so they can take their time, or should you lead a tour?" When showing vacant units, for safety reasons, if you feel uncomfortable with them, by all means have them walk it alone. However, since most tenants aren't out to get you and are simply looking for the next place to call home, a personal tour of the property is definitely beneficial. A personal tour gives the landlord the opportunity to point out all the specific benefits and features of the property, as well as to be available to answer any questions the prospective tenant might have while walking through the property.

Don't simply walk through the home and only remark, "Here's the living room—and the dining room. Bedrooms are in the back. Any questions?" Take this opportunity to really sell your property. "Here we have the kitchen. As you can see, it has received many upgrades, and the layout is wonderful with the open-concept kitchen and living room. It's perfect for having company over for dinner. Also, there is so much cabinet and counter space!" Don't overwhelm your prospective tenant or make your rental seem like something it isn't, but don't be afraid to highlight all the positive aspects about your rental either. Help them imagine themselves at home there.

Showing Units While Occupied

No tenant likes the idea of their life being interrupted by their landlord walking a complete stranger through their home. However, it is necessary, common, and expected. It should also be in your lease that you have the right to show the property. Assure your existing tenants that should you show the property while they are still living there, you will give them advance notice and respect their privacy as much as possible. It's a good idea to include this sentiment with your move-out instructions as well (included in the appendix of this book, as well as at http://www.BiggerPockets.com/LandlordBookBonus). We always give our existing tenants at least 24 hours' advance notice (which is the requirement in Washington for a "Notice to Enter") that we will be showing their unit—and usually try to give even more notice than that. Of course, if the tenant gives you permission, you may show the unit in a shorter timeframe, but the more courteous and respectful you are of their time, the more likely they are to accommodate your showings.

Materials

When showing available units to prospective tenants, you should have certain information about the property on-hand. We like to organize everything into convenient "Property Packets" and give one to every prospective tenant who walks through the door. The Property Packets include:

- **Page 1:** A picture of the exterior of the property with the location and rent amount. This is also a good place to attach your business card if you have one. If you don't, right now is a great time to consider getting some.

- **Page 2:** The description (we just use the description from our online ads) and all the specifics about the property, including rent, deposit, lease term, utilities, and any lease specifics, such as the pet policy. You should also include your qualification standards here. We like to begin this section with: "Below are the qualification standards for this home. You will not be approved if you do not meet the qualification requirements." End this page with an invitation to apply for the home if they meet your qualification standards.

- **Page(s) 3+:** The rental application (included in the appendix of this book, as well as at http://www.BiggerPockets.com/LandlordBookBonus).

Give every person to whom you show the property their own packet so they can take it home with them and have all of the information about the property with them to refer to later. Chances are, they have looked at many different rentals besides yours, so your handy informational packets will make it convenient to remember the details and to apply after they have walked out the door.

11 Most Common Questions Asked By Tenants —Answered

When renting out an available rental, you'll quickly notice that a lot of your time is spent answering questions from prospective tenants. Some questions are really easy, such as, "How much is the rent?" Others should be dealt with a little more carefully. Below are some of the eleven most common types of hard-to-answer questions you'll get when renting out your property with some responses you may want to consider.

1. "I can pay 6 months up front. Can I move in this weekend?"

Whenever a prospective tenant offers to pay "X" number of months up front, there is a reason, and it's usually not a good one for the landlord. In fact, it's a big ol' red flag. Usually it means they are aware of something that will affect them negatively in their background, and they are hoping the dollar signs will dissuade the landlord from properly screening them. Accepting prepaid rent from a risky tenant doesn't help the landlord at all. When that prepaid rent runs out, that tenant is still risky, and the landlord has no additional securities to compensate for that.

Furthermore, should the case arise where you are forced to evict the tenant, prepaid rent can definitely muddy the waters. If you are inclined to rent to someone who doesn't quite meet your qualifications standards, you would be much better off requiring an additional security deposit as allowed by your local laws. So, here's a good response for dealing with questions of this nature: "We don't accept prepaid rent; however, you are welcome to fill out our application, and after we have properly processed it and verified that you meet all of the qualification standards for the home, we would be happy to talk about getting you into the home by this weekend." After this response, chances are they will disappear and move on to the next unsuspecting landlord.

2. "I know you said you don't allow pets, but would a small dog be okay?"

The answer to this question should be easy; however, for some reason when people ask this question, it can be hard to be firm. Maybe it's because a lot of us are animal lovers at heart. If you really are uncomfortable with the idea of having pets in the property, a polite "I'm sorry, but this home is strictly a pet-free home" should be sufficient. However, if after meeting your prospective tenant and finding out they have a pet you decide to allow it, at least require additional securities, such as a pet fee or an additional deposit, and add a Pet Addendum to your lease. For more information on Pet Addendums, see Chapter 8.

3. "Can I pay my deposit in installments?"

The landlord should always collect all of the move-in funds in full prior to letting the tenant obtain occupancy. If they can't afford the security deposit, they probably aren't very good at handling their money. This is a good indication you'll have trouble later. Early in our career, we used to allow tenants to do this until we realized that it never worked, not even once! Unless you enjoy chasing down security deposit payments on your weekends and evenings, simply respond to this question with a firm, "Our policy states the security deposit must be paid in full prior to getting the keys. Do you have any family or friends who would lend you the funds?" Ending with a question of your own puts the ball in their court and allows you to move on to the next applicant. Amazingly, almost every time we have this conversation with a potential tenant, they come up with the money after all and were simply trying to prioritize their spending. In this case, you just made yourself the priority, setting a great precedent for the future of their tenancy.

4. "Can I take possession in two months?"

This question is a little bit trickier than the others because it depends on your rental market. You need to ask yourself this question: "How will I maximize my income?" For example, if our real estate market is soft and we have a reasonable expectation that the unit might sit vacant for another month or two, we might feel more inclined to hold the unit for the tenant. However, this is *seldom* the case due to our marketing machine and will likely be the same for you. It truly is a numbers game. If we feel we can make more in the long term by holding it, we'll do that; if not, we won't. Sometimes you won't be sure, and you'll have to trust your instinct.

Keep in mind, the tenant's move-in date is a point of negotiation. For example, the tenant may ask us if they can move in four weeks from the time they applied. If we really like the tenant and we think it's in our financial best interest, we will try to split the difference and reply, "We can only hold the unit for up to two weeks; however, we would require a deposit to hold the unit. Does that sound reasonable?" Nine times out of ten, the tenant will agree to this compromise.

5. "Can my due date be the 15th?"

"No." Trust us on this one. It might be fine on your first unit or two, but as you gain experience and build your portfolio, you will quickly regret your decision to allow your tenants to have different due dates. Having the rent due on the first is standard in the rental industry. Again, this question may indicate they are not good at handling their money. It's not necessarily a deal-killer, but it's definitely a sign that they live paycheck to paycheck (as many tenants do).

6. *"Do you accept the _____ Program?"*

We already talked about this earlier in this chapter, but let's touch on it again briefly since it's a common question. There are many assistance programs that are available to low-income tenants to help them with their rent. Personally, we've had issues accepting tenants on programs with the understanding that it was guaranteed income, only to discover how quickly and easily a tenant can lose the funding. This leaves the landlord holding the bag with a tenant who clearly cannot qualify on their own.

Of course, there may be excellent programs out there that we are not aware of, so we would recommend asking around to local landlords for advice. If you simply don't want to deal with these programs, your best response to this question may simply be, "Our policy states your income must equal three times or more the monthly rent." Keep in mind that Section 8 is a protected class in some areas, so do your due diligence and make sure you're not violating Fair Housing Laws before making any decisions.

7. *"Are you the owner?"*

This question also isn't as easy as it sounds, and it is completely up to you as to how you will answer it. Generally potential tenants aren't asking if you're the owner simply because they are curious, but because they see the owner as the ultimate authority and the person who can grant them special privileges or exceptions to the rules in regard to the rental. If you're a non-confrontational type of person, you may be tempted to make an exception (that you will quickly regret) to your rules or policies simply to avoid an awkward conversation. For this reason, you may want to consider adopting the name "property manager," rather than "owner" for your tenants.

If you are "only the property manager," tenants seem to have a much easier time understanding why you can't accommodate certain requests. We first heard of this strategy when we were new, 21-year-old landlords from Mike Butler's book *Landlording on Autopilot*, and it has helped us on many different occasions transform ourselves from the guy who can bend the rules to the guy who's simply doing his or her job in managing the property. So, if you'd rather not disclose that you're the owner, don't. When faced with the question "are you the owner," you may simply want to respond with, "I am the property manager for this home" and leave it at that. It's not a lie, simply an omission of all the facts, which they have no business knowing.

8. *"Will you consider a short-term lease?"*

Turnovers and vacancies can be two of the most expensive processes the landlord goes through, not to mention the time that goes into filling a vacancy, so most landlords look for long term tenants, and many refuse to do anything shorter than a year lease. However, if the rental market is slow and you can compensate for the fact that the lease would be short term by charging more for rent for that privilege, it's not necessarily a bad idea. Before making that decision, though, you will want to consider the time of year and the month the lease would be expiring. The last thing you want is to agree to a short term lease, only to have it expire in the dead of winter, which also happens to be the worst time to fill a vacancy. If we are not accommodating short term rentals and are faced with that request, we simply state: "Our lease is a minimum of one year, though we are always looking for tenants who plan to stay much longer."

9. *"I'm in a hurry. Can I pay the rent and move in today?"*

This question is a giant red flag and should always be met with extreme caution. There really are **no** good reasons for someone needing to be in that much of a hurry to move. A response along the lines of "You are certainly welcome to fill out our application, and after it has been properly processed to ensure you meet all of our qualification standards, we would be happy to discuss your move-in date in a couple days" should be sufficient to send them on their merry way.

10. *"My boyfriend/mom/sister wants to live with me, but I don't want them on the lease. Is that okay?"*

Let's start this paragraph off with a scenario. Say this tenant moves in as the only person on the lease, and you agree to allow her boyfriend/mom/sister/ whoever to move in with her *without* being on the lease. What happens if your tenant on the lease leaves and her roommates stay? You are left with a legal tenant(s) with whom you have no contract. Besides that, there are usually legitimate reasons the tenant doesn't want the roommate on the lease with them, and none of those reasons bode well for the landlord. In this situation, it's best to respond with, "Anyone over the age of 18 living in the home must fill out an application, meet our screening requirements, and be on the lease. I'm sorry, but we cannot make an exception to this policy."

11. *"What if I don't meet all of your criteria?"*

When prospective tenants ask this question, it's usually because they know they do not. Some issues, such as a lack of rental history, aren't necessarily a deal killer and can be compensated by requiring additional securities or a co-signer. In this situation, it's wise to get some more information from the tenant.

What if you don't know the answer?

Whenever you are unsure of your response to a question from a prospective tenant, especially if it has to do with special requests or alterations to your policies, don't feel bad about not answering right away; it is perfectly acceptable to let them know you will have to get back to them. This allows you to separate yourself from the immediate situation and go home and think on it. Ask yourself, "Is this decision the best one for my business?" This is also where the BiggerPockets Forums come in extremely handy. Post a question now, and within a few hours, you'll have potentially dozens of experienced landlords chiming in to help. Many of the questions that potential tenants ask are the same, and you will get them many times over in your landlording career. This allows you to determine your answer ahead of time, so you are prepared with your response before the question is ever even posed.

7 Tenants We'll Never Rent to

There are a lot of different types of people out there, with different personalities, quirks, attitudes, and opinions—and trust us, we've rented to them all! Over the past several years, there are certain character types we've learned to quickly run away from. These traits are not invisible and can usually be discovered by doing thorough tenant screening prior to approving a new tenant. Tenant screening involves more than verifying that your tenant earns an adequate income, has some references, and hasn't murdered anyone. You also need to make sure they aren't going to drive you crazy while they are your tenant! Hopefully this list of seven "fictitious, but totally plausible" tenant types will give you a good idea of who you should be watching out for when renting out a property.

Let's get started.

1. Entitled Tim

Entitled Tim grew up as the baby in the family, so naturally expects the world to be handed to him on a platter. Tim expects the landlord to abide by his every wish because Entitled Tim deserves it. Before even becoming a tenant, he shows up to the property showing and immediately informs the landlord that the stove and fridge have been used before, so they will need to be replaced. Clearly, Entitled Tim deserves only brand new appliances, carpet, countertops, and paint.

Only the best for Entitled Tim—because the world owes it to him.

2. Dirty Dan

Dirty Dan isn't just dirty—he's filthy and doesn't care.

Not only is Dirty Dan dirty, but his kids Rotten Roger and Grimy Gale also contribute to the mess. Every wall in the home will soon be covered in an artistic collage of mud, crayon, and hair (from Dirty Dan's oversized Dingy Dog). Dirty Dan doesn't understand that vacuuming needs to be done more than once a year and garbage tossed out the back window won't be magically placed in the garbage can. He laughs when his children pour red Kool-Aid all down the hallway, and he changes his motorcycle oil on the living room carpet.

Sometimes Dan's girlfriend Lazy Laura comes by and offers to help clean up, but usually ends up just making a bigger mess for everyone and joins in the filth. Dirty Dan knows he isn't the cleanest, so he avoids calling the landlord at all costs so his dirtiness will never be found out, even when a water supply line breaks in the ceiling and begins destroying the drywall in the kitchen. Eventually, Dirty Dan will move out and adamantly insist that he should get his entire security deposit back.

3. Lazy Laura

Laura hasn't held a job in more than six years because her employers have all demanded too much. Lazy Laura doesn't understand why everyone is always in such a hurry to do things! "Eat, drink, and be merry" is Lazy Laura's motto in life, and most of her days are consumed watching episodes of talk shows trying to determine who the baby's daddy is. Lazy Laura usually guesses wrong.

Between the frequent naps and endless time spent on Facebook, Lazy Laura sometimes remembers to pay the rent on time, but usually will pay it when it's most convenient or when the consequences of not paying become greater than the inconvenience of needing to get off the couch. Laura eventually leaves without giving notice, moving in with her boyfriend Dirty Dan, leaving the landlord with a mess and no rent.

4. Dave the Dealer

Dave the Dealer doesn't seem like such a bad tenant—on the surface.

It seems like he'd be a really fun guy to hang out with at a party, and he reminds you of the goofball in those '80s movies you used to enjoy so much. Dave is smart, articulate, and overly polite. Even better, as a tenant, Dave the Dealer always pays his rent on time and even goes the extra mile to get you the rent in cash before it's due. Although he gets a lot of foot traffic in and out of this property (several dozen shady-looking characters a day), he keeps a clean house and never causes problems.

However, Dave the Dealer's good streak can only last so long before the cops break down the front door and haul him down to the county jail. Suddenly, Dave's cash is a little tight, and some questionable people are hanging around his house while he's locked up. The house gets tagged with some explicit cartoon drawings, and the front window is smashed through with a rock from another dealer. It soon becomes clear that Dave the Dealer isn't such a fun guy after all.

5. Steve the Stoner

Steve the Stoner is another "fun" tenant for landlords.

He doesn't have the business sense that Dave the Dealer has, so he simply consumes the goods that Dave deals. Steve the Stoner isn't a violent fellow, but the neighbors complain of loud noises coming through the walls late at night and have even seen Steve jogging around the block in nothing but his underwear, waving a plunger. With only lava lamps to light the way, Steve tends to keep to himself in his dark apartment, Power Ranger bed sheets strung across every window making sure it's generally as dark as possible inside his place.

Steve eventually loses his job, but decides that there's a better alternative to job hunting: getting stoned. Luckily, you won't have to evict Steve 'cause he'll just trash the property and leave in the middle of the night.

6. Larry the Lawyer

There is nothing wrong with having a good attorney on your team, but Larry the Lawyer may not be the kind of tenant we want in our properties. Why? Because Larry knows how to work the system. Larry knows how to skip paying rent for six months and avoid prosecution by using obscure technicalities and irritating loopholes. Larry the Lawyer enjoys tormenting his landlord and making a game out of his misery. There are a lot of rentals out there where Larry might live—we just don't want him in ours.

7. Dramatic Darla

Dramatic Darla is the first to let you know about the talking she can hear through the walls of her apartment. She is also extremely nervous about the paint that got on the outlet cover in the kitchen during the last interior paint job, the neighbor (Dirty Dan) three houses down who has far too many cars parked in his driveway, and the nail hole in the ceiling that clearly will let bugs through.

Dramatic Darla spends a lot of time on WebMD, trying to determine the illness her child suddenly has—which was probably caused by faulty drywall in the home she is renting. Dramatic Darla demands that her landlord install a whole-house air purifier because of the toxic air quality and threatens to withhold the rent because she saw an ant in her pantry. Dramatic Darla has also Googled you, found your personal cell phone number, and makes every attempt to call at least once per day.

———

Whew! Of course, this section was meant to be exaggerated, but the fact remains: There are certain types of tenants you simply do not want to deal with. If there is one lesson we've learned as landlords, it's this: Wait for the right tenant and screen everyone, even if they seem nice at the beginning. We do not advocate ever discriminating against a tenant for any of the protected classes, but this doesn't mean you need to accept the first tenant who shows interest in your property.

By rushing and putting in a tenant who will cause you months or years of headaches, you are only costing yourself more money and stress in the long run. Do your due diligence with every prospective tenant. Dig into their background, their credit, their previous landlord references, their social media, their job history, and anything else you can (legally) find, and try to get a feel for what kind of tenant they are going to be.

Before you rent to any tenant, take a moment and ask yourself one important question: Is this a tenant I am willing to bet part of my financial future on? If not, move on and find a safer bet.

Wrapping it Up

Finding tenants is easy. Finding quality tenants takes a little more work. Hopefully the information outlined in this chapter gives you a few extra tools to add to your landlord tool belt to help you confidently navigate the pre-tenant stage of rentals. Now that we've talked about what makes a great tenant and delved into using your pre-screening skills and minimum qualification standards to filter out the duds, let's move on to deciding how to properly screen your applicants through your application. In Chapter 7 we'll dig into the application process—how it works, what information you should require, how to verify the information you receive, and finally, how to accept and deny applicants to approve only those who are great tenant material.

CHAPTER 7:
THE APPLICATION PROCESS &
TENANT SCREENING

The rental application is the second step in the tenant screening process and occurs after pre-screening, which we discussed in Chapter 6. The application is where you collect all of your prospective tenant's personal information from which you will conduct your screening. Never rely on an applicant's responses on their application when screening—it's easy to falsify information on paper. It's the landlord's job to take the information they have been provided and verify its legitimacy. It's during the screening process that you might discover an eviction or negative landlord references when the applicant has claimed to have none, addresses that do not coincide with what the tenant listed, a Social Security number that is invalid, a dog that was not mentioned, and much, much more. Or if you're lucky, you might discover the information on the application to be exactly so. The point is, you simply don't know until you see for yourself.

When collecting applications on your rental, here are a few key things to keep in mind:

- Make sure your application includes all the information you will need to conduct a proper screening and find a quality tenant. Don't make it too complicated or long; all of requested information should fit easily on one or two sheets of paper.

- Include your contact information and information about your application process for your applicants on the application itself. You will also need to disclose what types of information will be accessed during the screening and what cause for an application being denied entails. Make sure to list your minimum qualification standards as well.

- Make sure your applicant fills out the application *in full.* Tenants sometimes like to pick and choose what questions to answer or conveniently miss a question or two that they think will affect them negatively. We always let our applicants know that incomplete applications will not be processed. If there are blank spaces on an application, simply give it back to them and let them know it will be processed when it is complete.

- Always require a separate application (and application fee so it can be processed) for each person over the age of 18 who will be living in the home. This includes married couples, unmarried couples, roommates, family members, friends, Grandma—everyone.

- Be sure your application only requests information that will allow you to evaluate each applicant based on your qualification standards and whether their life exhibits traits of responsibility. Fair Housing Laws prevent discrimination based on race, color, religion, sex, national origin, familial status (including pregnant women, parents with one or more children under 18, and persons obtaining or who have legal custody of children under 18), and disability, as well as many other state and city specific protected classes. To avoid Fair Housing complaints—or worse, a lawsuit—make sure your application doesn't ask any questions that could be considered discriminatory.

- Never take the rental off the market and turn away would-be renters until you have an approved applicant and a Deposit to Hold the property in hand. Many times, an applicant will have second thoughts or change their mind even after being approved for a property, so it is vital to require the Deposit to Hold the property immediately after approval. If you don't and the tenant backs out a week or two later before moving in, chances are you will have turned away many would-be renters in the meantime. After approval, we always let our applicants know that we will hold the property for them for 24 hours, after which time the property will be open to other applicants unless they put down the Deposit to Hold (which we will discuss in more detail later).

- To avoid Fair Housing complaints, have applications available to everyone. A landlord may innocently deny someone an application because they already know they won't meet the income or some other requirement, only for the person to misunderstand their denial as being based on their particular protected class, leading them to file a complaint or lawsuit. Since the misunderstanding could easily have been avoided by simply providing the person an application, it would be in the landlord's best interest to provide applications to *all interested prospective tenants.* Then, when the landlord has verified the applicant doesn't qualify, they can simply send them a denial letter (Rental Application Response/ Adverse Action Notice), which we will talk about in more detail later on in this chapter, that states **in writing** they are being denied for not meeting the minimum standards for qualification. Easy peasy—and lawsuit averted.

The Application Form

The application form itself does not need to be complicated, but it does need to be thorough. To be successful in the business of landlording, you have to know that the person who you are entrusting with your investment is going to care for your property and help you prosper in this business, rather than assist you going down in flames. Your best chance of ensuring your success is through the screening process and the application. We've included a sample application for you in the appendix of this book, as well as at http://www.BiggerPockets.com/LandlordBookBonus. The application we use is designed to be easy to understand and easy for the applicant to fill out, and it includes all the vital questions we need answered to properly vet our applicants. We have put a lot of thought and time into making sure the information we request from our applicants is valuable in helping us make our decision. Next, let's go over the most important things that should be on every rental application.

Rental Application

Please return this application to _____ Application Fee _____
Address Applying for _____Desired Move-In Date _____

Important Note to Applicants Please fill this application out in full. Incomplete applications will be sent back to you to complete, causing a delay in the process and decreasing your chances of renting from us.

Personal Information *Please do not leave any blanks in this section.*
First Name _____MI. _____ Last Name _____
Social Security # _____Date of Birth _____ Driver's License # _____
Phone Number _____Alternate Phone _____Email _____
Who else will be living with you? _____
_____

Rental History *Please include all addresses you have lived at for the previous 5 years. Use additional paper if needed.*
Current Address _____City, State, Zip _____
Move-in Date _____Landlord's Name _____ Landlord's Phone _____
Monthly Rent _____Reason for Moving _____
Previous Address _____City, State, Zip _____
Move-in Date _____ Move-out Date _____ Landlord's Name _____
Landlord's Phone _____ Monthly Rent _____Reason for Moving _____
Previous Address _____City, State, Zip _____
Move-in Date _____ Move-out Date _____ Landlord's Name _____
Landlord's Phone _____ Monthly Rent _____Reason for Moving _____

Employment Information *Please include all sources of income. Use additional paper if needed. Self-employed: Please supply tax returns for previous two years and two most recent banks statements.*
Current Employer _____ Position _____
Employer Phone Number _____ Supervisor Name _____
Gross Wages Per Month _____ Hire Date _____
Other Sources of Income _____ Amount Per Month _____
Explain _____

Questionnaire *Please answer all these questions truthfully.*
How long will you live here? _____ What pets do you have? _____
How many evictions have been filed upon you? _____ How many felonies do you have? _____
Have you ever broken a lease? _____Do You Smoke? _____ How many vehicles do you own? _____
Is the total move-in amount available now? _____ When would you like to move in? _____
How did you hear about this home? _____ For what reasons could you not pay rent on
time? _____ Do you have a checking account? _____ Balance: _____
Do you have a savings account? _____ Balance: _____
Emergency Contact -Name _____ Phone _____ Relationship_____
(Including to contact regarding rent or tenancy.)
Why should we rent to you? _____

Additional Information Please use this optional space for additional information, comments, or explanations.
_____
_____

Please read carefully and sign and date below if you agree. Applicant certifies that the information contained in this application is true and correct. Applicant understands that false or misleading information is grounds for immediate disqualification. Applicant shall pay to the Landlord a nonrefundable fee to accompany this application to cover the Landlord's administrative costs and expense to verify the information submitted by the Applicant.

Authorization

Applicant authorizes the Landlord or Landlord's representatives to make any inquires deemed necessary to verify Applicant is the most qualified based on the below stated qualification standards. This verification includes, but is not limited to, direct contact with Applicant's employers, current landlord, previous landlords, friends, personal and professional references, law enforcement agencies, government agencies, consumer reporting agencies, public records, eviction records, and any other sources of information which the Landlord or Landlord's representative may deem necessary. Applicant verifies that the Landlord and Landlord's representatives shall not be held liable for damages of any kind that result from the verification of the information provided. This authorization shall extend through Applicant's tenancy to ensure continued compliance to the terms of tenancy or to recover any financial obligations relating to Applicant's tenancy, and beyond the expiration of Applicant's tenancy for recovery of any financial obligations, or for any other acceptable purpose. Should the Applicant be denied or face other adverse action based on information received in a consumer report, the Applicant has a right to obtain a free copy of the consumer report, and to dispute the accuracy of the information it contains by contacting the Consumer Reporting Agency: Address:_____. Phone:_____

Holding Fee

Upon the verbal or written approval of the Applicant's tenancy, if tenant will not be taking occupancy immediately, a Deposit to Hold Agreement will be executed and signed by all parties and a **non-refundable** holding fee shall be required within 24 hours, hereinafter referred to as "Deposit to Hold" in the amount equal to one month's rent to hold the property until a mutually agreed upon move-in date. Applicant understands that no rental will be held for more than 14 days. The Deposit to Hold removes the property from public offering and holds the home exclusively for the Applicant until all other requirements have been met. After all requirements have been met and a lease for the property completed, the Deposit to Hold will transfer to the security deposit to be held throughout the tenant's entire tenancy. If the Applicant fails to provide the Deposit to Hold within 24 hours of approval, the Applicant may be disqualified and the home will be offered to the next qualified applicant. After approval and before occupancy will be granted, Applicant must supply all the required move-in funds, including the security deposit, first month's rent, and any other additional deposits and fees, all tenant paid utilities must be transferred into Applicant's name, and a lease must be executed and signed by all parties. If for any reason, the Applicant fails to complete all move-in requirements the landlord will return the property to public offering and the entire Deposit to Hold will be forfeited to the Landlord for expenses including, but not limited to, lost rent, holding costs, advertising costs, and marketing costs.

Qualification Standards *Your Application will be denied if you do not meet the below standards for qualification.*
Applicant must have current photo identification and a valid social security number.
Applicant's monthly household income must exceed three times the rent. All income must be from a verifiable source. Unverifiable income will not be considered.
Applicants must receive positive references from all previous landlords for the previous 5 years.
Applicant may not have any evictions or unpaid judgments from previous landlords.
Applicant must exhibit a responsible financial life. Credit score must be a minimum of 600.
A background check will be conducted on all applicants over 18. Applicant's background must exhibit a pattern of responsibility.
Applicant must be a non-smoker.
Occupancy is limited to 2 people per bedroom.

At landlord's discretion, compensating factors such as an additional security deposit or co-signer (guarantor) may be required for qualification if Applicant fails to meet any one of the above requirements. In the event of multiple applicants, tenancy will be granted to the most qualified, based on the above criteria.

Applicant authorizes release of all information to Landlord and agrees that the information provided in this rental application is true and correct. This authorization extends beyond the end of Applicant's tenancy.

Applicant _____Date _____

The Application

Although we've supplied you with a sample application in the appendix of this book, let's dive into each aspect of the application so you'll fully understand each section and its importance.

Personal Information

First, you need to know who your applicant is and gather at minimum their name, Social Security number, date of birth, and contact information, including their email address, cell phone, and an alternate number. You will need this information to conduct their background and credit reports, and obviously you need to know where you can reach them should you have additional questions. The alternate contact information also comes in handy later on after they have become your tenant and you need to reach them. Some screening companies will also verify the applicant's driver's license number, so you can ask for that in this section as well. If the applicant leaves this spot blank, they probably don't have a driver's license—not a deal-killer, but information to file away in the back of your mind. So in total, you'll be seeking:

- Full Name
- Social Security Number
- Date of Birth
- Driver's License Number
- Contact Information
- Names of Everyone Who Will Live in the Home

This last question is extremely important to know who exactly will be residing with the applicant. While it is against Fair Housing Laws to specifically ask for the ages of the applicant's children or their relationship to the people listed in this section, they will usually volunteer this information here. It's okay for them to voluntarily give it, just not for you to ask it. Also, if they list six people and they are applying for a 2-bedroom unit, that's probably not going to work.

Rental History

To gain a perspective on the type of tenant your applicant will be, just ask their past landlords! It's a good idea to require information on all residences from the previous five years. If a previous landlord gives a less-than-stellar reference, that's your cue to move on. If your applicant has *less* than five years or *no* rental history, it may not be a big deal; just be careful. The point of rental history is to establish a pattern of responsibility and consistency as a tenant. Without that, it's essentially a shot in the dark as to what kind of tenant they will be for you. Two positive references are better than one, and one reference is better than none.

If your applicant has no rental history, but everything else on them checks out, you may feel comfortable renting to them with additional securities, such as a co-signer or additional deposit funds. Also, if the reason for their lack of rental references is because they are young, that is a much better scenario than someone older who has been "living with family and friends," as living with family and friends usually means something else is going on. No references are also better than a negative reference since at least with no references, you've got a 50/50 chance of their working out! It all comes down to what you as the landlord are comfortable with. Here's the information you may want to request about previous landlords. Make sure they know that if they have more references than the space provided, they can include additional pages.

Current Address
Move-In Date
Landlord's Name
Landlord's Phone Number
Monthly Rent
Reason for Moving

Previous Address
Move-In Date
Move-Out Date
Landlord's Name
Landlord's Phone Number
Monthly Rent
Reason for Moving

Previous Address
Move-In Date
Move-Out Date
Landlord's Name
Landlord's Phone Number
Monthly Rent
Reason for Moving

Employment Information

If your applicant is employed, you will need to verify their job stability and income. If they are self-employed or receive income from a source other than employment, you will need to verify that information as well. If they are self-employed, make sure to get at least the previous two years' tax returns, as well as their last two months' bank statements. If they receive income from another source, request documentation.

Current Employer

Position

Employer Phone Number

Supervisor Name

Gross Wages Per Month

Hire Date

Other Sources of Income

Your tenant may have sources of income that do not easily fit into the application form. Therefore, it's important to have a space for them to include other sources of income so you can decide if you'll include it or not. Examples could be government or student aid, child support, an online business, or something entirely different. If this income is stable and has existed for a significant amount of time (several years) we will typically choose to include it. If not, we likely will not.

Other Sources of Income:

Amount Per Month:

Explanation of Income:

General Information Questionnaire

In this section, you are asking questions about the applicant's life to determine their responsibility and further determine their candidacy for tenancy.

- **"How long will you live here?"**: Unless you are in the transient business, always look for tenants who indicate they are planning on staying in the home long-term. Because turnover and vacancy can be a couple of the most expensive things a landlord goes through, they should be avoided when possible. If the applicant writes down anything less than a year, that is probably your sign that they are not a good candidate.

- **"What pets do you have?"**: Whether you allow pets or not in your rentals, this question is phrased in such a way as to not appear negative. If you were to ask, "Do you have any pets?" they may write "no," thinking a "yes" will immediately disqualify them. Asking "what" instead of "do you" increases the chances of their being honest with this question.

- **"How many evictions have been filed upon you?**: We used to ask, "Have you ever been evicted?" until we read about this little gem in Mike Butler's book *Landlording on Autopilot*. In his book, Butler explains that landlords should phrase the question like this: "How many evictions *have been filed on you?*" Such wording will require the tenant to *think* and not write an automatic "no." Yes and no questions are much too easy to falsify, and tenants are used to questions being phrased that way. Also, an eviction filing identifies an irresponsible tenant as much as an eviction that proceeded to the point of the Sheriff escorting them out the door. Both are consequences of bad behavior that you don't need to deal with. Having them write an actual number also takes away their ability to claim they misunderstood the question.

- **"How many felonies do you have?"**: Once again, phrasing this question "how many," rather than "do you have" requires the tenant to stop and think about how they answer. Obviously, this information will be available on the tenant's background check, but by asking it here, you are able to determine whether or not the applicant is the honest sort or someone who has no problem falsifying answers to get what they want.

- **"Have you ever broken a lease?"**: This information should also be discovered when gathering your landlord references, but by asking here you again will be able to determine your applicant's honesty. If they have broken a lease, find out the details from the previous landlord and be prepared to require additional securities should you decide to rent to them.

- **"Do you smoke?"**: One of our qualification standards states that all applicants must be non-smokers in order to be approved. This is a fairly new standard we have added, and it may seem harsh, but it became necessary after getting unit after unit back that had smoke permeating the walls and carpet, despite having a "no smoking" policy. Smoke gets into everything and can only be remedied by re-painting with oil-based paint and replacing the flooring. Sometimes you may even need to oil-base prime the floor underneath your new carpet to seal out the odor. It's a hassle, and it's expensive. When we realized a "no smoking" policy was not enough, we took it one step further and eliminated smokers altogether. A "yes" to this question on the application will result in immediate disqualification from us—unless it's for medical marijuana, which as we talked about in Chapter 4, we may have to accommodate, though specific locations outside the interior of the home can be designated.

- **"How many vehicles do you own?"**: Do you want to be the landlord with four vehicles in the driveway and two inoperable vehicles in the yard? Neither do we. It's good to find out before you approve them how many vehicles they plan to bring with them. It's also a good idea to have a limit to the number of vehicles they can have on the property, but we'll go over that in more detail in Chapter 8.

- **"Is the total move-in amount available now?"**: The answer to this question gives you a good indication of whether your applicant is financially responsible and plans ahead. If they knew they would be moving and have gone so far as to apply for your rental, they should have had adequate time to prepare for the move-in money standards.

- **"When would you like to move in?"**: If your applicant answered, "Today," or "ASAP," be very careful during your screening process. A tenant wanting to move quickly could mean a few things: 1) they are being evicted, 2) their landlord asked them to leave, 3) they do not plan ahead, 4) they are not currently renters (everyone needs a place to live—where are they currently living and why?), or 5) a variety of other reasons that don't bode well for you. Another answer to be aware of is if they write a date in the *distant* future. For example, if they apply for your vacant rental in April saying they would like to move in come July, that's probably not going to work for you. It's highly unlikely it would be financially advantageous for you to hold your rental for three months! The answer you will want to see to this question is anywhere from 1–4 weeks out. Anything else you will want to scrutinize closely.

- **"How did you hear about this home?"**: This question helps you track what parts of your marketing are working and what parts are not.

- **"For what reasons could you not pay rent on time?"**: If a tenant states any reason other than "death," it should be noted. Again, you are looking for a tenant who is financially responsible, and while a lot of tenants live paycheck to paycheck, you don't want someone with the mentality that as soon as something goes wrong, the landlord doesn't get paid. Things go wrong all the time for everyone; plans change, cars break down, jobs are lost, medical emergencies happen, but even with these unexpected (but guaranteed) events, you want a tenant who pays their bills and doesn't let hardships interfere with their rent. The correct answer to this question is "nothing." If they answer differently, it doesn't mean they are going to be bad tenants, but it does indicate a mentality that you should be wary of when making your decision to approve or deny them tenancy.

- **"Do you have a checking account? Do you have a savings account?"**: When screening your potential tenants, always find out whether they have a checking or savings account. Having a bank account does not magically make your prospective tenant more responsible; however, not having a bank account is a definite sign that something might be amiss. Chances are, the reason they don't have a bank account isn't because they just never got around to it. It may be a sign of an irresponsible financial life—maybe they couldn't handle a bank account and got tired of all the bounced checks or overdraft fees—or it could also be a sign of garnishments due to judgments or illegal sources of income. A bank account versus no bank account is definitely not a deal killer, but something to keep in mind during your screening process.

- **"What is the balance of your checking and savings account?"**: This may seem like it's none of the landlord's business, but remember, we are asking questions that determine the applicant's suitability for the rental based purely on business reasons. If they have $20 in their checking account, things are not looking good for either of you. Job and income stability, income source, credit and background checks, and landlord references are sufficient to tell you whether they are the responsible sort, but again, if they are living paycheck to paycheck, then some unexpected financial emergency happens in their life, it's going to be difficult for them to make the rent payment. Look for tenants who have a comfortable amount of funds to their name.

- **Emergency Contact (Including to Contact Regarding Rent or Tenancy)**: The answer to this question can also be attributed to Mike Butler's book *Landlording on Autopilot*, and it's a good one. Every landlord has experienced a tenant (or multiple tenants) who are late on their rent and bury their heads, making it impossible for the landlord to communicate with them. That's where the emergency contact comes into play. Most applicants will list someone close to them, such as a parent or a close friend. These are people you want to know. Because you specified that the emergency contact was also a contact for rent or tenancy, you may contact that person in the event the tenant doesn't pay rent or has some other tenancy-related issue that a kick in the pants from the emergency contact may help solve.

- **"Why should we rent to you?"**: With this question, the tenant has the opportunity to tell you what makes them the best choice for tenancy. What every landlord wants to hear is: "I have great rental references and solid, consistent income. I always pay my bills before they are due, and I love the home you have available for rent. I would love to make it my permanent home. I also have a halo and wings and volunteer at the children's hospital every Saturday." Ok, maybe not that last part. If they answer, "I don't know," or "I need a place to live ASAP," they aren't very confident in their attributes as a tenant, are they?

- **Additional Information**: As stated on the application itself, the applicant is invited to "Please use this optional space for additional information, comments, or explanations." This is where a tenant can explain why they were evicted two years prior or the fact that their current landlord is a sleaze ball who won't fix anything. This section can give you a little more insight into the person you are screening.

Legal Stuff

This is the part of the application where the landlord covers their hiney and makes sure the applicant is fully aware of what happens with the information they supplied. To avoid any misunderstandings, make sure your application includes the following information.

- **The Applicant's Assurance:** The applicant agrees that the information in their application is true and that an incomplete application or information discovered to be false is grounds for denial. What landlord wants a tenant who lies from the very beginning?

- **The Application Fee:** This is where the applicant is told in writing that their application fee is non-refundable and will be used to cover the landlord's costs to verify the information they have listed on their application.

- **Permission to Contact:** Here the applicant is made aware of who the landlord (or the landlord's representative/agent) will be contacting to obtain information as to whether the applicant is a suitable candidate for tenancy. Really, the applicant simply gives the landlord permission to contact whomever they deem necessary.

- **Liability:** Make sure to include a clause that releases the landlord from any consequences that arise from screening the applicant.

- **Extended Authorization:** We like to include a line or two that the information supplied by the applicant on the application may be used at any time during their tenancy or after their tenancy has ended. The information on the application is especially helpful for collecting debts after a tenant has vacated.

- **Consumer Report Information:** If the landlord will be collecting a consumer report (for the background and credit check), the applicant must be given the name and address of the agency and told of their right to obtain a copy and dispute the accuracy of the report in the event of their denial.

- **Holding Fee:** If the tenant is approved, provide the terms of when the security deposit, also known at this point as the "Holding Fee," or "Deposit to Hold" must be paid to guarantee their position. We allow our tenants 24 hours from the time of approval to supply the holding fee and also sign the Deposit to Hold Agreement, which states the specifics of how long the unit will be held for the applicant, as well as the consequences should they fail to meet all of their obligations and perform by the given date. No tenancy is guaranteed to the applicant until they have been approved and have paid the holding fee.

- **Failure to Perform:** Should the tenant fail to supply the holding fee for the rental within the specified time period (24 hours), the applicant is made aware that the rental will be made available to other applicants.

- **Move-in Requirements:** This is where the tenant is made aware of what will be required of them after they are approved and before they are given keys, such as paying all move-in funds, deposits, fees, transferring utilities, signing a lease, and so forth.

- **Grounds for Denial:** Finally, the applicant needs to be made aware that if they fail to meet the minimum standards for qualification due to information received from any sources or if they fail to perform during the application process, they will be denied.

Qualification Standards

By now, the applicant should have seen the qualification standards in your advertisement, been told the qualification standards in their first phone call with you, been given the qualification standards in writing in person when they looked at the home, and finally, been given the qualification standards once more on the application itself. Should any applicant be denied tenancy for failing to meet the qualification standards, they can't say you didn't warn them. Your qualifications may read something like this:

"Your application will be denied if you do not meet the below standards for qualification.

- Applicant must have current photo identification and a valid social security number.

- Applicant's monthly household income must exceed three times the rent. All income must be from a verifiable source. Unverifiable income will not be considered.

- Applicants must receive positive references from all previous landlords for the previous 5 years.

- Applicant may not have any evictions or unpaid judgments from previous landlords.

- Applicant must exhibit a responsible financial life. Credit score must be a minimum of 600.

- A background check will be conducted on all applicants over 18. Applicant's background must exhibit a pattern of responsibility.

- Applicant must be a non-smoker.

- Occupancy is limited to 2 people per bedroom. *[Note on occupancy limits: When setting an occupancy limit, make sure the limit is based on legitimate reasons, taking into consideration the size of the rental and the number of bedrooms it contains. According to HUD, a reasonable occupancy limit is 2 per bedroom under the Fair Housing Act. viii]"*

We end this section by stating that tenancy will be granted to the most qualified applicant, based on our qualification standards, and that (at out discretion) compensating factors such as an additional security deposit or co-signer may be required for qualification if the applicant falls short of meeting any of the qualification requirements.

Release of Information Signature

Finally, make sure the tenant signs the application with a statement releasing the information within to the landlord. Besides protecting yourself from liability, you will have a hard time gathering income verification and landlord references without it.

Contact Information

Always include your contact information on the application with instructions for where and how to return the application upon completion.

The Application Fee/Identification

After receiving the application back from a prospective tenant:

- Look it over to make sure it's filled out completely. If not, hand it back and ask them to finish it.

- Get a copy of the applicant's photo identification card so you can verify that they are who they say they are. If they didn't bring you a copy, you can easily snap a picture with your phone.

- Collect the application fee. *Always* charge an application fee when collecting applications to rent your property. The application fee gives the prospective tenant some skin in the game and shows they are serious about wanting to rent the property. Processing an application takes time, and you need to be sure the person you are investigating is a legitimate candidate for your rental and not just someone who is out casually throwing in applications to every place they are mildly interested in. Some landlords will deduct the screening fee from the applicant's first month of rent if approved, though that is not required.

How Much Should the Landlord Charge for an Application Fee?

The amount you charge for your application fee should be minimal. Your state law should dictate an acceptable amount, though commonly landlords are legally allowed to charge the prospective tenant for the actual costs associated with obtaining a screening report if using a screening company, or if conducting the screening themselves, the landlord may charge an application fee that coincides with the "going rate" for screening in the area and allows for time spent obtaining background information, calling references and employers, etc. Generally application fees will range from $25–$50. We charge our applicants $35 per application, which is sufficient to cover the cost of screening and is still low enough not to have anyone balk at the price.

Always collect the application fee(s) prior to processing the application. Again, if the applicant doesn't have any skin in the game, there's a good chance they don't have any intention of following through. Also, if you go ahead and process the application without the application fee with their assurance that they will pay it later, good luck collecting it if they are denied. Make it easy on yourself, and let applicants know their applications will not be considered or processed until the application fee has been paid.

Application Disclosures

Prior to processing applications, the landlord must disclose in writing what types of information will be accessed to complete the screening and what will result in the applicant being denied housing. The tenant will need to sign a release of information to give the landlord the permission to access that particular information. To keep things simple, we include this information on the application itself, which the tenant signs. Also, since you will be running a background and credit check on the tenant, thus obtaining a "consumer report" whose information could result in the tenant being denied tenancy, the landlord must give the applicant the name, address, and phone number of the agency, as well as inform the applicant of their right to obtain a copy and dispute the accuracy of the report. This information should be printed on the application itself. If an applicant is denied, they must be sent an Adverse Action Notice, which we will discuss more later on in this chapter.

Digital Applications

Of course, there are several companies that exist, usually within large, expensive property management software, than can allow your prospective tenant to apply online for your property. Although we currently find that none of these systems work as well as a simple paper application, you may elect to use such a service. Our biggest complaint is that the questions are pre-written by the company, and it's clear most have never been landlords, so the application just doesn't ask the right questions. If you do decide to use such a service, just be sure that the fee is paid by the applicant and the information is forwarded to you.

How to Process the Application

Now the moment you've all been waiting for: Let's get down to the nuts and bolts of processing the application. Remember, before processing the application, make sure it is filled out completely and you have collected the application fee and photo identification. Next, look it over for any obvious red flags, such as gaps in rental history, insufficient rental references, lack of income, acknowledgement to a criminal history, eviction, or broken lease, pets (if you don't allow them), number of occupants, reasons for moving from their previous residences, and any weird comments under the space provided for additional comments.

If there are any obvious disqualifiers, such as lack of income, you can just hand their application right back to them; apparently they weren't listening when you previously explained and gave them your qualification standards. If there is nothing obvious that shouts, "Run away, run away!" you can move forward with the next steps. One last piece of advice: Don't hurry through this process in your excitement or desperation to find a tenant. Landlording is hard enough without the financial strain and stress a bad tenant can cause you. Take your time screening them to ensure you are doing your best to rent to qualified, *quality* tenants.

When processing an application, there are four main steps will you need to take.

1. Verify income.

2. Order a background check.

3. Order a credit report (often combined with the background check).

4. Get references from the applicant's past landlords.

There is definitely more to processing an application, which we will cover in this chapter as well, but these are the main steps that are probably the most important, and we will focus on them first.

Verifying Income

Your applicant will most likely have income from one of these categories: job, self-employment, or another source like those we talked about in the last chapter. Regardless of what type of income your applicant brings in, you will need to verify that it is adequate, consistent, and permanent. Some landlords will verify the applicant's income by having the applicant supply a paystub or two. While this may reveal whether the income is adequate, it will not tell you whether it is consistent or permanent. Also, if the applicant is dishonest, they can easily create a false paystub on their computer to satisfy the landlord's desire to see sufficient income.

To be thorough, the best option for verifying job income is by talking with the employer directly. This is another situation where a simple fill-in-the-blank form comes in handy to collect the needed information in an organized and efficient manner. When verifying income through an employer, they will probably request the Release of Information signed by the applicant before they will answer your questions. The bottom of your application should include this release. Additionally, you may want to send them a simple form that asks them for vital information from the tenant. We've included a sample Employment Verification Form that you can use for your landlording business. Get it in the appendix of this book or online at http://www.biggerpockets.com/LandlordBookBonus. Either fax or email it to them, then whether you send the form to the employer to fill out and return to you or you ask them the questions over the phone, these are the items you will want to cover:

- Position Held

- Rate of Pay

- Average Hours Per Week

- Hire Date

- Whether Applicant's Position is Considered Temporary

In addition, always give the employer the opportunity to offer additional thoughts or comments about the applicant if they wish, and be sure to get their name and title.

Background and Credit Check

A background check looks at the tenant's criminal history, as well as searches for any past judgments. It also will reveal any discrepancies in identity by verifying the Social Security number provided and will confirm the tenant's current and past addresses and reveal any discrepancies there. Why is it important to run a background check on all applicants? Because people lie. In the world of landlording, they lie a lot. Last week we ran a background check on someone who had a murder conviction on their background. Yes, murder. Denied.

Occasionally, we discover that our applicant's Social Security number is reporting them as deceased. Yet here they are, alive and kicking. Denied. Frequently, we discover judgments from past landlords or addresses the applicants failed to mention because they didn't want us talking to that landlord. Denied. Background checks reveal a lot of information about the applicant that can help the landlord avoid an expensive (or dangerous—c'mon, really... murder?) mistake.

A credit check looks at the tenant's ability and willingness to pay their bills and obligations responsibly. Some landlords don't run credit checks thinking they aren't important. We made that mistake, too. As a potential future debt collector for the applicant, you need to know that they lead a responsible financial life and pay their bills.

How to Run an Applicant's Background and Credit

For the background and credit check, you can search for this information yourself, though in order to gain access to an applicant's credit, you will have to jump through several hoops, including a home inspection. Or—and this is the avenue we take—you can take advantage of the many tenant screening services available that generate a report for you for a minimal cost. Keep in mind, some screening companies are going to be more comprehensive than others, so you may need to test out a few before finding the one that works for you. For the purpose of this book, we will look at an example using RentPrep.com. We are not affiliated with RentPrep.com in any way, but simply find them extremely easy and convenient to use after years of testing multiple companies. Of course, if you are reading this book in the future, this might change.

According to their website, each individual report that comes through their system is verified by a Federal Credit Reporting Act (FCRA) certified background screener. They have three packages to choose from currently, ranging from around $20 to around $40 in price: Basic, Pro, and Platinum. Since we do all our own income verification and rental history (which is included in the Platinum package), we always choose the Pro package, which includes the following:

- Social Security Verification
- Address History
- Eviction History
- Bankruptcy Search
- Judgment and Lien Search
- US Criminal Search
- US Sex Offender Search
- Global Homeland Security Search

To run the background, simply choose your package, then enter the applicant's name, Social Security number, date of birth, and current address, and in under two hours, they will email you a report that looks something like this sample found at http://www.rentprep.com/wp-content/uploads/2015/04/Sample-Pro-Package.pdf

4/21/2015	File # 69170 : MESS, HANK	

RentPrep
Screening Made Easy

Background Screening Report
Fidelis Screening Solutions
4534 Clinton St
Suite #2
West Seneca, NY 14224
Phone: 888-877-8501
Fax: 888-887-1491

FILE NUMBER	69170	REPORT DATE	04-21-2015
REPORT TO	JOE LANDLORD	ORDER DATE	04-21-2015
		TYPE	Landlord Pro Package

Application Information

APPLICANT	MESS, HANK	SSN	XXX-XX-1111	DOB	11-21-1983
ADDRESS(ES)	32 MAIN ST	CITY / STATE / ZIP	BUFFALO, NY 14206		

Identity Development

Person Search - SSN Validation

RESULTS	**Records Found**		
SSN SEARCHED	XXX-XX-1111	SEARCH DATE	04-21-2015 1:11 PM MDT

Applicant Information

FULL NAME / SSN	DOB	ADDRESS	PHONE	REPORTED DATE(S)
HANK M MESS		911 N DEADEND PLACE	(555)254-6011	First: 2007-08
XXX-XX-XXXX		MAPLEWOOD, NJ 07040		Last: 2007-08
		County: ESSEX		
AKA: MESS HANK				
MESSNER HANK				
HANK MESS				
HANK MESS		611 S LOSER ST		First: 2006-06
XXX-XX-XXXX		NEW YORK, NY 10031		Last: 2006-06
		County: NEW YORK		
AKA: HANK MESS				
MESS HANK				

WARNING: This search may not be used as the basis for an adverse action on an applicant. It should only be used to verify or correct an applicant's information, or as a tool to further research of public records or other verifications.

Investigative

Nationwide Criminal and Sex Offender Search

RESULTS	**Records Found**		
NAME SEARCHED	MESS, HANK	SEARCH DATE	04-21-2015 1:03 PM MDT
DOB SEARCHED	11-21-1983	SEARCH SCOPE	

To request a credit check in addition to the background check, you can add it on before submitting your order for the background check for an additional $10 or so. If you chose the Pro package for your background check, that brings your total charge to just over $30 for both the background and credit check. The application fee you charge your applicant should cover this fee.

When ordering a credit check from RentPrep, rather than receiving the applicant's actual credit report and exact credit score, you instead choose a credit score range that coincides with your qualification standard. Based on the criteria you provide, RentPrep will give you a simple "pass" or "fail" decision, including the TransUnion FICO Classic 04 scores that affected the applicant's score. Here are the current credit range options the landlord may choose at RentPrep.com:

Rating	FICO Score	Bankruptcies	Judgments
★★★★★	700-860	0 Bankruptcy	0 Judgments
★★★★	650-860	1 Bankruptcy	0 Judgments
★★★	600-860	1 Bankruptcy	0 Judgments
★★	500-860	1 Bankruptcy	1 Judgments
★	450-860	1 Bankruptcy	2 Judgments
0 Stars	397-860	1 Bankruptcy	3+ Judgments

If you choose to add on the credit check, it will be available within the same timeframe as the background check. Here's a sample of what the credit check from RentPrep looks like:

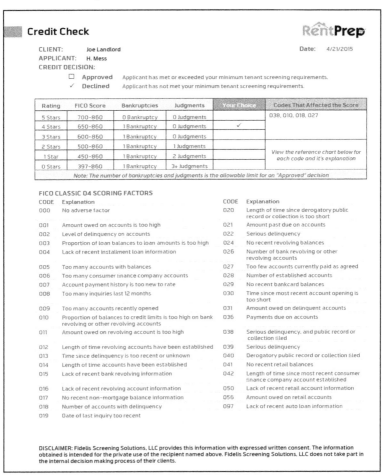

In this example from RentPrep's website, the applicant's credit score did not fall in the 650–860 range the landlord selected, so they were given a "declined" decision. You can also see where RentPrep lists the codes that affect the applicant's score. In this case you can see that the applicant was seriously delinquent with public record or collections filed, their credit balances were too high, they had multiple accounts delinquent, and too few credit accounts were paid as agreed. Sounds like a mess!

What to Do With the Background and Credit Check

After you have the results from your background and credit check, you need to decide what exactly to do with that information. First, you will want to:

- **Confirm they are who they say.** If they are listed as deceased or the Social Security number pulls up another individual's name, you can probably say bye-bye.

- **Confirm the addresses on their background check coincide with the ones they listed on their application.** If there are any discrepancies, you will want to make a note of that and ask the applicant about the addresses in question. Most likely the response will be something like, "Oh, I forgot." It is especially important to talk to the landlords the applicant tried to hide from you.

- **Look for any criminal convictions.** If there are any, you will need to decide if that criminal conviction makes the tenant a less likely candidate.

- **Look for any evictions.**

- **Look for any judgments or liens.** If the tenant has a judgment on their background check and you will be denying them because of it, one way to respond to the applicant is by putting the ball in their court. "Hey John, your background check revealed a judgment owed to Property USA, LLC in the amount of $4,200. What can you tell me about that?" Likely, they'll give you an excuse of some kind, but don't buy into it. Instead, ask them to have the company in question get in touch with you, but you will need to put their application on hold until you hear from them. Don't worry, you never will.

- **Finally, make sure they meet your credit requirement.**

If the applicant meets your minimum standards for qualification in their background and credit check, you can move forward with the next step of processing the application by getting rental references.

Getting References From Previous Landlords

Getting references from previous landlords is perhaps the most important of all the screening steps. A lousy tenant can disguise themselves in person and over the phone, but they can't hide from their past actions that the previous landlord can reveal. Remember, the references you receive from past landlords are the best indication of the way the tenant will behave for you.

Now, some tenants will try and be sneaky and have a friend pose as their previous landlord. One way to find out if the person you are speaking with is really a landlord is by first calling and asking, "Do you have any vacancies?" If it's a friend, they will quickly be thrown off, whereas a landlord will simply answer your question. Another way to verify the person you're speaking with is actually a landlord is by asking for verification of the tenant's rental specifics, such as the address, lease term, and rental amount. A friend posing as the tenant's landlord is most likely not going to have this information.

When calling for rental references, it's helpful to use a standard fill-in-the-blank form, such as our Previous Landlord Reference Form (Included in the appendix of this book, as well as at http://www.BiggerPockets.com/LandlordBookBonus). Be courteous and respectful of the previous landlord's time. Begin with who you are and why you are calling, then ask them if they have a moment to talk. The Previous Landlord Reference Form will keep you on track to cover the key information you will need without taking up too much of the landlord's time. Also, by asking the same questions like those on the questionnaire for any applicant that applies, you can be sure you are not violating any Fair Housing Laws by asking questions that could be considered discriminatory and could come back to bite you. Here are the important questions recommended for a thorough landlord reference.

- Did tenant stay for stated period? (Listed on the Previous Landlord Reference Form)
- What was the monthly rent?
- How much of the rent did the tenant normally pay?
- Did the tenant always pay rent on time?
- Did the tenant keep utilities on and paid in full at all times?
- Did anyone else live with the tenant(s)?

- Did the tenant(s) ever receive any legal notices (late rent, noise, unauthorized occupants, notice to vacate, etc.)?

- Did the tenant have any pets?

- Did the tenant maintain the home in good condition (housekeeping, lawn, etc.)?

- Did the tenant give proper notice before vacating?

- Did the tenant receive their entire deposit back after vacating?

- Would you rent to the tenant again?

The answers to these questions will tell you **a lot** about your applicant. Before ending the conversation, always give the previous landlord the invitation to offer any additional thoughts or comments about their experience with the tenant. When getting references from the applicant's previous landlords, always get a minimum of two so you can compare and check for consistency.

Remember, do not rely solely on a reference from a current landlord since you don't know their motivation for giving a good or bad reference. As we have stated before, a past landlord has nothing to gain or lose by being honest, whereas a current landlord may not want to lose a good tenant or may be overly excited to get rid of a bad one. Both situations may affect the legitimacy and integrity of their reference. Some landlords or property management companies will require the tenant's release of information signature before they will give out any information about that tenant. In this case, when faxing or emailing them the release of information from the applicant, you may also want to include the Previous Landlord Reference Form so they can simply complete the information you need and send it back to you. (The bottom of the application should have their release of information printed on it, along with the applicant's signature.)

If your applicant doesn't have any (or they have limited) rental references, usually due to their age or being prior homeowners, technically they don't meet all of your qualification standards for the home. Your options in this case are to 1) decline their application, 2) accept them without references and take the risk (assuming everything else about them is stellar), 3) require a cosigner, or 4) require an additional security deposit if that is allowed in your specific state. Personally, if an applicant meets all of our other standards, we will typically not turn them away due to a lack of references because of their young age or because they were previous homeowners unless there is a more qualified applicant available. Instead, if everything else about them indicated they would be a good tenant, we would simply require additional securities like those we just covered.

Advanced (& Sneaky) Ideas for Tenant Screening

So far in this chapter, we have covered how to process applications by verifying income, conducting the background and credit check and by obtaining rental references. Next, let's go over three additional ways to screen your applicants that are a little outside the box.

1. Social Media

In today's world, people often put more information publicly on their Facebook, Twitter, or other social network profile than they would even tell their own mother. This information is a goldmine for landlords to discover more about their prospective tenants. We always do an online search on our potential tenants and see if we can find any information that would help us make an informed decision. For example, a young couple once applied for one of our apartments that does not allow pets. However, upon checking her Facebook page, we discovered the applicant posing with a brand new puppy with the caption, "My adorable new puppy!!! Isn't she cute!?" Surprise, surprise. That information was definitely helpful.

By searching social networks, you might also discover information about their current living situation, roommates, or whether they complain all the time. Or maybe they seem just as great as they did in person and on their application. Another option for using social networks for learning more about your applicant is by looking for mutual friends or acquaintances and getting their opinion. In larger areas this may not work as well, but in small towns most people are connected in some way or another. If you notice your applicant is also mutual friends with "Sarah," an old friend from high school, consider shooting Sarah a message asking if she knows anything about the applicant that would be helpful in making an informed decision about their tenancy. Remember, the point of all this is to learn as much about the prospective tenant as possible before approving them so you can make an informed decision. There's nothing like approving your new tenant only to discover too late that you made a horrible error.

2. Google

Almost everything you've ever done publicly in your life is chronicled some-where on the internet. The same is true of your applicant. As of this writing, the best source for searching the internet is, of course, Google. Searching Google for a tenant's name is helpful for discovering little known facts about the applicant's life. You can also try combining the applicant's name with their city or county to narrow your search. You'll most likely get all sorts of information by Googling a person's name, but you are looking for infor-mation that specifically tells you a little more about the applicant, such as whether they were recently in the county's jail roster or have been involved in lawsuits.

To search Google, try entering their name within quotation marks, which causes the search to be narrowed down to only the the applicant's full name, or what you entered within the quotations. For example, entering "John Smith" will only show you results for "John Smith," whereas entering John Smith without quotations will show you results for anything contain-ing the name "John" and anything containing "Smith." Using quotation marks will significantly narrow your search.

3. Drive by Unexpectedly

Curious about how your prospective applicant will take care of your home should you approve them? A look at their current residence should give you a pretty good idea. Consider driving by or even paying them a visit at their home to get a good look at how much care they show (or don't) to their yard maintenance, housekeeping, and general cleanliness. If they live like slobs now or their lawn is two feet tall, that's not going to change anytime soon.

Once you have processed your applicant's application, you should have everything you need to either accept or deny them tenancy. If they have met your minimum standards for qualification and exhibit traits of depend-ability, reliability, and responsibility, you're off to a great start. If they have failed to meet your minimum standards of what you are looking for in a tenant, you will most likely deny them tenancy and wait for someone more qualified.

Denying an Applicant After Screening

When denying an applicant, make sure you have a logical business reason for doing so to avoid discrimination complaints. If faced with a Fair Housing complaint, you will need to be able to show proof that your decision was based on legitimate, fair business reasons like those outlined in your minimum screening standards, including references, income, background, or credit. Because of this, always make sure you keep notes of all your screening materials, including the reason the applicant is being denied. When we deny a tenant, we staple all the information we collected on them together with their application on the very top and file it away in a box labeled "Denied Applicants." In the event that we ever need a defense for our decision, it's all there.

Remember, even though tenants have many rights and there are many rules the landlord has to follow while being a landlord, ultimately the property still belongs to the landlord, and the landlord may set whatever terms and conditions he/she feels comfortable with, so long as they are legal and do not discriminate against the classes protected under Fair Housing. Also remember, just because a person is in a protected class does not mean you are obligated to rent to them. Everyone must meet the same standards to prove that they are qualified applicants.

Whenever you deny an applicant, always send them a Rental Application Response with the reason they were denied to avoid misunderstandings and further protect yourself against Fair Housing complaints. We've included a Rental Application Response in the appendix of this book, as well as at http://www.BiggerPockets.com/LandlordBookBonus.

If the applicant was denied based on information contained in a consumer report (which means a background or credit check that a company, such as RentPrep or MySmartMove, does for you), the landlord is legally obligated to send them:

- An Adverse Action Notice that states the name, address, and telephone number of the consumer reporting agency (such as RentPrep or MySmartMove)

- A statement that the consumer reporting agency did not make the decision to take the adverse action and cannot give the applicant any specifics

- A statement letting the applicant know of their right to dispute the accuracy of the report

- A statement letting the applicant know of their right to request a free copy of the report from the consumer reporting agency within 60 days

Our Rental Application Response doubles as the Adverse Action Notice. As you can see in the example of our Rental Application Response/ Adverse Action Notice, we include the option to check a box that states they were denied based on information in their consumer report, which is followed by the required information giving the applicant the resources for obtaining a copy or disputing the report themselves.

The landlord is also legally required to send the applicant an Adverse Action Notice if they were approved, but only if they agree to certain conditions (most commonly a co-signer, increased rent, or an additional deposit) due to information obtained in a consumer report. You can find our Rental Application Response/Adverse Action Notice With Conditions in the appendix of this book, as well as at http://www.BiggerPockets.com/ LandlordBookBonus.

Should You Allow a Cosigner?

A cosigner is an individual who agrees to become legally obligated for the payment and condition of a rental. A cosigner is used when the tenant cannot qualify by themselves, usually due to income or a lack of rental history. Whether or not you choose to accept a cosigner to help bolster your potential tenant's qualifications is up to you, but if you do, be sure to:

- **Screen the cosigner like a tenant.** They should fill out an application and be screened thoroughly, including background, income, employment, references, etc. Since the cosigner is guaranteeing the terms of the tenancy are consistently met, the landlord needs to be sure they are financially able to meet that requirement and that they exhibit the same responsible characteristics that are sought out in a tenant.

- **Be sure the cosigner owns property and lives in the county in which your rental is located.** By having these standards of a cosigner, you have a much higher likelihood that you will be able to locate them in the event that you need them to perform, since their address isn't as likely to change compared to a cosigner who is also a renter. Renters move much more often than homeowners, so there's a good possibility you will not be able to locate your renting cosigner when you need them.

- **Require an application fee from the cosigner as well.** It is the applicant's responsibility to meet your minimum standards for qualification. If they are unable to on their own, you should have no qualms about requiring the application fee to make it work with a cosigner since you have to incur the time and expense qualifying that person as well.

- **Fully explain to the cosigner that they are financially responsible for the property.** Let them know that you will hold them responsible should the tenant cause damage or refuse to pay rent. They need to understand that they are entering into a serious responsibility and not simply signing on the dotted line. You will need to have them sign a Cosigner Agreement, which will be included with the lease or rental agreement that states that they guarantee performance of the lease or rental agreement. You can find an example of a Cosigner Agreement in the appendix of this book, as well as at http://www.BiggerPockets.com/LandlordBookBonus.

- **When using a cosigner, some landlords will also require that the cosigner pay a "performance fee."** The performance fee is in addition to the normal security deposit and acts as the cosigner's personal skin in the game. They will receive the performance fee back when the tenant fulfills their lease, minus any amounts not covered by the tenant's security deposit. The performance fee gives the cosigner additional motivation to ensure compliance by the tenant since they will have to pay if the tenant does not.

When considering a cosigner, just remember that no cosigner, not even a great one, can stop a bad tenant from destroying a property. Avoid using a cosigner as an excuse to put in a terrible tenant that will just cause you headaches.

Co-Signer Agreement Addendum

This addendum is a part of the Lease Agreement dated: _____

Between (LANDLORD): _____

And (TENANT): _____

And (CO-SIGNER): _____

For the property located at_____

_____ (COSIGNER) understands and agrees to be jointly and
severely liable to the Lease Agreement listed above for the property located at_____
_____, guaranteeing performance of the Lease Agreement for it's entire
duration.

Co-signer agrees to pay a performance guarantee fee in the amount of $_____ (refundable at the
end of the lease, less any amounts not covered by the security deposit).

**ALL OTHER TERMS AND CONDITIONS OF THE ABOVE REFERENCED LEASE AGREEMENT SHALL REMAIN
THE SAME.**

Dated as of the _____**day** of _____, 20_____

_____   _____
Landlord/Manager   Tenant Signature

                                          _____
                                          Cosigner Signature

                                          _____
                                          Cosigner Social Security Number

                                          _____
                                          Cosigner Physical Address

                                          _____
                                          City, State, Zip

                                          _____
                                          Cosigner Phone and Email

---

Accepting a Tenant

Congratulations! You're (almost) officially a landlord and have hopefully approved someone who will make your landlording experience a breeze. However, after approving a new tenant, you're still not done. There are a few more things that need to be completed before your new tenant moves in. In this section we will talk about what the process looks like after you have approved a new applicant and the steps both the landlord and the tenant will need to take before the new tenant takes possession of the property.

Once a prospective tenant has applied, it usually takes us one to two days to fully process their application before we can reach a decision. If they meet all of our standards for qualification and we can reasonably assume they are great tenant material based on the techniques outlined in the last couple of chapters, they will be approved. So, first things first.

Next Steps After Approving a New Tenant

1. Decide on a Move-In Date

Once approved, not all tenants wish to move to their new place right away. Always discuss with your tenant when their desired move-in date is to prevent any misunderstandings, and preferably do this before accepting them. Some applicants may imply they want to move in right away on their application because they think that is what the landlord wants to hear, only to disclose after they have been approved that they aren't looking to move until weeks down the road. Every day a rental sits vacant is money out of the landlord's pocket. If a tenant wishes for us to hold a unit for them for an extended amount of time while they get their affairs in order, we let them know we can hold the unit for them for a very limited time. If they request us to hold the unit longer, we will generally hold the unit for up to two weeks and try to negotiate with them a compromise. Most of the time, this strategy works.

If you are unable to compromise on a move-in date, the final decision of whether or not you will proceed with the tenant is up to you and may depend on your current market. If decent tenants are hard to find, you may think holding your unit for your new tenant doesn't sound all that bad. However, if you have more than one promising applicant or can reasonably expect more, it may make more sense to let your applicant know you cannot hold the rental as long as they would like, but you would be happy to proceed if it is still available when they are ready to move. It all comes down to the numbers and your own personal preference.

2. Collect the Deposit to Hold

After you have approved a new tenant and have settled on a move-in date, you may want to collect a "Deposit to Hold" the unit for the applicant until they are ready to move. This deposit removes the home from public offering and holds it exclusively for your newly approved tenant until they fulfill the rest of their obligations, including:

- Turning utilities on in their name
- Paying all move-in funds

- Signing the lease or rental agreement

It is also their guarantee that they **will** fulfill all of their pre-tenant obligations and rent the home by a mutually agreed upon date. If for some reason they back out, the Deposit to Hold is forfeited to the landlord to use to cover lost rent during the holding period, as well as advertising and other costs associated with getting the home re-rented to another qualified applicant. However, when the new tenant fulfills their obligations, the Deposit to Hold usually transfers as their security deposit to be held during their tenancy. It is best to require the Deposit to Hold as soon as your new tenant has been approved.

On our application, we let our potential tenants know that if they are approved, we will hold the unit for them for 24 hours, during which time they will be expected to present the Deposit to Hold. Once they have officially been approved, we call them with our congratulations, remind them that they will need to pay the Deposit to Hold the unit within 24 hours, and make an appointment from there to collect those funds and sign the Deposit to Hold Agreement. Should they fail to provide the Deposit to Hold, we do not guarantee them the unit after 24 hours has passed and will continue to show the rental and accept and process applications.

To prevent any misunderstandings about what the Deposit to Hold is and how it will be used, always have a signed Deposit to Hold Agreement that both you and your new tenant(s) sign, and make sure they have a copy (one for each adult occupant) for themselves. (A sample Deposit to Hold Agreement is included in the appendix of this book, as well as at http://www. BiggerPockets.com/LandlordBookBonus.) The Deposit to Hold Agreement should include, at minimum, the following information:

- Date of agreement
- Complete address of rental
- Who the agreement is between (landlord and tenant)
- Acknowledgment of receipt of Deposit to Hold monies
- The specifics of the purpose of the Deposit to Hold
- Final date and time property will be held for prospective tenant
- Move-in requirements that must be completed during the holding period and before occupancy will be granted, including:
  o Rent paid
  o Deposit paid

- o Other Move-in funds paid (additional deposits, fees, etc.)
- o Tenant-paid utilities put into tenant's name
- o Lease signed by all (adult) occupants
- The consequences should they fail to perform by the given date and time
- Signatures of both the landlord and tenant (s)

Here is an example of the Deposit to Hold Agreement we use for our tenants:

Deposit to Hold Agreement

Date: _____

Property Address: _____

City: _____, State _____Zip_____

This agreement is between_____, hereafter

referred to as "Prospective Tenant(s)," and _____,

hereafter referred to as "Landlord."

Prospective Tenant(s) has been approved for tenancy at the above listed address.

Landlord acknowledges receipt of Deposit to Hold in the amount of $_____ from Prospective Tenant(s) as a **non-refundable** holding fee for the property listed above. Prospective Tenant(s) understands the holding fee reserves the property for the Prospective Tenant(s) until a lease and all move-in requirements have been properly completed. The lease and all move-in requirements must be completed before 5:00pm _____/_____/_____.

Move-in Requirements:
1st Months Rent must be paid in full in the amount of: $_____
Security Deposit must be paid in full in the amount of: $_____
Other Move-in Funds must be paid in full in the amount of: $_____
All tenant paid utilities must be transferred into Prospective Tenant's name.
A lease must be executed and signed by all parties.

When all move-in requirements have been met and Prospective Tenant(s) given possession of the property, the Deposit to Hold will be transferred to the Security Deposit to be held through the entire tenancy. Prospective Tenant understands and agrees that no possession of the property will be granted until all move-in requirements have been completed.

Deposit to Hold will be held in a trust account by the landlord. If for any reason, the Prospective Tenant(s) fail to complete all move-in requirements by the above listed date and time, the landlord will return the property to public offering and the entire Deposit to Hold will be forfeited to the Landlord for expenses including, but not limited to, lost rent, holding costs, advertising costs, and marketing costs.

_____   _____
Prospective Tenant   Prospective Tenant

_____   _____
Prospective Tenant   Landlord

Some landlords will require applicants to pay the Deposit to Hold at the time they submit their application. If that is the route you take, your Deposit to Hold Agreement will need to include verbiage that if the applicant is not approved, their Deposit to Hold funds will be refunded to them. The purpose of the Deposit to Hold is only to lock-in approved tenants.

3. Let the Tenant Know What Happens Next

Remember, the Deposit to Hold the rental should be collected as soon as possible after your new tenant has been approved. During this appointment to collect the Deposit to Hold, we also offer our new tenants a checklist of what needs to happen next. Since the move-in process may seem daunting, confusing, or overwhelming to a new tenant, this checklist gives them a play-by-play of what to expect. It also helps to reduce misunderstandings that can occur, such as forgetting to turn on all utilities or bringing a personal check instead of guaranteed funds to their lease signing appointment.

Here's a look at the New Tenant Acceptance Letter we provide to our new tenants letting them know what happens next. We've also included this form in the appendix of this book, as well as at http://www.BiggerPockets.com/LandlordBookBonus.

Dear_____: Date: ____/____/____

Congratulations on your approval for _____. We are looking forward to working with you and hope you will enjoy your new home.

We would like to make this as smooth a transition as possible for you. Below are instructions for the next steps you will need to take before moving into your new home. **We cannot give you the keys to your new home until all the steps have been completed.**

Step 1 - Deposit to Hold: The Deposit to Hold must be paid within 24 hours of approval and an Intent to Rent Agreement completed. The Deposit to Hold will remove the property from public offering to be held until a mutually determined move-in date. Note: We can only hold units for a maximum of two weeks. Your Deposit to Hold becomes your Security Deposit after you begin your tenancy. Your Deposit to Hold is $_____.

Step 2 - Utilities Turned On: All tenant paid utilities must be transferred into your name by moving day. For your convenience, we have included a list of local utility providers below, along with their contact information. The utilities you are responsible for have been highlighted.

Electricity   _____
Garbage   _____
Water/Sewer   _____
Gas   _____
Other   _____

Step 3 - All Move-in Funds Paid: Your first month of rent is $_____.
                                          Additional Deposits $_____.
                                          Additional Fees $_____.
                                          Total Amount Needed: $_____.

Please bring these funds to your New Tenant Orientation. All move-in funds must be paid by cashiers check or money order. We cannot accept cash or personal checks.

Step 4 - New Tenant Orientation/Lease Signing: Steps 1 - 3 must be completed by your New Tenant Orientation where we will go through and sign your new Lease or Rental Agreement. After this appointment you will receive keys to your new home. Please plan on this appointment taking approximately one hour. Your New Tenant Orientation is scheduled for ___/___/___ at _____am/pm. **All occupants over the age of 18 must be present at this appointment.**

We hope this itinerary answers any questions you may have about the move-in process. If you have any additional questions or concerns, please do not hesitate to let us know. Once again, congratulations on your new home!

Sincerely,

Management

After you have settled on a move-in date, you've collected the Deposit to Hold, scheduled the lease signing appointment, and communicated to your new tenant their pending pre-move-in obligations, you will also need to verify that they have transferred all the proper utilities into their name before their lease signing appointment. We'll discuss the actual signing of the lease and the lease itself in the next chapter.

Wrapping it Up

Hopefully, at this point you are comfortable with the process of finding and sifting through tenants. If you are working through this book at the same time you are screening a tenant for yourself, it's our hope that you've found the perfect tenant to rent your property. At the same time, we understand that the process can seem daunting, but it is not our goal to overwhelm you. We believe the application and screening process will become second nature to you in no time, but until then feel free to refer back to this chapter any time in the future when you have questions. Additionally, to help simplify the process, we want to encourage you to download a free flowchart poster to hang on your wall that covers all the major parts of the screening process so you can refer to it whenever you need a quick refresher. Just go to http://www.BiggerPockets.com/LandlordBookBonus.

CHAPTER 8:
SIGNING THE RENTAL CONTRACT

What did you have for dinner last October 3rd?

Having trouble recalling that little factoid? Don't feel bad—over time, it's easy for our memories to fade. The same is true with the facts in the agreement you make with your tenant concerning your rental property. The memory of exactly what was said will disappear from your mind (or your tenant's mind), and if it does, life as a landlord can get messy. Therefore, a lease should be signed for any rental property you own before allowing a tenant to move in.

A lease is a legal contract between the tenant and the landlord that states the terms, conditions, rules, and description of the rental relationship. It also spells out the duties and responsibilities of both parties and what could happen if either party fails to live up to their end of the bargain. The lease is a legal document, and its importance cannot be overstated!

The lease will help put all the facts on the table so there is no misunderstanding or forgetfulness regarding those facts. If nine months down the road a tenant decides to move in their drug-dealing nephew, the lease will help everyone remember who is supposed to be at the property and who is not. The lease helps keep both sides honest, and in case of a terrible tenant, the lease can give you the grounds needed to remove a tenant from your property.

Month-to-Month or Term Leases?

One of the largest expenses you will face as a landlord is tenant turnover. Every time a tenant packs up and moves, they leave a trail of dollar bills flowing from your bank account. Therefore, we landlords want our tenants to stay forever. Sadly, that's not going to happen, but we can have some influence over how long the tenant stays by signing the right kind of lease. However, does that mean you should put all tenants immediately on a long-term lease? Maybe not.

Your two choices when it comes to a lease are "term" and "month-to-month."

- In a term lease, the tenant is required to stay for a certain length of time. This term is usually one year in length, but some leases are signed for six months or nine months.

- With a month-to-month rental agreement, the tenant is not required to stay for any length of time, but proper notice (as defined by state-law) must be given before they move out.

It might seem obvious to use a term lease when renting to a tenant, but there is one major disadvantage to doing this: The landlord is also locked in to the lease. If you as the landlord don't like the tenant, you have to wait until the end of the lease to get rid of them. With a month-to-month tenancy, you can simply give the tenant proper notice (as defined by your state) that you will not be renewing their month-to-month lease anymore, and the tenant has to move. This is a BIG stick to carry around and ensure your tenants are behaving, especially if you are new to landlording.

That said, if you do your screening correctly at the beginning, chances are your tenant is going to be just fine, so this probably won't be an issue. Therefore, you will probably find it in your best interest to use term leases. For the first eight years of being landlords, we *only* did month-to-month leases with our tenants because we wanted the ability to ask tenants to leave if needed. Over those years, we've had to ask a very small handful to vacate, and most of them probably would have left anyway—with or without a lease. Now that we have mastered our screening techniques and are much more confident in our abilities to screen out the type of tenant who we would *want* the option to get rid of quickly, we have switched to term leases for most of our properties. Term leases also lower turnover of quality tenants moving elsewhere unexpectedly. If they know they are legally obligated to stay for a certain extended period, they (most likely) will, as opposed to having the freedom to move whenever they would like with a month-to-month lease.

Now, how long of a term should you sign? To answer this, look at the seasons. Certain parts of the year are incredibly difficult for finding tenants, so why not use the lease terms to your advantage and make sure possible vacancies always take place when the market is perfect for a new tenant? Let's say we needed to fill a unit on December 1st. There is no way we're going to sign a one-year lease with that tenant because we know twelve months down the road we are going to have a tough time finding a tenant during the holidays. Instead, we'll sign a six or nine-month lease to make the lease end in the summer or early fall, when units are easier to fill. Then, when the renewal time comes around, we'll put the tenant on a 12-month lease from that point forward. It's definitely our goal to make sure all our planned turnovers happen during prime moving season between June and September, so we work our leases around that goal.

Now that you've decided what kind of lease you should sign, let's talk about where to find that perfect, legal lease.

Where to Find a Good Rental Lease

In the late 1920s, President Coolidge invited some friends to dine with him at the White House. Not wanting to make a fool of themselves and being unsure of the proper etiquette for dining in such a setting, the friends decided to simply copy exactly what the President did at the table. The meal was served and the President took a bite, as did his friends. The President then took a drink, as did his friends. Then, the President poured some milk into a saucer, followed by some sugar. The friends did likewise with their own saucer. Then the President picked up the saucer, leaned over, and placed it on the floor—for the cat.

As the story above illustrates, sometimes imitation can be helpful in an unknown setting, but oftentimes it can make the imitator look like a fool. This is the case when a person simply copies another lease they picked up to use for their investments. Perhaps you'll be fine, but should the case arise where you need to use the lease for a big legal stick, the wrong lease could also cost you a lot of money.

Why the RIGHT Lease Matters

A common mistake made by many new landlords is to go online and simply Google "Free Rental Lease" and see what comes up. Typically, they'll print off whatever pops up and try to use it for their property. The problem with this, of course, should be obvious: You have no idea if that lease you found is legal and valid. A lease drawn up by a lawyer in one state might be totally different than a lease drawn up in another. Every state and even many cities have specific laws that govern what is and is not legal in a lease. Plus, the laws change all the time, so a lease that worked last year might not work this year.

Sure, if you never have a problem with your tenant, that lease you found on Google might be fine, but **we don't use lease agreements to prepare for the good times, we use lease agreements to prepare for the worst!**

What happens when you try to evict your tenant and you realize the lease has a provision that is not allowed in your state that delays or messes up the eviction process? What if your tenant tries to sue you because something in that lease was not legal in your state or city? These are real possibilities if you are using a boilerplate lease.

So where should you look for a good, legal rental lease agreement? Here are a few places.

1. Ask an Attorney

The first, most practical answer would be to ask an attorney in your city to draft up a lease. An attorney's job is to know the law, so if you want to ensure your lease is compliant with all current landlord-tenant laws, this would be a good place to start. Most lawyers who work with landlords on a regular basis will have a lease agreement already written up that they will likely give you (for a charge, of course).

You could also bring in a lease of your own (something you found online or through a friend) and have them review it, though check with them on the cost of this versus just purchasing a lease directly from them. It is for this reason that we included a sample lease with the purchase of this book, which you can find in the appendix or by visiting http://www.BiggerPockets.com/LandlordBookBonus. It is our hope that you will take this sample lease to an attorney to get reviewed and adjusted for your area.

2. Purchase From Online Legal Websites

If you don't want to spend several hundred dollars on a lease from your attorney, you can also purchase state-specific legal forms from numerous websites online. This would include EZLandlordForms.com, USLegalForms.com, or RocketLawyer.com. You could also pick up a copy of a lease agreement at many office supply stores, but make sure they are state-specific or offer an online state-specific version.

3. Use Property Management Software

Finally, if you are using property management software to manage your property, they may have state-specific lease agreements built into the software. This could be the most economical choice if you are already paying for the management software, or the most expensive choice if not.

When it comes to finding a great lease agreement for your property, don't be a copycat. Don't mess around. Spend the time and/or money up front to make sure you get a rock-solid lease agreement that will hold up no matter what your landlording experience throws at you.

22 Things Every Lease Should Contain

When you go to sign the lease, your tenant will likely have a lot of questions about what they are signing. As such, it's important for YOU to understand exactly what is being signed. So let's dive into the lease itself now and talk about the 22 parts every lease should contain and why it's important to have them. This will help you explain it to your tenant and also make sure your lease has everything it needs.

1. Names

At the top of the lease, be sure to include the names of all tenants who will be living in the property. We like to make sure the lease specifically states that only those listed are allowed to live in the home. This ensures that if Lazy Laura moves in her boyfriend Dirty Dan, she is violating the lease and could be evicted over it.

2. Dates

You must include the date that the lease has been signed, as well as the effective dates of the lease term. In other words, when does the lease actually begin and when does it end? Sometimes, you will sign a lease long before handing over the keys. (Such instances are rare for most landlords, but not unheard of. Perhaps the lease will begin on the 1st of the month, but the tenant will be gone on vacation during that time. So you may sign the lease before they leave, but make the effective date of the lease begin on the 1st of the month.)

3. Month-to-Month or Term

Is this lease a month-to-month lease or a pre-defined term? Six months? One year? Make sure the lease is clear.

4. Address of the Property

Of course, the address where the tenant will be living should also be listed on the lease. Some states might require the legal description to also be listed, though this is unlikely.

5. Guest Policy

For tenants, the distinction between a "guest" staying for a little bit and someone actually moving in can be a "gray area." To make this less gray, simply state in your lease how long a guest is allowed to stay. In our lease, that is 14 days. Anything longer and the tenant must be approved by management and added to the lease.

We once had an experience where a tenant of ours let her unemployed sister, unemployed brother-in-law, three kids, and a dog move into a small, 2-bedroom house. Of course, when we contacted the tenant to discuss the newly arrived "guests," she claimed they were only visiting. Fast forward to three months later when we followed up and discovered, not to our surprise, they were still there: three adults, three kids, and now two dogs in a little 2-bedroom house, along with ALL of their belongings.

Normally, if a tenant moved someone else in, we would have them submit an application and go through our approval process, then put them on the lease should they be approved. In **this** situation, however, that was obviously not going to work out. So we gave our tenant legal notice stating that all unauthorized occupants not on the lease must vacant within 10 days, or she'd be getting the boot. Just like that, they were gone. Should we have proceeded with the eviction, we would have had the legal documentation to follow through with removing the tenant and her "guests" permanently from the residence.

6. Subletting Policy

In today's world, subletting units for vacation rental use is growing exponentially, driven by sites like Airbnb.com and HomeAway.com. As a result, entrepreneurial tenants are finding that they can rent an apartment and then sublet that apartment to other guests as a nightly vacation rental. While you might think this doesn't affect your bottom line, remember that you have no idea who those nightly guests are, so you may want to hold a strict anti-subletting policy on your property. Your lease should lay out exactly what the subletting policy is.

7. Pet Policy

Will you allow the tenant to have a pet on the property, or are they strictly forbidden? If you are planning to allow pets, you will likely want to mention it in the lease but use a separate form known as a Pet Addendum to detail the arrangement. We've included a sample Pet Addendum with the purchase of this book that you can find in the appendix or at http://www.BiggerPockets. com/LandlordBookBonus.

8. Smoking Policy

Will you allow the tenant to smoke in the unit? (We recommend a firm NO.) What about smoking on the property? Is there a location where smoking would be allowed? We've found that a lot of tenants like to smoke while leaning out their bedroom windows, believing they are abiding by the "no smoking" policy we have in place. While this is definitely better than smoking directly in the room, the smell still drifts in, and it stays. Therefore, be specific in your lease as to your smoking policy. Remember, "smoker" is not a protected class, so you can discriminate against it—we do! If you smoke, you will not be approved for one of our rentals.

9. Rental Price

How much will the tenant pay in rent each month?

10. Where to Pay Rent

How should the tenant pay rent? Mail it? Drop it off? Specify *where* in your lease, but also be sure to mention that this could change if so desired by the landlord.

11. Security Deposit Amount

Be sure to specify how much the tenant is being charged for the security deposit, as well as under what conditions they could lose that deposit. In many states, the name and location of the bank (and sometimes the account number) for where the deposit is being held is required to be included on the lease.

12. Utilities

What is the tenant responsible for paying? Water? Sewer? Garbage? Electricity? Gas? Cable? Satellite? Spell it out in the lease.

13. Rent Due Date

When is the rent due? Monthly? On what date? Also, is there a "grace period" where the rent is not considered late? Most leases do contain a grace period, but only a few states actually require it. We offer a five-day grace period so the tenant can pay rent any time between the 1st and the 5th of the month without penalty. We don't need to do this, but since some of our tenants are on Social Security and they get paid on the 3rd of the month, we keep the grace period in to help them out. You may choose to not offer a grace period at all, and if that is allowed in your state, more power to you!

14. Late Fee Amount

If the tenant does not pay by the rental date, what kind of late fee are they charged? Also, if they pay with a check and the check gets returned, what kind of NSF penalty are they charged? You may also want to charge a "daily" late fee in addition to the set fee. For example, charge a $40 late fee the first day rent is late, with an additional $10 late fee each additional day rent is late. This encourages the tenant to pay their late rent quickly.

15. Access

The lease should specifically state the access rules for the landlord using the property. This includes emergencies, showing the unit, placing marketing materials in the windows, etc.

16. Attorney/Collection Fees

If the tenant is brought to court, who is responsible for paying those fees? Spell it out here in your lease to save lots of money if you need to ever evict or sue the tenant.

17. Rules/Regulations

In addition to everything else just mentioned, the lease should also contain the basic rules and regulations for using the property. You may choose to use a separate "Rules and Regulations" addendum and attach it to the lease (as we've provided in the appendix or at http://www.BiggerPockets.com/Land-lordBookBonus) or include the rules directly in the lease. Rules like "no cooking in the bedroom" or "don't go on the roof" may seem silly, but you'd be surprised what tenants do. Other rules you may want to discuss include:

- Firearms
- Fireworks
- Junk on decks, outside, on walkways, or in common areas
- Satellite dishes
- Cleanliness/housekeeping
- Fire/carbon monoxide detector operation
- Marijuana/smoking policy
- Vehicles (How many will you allow and where are they allowed to park?)
- Quiet hours
- Laundry room rules
- Illegal drugs
- Drinking
- Parties
- Window coverings
- Reporting water leaks
- Misuse of plumbing
- Satellite dishes (Are they allowed on decks? Attached to the building? Make it clear.)
- Mold/mildew
- Pets
- Vandalism

- Changing locks
- And more

18. Lawn Care/Pool Requirements

Who is responsible for mowing the lawn (and how often), weeding the flower beds, taking care of the pool, etc.? Spell it out clearly here and include what should happen if the tenant does not fulfill their end of the bargain (for example, the landlord will hire the lawn to get mowed and the tenant will be sent the bill).

19. Miscellaneous Addendums

You may also attach other addendums to the lease, including Federal and state-required forms (such as the EPA-required Lead Based Paint Disclosure) or additional things you want the tenant to know. For example, we include an addendum that simply explains in excruciating detail the process the tenant must go through when they want to move out. In Washington State, the requirement for giving notice is a little confusing for tenants, so we spell out exactly how it's done very carefully, and then have the tenant sign it as part of their lease. This helped us eliminate the "I didn't know!" excuse when they try to move out and don't follow Washington State requirements. Just be sure to run your addendums past your lawyer to make sure they comply with the law.

20. Move-In/Move-Out Checklist

In many states you are *required* to use a Move-In and Move-Out Condition Report for the property. Even in states where it is not required, it's a no-brainer. A Move-In/Move-Out Report simply allows the landlord and tenant to list condition and all known defects on the property at the start of the lease, so when the tenant moves out, both parties know how the unit should look, what damage was preexisting, and what damage the tenant should be charged for. We've included a Move-in/Move-Out Checklist with this book, which you can find in the appendix or at http://www.BiggerPockets.com/LandlordBookBonus.

21. Initials and Signatures

All parties should sign the lease, including separate signatures on all the addendums you might have. In addition, we like to have the tenant initial each and every page of the lease, just so they can't come back later and say that we added a page into the lease that wasn't there.

22. Legal Language

Finally, every lease agreement should have legal language at the beginning, end, and throughout that has been drafted by an attorney to make sure the lease is as binding as possible. We don't recommend writing up a lease from scratch because you will not know the legal way to write it.

Now that we've gone through the 22 things every good rental lease agreement should have, let's talk about the actual process of signing that lease.

How to Sign the Lease Agreement

Preferably, the lease signing appointment should take place at your office if you have one or at the property itself. Since we run our business out of our home, we prefer to do our lease signings at the property itself, which also makes it helpful for completing the Move-In Checklist. To keep this appointment as professional as possible, avoid signing on the top of your car or at your local coffee shop. You may also want to consider conducting this appointment in the meeting room of your attorney if that is an arrangement you can negotiate. Imagine the first impression you would be making on your tenant by conducting your appointment there! (Thanks, Chris Cloth-ier, for that tip on the BiggerPockets Podcast!)

When you are preparing for your lease signing appointment, always be sure to plan ahead. Dress and act professionally. The impression you give your tenant by the way you treat and handle your business will play a large role in how they treat their tenancy. If you are too casual or flippant, they may simply imitate the same behavior during their tenancy. "Rent's due? Oh well, the landlord won't care if I'm late." "The lawn needs to be mowed? Eh, I'll do it next week." Set the precedent from the beginning that you mean business.

Bring two copies of the rental agreement: one for the tenants to sign that you will keep and one to give them as a copy until you send them a copy of their signed contract. Always send your new tenant a copy of their *signed* contract. Not only is this likely a requirement in your state, but also the presence of their signature seems to make a bigger impact during their tenancy when they are questioning or are in disagreement about a particular rule. It's harder to argue when they can physically see their own signature, especially when they know that's the same thing the landlord sees and the same thing the judge will see if they don't straighten up.

Always prepare the lease ahead of time by verifying you have all the correct forms and filling in all the blanks and rental specifics, like the date, tenant names, lease term, deposit amount, and rent amount. You can also either highlight or place a signature sticker (you can get them at any office supply store) on each spot where the tenant needs to sign or date. This helps ensure that a signature doesn't get missed at the lease signing appointment.

Make sure you bring enough pens for all tenants who will be signing. While we're on the subject of pens, think about when you go to the bank to sign documents for a new loan, to the escrow company to close on a new property, or to your attorney's office to sign legal documents. What do they all have in common that probably stands out in your mind? They all have beautiful, fancy, blue ink pens ready and waiting for you to use. You know, the kind you inwardly "ooo" and "ahh" over and secretly wish you could take home. So you see, even the choice of pen makes an impression. Avoid using the pen your dog got ahold of and chewed the cap off or pens with advertisements from your insurance agent. Plan ahead and pick up a box or two of nice, blue ink pens for your lease signing appointments and make sure every tenant gets their own.

Always bring your camera and/or video camera to record the condition of the unit at the time your new tenants obtain occupancy (a smartphone camera works just fine). You will be recording the condition in writing in your Move-In Condition Report in your lease as well, but pictures and video speak volumes more than words. The more documentation you have of the move-in condition of your rental unit, the better.

If you will be conducting your lease signing appointment at the property itself, arrive to the appointment early enough that you can turn on lights, open blinds, and turn on the heat or air conditioner (depending on the season). This also gives you the opportunity to take your pictures and video of the interior and exterior of the property before the tenant arrives.

Before giving your new tenants the keys to their new home, ensure that:

1. They have transferred all the utilities they are responsible for into their name.

2. They have brought you their remaining move-in funds in a guaranteed form: cashier's check or money order.

3. All occupants over the age of 18 who will be living in the home have signed the lease, including the Move-In Condition Report.

When going through the lease with your new tenants, spend some time on this. Their understanding of the particulars of the lease now will determine their compliance with it later. You don't need to read the lease word for word (unless you want to), but at minimum go through the lease point by point. It's okay to summarize each section, as long as you cover each section thoroughly. Before going over the lease with our new tenants, first we like to go through a short presentation called New Tenant Orientation.

New Tenant Orientation

Our New Tenant Orientation is a short, presentation we go over with all new tenants that reiterates the important things we really want them to remember, clarifies both the landlord and tenant's roles and responsibilities, and tells the tenant a little bit of what we are about. The main points we cover in the New Tenant Orientation are:

1. Our Mission Statement

2. Tenant and Landlord Roles

3. Maintenance

4. Tenant Repair Responsibilities

5. When Rent is Due

6. What Happens When Rent is Not Paid on Time, and

7. House Rules

The New Tenant Orientation is valuable because it reiterates the terms that tenants seem particularly prone to forget, neglect, or ignore, and it clarifies what exactly is expected of them while they live in the home. It shows them that this relationship is not about simply signing on the dotted line and forgetting about it. It shows that you take your business seriously and so should they. Our presentation is simple: 8.5"x11" papers, in a binder with a clear, laminated cover. When going over this with our new tenants, we might lead into it with something like: "We've created a short tutorial for you to help with commonly asked questions and issues related to your tenancy. Let's go over that together right now."

Here's a look at our New Tenant Orientation (you can find the entire presentation in the appendix of this book, or download it at https://www.

BiggerPockets.com/LandlordBookBonus.)

New Tenant Orientation

Mission Statement

Open Door Properties strives to provide, maintain, and improve affordable homes with exceptional service.

Open Door Properties LLC is a professional property management company that takes great pride in offering clean, quality rentals at an affordable rate. We are committed to this goal long-term and seek to provide the best property management in Western Washington. At Open Door Properties, we promise to:

- Return all phone calls within 24 business hours
- Complete all maintenance issues and repairs efficiently, quickly, and courteously
- Consistently improve the aesthetic look of any property we manage
- Maintain affordability in rental rates
- Provide exceptional service and support to residents

What Is a Lease?

A lease is a legal contract between the landlord and tenant. When you lease a home from us, this is what you can expect. At the commencement of your tenancy…

The landlord (Us) will provide a home that is clean, sanitary, in good cosmetic shape, and in good working order. The landlord will continue to keep the home in good working order and abide by the terms in the lease throughout the length of your tenancy.

The tenant (You) is responsible for keeping the home in good condition by practicing good housekeeping habits, including to prevent leaks, mold growth, rodents, and pests, treating the property with care to avoid preventable damage or maintenance needs, reporting maintenance issues in a timely manner, paying rent when it is due, and abiding by the terms of the lease throughout the length of your tenancy.

Maintenance

Please call us promptly with any maintenance requests. Your home has been thoroughly cleaned and inspected for any maintenance issues prior to your taking occupancy. However, we do not live in the home and therefore will not be aware when you have a future maintenance concern unless you tell us. It is 100% your responsibility to report maintenance issues.

Here is a list of items we want to know about immediately:

1. Mold (within 48 hours)

2. Drippy faucets, drippy pipes, or "running" toilets (within 48 hours)

3. Moisture where there should be none (roof, under the sink, etc.)

Your Repair Responsibility

- **Mold (from living conditions):** Mold will grow if given the opportunity. Keep your home clean and dry, with adequate ventilation and air movement. This means making sure all rooms receive heat and airflow on a consistent basis. Immediately clean up any sign of mold or mildew growth to prevent damage to the building. This includes behind furniture, in windows, in corners of walls, etc.

- **(Some) Leaks:** You are responsible for leaks caused by misuse or neglect (such as knocking drain lines loose). Report **all** leaks immediately, as they can become a very big problem very quickly.

- **Faucets/knobs:** Faucets and knobs can break easily if not handled properly.

- **Broken windows, blinds, doors, glass, locks, or any other damage** caused directly/indirectly by you or your guests.

- **Light bulbs:** These are your responsibility to replace.

- **Batteries:** It is your responsibility to keep your smoke detector and carbon monoxide detector in working order by replacing the batteries on a regular schedule.

- **Clogged** toilets, bathtubs, sinks, and other drains.

Unreported repair needs that lead to preventable damage, such as:

- Mold: Once again, mold and mildew will grow if given the

opportunity. It is your responsibility to prevent mold and mildew and to clean it up at the first sign to avoid costly liability. If you do not kill mold and mildew immediately, it will continue to spread, leading to damage, damage that could have been prevented, therefore making you liable for the repair.

- Rot/damage from leaks: It is your responsibility to report all drippy faucets and pipe leaks within 48 hours. Non-reported leaks lead to damage that could have been prevented, therefore making you liable for the cost to repair the damage.

What is Emergency Maintenance?

An emergency maintenance problem is something that if not taken care of IMMEDIATELY will cause significant damage. Emergencies usually involve water or fire. If it involves fire, call 911.

When is Rent Due?

Rent is always due on the 1st of every month. Rent payments must be paid in full at all times to avoid a late fee. Past balances are considered rent due. For example, if you owe a balance in addition to rent, on the 1st the full amount is due, with the payment being applied first to the previous balance. To further break this down, if on June 15th you were billed $41.50 for a maintenance repair you were responsible for, and on July 1st you only paid your regular rent payment, your rent payment would be considered $41.50 short.

Paying Rent on Time is a BIG DEAL. No excuses.

Rent is due on the 1st of each month, and it is solely your responsibility to be sure your rent gets to us in time. You will need to plan ahead to be sure you pay your rent on time. We understand that sometimes you may need a little more time; therefore, we give an additional 5 days' grace period each month for instances when you cannot pay by the 1st.

If you do not pay your rent by the 5th of the month, this is what to expect:

- On the 6th, $50 will be added to your total due.
- On the 6th, you will be given Eviction Notice, at which time you have 3 days to pay your rent and late fees in full, or you will have

to move.

- On the 7th, an additional $10 will begin accruing each day until your rent is paid in full.

- By the 10th, if we have still not received your rent payment and late fees, you will be evicted.

What's Going to Happen if You are Late with Rent

- It gets expensive! Plan ahead to avoid costly late fees.

- Eviction will be filed on you immediately.

- When you are evicted, it goes on your permanent record, and it will be extremely difficult to find another home to rent.

- When you are evicted, you are billed for our attorney's costs.

- When you are evicted, you create a substantial monetary judgment against you, which if remains unpaid is sent to a collection agency and affects your credit and credibility.

Policies

Your lease outlines our policies in detail, so please be sure to become familiar with them to avoid a phone call or worse, termination of your tenancy. Below are the policies that we would especially like you to remember.

No Smoking

One of the reasons you were chosen as a tenant is because you do not smoke. We do not allow smoking in any rental or within 20 feet of our buildings. Smoke permeates and damages ceilings, carpets, walls, and floor coverings. You will be held liable for any smoke-related damage within the rental.

No Pets

Pets are not allowed without written approval from the landlord and are subject to additional fees. If you intend to hide a pet within your unit, please reconsider to avoid causing your own eviction.

Window Coverings

Bed sheets or other similar objects may not be used as curtains or window coverings. Broken blinds must be replaced immediately. If we notice your blinds are broken, we will hire a contractor to install new ones at your expense.

Decks/Balconies

Decks/balconies must remain clear of debris, garbage, bicycles, toys, furniture, tarps, and other clutter. Do not use your balcony as storage or to dry clothes. Decks/balconies are meant for your enjoyment. A barbecue, lawn furniture, and small plants are the only acceptable items. Failure to abide by this policy will result in termination of your tenancy.

Guests

Please limit your guests to 1-3 per day.

Noise Levels

Out of respect for your neighbors, please keep all noise to a minimum. Your neighbors are entitled to the quiet enjoyment of their home at all times.

Parties

Loud parties are not allowed.

Occupancy

Occupancy is limited to ONLY the people we listed on the lease agreement. If you decide to get a roommate after you move in or you have a guest staying for more than 14 consecutive days, you must notify us, and they must fill out an application and go through our approval process. All occupants must meet our screening standards. Keep in mind there is an occupancy limit for the home you rent.

Notice to Vacate

When you decide to move, remember to first take a look at the terms in your rental agreement or lease for how to proceed. If you are on a month-to-month rental agreement, you must give a minimum of 20 days' written notice before the end of the month. If you have a lease, you must give a minimum of 30 days' written notice before the expiration of your lease.

We hope this presentation has helped clarify any questions you may have had. Thank you for your tenancy and congratulations on your new home!

————

Having a presentation such as the New Tenant Orientation keeps things professional while reiterating and driving home your point that you run a tight ship, which hopefully helps to avoid common tenant violations in the future. During the lease signing appointment and New Tenant Orientation, make sure you give your new tenant the opportunity to ask questions. You may know your lease and policies like the back of your hand, but your tenants will not. It's your job to teach them.

Once you have collected the rest of the move-in funds, verified tenant-paid utilities have been transferred, all adult occupants have signed the lease, and you have completed your Move-In Condition Report, your new tenants can finally be given the keys to their new home. Congratulations, landlord! So, now what?

The Tenant File

Be sure you make a copy of the rental agreement and send it to your new tenants for their records. Supplying a signed copy of the rental agreement is a requirement in most states. Some states also have a timeframe in which the tenant must receive the copy, as well as a requirement that each person who is on the contract receive their *own* copy.

Next, create a tenant file for all your documents related to your new tenant's tenancy. This includes their application, all your screening documents, their rental agreement, and move-in condition pictures. If you keep your tenant's move-in condition pictures and video on your computer, make a note in the file of where exactly they are located. You may find it best to put them on Google Drive, Dropbox, or another cloud-based service, and simply print off the URL for the file and place the URL in their folder.

The tenant file is also where you will keep all phone messages, correspondence, emails, notices, maintenance requests/resolutions, and anything else having to do with your tenant during their tenancy. It is essentially their "diary" file. For organization and accessibility, consider keeping everything inside the tenant's file in chronological order, beginning on the bottom with their screening and move-in documents and ending on the top with whatever is most current. Make sure each file is labeled on the tab with the tenant's name and address. We also label the front of the file with what we call "Quicklook Information," which includes their:

- Name, address, and contact information

- Names of all occupants

- Move-in date

- Lease term

- Deposit amount

- Rent amount

Of course, we also keep all of this information in their file and in Google Drive so it can be accessed from anywhere, but having it on the front of the file is helpful as well. You should use the system that works best for you for keeping your tenant's information organized and easily accessible.

Wrapping it Up

Now that you have your tenant in place and have their file nicely organized and safely tucked away, in the next chapter we will dive into how to manage your tenant during their tenancy by training them correctly, accepting rent, operating your business efficiently, and minimizing risk.

CHAPTER 9:
MANAGING TENANTS

I (Brandon) would squirm, I would cry, I would complain—but my parents were unrelenting.

For five whole minutes of torture, I needed to keep my nose touching the small, pencil-drawn circle on the wall. As you likely remember, to a child, five minutes can feel like an eternity. But that's the punishment my parents saw fit to discipline my five-year-old self when I got into trouble. And boy, did I ever get in trouble! After my punishment was done, my parents would take time to explain why I was being punished to make sure I understood the right way to act in the future.

If you've ever raised kids, you'll understand that by nature kids can be pretty naughty. They don't come out naturally knowing how to abide by all the rules and processes of life. Instead, they need to be *trained*.

The same thing is true for tenants. Most tenants do not naturally know how to behave according to your rules because they've never lived under your rules before! They've likely been raised under the rules of other, less effective landlords and have picked up some bad habits in the process. Therefore, it's up to you to train them in the way they should act.

People tend to get offended when we use the word "training" in regard to tenants. However, we've found no phrase that more accurately defines what a landlord's job should be. Training is not a derogatory concept. As children we are trained to behave well in society. In high school we are trained to drive a car. In our adult life we are trained to obey laws, pay taxes, and work hard at our jobs. Training is a part of life because very few things in life come naturally. Instead, most things require training.

Being a good tenant is no exception; tenants MUST be trained if you want to decrease the level of work needed to manage your properties. Yes, you could toss tenants into a rental and hope for the best, and this is what most landlords do (and why most landlords fail). Soon, the tenants will be paying rent when they get around to it, calling at all hours of the day and night, trashing the property, and driving you crazy. Does that sound like an ideal lifestyle to you? Didn't think so.

Training begins with the first interaction your tenant has with your company and continues until the day they hand over the keys on their move-out day. Of course, the bulk of that training takes place at the beginning of the tenancy, as we discussed earlier in Chapter 8 regarding the new tenant orientation, but it also exists while the tenant lives in the property. Every action you take as a landlord is training the tenant, either positively or negatively. Training a tenant is similar to training in any other aspect: The correct way to do something should be taught clearly and reinforced with either positive or negative consequences. If the tenant pays late and is hit with a late charge, they are being trained that paying late is bad. If the tenant renews their lease for another year and receives a thank you note, they are being trained that staying put is good.

If you want to make your landlording as successful and stress-free as possible, pay close attention to the tips you'll find here. Always be aware that every action you take is training your tenants in one way or another, so focus on training them to be the kind of tenants you love to manage. Throughout the next two chapters, we'll dive into the nitty gritty on how we manage tenants and deal with problems when they arise.

Setting Office Hours

One of the easiest ways to begin training your tenant is by setting office hours. It may seem counterintuitive to give yourself hours where you *have* to work, but setting office hours will benefit both you and your tenant in significant ways. Office hours help YOU keep your business and personal life more separate. It will help your tenant to learn to respect your boundaries, and if they want something done, to ask during the proper time.

Back in the beginning of our landlording career (before we had our hours of operation), we had a tenant call us at 2:00 a.m. to report a water leak. Now, a water leak can be a big deal, but this was not one of those instances. Brandon crawled out of bed at zero-dark-thirty and drove to the tenant's home expecting to find water exploding all over the kitchen.

Instead, what he found was the tenant doing her dishes—with an unconnected pipe beneath the sink. Had she simply stopped washing her dishes (at 2:00 a.m.) and waited to call until the next morning, the problem would have still been fixed and her dishes would have still gotten done—only during normal hours!

Keep in mind, those office hours do not need to be 9:00 a.m. to 5:00 p.m., and in fact we don't recommend that they are. As Tim Ferriss pointed out in the classic entrepreneurial book *The 4-Hour Workweek*, people tend to fill the amount of time they have with the tasks they need to do. This is known as Parkinson's Law, and it's something we've found very true in our business. Who ever declared that 99 percent of human jobs take exactly eight hours to accomplish each day? No one! Our office hours are generally from 10:00 a.m. to 4:00 p.m., and we make sure our tenants know that those are the hours during which they can reach us. It's stated on the application, on our business cards, on our website, and on the voicemail.

All the tenants know that we are available to answer phone calls between the hours of 10:00 a.m. and 4:00 p.m., and if they call outside those hours, they'll be met with a voicemail telling them to leave a message or call back the next day between 10:00 a.m. and 4:00 p.m. In reality, we probably could make those hours shorter, but we also want to make it convenient for the tenant as well. Of course, we don't need to sit in our office for those six hours waiting for the phone to ring, but those are the hours during which our tenants know they can reach us and during which we will address their issues.

Furthermore, when you own rental properties, it's wise to have an emergency number for tenants to call when they have a problem outside of normal office hours. For example, if a waterline breaks in the ceiling of their unit, hundreds of dollars in damage can happen for every minute that leak goes unfixed. There are few options you can do in this case:

1. Give your tenants an "emergency number" that they can call in case of an emergency.

2. Put the emergency number in the voicemail for your regular phone line.

We have found option 2 to work the best in our business. The interesting thing is, with hundreds of tenants over the past decade, we have yet to receive a middle-of-the-night emergency call. However, should the need ever arise, we have a system in place to handle it.

Remember, it doesn't matter what your office hours are. They could be

8:00 a.m.–5:00 p.m., 5:00 p.m.–8:00 p.m., 9:00 a.m.–3:00 p.m. on Mondays, Wednesdays, and Fridays, or whatever you prefer that works well in your life and for your landlording business. Just make sure you have them; it will make your entire landlording life much easier to handle.

We'll talk a bit more about setting up your phone system in Chapter 14 and how we use Google Voice to manage this process for free. But we'll leave you in suspense for now and move on to one of your favorite activities: getting paid!

How to Collect Rent

"Charlie, give that back right now!" we shout to no avail. He's already gone, running like a madman through the house and out the back door.

It's another day in the Turner household, raising the world's cutest Yorkshire Terrier.

Charlie's favorite game is "catch me if you can!" He'll grab something he probably shouldn't have, get our attention with a bark or growl, and then scurry through the house like a bat out of hell, waiting for one of us to chase him. Shoes, eyeglasses, frisbees, socks, bills, whatever he can find. And of course, we chase him. How could we resist, with those big brown eyes and fluffy face?

Tenants, on the other hand, are not so cute. We don't play "catch me if you can" with a tenant's rent, and neither should you. We train them to bring us the rent every time, though the technique to do this has changed over the years, based on trial and error. Below we've listed several ways that you could collect rent, and we've given the pros and cons of each. You'll likely test out a few options over the coming years to develop a plan that works for you and your tenants, so don't be afraid to try things out. For example, in a perfect world, all of our tenants would pay rent online, but we've discovered that many of our tenants do not have a computer or don't know how to use it if they do. (We know that sounds crazy, but a huge portion of the US population doesn't!) Therefore, we've had to come up with solutions that work for the tenant *and* that require the least amount of work for us, the landlords.

In-Person Cash

Let's start with the big "no-no." **Don't collect cash in person.** Not only is it the most time-consuming way to get rent, it's also the most dangerous.

When landlords go door to door and pick up rent on a monthly basis, people notice. "Oh, here comes the landlord doing her rounds. I wonder how much cash she's got in her purse?" It's just asking to get robbed. Some landlords boast about the gun they carry around so they can pick up rent in cash and fight off the thugs, but… is that the kind of life YOU want to lead? We sure don't. Picking up rent in person also puts you into the "chasing rent" category, where you are training your tenant that they can tell you to jump and you will to ask, "How high?" You don't want this kind of landlord-tenant relationship. Maintain authority and don't pick up rent in person.

The only benefit to picking up rent in person is the ability to check up on your property to see how it's performing. We get this, the desire to know what's going on with your tenants and build a relationship. But there are much more efficient ways to do this than picking up rent in person, and we would encourage you to explore those.

Letting Tenants Drop the Rent Off at Your House

Don't do this. Please. In fact, never give out your home address to tenants. Your tenants might be great people when they move in, but you never know the true character of someone until they are under incredible pressure or going through a difficult time. We once let a great tenant drop off rent in person to our home because he lived just a few blocks away. However, when he was late on his rent and we sent him the late notice, he stormed over to the house and started making a scene on the front porch, hollering and swearing. Of course, it didn't do him any good, but having this take place on our doorstep was not an ideal situation.

Remember, you run a *business* not a hobby. The manager of the local pizza place wouldn't give you his home address, right? When you have a problem with the pizza, you wouldn't dream of driving to the pizza owner's house to complain. You deal with business *at* the business. The same is true for your landlording business. If you have an in-home office like we do, this means issues can be dealt with over the phone or email during business hours. In the event a face-to-face encounter needs to happen, it can take place at the rental. Keep your business and personal life as separate as possible. This will ensure less stress and more safety for your family.

Mailing Rent

One of the most popular ways among landlords to get rent is through the mail. Tenants simply place their rent in an envelope and mail it to you. By having the tenant mail the rent, you don't need to go pick it up; it simply is delivered to you. If you have a lot of tenants, picking up rent can be a five-minute task with one trip to your PO Box. (Because, of course, you wouldn't think about giving your home address to all your tenants.)

We actually ran our company this way for a number of years, but have recently stopped accepting checks in the mail. On the 6th of the month, we would head to our PO Box and 90 percent of the rent would be there, but the other 10 percent would not. We would call the tenant and hear the same line over and over: "I mailed it! It must be lost in the mail!" Luckily, the post office places a date on every piece of mail the day it is sent (the postmark), and we could see the date the tenant mailed it.

Much of the time, of course, the tenant lied and simply claimed that they mailed it, when the postmarked date was after we called. But other times, the postmark date was actually early enough, and the post office simply delayed the letter for some reason or another. We've even had checks lost for several weeks in the mail, all the while thinking our tenant was trying to stiff us. Every month we ran into these problems, never knowing if the tenant was lying or if the rent really was lost. We would issue an eviction notice, only to get the check a few days later, after many heated conversations with the tenant. Or we would take the tenant's word for it, only to discover later they lied. It was simply too irritating to deal with, and we needed to find a more immediate solution.

That said, if you plan to accept rent by mail, here are a few tips to follow:
- Get a PO Box and don't give out your home address.
- Require that the rent be **received** by a certain date, not just sent. If rent is due on the 1st of the month but you have a five-day "grace period" (which just means rent is due by the 5th!), then the tenants must mail the rent so that you receive it by the 5th. If they mail it on the 4th, they should know they will likely get a late fee. If they mail it on the 5th, they will get a late fee.
- Make sure the tenant knows NOT to send cash. Yes, you will need to spell this out for them.

A Local Dropbox

If you own a larger multifamily property, you may consider installing a rental dropbox on the premises so tenants can pay their rent there. We once had a dropbox installed at our apartment complex but began to worry about the security of the box. If people want to break into something, they will. It doesn't matter how secure it is. Although we didn't allow tenants to drop off cash in this box (just money orders, cashier's checks, or personal checks), it would still have been a nightmare if someone broke into the box and stole those checks. The risk was just too great, so we moved on from the dropbox and decided to implement other, more modern, solutions. Let's talk about those now.

ACH Payments

ACH, which stands for Automated Clearing House, is the system that banks use to talk to one another and send money from one checking/savings account to another. If you have automatic payments set up for some of your home bills (cable, utilities, etc.) and that payment is deducted directly out of your checking account, it's likely they are using an ACH processor.

The problem with ACH processing is that, while it can be incredibly cheap to do an ACH transfer, it may not be cost-effective for a small-time landlord to set up. You must set up your ACH through the merchant services department at a bank or other financial institution, and there may be large setup fees or ongoing monthly fees. For example, some banks we've looked into charge $40 per month for the ability to do ACH transfer, plus another $0.25 per transaction. The $0.25 might not be a big deal, but the $40 per month might be crazy if you only have a few units. Therefore, doing ACH transfers directly might be best used when you have dozens of units or utilize a third-party to handle your ACH transactions online. Let's talk about that next.

Online Payments

In the future, there's a good probability that *all* rent is going to be paid online. However, that future is not quite here, so the process of collecting rent online is still a bit muddied. New startups in Silicon Valley are being founded on an almost daily basis to address this problem, but no one yet has the perfect solution (though depending on when you read this book, perhaps someone has emerged as the leader).

Therefore, there are dozens of different companies that you can work with to accept online payments, some better than others. With the huge failure rate of startups, however, most companies won't be in operation by the time this book is published, so we won't bother listing our favorite companies here in this book. Instead, we would like to direct you to a page on BiggerPockets that chronicles the best online rent payment companies right now, which we will continually be updating as new companies come and go. To see this list, just head to http://www.biggerpockets.com/payrentonline.

PayNearMe

Now, if a tenant does not have a bank account or will not pay rent online, there is another solution that may come in handy: PayNearMe.

PayNearMe is a way to let your tenants pay rent in cash at a local 7-Eleven, ACE Cash Express, or other business that partners with the company. When the tenant takes their assigned PayNearMe Card with their unique barcode to one of PayNearMe's payment locations and pays their rent, the landlord is instantly notified when the rent was paid (no more "it's in the mail!"), and the money is then deposited into the landlord's bank account. In other words, your tenant doesn't need to go get a money order, write a check, get a stamp, address an envelope, or mail the rent. You as the landlord don't need to wait around and wonder if your tenant really sent it or if they are simply lying so they can wait for their next pay day.

When a tenant uses PayNearMe, they simply go through the following four steps:

1. The tenant takes their cash to an approved retailer.
2. The tenant allows the cashier to scan their unique barcode that you supply them (or they have on their smartphone).
3. The tenant hands over their cash to the cashier.
4. The tenant gets a printed receipt right then and there, while you get instant notification that the rent was paid.

Each tenant's account is managed online by the landlord, where the landlord can easily issue replacement cards, change the amount owed, enforce the amount owed (meaning PayNearMe will not accept anything less than what is owed), and even suspend payments (preventing, say, a tenant who is being evicted from making a one dollar payment and screwing up the process).

For the landlord, PayNearMe is free, though there may be a small setup fee. For tenants, there is, as of the writing of this book, a $3.99 charge to use the PayNearMe service. In other words, if the tenant chooses to live their life without a bank account, it's fine—but it's going to cost them $3.99 a month to pay their rent. This gives the tenant options without hurting you (the landlord) at all.

Collecting Rent: Summary

As you can see, when it comes to collecting rent, landlords have a lot of options besides knocking down doors. Not every option is going to work for you, and you'll likely develop your own system as you move forward and as technology progresses. Since the day we started landlording, we've used every single strategy we've talked about in this chapter and are continuing to test new ideas. Currently, we accept online payments through two different online companies (giving the tenant the option to choose which one they like better), and we also use PayNearMe. All three methods have proven to be very successful, all three are very simple, and all three give us almost instant notification of when rent was paid and automatically deposited into our bank account. The important thing is that you create a **system** for paying rent and continually try to improve that system to decrease your stress, boost your bottom line, and get paid, every time, on time.

Grace Periods and Rent Extensions

A grace period is additional time given to the tenant to pay their rent before they will be charged a late fee or given eviction notice. For example, rent may be due on the 1st of every month, but the tenant has until, say, the 5th to make their payment. Grace periods can be anywhere between 2–"X" number of days. They are actually a requirement in some states, and in others they are not, but we have found that they are useful for a couple reasons: 1) Many tenants are on a fixed, government income and don't get paid until the 3rd of the month, and 2) it shows the tenant that the landlord gives them flexibility in when they make their payment. Nice guy. However, the flexibility is on the landlord's terms. We always let our tenants know that rent is still **due** on the 1st, so technically if they take advantage of the grace period, they are considered late, though we won't initiate eviction notice and penalties until the 6th of the month.

Whatever you do, make sure all your tenants are on the same schedule. Don't change due dates and grace periods to suit the tenant when they move in (because they will ask). It may work out fine for the first few tenants, but as you continue to acquire more rentals, you will want everyone to be paying at the same time so you can keep track of who has paid and who has not.

Our grace period goes through the 5th of the month. If rent has not been paid by the 5th, they will get a late fee, currently $50. Additionally, we charge them an extra $10 *per day* after that until they have paid their rent in full. For example, on the 6th they receive a one-time $50 late fee, on the 7th an additional $10 is added to the $50, on the 8th an additional $10 is added to the $60, and so forth. Every day gets a little more expensive.

When your tenant pays late, it is vital that you follow through with the late fees. This bears repeating: *It is vital that you follow through with the late fees.* Don't waiver, as the late fee's sole purpose is to motivate your tenant to pay as quickly as possible. Take away that motivation, and good luck getting your rent—that is, until the tenant gets around to paying it. If there is one simple piece of advice in this entire book that you should listen to it is this: always follow through with late fees.

Let's be real: The number one reason most tenants are late on their rent is not because of an emergency or some unforeseen necessary expense, but because of priorities. They are late because paying rent on time has not been made a priority. The best way to make timely payments a priority is by following through on the late fees. Tenants, and America in general, usually live above their means. In other words, there's always more month than money. Therefore, every month requires sacrifice and prioritization of bills: food, clothing, rent, cable, a new TV, a game console, tattoos, medical bills, Starbucks—these are all expenses your tenant is internally trying to prioritize.

Naturally, the bills with the highest penalty for negligence are usually prioritized the highest. Those will be the bills that get paid first. So the question is, is the consequence for paying rent late greater than or less than the consequence of having the cable turned off or having to go without their daily coffee or smoke fix? Despite what tenants think, late fees are not about lining the landlord's pockets. Late fees are designed to give rent a place of high priority because of the consequence. You may feel bad or think you're being cruel by charging a late fee, but by following through, you are helping your tenant prioritize the most important bill they have: their housing.

This last month we had a tenant call us a couple days before her grace period was up to let us know that she had some unexpected expenses come up, wouldn't have the full rent in time, and wanted to know if she could pay the rest at the end of the month. We told her we needed to follow her lease, and the lease says her full rent payment is due the 1st and late after the 5th.

Any rent not paid would trigger both late fees and eviction notice. Guess what? On the 5th her priorities suddenly changed, and she paid her entire rent payment. From past experience, this particular tenant knew that we take non-timely rent payments seriously.

We do offer our tenants one alternative to the late fee penalty, but it requires their planning ahead and communication. We call it the rent extension, and it is not something we advertise to our tenants. However, if a tenant calls us *before* the 1st to let us know they will be late on their rent, we will offer them a rent extension up to the 10th for a $20 penalty. If they don't follow through on the 10th, they are hit with the full late fees and eviction notice. The reason for the rent extension is to reward responsible behavior: 1) they planned ahead to deal with the problem, 2) they communicated, and 3) they initiated the communication, rather than waiting for us to call them once the rent was already late.

Raising the Rent

Raising the rent on tenants is never a joyful task, but it is one of the most important things you can do to build wealth through your rental properties. Rents generally go up over time, and everyone (including your tenant) expects it. That's right: Your tenant expects a bump in their rent, probably on an annual basis, and although they'll gripe a little to themselves, it's unlikely they'll move out, as long as you are competitive.

And what if they do move out? You may be inclined to keep the rent low, as to avoid too much turnover, but we would encourage you to look at the bottom line and decide, "Am I really saving money this way?" For example, let's say you have four units, and each is underpriced by $50 per month. By raising the rent on each unit, that's an extra $200 per month, which equates to $2,400 per year or $24,000 per decade. By raising the rent, even if a tenant or two were to move out, it's likely the increased rent would more than make up for the difference.

Many landlords refuse to raise the rent for many years, only to find themselves hundreds of dollars below market value and missing out on tens of thousands of dollars in potential rent. To combat this, we recommend raising the rent on an annual basis (if possible) with your market. Even a small raise of just $5 or $10 a month will keep your rental going up slowly, rather than a large $50 bump every five years. And few tenants will ever move over such a small raise. These bumps are often known as "nuisance raises" and depending on how many units you manage, could make a big difference to your bottom line.

That said, the goal is not simply to "raise the rent," but to make sure your rent is at (or perhaps *slightly* below in order to stay competitive) the market rent. We talked about in Chapter 3 how to determine the market rent for a property, so we won't rehash it now, but make sure you take an honest evaluation of the market every several months to make sure you are still in-line. Furthermore, if you have a dozen qualified people wanting to apply for your property, there is a good chance you could raise the rent slightly. On the other hand, if you are having trouble finding applicants who can qualify, perhaps it's time to lower the rent (or increase your marketing).

How to Raise the Rent

First, you need to find out if you even **can** raise the rent. When a tenant is in a lease, the rent is fixed for the term of that lease and cannot be raised until after the lease is over. This is why rent raises are most common upon the renewing of one's lease. If you are in a month-to-month agreement with your tenant, you can likely raise the rent on the tenant as long as proper notice has been given. (Usually 30 days', but sometimes 60 days' notice is required. Check with your landlord-tenant laws as to the required notice to change the terms of a month-to-month agreement.) Also, if you are in an area with rent control, where the government controls rental prices, check carefully with your local laws. There is a good chance you won't be able to raise the rent at all.

When raising the rent, try this trick often used by marketers: Don't tell them what the new rental price is going to be, but give them three price options to choose from. Think about it. Almost every big business offers three price tiers:

- Small, Medium, Large

- Basic, Premium, Platinum

- Bronze, Silver, Gold

- Regular, Premium, Plus

By offering three choices, individuals tend to compare the choices given, rather than comparing the price to other businesses. A coffee at Starbucks may be ridiculously priced, but by giving the customer options—the "Tall" for $3.25, the "Grande" for $3.75, or the "Venti" for $4.25—people rarely even consider the $0.99 cup of coffee they can get at the local diner across the street. Instead, they choose from the options they have been given. Of course, there are other reasons a person pays $4.00 for a drink, but the pricing tiers help to take attention off the price and give people the power to choose what price they want to pay. Additionally, that Venti drink priced at $4.25 doesn't cost Starbucks much more to make than the Tall drink at $3.25, so the higher tiered product just produces more income for the company, as some people will always choose the "premium" option, and others will always choose the "regular" option. This way, Starbucks can make a profit on everyone, while still allowing the customer a choice. And you can do the same with rent raises.

To raise the rent, simply send a Lease Renewal Decision form such as the following. (We've also included this letter in the appendix, as well as online at http://www.BiggerPockets.com/LandlordBookBonus.)

Lease Renewal Decision Form

Date ___/___/___

Dear _____,

Thank you for your tenancy at _____! We've really appreciated having you here this past year and look forward to continuing our relationship with you. It is a privilege to be able to work with you and we thank you for your business.

According to our records, it appears that your lease-term is coming up at the end of next month and, as such, we need to discuss your future plans with you and make sure we are all on the same page. Due to naturally increasing expenses for the owner, it is necessary to gradually increase rent over time. Therefore, a slight bump in your monthly rental rate will take place soon. However, we would like your input on where to go from here.

Please choose from one of the following options for your future at your home. Simply circle the option below you would like to choose, and send this form back to us. We will prepare a new lease with the proper information and mail it to you within seven days.

Sign a new **one-year lease** at $_____ per month, which will begin on _____ and end on _____. This is an increase of $_____ per month.

Sign a new **six-month lease** at $_____ per month, which will begin on _____ and end on _____. This is an increase of $_____ per month.

Sign a **month-to-month lease** agreement at $_____ per month, which will begin on _____. This is an increase of $_____ per month.

Although we hope you'll stay with us forever, if you do not plan on renewing your lease and staying with us any longer, please let us know immediately. Our state law requires tenants to give ____ days written notice to vacate before the end of their lease. Therefore, please return this form and let us know your plans by _____ so we can make plans that work for everyone.

Once again, thank you for your residency here at [address or apartment complex name]; we look forward to many more years of working with you.

Sincerely,

Management

Of course, some tenants may still call and complain about the rent being raised, or they may even decide to move, but most likely they will simply chalk it up to one of the realities of renting. Over the past decade of raising the rent on approximately 100 or more tenants, we've only ever had **one** tenant call to complain (a grumpy old man in his 80s), so we compromised and agreed to give him six more months before raising his rent. See? We're not all bad guys!

Periodic Inspections

Several years ago, I (Brandon) was walking across the parking lot of our apartment complex, when a young boy from one of the apartments came down and asked me to come look at his apartment. I followed him to his unit, where I met with his parents, who sheepishly walked me to the back bedroom. When I stepped foot into the room, my jaw hit the floor. The entire ceiling was covered in a layer of disgusting green mold. Apparently the roof had been leaking for many months, possibly several years, and the tenants did not want to call and report the problem. You are probably wondering why any tenant would let a problem like this go on for years, but it's not that uncommon with rental properties. Many tenants are afraid to report maintenance issues, so instead they simply keep quiet. Perhaps they:

- Have had a bad experience with a previous landlord

- Fear they will be charged for the damages

- May not like having people in their home

- May not want the landlord to see the condition in which they keep the rental

- May fear that reporting a problem would "rock the boat" and trigger a rent-raise letter

Of course, in this situation we moved the tenant out to another unit, fixed the roof leak, and remediated the mold (after a complete tear-out of drywall and insulation)—all to the tune of about $5,000. Ouch. Had the leak been dealt with sooner, the problem could have been fixed for a couple hundred bucks. While we were clearly upset with the tenant over not reporting the issue, *the fault was ultimately ours.* We should have performed regular inspections. Since that date, all of our units get inspected on a six-month rotation. Our lease also now states that any maintenance issues that are not reported that result in further *avoidable* damage will be billed to them.

When you hand over the keys to a tenant, you are also handing over the trust that they will take care of your investment for you. Of course, that's a lot of faith to put in someone you just met and don't know very well! For this reason, it's important to do regular inspections of your rental units to make sure that the tenant is taking proper care of the property, the tenant is abiding by their lease, and that maintenance problems are being accurately reported and addressed. The inspection doesn't need to take long (usually less than 10 minutes), so you can bundle multiple inspections at one time. Additionally, we would recommend NOT doing the inspection yourself, as a tenant may be more likely to complain about problems to a third party, such as a handyman. If a problem is discovered, the handyman can also give you a bid to fix the problem and maybe take care of it right then and there.

When doing the property inspection, take note of the following things:

- Mold and mildew

- Undocumented pets

- Broken window blinds

- Holes in doors or in walls

- Evidence of extra people living in the unit

- Smoke detectors and carbon monoxide detectors (if required) - make sure they exist, are up to code, and work

- Leaks under the kitchen and bathroom sinks

- Dripping water from the bathroom or kitchen sink

- Dripping water from the bathtub

- Whether the toilet is continuously running

- General cleanliness of the property

- Items piled against heaters or other fire dangers

You may have more items to add to this list or some that might not apply. The important thing is to look for things that, if left unchecked, can cause damage to your property over the long run. This is also a good time to see how your tenant lives, so you can make good decisions on whether or not you want to renew their lease the next time around, or if there is anything they need to remedy. Also, be sure to remedy any problems found during the inspection, including damages caused by the tenant, so your tenant knows you are not the type of landlord who will allow their property to be treated poorly or fall into disrepair. Be sure to send the tenant the bill for any repairs for damages they caused.

When we hire our handyman to do an inspection, we give him a stack of the following form to fill out for each property and return to us. You can find this form in the appendix of this book or online at http://www.BiggerPockets.com/LandlordBookBonus.

Property Inspection Checklist

Address: _____ *Date:* _____ *Time:* _____

- *Smoke detectors* - Make sure there is a working smoke detector in each bedroom and one additional smoke detector elsewhere in the property per floor.

- *Carbon Monoxide Detector* – Washington State Law requires a working carbon monoxide detector in all residential rental properties, regardless of the heating source. Make sure there is at least one working on each floor.

- *Mold* - Look for any signs of mold in each room, especially in corners, behind furniture, near windows, on walls, in closets, or under cabinets. Ask tenant if they have seen any mold. Look for anything as small as a few specks, slight wall discoloration, or obvious patches of mold growing. Make note of any problem areas, take a picture and write the description of location and size of the area.

- *Leaks* – Even the smallest drip from a faucet can cause hundreds or even thousands of dollars in damage. Please make note of any leaks in the following areas:

  o *Kitchen:* Is the kitchen faucet dripping? Y/N

  o *Kitchen:* Is it dry in the cabinet beneath the kitchen sink? Y/N

  o *Kitchen:* Under the sink, are there any signs of rot or of being recently damp?

  o *Bathroom(s):* Is the bathtub faucet dripping?

  o *Bathroom(s):* Is the bathroom faucet dripping?

  o *Bathroom(s):* Is it dry in the cabinet beneath the bathroom sink?

  o *Bathroom(s):* Under the bathroom sink, are there any signs of rot or of being recently damp?

  o *Bathroom(s):* Is the toilet making a continuous sound like "running water?" If so, make a note.

- *Water Damage:* Check the ceiling throughout the property. Are there any signs of water from a roof leak (brown spots, rings, saggy drywall)? Y/N

- *Caulk* - Is the caulk around the shower/along the bottom of the tub good?

- *Interior Lighting* - Do all interior lights work? (Bedrooms, bathrooms, kitchen, etc.)

- *Exterior Lighting*: Do all exterior lights work? (Decks, porches, garages, etc.)

- *Blinds* - Are all blinds in good condition?

- *Decks/Porches* - Is the deck, porch, or other outdoor areas clear of unapproved items? (Anything that is not a BBQ, lawn furniture, or plant.)

- *General Condition* - Is the tenant keeping the unit clean and in good condition?

  Yes_____ No _____

Please list any additional important details:

Inspection completed by:

Signature: _____   Date: _____

Communicating With Tenants

As a landlord, one of your primary responsibilities will be to maintain open communication with your tenants. One of the top reasons tenants move from one place to another is because of their non-responsive landlord. Therefore, it's not just cordial to have good communication, it's also good for business.

When communicating with tenants, the telephone will obviously be used often, but we still recommend making a policy that **everything** gets written down, even if someone calls or tells you something in person. Should something bad happen in your business and you are forced to appear before a judge, generally the rule holds true that "he who has the best paperwork wins." Written communication is also helpful for keeping yourself organized, as less is rattling around inside your head. Therefore, when a tenant calls and complains about a leak in their bathroom, write it up on a Work Order form. When you deny a tenant due to insufficient rental history, write down the reason and keep it with their paperwork. If your tenant is piling up garbage on their deck, rather than taking it out to the dumpster, send them a written notice!

Text messaging with tenants can also be helpful, as most people today prefer text over phone calls, but treat the text exactly as you would a phone call: Document it in writing in their file. Never send important notices via text. And remember, if you want to get your point across to a tenant, nothing says business like a certified letter through the mail.

Finally, if you and your tenants are tech-savvy enough, encourage the use of email to communicate with you, but be sure to print out all email conversations in case you need them in the future. Place those conversations in the tenant's file to refer to later. Lastly, when a tenant moves out, don't throw away their file. Keep all tenant files for at least 10 years. You never know when you might need them, and rubber bins are cheap and can easily be stored in your attic or garage.

Hiring a Resident Manager

As you grow your real estate portfolio, you may want to consider the idea of a "resident manager" to help look after your properties. This is most commonly found in apartment complexes, but it doesn't have to be. In fact, in some areas like California or New York, a resident manager is required for buildings with a certain number of units (16 in California, 9 in New York).

A resident manager is someone who lives at your property and has certain duties to carry out in exchange for either a salary or reduced/free rent. We've used a resident manager several times at our apartment complex, with mixed results.

Resident managers can definitely lighten your load and help you become a more "stress-free" landlord. They can be assigned numerous tasks, such as lawn care, small maintenance, signing leases, sweeping parking lots, serving legal notices, answering phones, or whatever else you decide. Obviously, this can help you spend more time working ON your business, rather than IN your business. They can handle the direct tenant contact, while you work on acquiring more properties or relaxing on a beach—whatever floats your boat. Resident managers are typically less expensive than hiring a professional property management company and allow you to maintain more direct control over your investment property.

Resident managers have the capability to reduce your workload and stress, but the most important thing we've noticed is that resident managers, if not managed carefully, can actually increase your workload and stress level. You see, when you hire a resident manager, you shift roles. You are likely no longer dealing directly with your tenants, but instead you are now a boss with a sort-of employee. We've had to cut ties with a couple resident managers who were not doing their jobs correctly, but we place most of the blame on ourselves for not taking the time to correctly train and manage them. As any business owner knows, if you don't train your employees—and monitor and offer feedback on their actions—an employee will likely cause more damage than good. This is the danger with resident managers. Therefore, if you plan to use a resident manager, look at your own management skills and ask yourself, "Will I be a good boss?" If so, proceed. If not, either avoid bringing on a resident manager or improve your management skills.

We once hired a resident manager who seemed fantastic at the start. He was good at maintenance, ambitious, and friendly. We gave him a detailed manual on how things should be done, briefly trained him, and then let him at it. He took the reigns with joy, freeing us up from phone calls, lease signings, and maintenance. It was a huge stress relief. However, soon things turned south. He began acting as the "king of the complex" and was rude to tenants (and sometimes us!). Soon, he started breaking many of the apartment rules (like piling junk on his deck, parking an RV in the lot, and getting a dog), and after several talks with him, we had to let him go.

But it was after he left that we saw the true damage of this situation. He approved tenants who didn't meet our minimum screening standards (including renting a unit out to a couple who made just $600 per month—and the rent was $525!) and allowed tenants to get away with things we never would. Tenants began coming out of the woodwork complaining about his rudeness, fits of rage, and repeated calls for maintenance fixes that were never done, leading to further damage. The work that was done was shoddy (at best) and sometimes downright wrong! To this day, we're still dealing with the results of his actions and still finding things that need to be re-repaired because that resident manager had *too much power* and *not enough accountability.* Don't make our mistake. Train, manage, and control your resident manager. For the best book ever written on dealing with a resident manager, be sure to read John T. Reed's book *How to Manage Residential Property for Maximum Cash Flow.* Reed goes into great detail on the process of finding, screening, and managing these employees.

Also, make sure you understand the tax ramifications of hiring a resident manager. A resident manager IS an employee of your company, and as such, the same laws that govern other businesses govern your relationship with your resident manager, especially the taxes and paperwork. This means when the manager is hired, the owner must file form W-4 (Employee Withholding Allowance Certificate) with the IRS, and a form W-2 must be given to the resident manager at tax time. Luckily, the IRS has ruled that the payroll taxes (the 15.3 percent tax comprised of Social Security and Medicare taxes that are split between employers and employees in the US) are not required for the price of the reduced (or free) rent but IS required for any salary paid to the manager. In addition, you may need to purchase "worker's compensation insurance" for your resident manager. Check with your state's requirements for hiring employees and follow those rules carefully.[ix]

If you plan to hire a resident manager, make sure you continually brush up on your management skills and don't give away too much power without some heavy accountability. Read books on management and hiring the best employees. Continually check in on them and make training a regular thing. Make sure they are someone you feel comfortable being a "boss" to—in other words, not your grandma. And finally, make sure you sign a contract with the resident manager that outlines the duties and responsibilities of that manager, as well as the compensation being given and the consequences should they fail to perform.

6 Ways to Keep Yourself Free From Lawsuits

In our litigious age, it's impossible to keep yourself 100 percent free of a lawsuit. As a landlord, the chance of getting sued actually increases. However, there are some actions you can take to decrease your chance of being hit with a lawsuit. This section is not designed to scare you, but lawsuits are a real thing, hence the need for great insurance on your property. But besides insurance, let's talk about six of the easiest ways to reduce your liability.

1. Provide Housing That is Habitable

As a landlord, it is your legal responsibility to provide housing that meets a certain level of cleanliness. If you rent properties that don't meet basic standards, your risk of getting sued increases greatly. So don't be a slumlord! Fix up your properties and make sure they are in good, livable condition for the tenant. Be sure to investigate and comply with federal, state, and local housing codes to ensure your property is in good enough condition to rent.

2. Provide Housing That is Reasonably Safe

If you fail to provide a reasonable level of security for your tenants, you could be sued. For example, if a tenant calls with complaints about their door lock not working, and before you can fix the problem someone breaks in and attacks the tenant, you could face a lawsuit. Therefore, make sure safety-related concerns are addressed promptly. And, of course, don't rent to people who might hurt other people.

3. Get Repairs Taken Care of Quickly

If a tenant has an issue that must be fixed and you refuse to, you are opening yourself up to a lawsuit or at minimum, the tenant legally being able to withhold the rent and using their own money to pay for the repairs. So don't let things get to this point. Hire qualified people to repair your properties immediately.

4. Maintain the Property Well

One of the primary causes of lawsuits in the real estate space is due to injury sustained on the property by a tenant or a guest. Therefore, it is imperative that you continually make sure there are no hazards on the property that could harm a tenant, such as defective or missing handrails, slippery staircases, or dangerous pets.

5. Disclose and Handle Environmental Concerns

Landlords can also be sued over environmental concerns, such as asbestos, lead-based paint, mold, bedbugs, or other local environmental issues. The key to avoiding lawsuits is disclosure and fast action. If you know of a problem, disclose it. For example, if you know asbestos or lead-based paint was used in the property, let the tenants know. If mold, bedbugs, or other similar issues creep up, deal with them swiftly.

6. Follow the Lease

When you sign a lease with a tenant, you are signing a contract that is binding for BOTH parties. In other words, you have some duties and responsibilities as well, and if you break your end of the contract, you could get sued. Therefore, understand the lease that you are signing and stick to the contract.

Generating Extra Income and Reducing Expenses

No one enters the real estate investing niche because it sounds like a fun thing to do. (Okay, maybe some do.) Instead, the goal is to *make a profit*. No doubt you've heard the saying, "You make your money when you buy," which is no doubt true. If you buy the wrong property for the wrong price, it's unlikely you'll ever make a profit. However, there are other ways besides the purchase that can help you make more money from your property, and that's through increasing the income and decreasing the expenses. In this section, we're going to look at some of the most common ways you can squeeze more income from your rentals while decreasing the amount you need to pay out, resulting in more cash in your bank account.

Increasing Income

Raise the Rent: The easiest way to get more income is by raising the rent, which we talked about in this chapter. Just make sure that your rental price isn't so high that if affects your vacancy rate in a significantly way.

Charge Fees: We started out this chapter talking about training your tenants. One of the primary ways this is done is through the use of fees. In addition to training your tenants, charging fees can also add income to your bottom line. For example, if a tenant is late, charge a late fee. Or if a tenant locks themselves out of their unit, charge an "unlock" fee. Of course, make sure all of your fees are spelled out in your lease and are allowed by your state's laws.

Charge for Extra Services: There could be several services that you could charge for with your tenants, such as annual carpet cleanings, window washing, or even maid service. Of course, you can figure out the costs of these amenities and charge the tenant for the cost on a monthly basis. For example, for $20 per month added to their rent, they'll receive one carpet cleaning service per year (bringing in $240 per year but only costing you around $100 for a 2-bedroom apartment).

Laundry Income: If you own a multifamily property, installing a coin-operated laundry machine can help bring in additional income. Just make sure the cost of maintaining those machines and the added electricity costs don't trump any profit you might make. There are also laundry servicing companies that will bring their own machines in, collect the coins, and do maintenance on the machines for a share in the profits—usually 50/50. We currently have three sets of washers/dryers at our apartment complex under this arrangement and make around $350 per month in extra income with no added stress (and the tenants love it).

Extra Storage: Self-storage is a $6 billion business in the US alone.[x] As a landlord, you can get in on some of this if you have any clean, dry locations that can be leased to the public (or to your own tenants).

If you are looking for a large collection of other unique ways to make more income as a landlord, be sure to read Al Williamson's excellent book *40 Ways to Increase the Net Income of Your Rental Property*.

Decreasing Expenses

Water: If you are responsible for paying the water bill at your property, you've likely already discovered that this bill is one of your largest expenses. Luckily, you can reduce this cost in several ways. First, fix leaks and drips immediately. A dripping faucet may not seem like a big deal, but just one small drip can cost you hundreds of dollars per year. The same goes for running toilets. If you hear a quiet trickle in the bathroom or the toilet needs to run occasionally to "fill back up" despite not being used, it's likely your flapper on the toilet is damaged. This is a five-minute fix, costing less than $5, that can save you hundreds.

Sub-metering: If you own a multifamily property and the utilities (water or electricity) are "master-metered" (meaning, there is only one meter and the landlord pays everything), you can significantly cut your costs by shifting the responsibilities of that payment onto the tenant. Of course, this may be easier said than done, as rewiring an old property could cost tens or hundreds of thousands of dollars (but might still be worth it).

Water is a little easier to sub-meter, even without redoing all the pipes. There are electronic meters that can be placed on the water heater that record the water usage and in turn allow you to bill each tenant for their portion of the water used. Of course, you'll want to make sure that by charging your tenant for water, you aren't going to price yourself out of your market and be forced to drop rent by a similar amount.

Cheaper Advertising: Advertising a vacant property can be expensive, so be sure to explore the lower cost advertising methods like Craigslist or Zillow before using paid sources like the newspaper.

Challenge Tax Assessment: One of the largest expenses you'll pay each year is the annual property tax bill. If you feel that the value that your County's Tax Assessor has given to your property is too high, you can challenge it and ask that it be changed. There is no guarantee that it will be, but if your case is strong enough, you might be able to save hundreds or thousands of dollars per year.

Electricity: If there are areas at your property where you must pay the electricity bill, replace any light bulbs with Energy Star Certified Light Bulbs. Not only will this help cut down on your monthly bill (they use 70–90 percent less energy than traditional incandescent bulbs), they also have a lot longer life (10x - 25x longer), meaning less time changing light bulbs in the future.[xi]

Trash: If you are responsible for paying the garbage bill at your property, make sure you are getting the best deal by shopping around to all the local garbage companies. Then make sure you are paying the most efficient pricing. For example, is it better to have a small can picked up weekly or a large can picked up every other week? Doing the research once can save you significant cash over the long run.

Wrapping it Up

In this chapter, we focused on the day to day structure of managing your tenants. We looked at the importance of training tenants and how that can help reduce your workload as a landlord. We also looked at the many different ways to collect and raise rent, as well as some of the best methods for keeping communication flowing between you and your tenant. Finally, we concluded with discussion on hiring resident managers, avoiding lawsuits, and making more profit, all topics that are important to know as you build your real estate portfolio.

Managing rental properties is not an impossible or scary task, but as you can see from this chapter, there are a lot of moving parts. Don't get overwhelmed, though. The process does get easier; with practice, these tasks will become second nature. The systems discussed here are designed to help your business run like a smooth, well-oiled machine. However, even the best-running machines have problems and need routine maintenance. The next chapter will focus primarily on this topic of problems and how to deal with the issues you are bound to face.

CHAPTER 10:
DEALING WITH PROBLEMS

Even with proper screening, you're sure to have problems during your landlording career since there is no foolproof way to know with 100 percent accuracy that your tenant will always make the right choices. Many of them will not. In fact, *you* will probably not always make the right choices. The truth is, your business will not always run smoothly *because landlording involves people*. However, when problems arise, it's not the end of the world; the landlord just needs to know how to deal with them quickly and legally. You may be asking yourself:

- What if my tenants don't pay rent?
- What if they paint the walls?
- What if they get a dog without my permission?
- What if they are too rough on the house?
- What if they don't maintain the house?
- What if they change their oil in the living room?
- What if they burn down the kitchen?
- What if, what if, what if...

There are a lot of "what ifs" that go along with being a landlord when putting your investment in the hands of strangers. But with every question, there are answers. And while each tenant and rental situation is unique, most of the problems or issues you will face with your tenants are not. You'll quickly learn there are recurring themes that have been dealt with by millions of landlords for thousands of years. In this chapter we will talk about the most common problems you are likely to face as a landlord and how you might deal with them. Without further ado, let's begin.

What to Do When Tenants Don't Pay Rent

Perhaps the most common problem landlords have with their tenants is late payments. If your tenant does not pay their rent when it is due, it is important that you deal with it immediately. The only way to combat late paying tenants and discourage the same behavior in the future is to have a consequence: the late fee. Your lease should describe exactly the terms for paying rent, when it is due, and the consequences for delinquency.

Understand that not paying rent is a serious thing; the tenant is stealing money from your bank account. You wouldn't let your neighbor, friend, or even your own family gain access to your checking account to remove hundreds of dollars against your will, so why would you allow a stranger to do so? You may think we are being dramatic, but think about it; it's the truth. Don't think of late rent as a mere inconvenience, but recognize it for the serious issue that it is.

Of course, the simple answer to a late or non-existent payment is "evict them!" And that may be what needs to happen, which is why the next chapter of this book is focused on that task. However, evicting a tenant is messy business. It can be expensive, stressful, and overwhelming—especially if you are new to the process. Therefore, we feel it's in the landlord's best interest to solve the problem **outside** of the eviction courts first, if possible. This doesn't mean letting the process drag on for weeks, but there are some quick actions you can take to avoid an eviction when a tenant doesn't pay rent on time. Let's talk about those now.

The Phone Call

When a tenant's rent is not received by the due date, the first thing we do is call them. Of course, many landlords skip this step (and with repeat offenders, we skip this step also). But most of the time when the rent is late, it's because the tenant simply forgot or they have another easy-to-explain reason. If you can get in touch with them, usually they'll say something along the lines of, "Shoot, okay. I'll pay that today. I forgot, sorry." We always remind them to be sure and include the late fee with their payment. As much as you might want to be the "nice guy" here and waive that late fee, remember that late fees are designed to train the tenant to make rent a priority. By waiving it, you're negating its purpose.

If you cannot get in touch with the tenant via their phone, you can try emailing them as well if you have their email address. Text messages also seem to work well, as tenants, when they are at fault, will feel less sheepish about responding via text than answering their phone. If you are able to get in touch with the tenant and they don't have the rent, now you have a more serious problem. Most likely, you are going to hear the words "can you work with me" at some point in the conversation.

Should you? Maybe, maybe not. Let's talk about that next.

Should I Work With My Tenant or Evict Them?

Many tenants will request that you "work with them" when their rent is late. Deciding to work with them is a bit of an art form, and there is a strategy for doing so that won't leave you in the lurch if something goes wrong. Before we get there, let's talk about the two most common reasons why rent is usually late:

1. Priorities: There is a common pattern we see with late rent, and it's caused by the fact that there are more than four weeks in a month. In other words, in April the tenant might get paid on the 3rd and 17th, then in May their paychecks would land on May 1st, 15th, and 29th. June would be the 12th and 26th, and July would be 10th and 24th. As you can see, for those who are paid every other week, paydays come MORE often than twice a month, and tenants sometimes have a hard time getting used to that. In the dates above, the tenant would likely use their May 1st paycheck for rent for May. Then they hopefully would use the paycheck from the 29th of May to pay their June rent.

But then that check on June 26th comes around, and the tenant realizes they still have a full week until rent is due, and they really need that money for something else, so they say, "I'll just spend this paycheck and use the next one for rent." But the next one doesn't come until July 10th, so the tenant calls on the 5th of July and says, "My rent is going to be late because my paycheck doesn't come until Friday," as if some freak occurrence caused their paycheck to be delayed. Not placing their rent as a priority in their life is the number one reason why your tenant cannot make their rent payment on time.

2. Illness or Job Loss: Despite what the media might have you believe, this is actually a pretty *uncommon* reason for not paying the rent. Usually, like we just discussed, tenants just haven't made rent their priority; therefore, other things take precedence over a timely rent payment. However, when a tenant truly is struggling, it's incredibly difficult for the landlord to know how to navigate. Our nature is to be kind to people and help them. After all, we are not machines; we are human beings and can sympathize with their situation. However, it can be tough to know what is true and what is just an excuse. Even if it is a true problem, how much is your responsibility? You are running a business, and you cannot be profitable if you cater to everyone's problems. In fact, by being strict during difficult times, you might just help them keep their priorities straight and encourage them to work harder to get a new job or pay their other bills some other way.

Generally, the way we've looked at this situation is as follows: When someone is going through a tough time, the rent **MUST** be paid. The question is, will we pay it *out of our own personal bank account*, or will we hold them to their obligations? This mindset helps us separate our feelings from reality. If we would be willing to hand the struggling tenant $1,000 out of our own pocket, outside of the business, that is the only time when we would be willing to work with them on their rent. There are plenty of people in our own network of friends and acquaintances who are struggling financially, and if we had an extra $1,000 laying around, of course we would rather hand it over to them than to our tenant who may or may not be telling the truth. Unless you're running a charity, the rent must be paid *at all times*.

Sometimes when the tenant realizes they have no other options, they will work it out, especially if you've made the rent a priority. Most of the time in a situation as extreme as illness or job loss, it does not, leaving the tenant with the choice of either moving willingly or being escorted out by the Sheriff post eviction. Next, we'd like to share two real-life case studies of tenants who have paid rent to us late recently.

Case Study #1

Luis was a single, hard-working guy who rented a small, 1-bedroom house from us. One month, he called to explain that his paycheck wasn't coming for several days (the mystery of the "disappearing previous paycheck") and needed a few more days to pay. We explained that he would still need to pay the late fee ($50) and the daily late fee ($10 per day), and we asked him for an exact date for when he would be paying the rent, which he stated would be on the 10th. We told him, "That's your choice to pay then, but you will receive a Pay or Vacate Notice from us, and that starts the clock ticking. On the 10th we have to file for eviction, so just make sure it's paid by then, with the late fees." The rent came in on the 10th, along with the late fees, and Luis was back on track.

Case Study #2

When they moved into our apartment complex, Lana and John were both employed and the parents of two children. A couple of years into their tenancy, John took off, leaving Lana a single mom, with a single income, and now *four* kids (we don't know how she picked the extra two up!). Although she was a nurse and made good money, she always struggled with paying the rent on time, receiving Pay or Vacate Notices numerous times. In addition, her apartment became increasingly messy: garbage everywhere, broken blinds, Mickey Mouse sheets in the windows—everything that drives us crazy—only to be fixed "just enough" when we would call and make her.

Two months ago, the rent didn't show up (as usual), we received no phone call, and she refused to return our voicemails or text messages. We served the Pay or Vacate Notice (giving her three days to pay her rent before eviction proceedings would start), but again, we heard nothing. The 10th of the month came, and still, after repeated phone calls, text messages, and even personal visits to her apartment, we could not get in touch. Finally, on the 10th, we sent her a text message that said, "Eviction is being filed tomorrow, and it will be too late to stop. Can we talk?" We finally received a call back within a few minutes (apparently she realized she could bury her head no longer!), where Lana stated that her paycheck was late and asked if we would work with her. When we asked about the exact date that she could pay, her response was, "I don't know, maybe the 28th of this month." We told her that would not work for us, and we would have to file for eviction, so she hung up on us. Eviction was filed on the 11th, and within three weeks she had moved out, leaving us with a disaster of a unit.

As you can see in the previous two examples, we are not opposed to working with someone as long as we are protecting ourselves against loss; we still served the Notice to Vacate, and we still charged the late fees in both cases. In case #1, we worked with the tenant, as he maintained communication with us and didn't demand an excessive amount of time, paying within the required three days. We might have even waited a couple extra days before filing for eviction had it been necessary. Working with case #2, however, would have resulted in disaster. We *may* have received the rent on the 28th, of course, but by then, the rent would be almost a month late. Would she have rent for the next month, due just four days later? Of course not. And the pattern would repeat indefinitely until she would flat-out stiff us, and we would be an entire month behind in rent before starting her eviction.

If you are going to "work with a tenant" and their late rent, only do so if you fully understand the situation. In other words, ask them why the rent is not paid and explain the "two-week paycheck problem" to them, as we discussed above. Make them walk backwards with you through their paychecks if needed so they understand that getting paid every other week actually means they should be ahead on their rent. Then, find out exactly what day their paycheck will come and hold them to that. Or if their paycheck is still a couple of weeks away, encourage them to borrow the money from a family member, friend, or cash-advance service. If you do decide to work with your tenant in regard to their late rent, never let them get more than two weeks behind, don't make it a habit, and only "work with them" within the bounds of the law, protecting yourself.

Dealing with late rent is never fun, but you'll likely find as we have: The more strict you are, the easier it becomes. Tenants pay on time most of the time, especially when they know you are serious about it. Most of the horror stories we hear from ex-landlords involved them being too soft on late rent. Adopt a policy of fair-but-firm when dealing with late rent, and the issue won't leave you bankrupt. Yes, you might have to evict, but it will be better than losing your whole business. The next chapter will deal with the topic of evictions, but first, let's look at some of the other problems you'll have to navigate through on your landlording journey.

Handling Tenant Maintenance and Repairs

Last week, we received a frantic call from one of our tenants who said water was pouring through the ceiling in their hallway. A few days later, another tenant's dishwasher was leaking. Yesterday, yet another tenant called to let us know one of their stove burners stopped working and their front door would not lock correctly anymore. Maintenance issues in a rental come with the territory. However, before ever receiving that first maintenance request, it's important to have a plan in place for how to deal with them. Here are a few things you can do to prepare for maintenance issues within your rental business:

1. Have a reliable list of go-to contractors and handymen that you trust. Dealing with contractors is such a vital part of your business

that we'll dedicate the entire next chapter of this book to it.

2. Create a system for documenting and tracking maintenance requests.

3. Become familiar with your local laws on the landlord's responsibility for responding to and dealing with maintenance issues.

4. Keep a detailed record of all maintenance requests and their resolutions.

You will likely notice over the course of time that there are three types of tenants when it comes to maintenance:

- **Tenant A** reports only important maintenance issues when they occur. We like them.

- **Tenant B** reports every little thing at least twice a week. Light bulb burned out? Cabinet knob is loose? Don't worry, they'll call!

- **Tenant C** never reports anything, even when it's important.

Tenant C is fairly common among tenants. They are the ones who, for whatever reason, fail to let you know about problems until they have turned into much bigger problems that could have been avoided by simply notifying the landlord sooner. It's specifically for these tenants that it's a good idea to offer a few different options for reporting maintenance concerns, including by telephone, text, email, snail mail, or via a quick fill-in-the-blank form on your website. For an example of a website version, check out our Maintenance Request tab at our company website, http://www.opendoor-propertiesllc.com. By giving your tenants multiple avenues for reporting their maintenance issues, you increase the likelihood that they will report it, and you also give them the accurate impression that you care about your property and want to know when things aren't working as they should.

The Work Order

Whenever we get a call (or are notified via some other avenue) from a tenant who has a maintenance issue or concern, the first thing we do is pull out our Work Order form (included in the appendix of this book, as well as online at http://www.BiggerPockets.com/LandlordBookBonus) and note the following information:

- Date/Time
- Tenant Name

- Address

- Phone Number

- Email (if applicable)

- Description of Maintenance Request

Water pouring through the ceiling sounds pretty serious, but was water literally pouring from the ceiling in gallons, or was there a slow drip, which also might be described by a frantic tenant as "pouring"? Was the dishwasher leaking around the top, side, or bottom? Was it simply overloaded? Was the stove element truly broken, or did it possibly just become unplugged? When you receive a maintenance concern or request from a tenant, find out how long the problem has been occurring and get as many details as possible so you know how to proceed. After a few questions, you may even discover that the maintenance concern isn't really a concern at all and can be handled over the phone.

After gathering all the information you need to proceed, get the tenant's permission for you or your workers to enter the rental with or without their being present and note this on their Work Order. Note: If there are going to be underage children home alone, do not send a maintenance person inside without another adult present, for liability reasons.

Once you have as many details about the problem as possible from your tenant, you should have enough information to hire the appropriate contractor. If not, either check it out yourself or have your handyman investigate. Always keep communication open between you and the contractor, as well as between you and the tenant, so you can remediate the problem as quickly as possible. Keep in mind, the landlord is required by law to maintain the integrity of the home and respond to maintenance issues within a certain timeframe. In Washington State, the law[xii] states that landlords must respond within the following parameters:

- Within 24 hours when the maintenance issue deprives the tenant of hot or cold water, heat, or electricity, or is immediately hazardous to life.

- Within 72 hours when the maintenance issue deprives the tenant of the use of their appliances (refrigerator, stove, or oven), or other major plumbing fixture that the landlord supplies (such as a toilet).

- Within 10 days for all other maintenance issues.

For *all* maintenance issues, the burden of proof is on the landlord to ensure proper completion, so always keep detailed records of the date and time the problem was reported, the repair particulars, and the date of completion. If proper completion is delayed for some reason (such as waiting for material to be delivered or the tenant won't allow access) and cannot be completed within the required timeframe, the law states that the issue must be remedied as quickly as possible. Make sure to become familiar with your legal duties as a landlord in your local area so you can be sure you are dealing with issues legally and in a timely manner.

Once a maintenance issue has been completed, we always follow up with the handyman or contractor to note the repair that was made (this goes on the Work Order for our records). We then follow up with the tenant to ensure their satisfaction with the work that was completed. The next part of the Work Order looks like this:

- Date of Maintenance Completion
- Description of Maintenance Completed
- Follow-up with Tenant: _____Date: _____
- Notes From Follow-up

If you follow a similar strategy for dealing with maintenance issues, once the Work Order is complete you will have an accurate, organized, detailed account of the entire incident for your records, including the date the issue occurred, the issue itself, the repairs that were made and by whom, the date the repair was completed, and notes from the follow-up with the tenant. From there, it can be added to the tenant's file. This information is helpful for proving the work was completed in a timely manner, and it also helps to track the maintenance work at each property. For example, if the same tenant called multiple times over the course of a few months about repairing the same appliance, you would know that it may be time to replace that particular appliance.

One last thought on dealing with maintenance issues: Always pay your contractors and handymen quickly so they respond quickly when you need them. If you have a reputation for taking your sweet time paying your bills, they will remember that when you call them for help.

Work Order/Maintenance Request

Date: ___/___/___ Time: ___:___am/pm

Tenant Name: _____

Address: _____

Phone Number: _____

Email: _____

Description of Maintenance Requested

```



```

Office Use Only

Maintenance Request Notes
Received ___/___/___ Time ___:___am/pm

```



```

Date of Completion ___/___/___   Follow-up with Tenant: _____ Date: _____
Notes from Follow-up:

Bounced Rent Checks

If you allow your tenants to pay their rent via personal check, you are bound to run into a bounced check at some point, also known as "NSF" or "Non-Sufficient Funds." For those of you who are lucky enough to have never dealt with receiving a bounced check, basically it means the tenant doesn't have the funds in their account to cover the rent. Therefore, the check you deposit into your bank doesn't clear, causing the funds from your tenant to be withdrawn, or "bounce." Besides the rent not actually being paid, bounced checks are frustrating because it can take up to a couple weeks to receive notification that it bounced, putting you well into the month and well past your tenant's due date.

We deal with bounced checks the same way we would deal with late rent. As soon as we are aware that the rent check did not clear, we notify the tenant and give them instructions for repaying immediately (in guaranteed funds), along with a late fee. If the tenant cannot pay immediately (which is sometimes the case), they are issued a Pay or Vacate Notice and must pay within the parameters of the notice or deal with the consequences. Bounced checks are not to be taken lightly and need to be dealt with swiftly and seriously. The bounced check will likely throw your tenant off track financially, and it is imperative to ensure the tenant gets back on track ASAP so they can make their future rent payments on time. One last thought on bounced checks: If you receive a bad check from a tenant, it would be wise to require guaranteed funds, such as a cashier's check or money order, for all future payments from that particular tenant. Make sure your policy for dealing with bounced checks is included in your rental agreement or lease.

Abandonment

Last month, one of our tenants failed to pay rent. On the 6th, a Notice to Pay or Vacate form was served to his home and mailed to him. We tried contacting him multiple times in the following days, to no avail. Our first sign that something was amiss was the obvious lack of rent, the second sign was his lack of response or communication, the third sign was the overgrown lawn, the fourth sign was the overflowing garbage can with items you wouldn't normally see in the trash, and the fifth sign was from his boss at work—he didn't work there anymore. Oh boy, here we go. All of these signs added up to one thing: The tenant moved without telling us.

A rental is referred to as "abandoned" when the tenant defaults in rent and implies by words or actions that they have moved. If you have reason to believe your rental has been abandoned, first try and contact your tenant. If you are unable to reach them via any of the contact information you have for them, look for indications that the unit has been vacated, such as signs that no one has been caring for the property (including an overgrown lawn), no activity in or around the rental, disconnected utilities, or word from the neighbors that they saw the tenant move out. If you are unsure if the unit is abandoned, you can always post a legal notice to enter the property based on the legal timeline allowed by your state. Call it an "inspection," and at the appropriate time, enter. If the tenant has cleared out all of their belongings, that's a pretty clear sign they are gone. Sometimes it can be tough to know if the tenant has abandoned the property and left a lot of junk or if they simply live with few possessions, so we would err on the side of caution and try to get a solid confirmation that they are, indeed, gone before performing the following steps.

Upon discovering an abandoned unit, the landlord has certain legal steps he/she must take before re-renting the property. The first step you must take is to become knowledgeable about your state's specific process for dealing with abandonment. In Washington State, if a rental is discovered to be abandoned, the landlord may take immediate possession, change the locks, and must post a notice at the rental declaring it to be abandoned. If the tenant has left behind any furniture or personal items, the landlord must store these items in a reasonably secure place and notify the tenant in writing (to their last known address) of the physical whereabouts of their property and how long it will be stored (7 days for property valued under $250 and 45 days for property valued over $250, including personal papers, family pictures, and keepsakes) before it will be disposed of or sold.

When dealing with an abandoned rental, be sure to document the condition of the unit, as well as any items left behind by the tenant, in writing and with pictures. The last thing you want to deal with from a tenant who abandoned your rental is for them to later accuse you of stealing or losing their precious family heirloom. If the tenant requests the return of any personal items left behind before they are sold, they must first pay all the costs associated with the storage of the items before the items will be returned. After the landlord has stored the items for the legally required period, the items may be sold and the funds applied to the tenant's balance. Any funds above and beyond what the tenant owes must be held for one year, after which time those funds are forfeited by the tenant, and the landlord may keep them.

Even though the rental has been abandoned, the tenant is still liable for lost rent, costs associated with getting the unit rented again, and legal fees. In Washington State, if they were on a month-to-month rental agreement, they are liable for rent for the 30 days following when the landlord learned of the abandonment or for 30 days after when their next rent payment would have been due, whichever comes first. If they were on a term lease agreement, they are liable for the rent for the remaining term of the lease, though the landlord does have the legal responsibility to try and re-rent the property as soon as possible to mitigate the damages.

What to Do When a Tenant Dies

A few months ago, one of our best tenants passed away unexpectedly. She was a dear, sweet, and feisty woman who had been with us from the beginning of our landlording journey. When she passed away, not only were we heartbroken, but we were unsure what our responsibilities were concerning the rental and her house full of personal property. So, we did some research on how we should proceed. What we found out was that there is a legal process the landlord must follow in order to reclaim their property. It's important that you research your state's particular laws in the event you are faced with the death of the tenant; however, the following is how a landlord in Washington State currently handles this type of situation.

If a tenant passes away at the residence itself, the police and coroner will secure the home, conduct an investigation if necessary, remove the body, and notify relatives. If there are other tenants still in the home, the landlord and remaining tenants can resume their arrangement as before. The deceased tenant's belongings become the responsibility of the remaining tenants, and the landlord does not need to get involved.

If the deceased tenant is the only tenant and they passed away at some other location, the landlord should secure the premises and attempt to get in contact with the executor of the estate since the rental becomes the estate's responsibility at this point. The landlord should not give anyone access to the tenant's personal belongings unless they are the executor.

Should no executor be forthcoming, once the rent is in default, the landlord may proceed exactly as if the house were abandoned by:

1. Posting notice

2. Changing the locks and taking immediate possession

3. Itemizing and storing the tenant's belongings until the required amount of time has passed

4. Selling, disposing of, or donating (to family or charity) the tenant's property after the required amount of time has passed, and

5. Setting aside any overages from the sale after paying the deceased tenant's debts to the landlord (for rent, storage of the tenant's belongings, and any other costs incurred by the landlord as a result of the tenant's demise) for one year should an executor come forward during the time period.

Once again, this is how a death of a tenant is handled in Washington. The specific legal process in your area is likely different. The death of a tenant is a sensitive subject and needs to be handled very carefully to avoid mistakes that put the landlord in a vulnerable position. The last thing any landlord wants in this type of situation is a lawsuit from the deceased tenant's family. The point of this section is simply to make you aware that you need to do your research in this type of situation to be sure you are proceeding legally and to reclaim your property as quickly as possible.

Dealing With Drugs

Even with proper screening, it may come to light during your tenant's tenancy that they are involved with illegal drugs, either selling or using. Not only will drugs ruin your tenant's life, but they will significantly affect yours as well. With drugs come late rent and a neglected house—usually accompanied by filth, suspicious burn markings in the flooring, an overgrown lawn, and frequent shady visitors. Tenants on illegal drugs or dealing illegal drugs are bad for business. Not only will they ruin your property, but in a multi-family property, they will drive other good tenants away. When it comes to illegal drugs, there are some signs that indicate there is a problem:

- Tenant begins paying rent later and later every month
- Tenant falls behind on utility payments
- Tenant ignores problems
- Tenant ignores the landlord
- Tenant won't let maintenance inside the rental
- The exterior of the property shows neglect: garbage, junk, or overgrown lawn
- Tenant has multiple visitors at all times of the day who come and go quickly
- Tenant's housekeeping shows severe neglect
- Tenant uses extreme security measures
- Tenant keeps their blinds or curtains closed at all times
- Tenant exhibits illogical behavior

Of course, though none of these activities or actions in and of themselves are *proof* that your tenant is involved in shady dealings, they can be *evidence* of it. If you have legitimate reasons for believing your tenant is involved with drugs, you have a serious and potentially dangerous problem on your hands. If they are on a month-to-month agreement, simply do not renew it. If they are on a term lease, you have a couple options: Cash for

Keys or eviction (both of which we will talk about later). Your lease should have a clause or addendum that prohibits drug use, dealing, and any other illegal activity. However, trying to *prove* a tenant is dealing drugs can be difficult, which is why in our business, we prefer to use the Cash for Keys option rather than eviction when dealing with situations such as this.

Cash for Keys is simply the practice of paying your tenant to move out, knowing that the cost of paying a tenant is cheaper and easier than trying to evict. In the past when we have become suspicious that the tenant is involved with illegal activity, we contact them and let them know their tenancy is not working out, but we would like to help them get into a new place. This is where the cash comes in—we offer them a set amount, generally between $300–$500 to be completely moved out of the home by a certain date, usually within 7–14 days. We explain that in order to receive the cash, the home must be free of all personal belongings and clean. When dealing with a tenant involved with drugs, this method has almost always worked for us. Because a tenant involved in this type of activity cannot keep their life together, if they *didn't* bite at our offer of cash, we would simply find some other form of lease non-compliance and evict them over that as quickly as possible. Offering cash is simply the easiest and quickest way to remove them from the property. We'll talk more about Cash for Keys in Chapter 11.

Lease Compliance: The 10 Most Common Problems You'll Encounter

In this next section, we will cover the ten most common lease compliance problems landlords face and how to deal with them. A lease compliance issue is just that—when the tenant doesn't comply with the rules outlined in their lease. As you'll see, most non-compliance issues can be dealt with first by contacting the tenant, and if the tenant does not remedy the problem within a reasonable amount of time, it should be followed up with a written notice demanding their compliance.

In Washington State, the law states that after receiving written notice to comply with their rental agreement or lease, tenants have ten days to remedy the problem or they can be evicted. Make sure you know your own local law in regard to lease compliance before proceeding. If they are responsible, your tenant will hopefully take care of the issue after a simple phone call, email, or letter. If more force is required, send them a notice. Usually, a notice stating that they must comply within "X" number of days (whatever your local laws require) or be forced to vacate the premises is enough to generate their compliance. Now, let's get to the list of the ten most common lease-compliance issues.

1. Junk Outside

Nothing screams "slum" like piles of junk cascading over the balcony, down the driveway, and pouring out the front door of your rental unit. While we are sure YOU would never live this way, there is a good chance your tenant will have no problem with that lifestyle. Piles of junk drive away other tenants in a multifamily situation, encourage similar behavior from neighbors, and can permanently damage your house by inviting rodents, bugs, and mold to move in.

The first step in dealing with excess junk is to make sure your lease includes specific language requiring that garbage may not be piled up and it must be placed in proper receptacles. Furthermore, your lease should state what items are appropriate to be kept outside. This is a bit easier to enforce in a multifamily situation, but even single family homes should have a standard as to what is and is not allowed. As we discussed back in Chapter 8, our current lease states the following: "Outside areas must remain clear of debris, garbage, bicycles, toys, furniture, tarps, and other clutter. Do not use your balcony as storage or to dry clothes. Decks/balconies are meant for your enjoyment: A barbecue, lawn furniture and small plants are the only acceptable items. Failure to abide by this policy will result in termination of your tenancy."

When we notice a tenant has junk or garbage piling up (usually on a deck, patio, or front porch), we will either call or send a letter, depending on the relationship we have with the tenant. Sometimes a phone call is enough to elicit the needed action, and other times a letter (or better yet, a certified letter) is required to get the tenant to take the appropriate measures. This letter should have a deadline for getting their trash removed, based on the legal number of days to correct a lease violation as outlined by your state's landlord-tenant laws.

2. Unapproved Roommates

Tenants often move in or move out individuals without notifying the landlord. We take this very seriously, as we need to always have a clear understanding of who is and isn't living on the property. It's important to require that each adult individual living in the property be screened properly, ensuring they meet your minimum qualifications and that they be listed on the lease. You might really like that tenant Betty, but when she moves in her new boyfriend Barney, how do you know he is not an ex-con who just finished serving 18 years for the murder of his cousin? Also, if Betty moved out, leaving you with Barney as your sole tenant, you need to be sure that 1) he meets your qualification standards, and 2) he is legally bound by the terms in your contract.

If you believe your tenant has moved someone into the unit, the first step we take is to place a phone call to the tenant. Nine times out of 10, the tenant will quickly say, "Oh, they are just staying with me for a little while," to which we respond, "Well, your lease, as well as our company policy, only allows guests to stay for up to two weeks before they must be added to the lease. Has your guest been with you that long?" After some fumbling around, the tenant will finally admit that the person *is* moving in, and they will usually ask, "So, how do I add them to the lease?"

Technically speaking, if the tenant is in a lease and their term is not up, the tenant does not have the right to move someone in. However, they'll likely do it anyway, so we find it best to allow the new guest to *apply* to become a tenant. The process for allowing a tenant to add someone to the lease is fairly similar to the process of renting it out in the first place:

1. Give the new "tenant" an application to fill out and require that they fill it out in full and include the application fee.

2. Complete the full screening process that we outlined in Chapter 7, including the background check, credit check, landlord references, and income verification (though if the tenant living there already meets the income requirement, technically the new tenant will not need any income, as the income requirement is based on total household income).

3. If you approve the new tenant, you have a couple options as far as getting them on the lease. 1) Sign a new lease with all the tenants. Walk both the original tenant(s) and the new tenant through the entire lease, just as you did with the original tenant when they moved in. Then, make sure all adults sign the new lease. Or, 2) Walk all tenants through the old lease then have them sign a new addendum to change the terms of the old lease, which in this situation would be adding "so-and-so" to the lease. Be sure to spell

out exactly what the change in terms are and state that all other terms and conditions will remain the same and in full force.

In the event the tenant's guest does not meet your minimum screening standards, you will need to immediately give the tenant an ultimatum: Either the guest vacates, or everyone does. This situation can be dealt with the same as any other non-lease compliance situation, by giving the tenant a legal written notice to comply with their lease or face eviction. The tenant will then be legally required to comply within the number of days outlined by your state's landlord-tenant laws, and if they choose not to, you can evict them and start over with a new tenant. We have never had it come to that, though; most tenants in this situation aren't going to willingly lose their home over a roommate.

3. Smoking

If you suspect a tenant is smoking in their unit (usually from cigarette butts around their property or by the smell when you have an inspection done), provide them with the notice to comply letter immediately. Smoking can cause thousands of dollars in damage to your property, so deal with the situation immediately. Most of the time, the tenant is going to lie and say, "I wasn't smoking!" or they will blame it on a friend or guest. Send the letter anyway (they are responsible for the actions of their friends and guests as well), and then call the tenant and make sure they received the letter and they understand the seriousness of the situation. Let them know you are scheduling someone to check out the property and ensure that the problem has been fixed.

If after the inspection there is still evidence of smoking in the unit, you have the decision to either get rid of the tenant, or simply let it go and hold the tenant liable for the damages when they eventually move out or when their lease ends (be that month-to-month or further down the road). Let's be honest, the cost of an eviction and the turnover might be just as much, if not more, than the damage from the smoke smell. Once the damage is already done, it's up to you to decide how hard you want to push. Just remember, cigarette smoke permeates everything—so the sooner you can take care of the situation, the better. Of course, the easiest way to avoid this problem altogether is by not approving anyone who smokes in the first place.

We have one tenant who currently smokes in his unit and has since long before we took over. There is no point in forcing him to stop, as the carpet and paint are already ruined. If we were to evict him, we would still need to make all the repairs, but we would lose an otherwise good tenant. These are the "gray areas" of landlording and something you'll likely encounter as well.

4. Pets

Unapproved pets are another common lease compliance issue landlords face. For whatever reason, tenants think they can hide their 70-pound chocolate lab in their unit and the landlord will never notice. In a situation such as this, you have a couple options: Let them keep the animal and consider charging them a one-time fee or monthly rent for the privilege of keeping an animal on the premises (if you do this, make sure to add a Pet Addendum to their lease), or send the tenant a notice demanding their compliance with their lease, specifically removing the animal from the premises. In a multi-family situation, just remember that if you make an exception for one pet, other tenants will expect you to make an exception for theirs as well.

5. Bugs

Last year a family moved into one of our rentals, immigrating to the US from another country halfway around the world. Then, several months ago, one more family member from that country came to live with them, which we allowed. Within a few weeks, the tenants began calling about a bug infestation in their property and blaming us for the problem, threatening to call the city, the state, the health department, the FBI, and anyone else because of our bug problem. Of course, we immediately sent out the best pest controller in our area, and indeed, there were bugs. However, he had never seen this kind of bug before and had no idea what they were. After taking them home to investigate, guess what he discovered! Yep, the bugs were found in only one part of the world: the home country of the family.

Bugs are frustrating because most of the time they are caused by your tenant, but the tenant will never believe that. They'll complain and bad-mouth you to everyone until the problem is fixed. Even in the story above, the tenant still believes it is our fault for the bugs, but they got to foot the bill for the exterminator.

The truth about bugs is this: They are everywhere! Bugs live in nearly every square foot of your property, but they tend to come out into our world when there is food for them. When there is no food, they tend to disappear. Therefore, the first way to cure bug problems is to educate tenants on the best way to avoid them. A clean house is the best way to avoid bugs. That said, infestations do happen, and sometimes it is outside the fault of the tenant. This could be due to improperly sealed indoor spaces, ground infestations, wall infestations, neighbors, or other circumstances.

The good news is, most bug problems can be easily remediated by a professional pest inspection company. If the problem is minor, you might even be able to do it yourself with some chemicals bought at the hardware store, but in our experience, those only work some of the time, and it's best to call the professionals.

Some landlords will include a clause in their lease stating that the home is bug-free at the time of move-in and any pests discovered in the home after so many days of occupancy (this can vary from a couple of weeks to a couple of months) are the tenant's responsible to remedy. It's logical to assume that if the rental has no bugs before the tenant moves in, then bugs appear after the tenant has moved in, they are a result of the tenant. Our lease states that the tenant will be liable for all expenses associated with the extermination and fumigation for infestations that are a result of the tenant. Of course, before implementing any changes to your lease, be sure it is legally allowed by your state-specific landlord-tenant laws.

6. Mold

Mold is everywhere, especially if you live in a wet climate; there is simply no way to escape it. Mold spores drift through the air and settle on the couch, on your face, on the floor, everywhere! The problem, however, is when mold spores are given an environment where they thrive and begin to grow on surfaces. This is when the dreaded "black mold" shows up, something that strikes more fear into the hearts of tenants than anthrax or Ebola. The truth is, black mold is just a naturally occurring fungus that, when highly concentrated, can cause allergic reactions for those with weak immune systems. That said, if your tenant sees a small amount of mold on their bathroom wall, you can bet they'll be calling you telling you about their leg pain, their headaches, their sleepless nights, and their hepatitis—all caused, of course, by that dreaded "black mold."

All joking aside, the presence of visible mold is a serious issue landlords need to deal with swiftly. As stated by NOLO.com, "across the country, tenants have won multimillion-dollar cases against landlords for significant health problems—such as rashes, chronic fatigue, nausea, cognitive losses, hemorrhaging, and asthma—allegedly caused by exposure to 'toxic molds' in their building." Some states, like Washington and California, actually have laws that require certain disclosures be given to all tenants when they sign a new lease. Besides the health concerns for those with weak immune systems and hypochondriacs, mold will also cause significant damage if left untreated (and many times, because of the stigma behind mold, tenant's won't go near it with a ten foot pole, even when it's an easy fix). Therefore, mold IS your problem, whether or not it is caused by the tenant or your building. If it's caused by your tenant and they fail to remedy the problem, deal with it swiftly, hold your tenant responsible for the damages, then educate your tenant on how to prevent future occurrences.

Mold tends to grow where there is poor airflow and moisture. This is why bathrooms are the worst culprits for mold, usually due to the lack of a window and the continuous steam from hot showers. Mold also can grow easily behind furniture that is pushed too close to a wall, if there is a heavy level of moisture in the room air. Notice that in both of these cases, the mold is NOT a disease, mischievously planted by the landlord, despite what tenants might think. Mold is commonly caused by the tenant, but as the quote above by NOLO shows, this doesn't mean it's not your responsibility to deal with it.

Step one in dealing with mold is making sure you and your tenant are properly educated on what causes mold and how to clean it. We would recommend printing out the PDF produced by the United States EPA titled, "A Brief Guide to Mold, Moisture, and Your Home," which you can download for free at http://www.epa.gov/mold/pdfs/moldguide.pdf. We've also included this in the appendix of this book, as well as online at http://www.BiggerPockets.com/LandlordBookBonus. Make sure your tenant gets a copy of this document when they move into their unit. Also, explain to the tenant that mold is most commonly caused by three things:

1. Steamy showers

2. Furniture against walls

3. Leaky pipes, ceilings, faucets, etc.

Explain to them that numbers one and two are their responsibility, and number three is yours IF they report issues. If they don't report a leak that results in mold growth, this falls under the category of **avoidable** damage, most likely making them liable for the expense of the remediation. Encourage your tenant to run the bathroom fan at least one hour after every bath or shower and run their kitchen fan while cooking. This is probably the number one reason why tenants have mold; if they do not use proper ventilation during these activities, all that warm, moist air will settle throughout the house, creating a prime environment for mold and mildew. If the tenant's bathroom or kitchen does not have a vent, install one. Be sure they understand the need to properly ventilate their home by opening windows and airing it out on nice days, make sure they keep their couches, their beds, and their clothes away from walls, and they don't cram items into corners or against walls in non-ventilated areas (such as closets, cabinets, or attics). And of course, be sure leaks are fixed immediately.

According to the EPA, mold that covers less than 10 square feet (an area about three feet by three feet) can be easily cleaned up by a non-professional. Therefore, if the mold already exists in small amounts (on windowsills, behind a bed, on the shower tile), the following five-step process, as given by the EPA, should take care of the problem:

1. **Act Quickly:** The faster you deal with mold, the less damage it can cause.

2. **Fix the Cause:** If the cause is a leak, get that fixed as soon as possible. If the cause is heavy moisture, encourage the tenant to open windows more often or run their fan(s) more often. Also make sure the tenant's furniture is moved away from the walls.

3. **Clean It:** Scrub mold off hard surfaces with detergent and water, and dry completely. Be sure to wear gloves, goggles, and possibly a respirator if you are concerned about breathing in spores.

4. **Toss Porous Stuff:** Porous materials, like ceiling tiles or carpet, may need to be thrown away if they are moldy.

5. **Paint:** Never paint over mold (it'll just grow over the new paint), BUT after it is cleaned and dry, you may paint it if desired.

Remember, mold is not a disease or a chemical that is likely going to kill you or your tenants. However, it is a serious enough issue that you need to understand how to deal with it to keep your tenants safe and happy, and to prevent damage to your property. It's also important to understand mold and mildew so you don't get stuck footing the bill for tenants whose living conditions are the result of the problem.

7. Housekeeping

It's not your job as the landlord to be the tenant's mother and insist that they clean their room, but it is your job to ensure your investment is not being destroyed or being introduced to mold, pests, or rodents because someone chooses to live like an animal. Periodic inspections can let you know how your tenant lives, and if a major problem is found, you can give the tenant a Notice of Compliance to tidy up. If they don't, either evict them over non-compliance or wait until their lease ends and don't renew it.

8. Noise

If you own a multifamily property, chances are you will have to deal with noise complaints. We once had a tenant who would complain because she could hear her neighbor singing in the shower every morning at 5:00 a.m. These situations do happen often when people live in close proximity, and as the landlord, you'll be the first one they call. When we get noise complaints, typically this is the three step process we follow:

1. Thank the tenant for letting us know about the issue and encourage them to deal with it themselves. Many times, the tenant is just nervous to talk to the other tenant, but with some encouragement from the landlord, they will usually approach the situation with the other tenant without having to involve the landlord directly.

2. If #1 doesn't work, we simply call the tenant making the noise and explain the problem and ask them to keep more quiet.

3. If #2 doesn't work, we send a formal Notice to Comply letter to ask them to stop.

If that doesn't work, it might be time to either pursue eviction or wait for their lease to end and not renew it, depending on the situation. Sometimes there is nothing you should do, and the tenant being bothered simply needs to suck it up. For example, if you have a multifamily property and the upstairs tenants have children who continually walk around on the floor, bothering the tenant below, what can you do? You can't tell the upstairs tenant to tie their children up, and asking them to leave because of their kids would violate Fair Housing Laws. People will always complain, and it's your job to decide if the complaint is warranted and worth trying to solve.

When dealing with multifamily units, it's natural to have some tenants who just don't get along with one another, creating other conflicts. As long as these conflicts are normal, they can be handled the same way a noise complaint would be handled:

1. Encourage them to work it out amongst themselves,

2. Contact the offending tenant and ask them to correct the issue, then

3. Send a Notice to Comply.

However, if the conflict is of a dangerous or criminal nature (such as getting into physical fights or threatening each other), it would be best to simply get rid of those tenants. Ain't nobody got time for that.

9. Window Coverings

One of our biggest pet peeves as property owners is driving up to our apartment complex, with the beautiful lawn, pristine paint job, and impeccable landscaping, only to see bed sheets hanging in the windows of the units. Tenants often choose not to "invest" in curtains (why would they, when bed sheets do the trick?) and instead put up bed sheets to block out the light.

To combat this, we install inexpensive white mini-blinds in every single property we own (the kind that can be purchased from any big-box home store for $5–$20) and install them before a tenant moves in. However, even this only solves half the problem, as those blinds are commonly damaged by irresponsible tenants, children and pets. Even so, we require that all blinds be in good operating order, and if any are damaged, the tenant is responsible for either installing new ones, or we will install new ones for them, billing them for the cost. After getting a $50 bill for new blinds (materials and labor) a few times, they find a way to keep them intact.

10. Breaking the Lease

Finally, let's talk about what happens when a tenant wants to break a lease. Perhaps they got a new job elsewhere, they broke up with their significant other, or they simply found a better place to live and want out. The purpose of a lease is to stop this kind of thing from happening, but tenants tend not to care about the lease as much as the landlord and they'll break the lease anyway. So what then?

First, we tell tenant that they are legally required to continue paying the rent up until the end of their lease. Oftentimes, it just never clicked with them how a lease really worked (or never thought we'd care), and this revelation is enough to keep them in place. Other times, however, they simply move. When the tenant leaves, this can leave you scrambling to find a new tenant, but hopefully you have a hefty security deposit to help cover some of the unexpected financial loss. Be sure to check with the laws in your state on what you can and can't do with their deposit, but chances are you can use this to cover the lost rent for the property. Just like with any unit whose tenant has vacated, keep detailed records of the condition of the rental and the cost associated with making it rent-ready again. Then, add in the utility bills, lost rent, and any other charges that are the tenant's responsibility during the remainder of their lease and hold them to it. If the deposit doesn't cover it, be sure to send them the bill, and if necessary, contact your attorney for help with trying to collect the balance.

One tactic that has worked well when a tenant wants to break their lease with us is this: We tell them that they need to keep paying rent, but the day that we get their unit re-rented out is the day we'll let them out of their lease and refund any portion not used. For example, let's say that Tenant John broke his lease and left his apartment on the 31st of March, but he's responsible for April rent and agrees to pay it on the 1st. You immediately get the unit turned over and get the unit re-rented to Linda on the 9th of April. Because Tenant John had paid for the month of April at the beginning of that month and Linda moved in and paid rent on the 9th, you only lost eight days' worth of rent (from April 1st through April 8th), so that's all you charge Tenant John, refunding him back the difference. In this case, April had 30 days, and eight of those were Tenant John's responsibility, or 26.66 percent of the month. If Tenant John's rent was $600 per month, then John would be responsible for $160, but because he paid $600 on the 1st, he would receive a rent refund of $440, along with his deposit refund. Tenant Linda would cover the rest of the month, and we would have no lost rent from that broken lease. Sometimes, of course, Tenant John will refuse to pay for the next month's rent, though he is still liable for it. Either way, as long as we get the unit re-rented fairly quickly and the unit does not require an expensive turnover, we won't lose any money on the broken lease, which is good for me and good for the tenant who vacated.

Wrapping it Up

The above ten examples of lease violations are the most common for landlords, and you will most likely run into some, if not all, of these same situations in your landlording career. You may have noticed that each non-compliance issue gave the landlord three options:

1. Ignore it

2. Attempt to solve it

3. Get rid of the tenant

The next chapter is going to focus on #3—removing a tenant from your property who either stopped paying their rent or is otherwise in severe violation of their rental contract. We'll focus on the topic of evicting tenants, as well as some alternatives that could save you a lot of time, money, and stress. Because frankly—those are three things every landlord wants to save.

CHAPTER 11:
GETTING RID OF BAD TENANTS

Pink slip.

Gettin' canned.

Let go.

"It's just not working out."

We all recognize these words and know exactly what they mean: *You're fired.*

These are two of the most painful words a person can hear from their boss, but as any business owner knows, they are often required to maintain a profitable and effective business. And in our book, landlording IS a business, and anyone who treats it otherwise is setting themselves up for a disastrous (or at least stressful) adventure. But this section is not about firing *employees*; instead, we're talking about *firing our tenants.* Yes, you read that right. Sometimes we fire our tenants. Pink slip, gettin' canned, "it's just not working out."

There are several ways to fire a bad tenant, and this chapter is going to focus on those options. There is no one-size-fits-all solution for getting rid of a bad tenant, so we'll give you several options to make sure you have the knowledge to take the path that will save you the most time, money, and hassle.

Why Tenants Need to Be Removed

If you have been in the residential rental business for any significant amount of time, eventually you'll discover that one tenant whose life mission appears to be to send you to an early grave. We've all been there, and it is frustrating, believe us. They can do this in ways big and small—and usually in a lot of different ways at once! Here are a few examples of ways your tenant might be driving you nuts.

- Paying their rent late.
- Paying their rent late with an incredible, sad story as to why it's late. (Tenant: "You see, my great uncle Jimmy passed away, and I had to fly unexpectedly to North Dakota for the funeral. But then when I got there, a massive tornado blew in and took out the whole town. Then my car broke down on my way home." Landlord: "Didn't you fly?" Tenant: "Oh, that's what I meant. After I *flew* home, my car broke down, and I couldn't get to work, so I was out of work for three weeks!" Landlord: "Is that the box to a new 60" big screen TV out by your garbage can?" Tenant: "What box? Oh that. That's… not… mine.")
- Or on the flip side, playing ostrich and burying their head when the rent is due.
- Smoking in a non-smoking unit.
- Smoking out the window in a non-smoking unit. (It's not "technically" smoking in the unit if their hand is out the window.)
- Getting a pit bull in a no-pet unit.
- Getting a pet of any kind in a no-pet unit. *(But it's so cute!)*
- Not taking care of or cleaning up after animals in a pet-friendly unit.
- Noise complaints from the neighbors.
- Turning the backyard into a vehicle cemetery.
- Not mowing the lawn.
- Letting their sister and Joe Blow move in.
- Changing the oil in the living room. (Yes, this has happened.)
- Not reporting maintenance issues that turn into major problems.
- Using their decks as a catch-all.
- Using Mickey Mouse sheets as curtains (after they broke the blinds).

You get the idea. There is a popular business principle often discussed called "The Pareto Principle," also known as "The 80/20 Rule" that has been attributed to Italian economist Vilfredo Pareto. Wikipedia explains it well by saying, "The Pareto Principle...states that for many events, roughly 80 percent of the effects come from 20 percent of the causes." In the world of landlording, this can be applied to mean that 80 percent of your problems (or stress) comes from 20 percent of your tenants. The percentages don't have to be exact, but it comes down to simply eliminating those problem tenants from your portfolio.

By firing the tenants in your irritating 20 percent, you will be a happier landlord, your other tenants will be happier, and your business will run much more smoothly. There are a lot of qualified people out there who are great tenants, so why put yourself through the hassle of trying the deal with someone who simply doesn't care? Life's too short to rent to people who will shorten your life even further. So, let's get rid of them, shall we?

Not Renewing the Lease

In the beginning, the tenant probably looked great! You likely did everything a good landlord is supposed to do to find qualified tenants. Maybe they even had good intentions, or maybe they just hadn't been caught yet and were really good at getting through the screening process. Either way, eventually you realize that they are driving you bananas and they have to go. Of course, if they are in violation of their contract, you could evict over that issue. However, there is an easier method that is far cheaper that might work for you: simply not renewing their lease. After all, whether they have an annual lease, a month-to-month lease, or something else, their lease does have an end date. You can simply let the tenant know that you will not be renewing their contract for another month, and they'll need to find a new place to live.

(Keep in mind, if you live in a location where a tenant cannot be asked to move from their property, like San Francisco or New York City, this next small section may not apply to you.)

If you do decide not to renew a lease, be sure you notify the tenant in writing within the required amount of time *before* the end of their lease expiration. If you have a month-to-month agreement, give them the required notice in writing that you won't be renewing their agreement for the following month. In the State of Washington where we operate, you can give the tenant a minimum of 20 days' notice before the end of the month to end their contract—and we have used it! There is also a bit of fancy footwork needed here. If you give the notice too early, the tenant may not pay their rent for the current month, so if possible, give the notice after the rent has been paid. For us, because we only need to give 20 days' notice before the end of the month, we will wait for the rent to come in on the 1st (through the 5th) and give them notice the next day. Of course, if your area requires 30 days' or longer notice, this may be a luxury you won't be able to take. This is just more reason why you need to understand your local landlord-tenant laws. Let us tell you a quick story about the last tenant we fired.

Her name is Stephanie. Her deck and surrounding yard look like a dumpster—again. Seriously, who drinks that much soda? And why do they throw it off their balcony? Another call from the neighbor next door comes in about Stephanie's garbage blowing into her part of the lawn. And then the rent is late again. The tenant downstairs is calling about all the noise coming from the upstairs unit. Oh, and the soda cans, toys, and garbage from Stephanie's deck keep falling into the good tenant's outdoor living space. She is NOT happy.

Stephanie was an ideal tenant—on paper. She (somehow) met our rental criteria, and in the beginning, she looked like a good fit for our property. Oh, how wrong we were. For six months we were plagued by the drama surrounding Stephanie and the stress that comes along with a negligent tenant. Not a week went by where were weren't calling Stephanie regarding her non-compliance in some way. Every phone call was followed up by a letter. Every letter eventually needed to be followed up with a notice. Whenever we were on our last straw, she would quickly fix the problem to avoid eviction.

Until one day we had enough and fired her. We gave her a 20-day notice to move (per our state requirements), and in less than a month, she was gone. Ah, peace and quiet. We immediately replaced Stephanie with another tenant who has been perfect from the day they moved in.

Now, what would have happened if Stephanie had not left? Yes, we could have pursued an eviction, but besides being expensive, we also don't want to be in a position where the judge may decide to grant Stephanie more time to clean up her act, only for us to end up back in court the following month. In these kinds of cases, as well as situations where we want to remove a tenant and their lease is not ending any time soon, we generally look toward the Cash for Keys strategy.

Cash for Keys

Cash for Keys is a controversial process debated often in landlord circles, but something we LOVE and use. Cash for Keys is the strategy of giving your tenants money to leave the property, avoiding the eviction process altogether. We have used this technique several times over the past few years and found great success. However, before throwing money at your tenant, let's talk about the specifics.

The theory behind Cash for Keys is simple: Giving the tenant money to leave is cheaper than paying an attorney for an eviction. Think about it: Evicting a tenant will likely take a month or longer, depending on your state. It could cost you several thousand dollars in legal fees to do so, on top of the lost rent for at least a month, maybe two, three or more. Then, you have to deal with the clean-up of a tenant who was just evicted, which is never very pretty. All in all, a normal eviction could cost you around $5,000 or more. But what if you could just offer your tenant $500 to leave the property in good condition? Exactly. That's Cash for Keys.

Of course, $500 is just an example. Maybe you want to give more. Maybe less. It will depend on the unit, the tenant, and the motivation. However, $500 is usually enough to encourage someone to leave, especially someone desperate enough to be facing an eviction. If you are going to try Cash for Keys, the following seven principles should be followed:

1. **Explain to the tenant in detail what they need to do.** We tell them that the unit must be in move-in ready condition when they leave, so they have to clean it and repair any damages. This saves us clean-up costs and reduces the chance that the tenant will damage the property on the way out.

2. **Give the tenant a specific date they need to move out by.** Typically, we will not give any more than four days to move. The point of Cash for Keys is to get them out of the property *quickly.*

3. **Give a Pay or Vacate Notice anyway.** We'll talk about this form in a moment, but just in case they don't leave, you will not have lost much time. This is typically the first step in the eviction process, and you should get it started in the event that the tenant does not leave.

4. **Meet with the tenant.** Next, meet the tenant at the property and verify that the unit is, indeed, "broom clean." To be safe, make sure to take someone with you.

5. **Inspect the property.** Make sure the tenant lived up to their end of the bargain. The home should be cleaned out and in good

shape. If not, show the tenant what needs to be done, and tell them you'll come back in several hours to try again. Never give the tenant money until they are 100 percent out and have turned over the key.

6. **Sign the paperwork.** Have them sign a simple document that relinquishes their tenancy at the property. This will protect you in case they later say you changed the locks on them or that they did not really move out. Make sure they sign and date the document.

7. **Hand over the cash.** If the tenant has held up his or her part of the deal, hand over the money and thank them for a positive transition. Wish them well on their way! Then get into the house and change the locks immediately.

Yes, Cash for Keys stings your pride. It feels so "un-American," like the bad guy is getting away with the crime. Some landlords flat-out refuse to even consider this idea because it feels so wrong, but remember, Cash for Keys isn't personal; it's business! Brad Pitt sums it up well in a phone call to Andy Garcia in one of our favorite movies *Ocean's 11*, when he is stealing a large sum of cash from Andy Garcia's casino:

"Are you watching your monitors? Okay, keep watching. In this town, your luck can change just that quickly. Take a closer look at your monitor. As your manager's probably reporting to you now, you have a little over $160 million in your vault tonight. You may notice we're only packing up about half that. The other half we're leaving in your vault, booby-trapped, as a hostage. You let our $80 million go, and you get to keep yours. That's the deal. You try to stop us, and we'll blow both. Mr. Benedict, you could lose $80 million tonight secretly or you could lose $160 million publicly. It's your decision."

Mr. and Ms. Landlord: You could lose $500 this month secretly, or you could lose $5,000 this year publicly. It's your decision.

That said, Cash for Keys doesn't always work. Some tenants will refuse it. Some tenants will ignore it. Sometimes you just won't want to try it. In that case, you'll need to continue the eviction process.

Evicting a Tenant

After you've tried everything you can to rectify a situation and explored all other options to get the tenant out of your property, you will likely be left with one option: eviction. The process of evicting a tenant can be complicated and expensive, but it's also not impossible to learn. Don't let the idea of an eviction scare you from managing tenants. Instead, understand that evictions will be part of your business and just another day-to-day task you'll need to learn. The rest of this chapter is designed to help you do just that.

Two Facts About Evictions

Before we jump into the specifics regarding the eviction, let's put two important facts on the table.

First, understand that this WILL happen to you, but it's not that big of a deal. Non-paying tenants are a very normal thing, so don't freak out. You'll get through it. Nevertheless, it's best to have a system in place and know exactly how to deal with it when it eventually happens. This way, you can jump on it immediately and have the best chance for recovering that rent and reclaiming your property.

Second, evictions are incredibly state-specific. In other words, the entire eviction process is governed by the rules and laws of each state. Everything we are about to discuss regarding the eviction of a tenant is just general knowledge, but the specific days and dates will require you to do a little more homework into your state's landlord-tenant laws.

How NOT to Evict a Tenant

Recently, we heard the tale of a landlord in our town who was dealing with a delinquent tenant and decided to take matters into his own hands. He waited until the tenant was gone, went into the property, and began taking stuff. *Stupid!* Not only is this tenant still in the property, but the landlord now has a lawsuit on his hands.

Please, please, please *don't* go vigilante and take the eviction process into your own hands. Just don't. This is known as a "self-help" eviction, and it's illegal in most states and stupid in all of them. Don't change the locks. Don't remove the windows and doors. Don't shut off their utilities. Don't take their stuff. You'll have enough drama trying to evict the tenant; you don't need to compound it by making yourself look like the bad guy when standing in front of a judge. Follow the rules, follow the laws, and let the eviction process work. Remember: This is a business.

Should You Hire an Attorney to Evict the Tenant?

In most cases, yes, you should hire an attorney to evict your tenant. Yes, you can do the job yourself and save a lot of money, but you could also cross one "t" incorrectly or forget to dot one "i" and lose weeks or months of work. The eviction process can be complicated, and in most areas, the courts are not as friendly to the landlord as they are to the tenant. As the landlord, you are already facing a battle, and going it alone is dangerous unless you know exactly what you are doing.

To find a good attorney, ask for references from other landlords. This is one of the benefits to jumping into the BiggerPockets Forums and building relationships. If you are a BiggerPockets Pro member, you can also use BiggerPockets Meet to find investors in any zip code in America and send them a message asking for a referral to a good attorney. Another way to find a good attorney would be to call your local county administration building and ask to speak to the person in charge of evictions. When you get them on the phone, ask them which attorney files the most evictions in your area. They would likely be a good attorney to talk with about your situation. As you get more experienced with evictions (or if you are broke and you absolutely cannot afford an attorney), you might choose to do the eviction yourself, but we don't recommend it.

How to Evict a Tenant: The Step-by-Step Eviction Process

At this point, you are ready to evict your tenant. They have either refused to pay their rent or are in violation of their rental contract in some other way. As tough as it might sound, it's time to begin the eviction process. Let's walk through that process now, step by step.

Step 1: Post or Deliver the Notice

The first "legal" step in evicting a tenant comes in the form of hand-delivering (serving) a notice to the tenant, letting them know of their grievance and what happens next. The kind of notice served will depend on the reason they are being evicted.

- If they are being evicted for non-payment of rent, you will serve a Pay or Vacate Notice, also known as a Pay or Quit Notice, to their home. This notice lets them know that they have "X" number of days (depending on your state's laws) to pay the rent or they will be evicted. The notice also should explain any rental amount due, along with the late fees or penalties that are being charged.

- If they are being evicted for violating any other terms of their lease (they moved in a pet, late-night partied, trashed their unit, etc.), then they are served a Notice to Comply, which states that they have "X" number of days to rectify the situation or they will be evicted.

Each state has different requirements for the notices that must be served, so be sure to check out your state's process (you can find the requirements for all fifty states by visiting www.BiggerPockets.com/eviction, or check out the section we included in the appendix of this book.) so you will know the right form to serve.

In most states, the notice can be attached to the door of the rental unit if no one answers the door, but if posted, most states require that a copy of the notice also be mailed to the tenant. If you mail the notice, be sure to send it "Certified, with Return Receipt" from the US Postal Service, so you can prove the document was delivered. Be careful to follow the exact rules of your state in regard to how this notice must be served. In some states, the owner of the property may not be allowed to serve the legal notice themselves. Also, always be sure to only hand the notice to an adult in the home or someone of suitable age—never the tenant's children. The point of hand-delivering the notice is to ensure the tenant receives it; if the notice is handed to a child, who knows where it might end up. It's also a good idea to record the date and time that the notice was served and who the notice was handed to. (If posted to the door, a quick picture with your cell phone of the notice on the door is a great idea for your records.)

When it comes to the late-rent Pay or Vacate Notice, understand that once a notice has been served, collecting any amount of rent afterwards will likely start the clock ticking again, and new papers must be served. Therefore, think twice before collecting a small amount from the tenant.

In addition to this notice, we like to include a letter to the tenant with the official notice (given separately but at the same time) to soften the blow a little. Legal notices can be very cold, causing the tenant anger and confusion. The goal of the letter is to get the tenant to communicate with us and not simply bury their head in the sand (which is the common reaction for tenants going through hard times—they simply shut down). We want to encourage communication with the tenant that will hopefully assist in avoiding the eviction and our lawyers altogether. Here is an example of this letter, which you can also find in the appendix of this book or online at http://www.BiggerPockets.com/LandlordBookBonus.

Courtesy Late Rent Notice

Dear Tenant: Date: ____/____/____

This is a courtesy notice that we have not yet received your rent payment for this month. As a reminder, rent is always due on the 1st of every month and considered late if not received by the 5th of the month. Please be sure your full payment is paid no later than 5:00pm today to avoid eviction proceedings.

Balances Owed

Rent for the month of _____ in the amount of $_____

Late Fee in accordance with Lease Agreement $_____

Other amounts owed for _____ $_____

Total Amount Due $_____

If you believe you have received this notice in error, or you cannot make your payment by 5:00pm today, please contact us at (___) ____-_____ as soon as possible to discuss your plans. Communication is extremely important. We are looking forward to hearing from you.

Sincerely,

Management

Step 2: File Eviction With the Court

After the minimum number of days have passed (as defined by the notice you served), it's time to move forward with the eviction. If you hire an attorney, this is where the attorney will likely take over the process, letting you get back to your life. Be sure to give your attorney all of the information they will need to get the whole picture, including:

1. A copy of the tenant's lease

2. A copy of the notice that was served

3. A brief summary of the situation

If you plan to do the eviction yourself, the second step is to officially file the lawsuit with the court. (Yes, this is a lawsuit you will be filing, and it is also known as an unlawful detainer.) This is done at your local courthouse, though you may need to make some phone calls first to find out exactly where to go and what paperwork they need. Once filed, the court administrator will issue a court date for you and your tenant to show up in court and plead both sides in front of the judge. Of course, if you are using an attorney, the attorney will show up in court. If you're doing the eviction yourself, you will likely need to be present.

Step 3: The Lawsuit Is Served

Once the lawsuit has been filed in court and the court date set, the tenant will be served the official "unlawful detainer" lawsuit. Most likely, this will need to be served by a third party. This lawsuit usually must be delivered directly to the tenant—posting it to the door is generally not allowed unless special permission is given by the court, which could set the eviction back several weeks. So hopefully the server can get the document directly into the hands of someone of suitable age living at the property.

Step 4: The Court Date

When the court date comes, you will need to be prepared (or your attorney will need to be!). If you are doing the eviction yourself, make sure you bring with you:

- The lease agreement
- Any written communications between you and the tenant
- The tenant's original application, if you have it
- The notice paperwork that was served
- Written documentation of everything you've done so far with the tenant in regard to the grievance and eviction
- The lawsuit that was filed

Generally, if the tenant does not show up to court and doesn't respond to the lawsuit, they automatically lose, which in our experience is generally how standard evictions usually go down. We've done a handful of evictions, and only once did the tenant show up in court—and she lost.

If the tenant does show up, the judge will hear both sides and rule either in the favor of the landlord or the tenant. If you, the landlord, lose the eviction, well, that sucks. It likely means you or your attorney didn't have all your paperwork in order, or you or your attorney didn't follow the correct eviction proceedings. You will likely have to start over at the beginning. However, if you (or your attorney) did everything right and you win the case, a judgment will be issued against the tenant for the amount of money owed in rent, back rent, court costs, attorney's fees, and late charges.

Additionally, the court will order the tenant to vacate the premises within a certain number of days (depending on the state). This is done through a document known as a Writ of Restitution or Writ of Possession. This writ gives the landlord the legal right to remove the tenant. Usually the writ will give a certain number of days to the tenant, usually between 24 hours and one week, to completely vacate. Keep in mind, in some Northern states, evictions during the cold winter months can be put on hold until warmer weather. There's simply not a lot you can do about that.

Step 5: Schedule With the Sheriff

Once the tenant loses the eviction, the landlord (or attorney) will need to take the Writ of Restitution to the Sheriff. That's right: You cannot physically go and remove the tenant and their belongings from the home without a Sheriff. You (or your attorney) will have to pay another fee to the Sheriff and fill out some more forms. Finally, a removal date will be set. The Sheriff's department will likely go to the home and post their own notice, giving a date and time that they will be at the home to remove the tenant from the premises.

Step 6: Remove the Tenant (With Help)

Generally, the tenant will leave before the Sheriff shows up, but it's entirely possible to have the tenant still there—and angry—when the Sheriff arrives. The Sheriff's job is to keep the peace and physically remove the tenant if needed, but it is **not** their job to change the locks or remove the contents of the property. They will simply supervise you and/or your "crew" as you secure the property, after which you will need to itemize, photograph, and remove all of the tenant's remaining property. We also recommend taking a video camera with you and recording the contents of the property the moment you enter behind the Sheriff, as well as doing a complete walkthrough, before removing the tenant's belongings from the premises.

Usually, the tenant's property will be placed outside on the nearest public roadway, but not always. If they don't claim it, it can be discarded and likely picked through by the homeless in the area. The tenant *can* request through the court that the landlord store their personal things (yes, really); if this is the case, you will need to store the tenant's things in a secure location. Of course, the tenant would be required to pay for the expense accrued for the storage before getting their things back, but there is no clear rule on *when* they need to pay for it, so if the tenant never claims it, you may up eating this expense and simply having to discard the property at a later time.

At this point, you've likely spent a good amount of cash and time to get this tenant removed. Is there any way to get paid back for this trouble? Maybe. After all, you do have a judgment from the court, which can be used to collect debts. However, collecting judgments is like trying to squeeze blood from a turnip. We've never collected a penny—yet. We still report our judgments to debt collectors, who take a portion of any money they recover for their trouble. At the very least, they'll hound the tenant for many years to come. It's a small win, but after a lengthy eviction, we'll take it! Additionally, there are ways to garnish wages and even garnish a tax return, so you may want to consider those options as well.

Frequently Asked Questions on Evicting a Tenant

How long does an eviction take?

In most states, as long as everything goes as planned, an eviction takes about a month. However, in some "tenant-friendly" states, evictions can take up to six months.

How much does an eviction cost?

The state-required legal fees involved with an eviction are fairly light, usually no more than a few hundred dollars. However, the attorney fees and lost rent are the big cash flow killers. You'll likely spend between $1,500 and $3,000 on attorney's costs, plus several months of lost rent and damages done to the property. Cash for Keys doesn't sound so crazy now, does it?

Is it possible to evict a tenant without a rental contract?

If you don't have a rental contract with your tenant, it is still possible to evict. In most states, a tenant without a rental contract is treated the same as a tenant on a month-to-month lease. This can actually be a good thing for you, in that an eviction could be avoided by simply "not renewing the month-to-month lease" and asking the tenant to leave with a Notice to Vacate (according to your specific state's laws). Of course, if you have to evict without a rental contract, just bring every bit of paperwork and information you can about the tenant.

Where do I get an eviction letter?

Before filing the lawsuit, you will need to serve the tenant with a notice, also known as an "eviction letter." This is either the Pay or Vacate Notice or the Notice to Comply. These can be obtained from an attorney or online through sites like EZLandlordForms.com. We also included samples of the forms we use in the appendix of this book and at http://www.BiggerPockets.com/LandlordBookBonus.

Final Thoughts on Tenant Evictions

Evictions are annoying, but they are part of doing business as a landlord. Don't panic when you need to do an eviction—just move forward with confidence and take care of the problem. Once again, we do recommend you contact an attorney to help you with your eviction, at least until you are confident that you can complete it correctly yourself.

Wrapping it Up

As we mentioned earlier, there is no one-size-fits-all solution for getting rid of a tenant. Hopefully you are well aware of the many different options you have for removing a tenant from your property, so getting rid of a bad tenant should not be an issue going forward. And speaking of going forward, let's move on and talk about another common task you'll spend much of your landlord days doing: dealing with contractors.

CHAPTER 12:
DEALING WITH CONTRACTORS

Contractors can be a difficult bunch.

If you are a landlord (or any kind of real estate investor), dealing with those in the construction trade is part of daily life. This is especially true for landlords like us who choose to invest in fixer-upper rentals to gain that extra equity push. But how do you **start**? Where do you find the best contractors? How do you know they aren't ripping you off?

Before you can start making phone calls, hiring contractors, getting bids, and swinging hammers, you must first identify what kind of contractor you need. Let's look at that first.

Types of Contractors
The General Contractor

The general contractor (often referred to as a "GC") is a specialist who oversees entire jobs, hiring other contractors (known as subcontractors or "subs") to do various tasks. For example, you might hire a GC to remodel a property, and the GC will be responsible for hiring the subcontractors, such as the plumber, the electrician, the carpenter, the painter, etc. To complicate things a bit, both the GC and the subs are often just referred to as the blanket term "contractors."

Sometimes the GC does very little of the work himself, acting almost exclusively as a project manager. Other times, the GC will do the general rehab work (demo, carpentry, roofing, painting) and hire out the specialty tasks that require a special license, like plumbing and electrical. It really depends on the GC and the agreement you have with them.

Hiring a general contractor will likely be the most expensive option, as they must pay for their overhead and for their supervision on the project, but hiring a GC is also usually the easiest option, as they handle the majority of the hassle and coordination. As a landlord, it's most common that YOU will act as the general contractor on most projects, rather than paying the big bucks a GC will charge. It will be your job to find the right subcontractor to do the right task for you.

The Handyman

One of the most valuable subcontractors you will use in your landlording business is commonly known as a "handyman." These contractors are not specialists in just one field of construction, but many different areas of the job site. Finding a great handyman to help you in your landlording business will be one of the most impactful things you can possibly do.

A great handyman will know how to diagnose a problem and hopefully will know how to fix it (or know who to call). They can paint, patch a drywall hole, tear out a sink, clean gutters, and perform numerous other tasks around your rental property. However, good handymen can be incredibly hard to find. The good ones tend to become general contractors; the bad ones will claim to be amazing, only to destroy your property, take your money, and leave you penniless.

Specialists

Certain types of activities, including plumbing, electrical, HVAC, and more, will require specialty contractors who must hold special licenses within their field. For example, in most states, even the landlord can't work on the electrical system of his or her own property—they must use a licensed electrician. One misstep in the wiring can burn down a neighborhood, so these laws are in place to protect everyone. These types of contractors will likely be your most expensive, as the price of a good specialty contractor usually starts at around $100 per hour and only goes up from there. However, because these contractors are trained in one exact field, they usually can diagnose problems far faster and more easily than general contractors or handymen.

Licensed vs. Unlicensed Contractors

There are a LOT of unlicensed contractors out there. Anyone who can (or can't!) swing a hammer can claim to be a contractor, but few are licensed to do so. A license is obtained by a contractor after they have filled out the proper forms with the state where they are doing business, paid the appropriate fees, taken the appropriate tests, and obtained the correct insurance and surety bond required by the state. (A surety bond is similar to insurance, where the contractor pays a fee to a bond company, and if they don't complete the work that was agreed upon, the bond can come in to pay for the work to be finished, and the bond company will go after the contractor.) We will refer to licensed, bonded, and insured contractors as simply "licensed" for the purpose of this book.

That said, because of the costs a licensed contractor must pay to maintain their standing, licensed contractors tend to have higher overhead costs than their unlicensed counterparts. Translation: *Licensed contractors are more expensive.* Now, if you are anything like us, you are probably a penny-pincher who loves to find a good deal. So, if two guys can both do the work, and one is $25/hr (unlicensed) and the other is $45/hr (licensed), is it a terrible idea to go with the cheaper guy? In other words, as a landlord, does it really matter if they are licensed, as long as the work gets done?

YES. IT MATTERS.

Here are four major reasons why:

- First, when a contractor is licensed, it means they are legitimate about wanting to be in the game for the long-haul; they are not simply taking your money and running. After all, a license likely cost them hundreds or even thousands of dollars and requires mounds of ongoing paperwork. The licensed contractor at least *wants* to be legit, which means a lot. If nothing else, it demonstrates that the individual doesn't cut corners when it comes to their legitimacy, and it increases the likelihood that they won't cut corners on your project either.

- Secondly, their legitimacy also gives you a "big stick" to use if the contractor doesn't live up to their end of the bargain, as you can report the contractor and even go after their surety bond. If accused of wrongdoing, the contractor could lose his or her license and subsequently, his or her livelihood.

- Third, a contractor who is licensed by law must have workman's compensation insurance on themselves and their employees. This insurance helps to protect you, the owner, in the relatively frequent occurrence that someone gets hurt on the job. Without that insurance, it's likely the hurt individual will go after YOU to pay their medical bills. How would you like a $40,000 lawsuit on top of that $400 paint job?

- Fourth, hiring an unlicensed contractor may void any warranties on the products they installed.

If you still aren't convinced that it's worth it to hire a licensed contractor, consider the following real-life example from our landlording career of what can happen if you hire someone who is not licensed.

*He seemed great, at first. Walked the walk, talked the talk, drove a nice truck, looked us in the eye, and assured us he could complete our project within our five-week timeframe. He was also "licensed." This guy was legit, or so we thought. After signing a contract and giving him a $5,000 down payment for materials, we let him at it. A week into the project, we started feeling like something wasn't right. Nothing was getting done, and the clock was ticking. After repeated calls, he again assured us all was well—he was just waiting on the materials he ordered to arrive and finishing up a couple loose ends on another project before starting ours; not to worry, it would get done. A few days later, after no progress on our project, we **knew** something was wrong.*

We drove to the building supply store that he supposedly ordered our supplies from, only to discover that they had no record of his order. "Are you sure?" we questioned. They were sure. Our materials were never ordered, and this stranger we gave $5,000 of our hard-earned money to just two weeks prior was suspiciously MIA. We went online to do a little research and learned not only was this particular contractor NOT licensed, but he had been accused of stealing $3,000 from another unsuspecting homeowner just 10 months earlier. Ugh. When we finally got ahold of him over the phone and confronted him about his lies, he admitted that, indeed, our money was gone. He had spent it.

We are the first to admit we made many mistakes when it came to hiring this "contractor," but our biggest mistake was that we should have *verified* that he was licensed and not simply taken his word for it. By doing a simple search online, you can discover all kinds of information about your contractor, including if they are licensed, bonded, and insured; if they are active (and not suspended); if they have any infractions; and if they have any lawsuits against their bond. You can also verify that your tradesperson (such as your electrician or plumber) is certified.

In our situation, had our "contractor" actually been licensed, bonded, and insured, his bond would have (hopefully) covered his dishonesty, and we would (hopefully) not have been out $5,000 dollars. Furthermore, if he was licensed, it would have been harder for him to swallow stealing that much money, knowing he would lose his license, and hence his livelihood, when we complained. Finally, we should never have paid such a large down payment to a contractor with whom we had never done business. Looking back, it would have been much smarter to order the materials ourselves and simply pay him for his labor at certain benchmarks. But alas, our money (and a piece of our faith in humanity!) was gone like the wind.

Hopefully by this point we've convinced you of the importance of hiring a contractor who is licensed. As you can tell from the story we just shared, it's also not enough to simply take them at their word. Just last week we talked with a contractor about doing some work for us on a rental property, and he swore up and down he was licensed, bonded, and insured. He even went so far as to bash all those "under the table" guys who take work away from him, "the legit guy." However, when we went online and checked, he was not licensed at all. A complete fraud. We won't be working with him—ever. (He seemed like such a nice guy, too. His loss!)

Please, verify that your contractor is, indeed, licensed. Luckily, like we previously mentioned, this can be done fairly easily online by searching your state's website. Find it by Googling "[your state] contractor license search," and it should pop up first. You should also ask to see a copy of their insurance and bond, just to make sure they have not lapsed. Don't feel bad for asking—it's just business. Any good contractor will respect you for asking.

Keep in mind, a license does NOT mean the contractor is going to be good. Not all states require a general contractor to know *anything* about construction to get a license, so being licensed does not guarantee expertise. (Of course, with certain trades like electrical or plumbing, a license shows that they have had training and at least can pass a test demonstrating they know what they doing.) A license doesn't show you the level of quality the contractor can do nor the speed at which they will do it. For that, you are going to have to do some research, which we'll talk about in a moment. First, you need to find those contractors. Let's talk about that now.

5 Ways to Find Great Contractors

Finding contractors begins with proactively going out and looking for them. The following are five ways you can do that.

1. Personal Referrals

By and large, the #1 tip offered by guests on The BiggerPockets Podcast for finding contractors is through referrals from others. This is obvious, of course, but so few of us really go out of our way to ask people. We make it a habit to ask every single homeowner we talk to in our area if they know any good contractors. We could be in a conversation at the bank, the post office, or on Facebook, and we'll typically find a way to ask, "Do you know any good contractors in the area?" People love to recommend others who have been good to them and will likely not recommend a jerk, so pay close attention to those who come wholeheartedly recommended.

And speaking of Facebook, try this: Head over to your Facebook page right now and post a simple status that says, "Hey, everyone in [county or city name], I'm looking for an incredible [handyman/contractor/painter/etc.]. Anyone know someone amazing I should talk to?"

You'll likely get some great personal recommendations without even leaving your chair.

2. Other Contractors

Another tip we like rather a lot (which we heard from a guest on the BiggerPockets Podcast) is to ask subcontractors *who they like to follow*. When rehabbing a property, the construction moves in phases. Demo, then drywall. Drywall, then painting. Painting, then trim. On and on it goes until the project is done. Therefore, if you want to find a good contractor for one part of the job, ask the contractor next in the lineup. For example, if you want to find a good framer, ask the drywall person. If you want to find a good drywall person, ask the painter.

3. Craigslist

Craigslist is a double-edged sword. On one hand, it's the place where everyone seems to be. You can find anything from used bikes, to prostitutes, to contractors, and everything in between. However, Craigslist is also generally free to post and search on, which means the very bottom of the barrel tends to use it alongside the best. The dishonest contractor we mentioned a moment ago came from a Craigslist ad we posted. However, while that guy didn't work out, another respondent worked out great (and he IS licensed, bonded, and insured). So Craigslist *can* be a good tool; just be extra diligent when screening contractors found there.

4. Ask Store Employees

Our friend Darren Sager (a landlord from New Jersey) recently suggested visiting construction supply stores (for example, a tile supply store if you need tile work) and asking the employees who work there who they would have work on their houses. These employees have a unique view of the quality of materials that their customers (contractors) use, as well as the experience level and management style of those who buy from them.

5. Home Stores

Contractors and handymen need to purchase supplies, right? So why not hang out where they hang out and do some good ol' fashioned networking? As J Scott, author of *The Book on Flipping Houses*, recommends, head to a big box home store like Home Depot or Lowes early in the morning, perhaps 6:00 a.m. and see who is checking out at the contractor's desk. Those contractors are typically the "go-getters" who are up early to get their supplies and get to the job site. You don't typically see hungover contractors out at that time of the day!

Screening Contractors in 5 Steps

To be blunt, most contractors are going to be terrible for your landlording business. For this reason, you need to screen those contractors just as carefully as you might screen a tenant. Very few people put the work into finding a great contractor, so they struggle along with bad ones for years. This was our story as well! If only we had realized that by doing the careful work up front to find a great contractors, our lives would have been so much easier for years to come. Screening contractors takes time, but think of it as an investment that will pay off 1,000-fold if done correctly.

The following is a five-step process we use to screen contractors.

1. Pre-Screen on the Phone & in Person

Just as with tenants, our opinion of the contractor begins the moment we begin talking with them, whether over email, phone, or in person. Do they carry themselves professionally? Do they respond well to questions? Ask them some general questions, such as:

- How long have you been in this line of work?
- What skill would you say you are the best at?

- What job tasks do you hate doing?

- In what cities do you typically work?

- How many employees work for you? (Or *"work in your company" if you are not talking to the boss.*)

- How busy are you?

- Do you pull permits, or would I need to?

- If I were to hire you, when could you start knocking out tasks?

Then, set up a time to meet and show them the project, if you have one. Set an appointment and be sure to show up a few minutes early, just to see exactly what time they arrive. Are they on time? Late? Early? Do they look professional? How do they act? If everything feels ok after this first meeting, move on to step 2.

2. Google Them

The first thing we do now when looking for information on a certain contractor is to simply search Google for their name and their company name. This can often unearth any big red flags about the person. You'll also want to add your city name and some other keywords to the search, such as "scam" or "rip off." For example, if we wanted to find out more about First Rate Construction Company in Metropolis, we would search things like:

- *First Rate Construction Metropolis*

- *First Rate Construction scam*

- *First Rate Construction sue*

- *First Rate Construction court*

- *First Rate Construction evil*

These terms can help you discover major complaints about the contractor, but keep in mind, not all complaints are valid. Some people are just crazy. What it will do, however, is give you direction on what steps to take next.

In addition to Google, there are numerous websites (such as Criminal-Searches.com) that allow you to research more deeply into someone's past to discover little-known information about them. You could also run a background/credit check on your contractor, exactly the same way you would with a tenant. The choice is yours on whether or not you run a background check, but just know you can never be too careful.

3. Ask for References

Next, ask the contractor for references from previous people for whom they have worked. Photos are nice, but names and addresses are better. Then, do what 90 percent of the population will never do and **actually call those references!** You may want to ask the reference several questions, like:

- What work did they do?

- How fast did they do it?

- Did they keep a clean job site?

- You are related to [contractor's name], right? *(If they are, they will think you were already privy to that information and will have no problem answering honestly!)*

- Any problems working with them?

- Would you hire them again?

- Can I take a look at the finished product? *(This could be in person or via pictures.)*

These questions will help you understand more about the abilities and history of the contractor. Then, if possible, actually check out the work the contractor did and make sure it looks good.

Another tip recently given to us by J Scott was to ask the contractor to tell you about a recent big job they've done. Contractors love to brag about their big jobs, so he or she will likely regale you with the story of how much work they needed to do and how great it looked at the end. Find out the address, and then go to the city and verify that a permit was pulled for that project. If not, the contractor did all the work without a permit, which is a good indication they are not a contractor you want on your team.

4. Verify

We talked about this earlier, but we'll repeat it here for good measure. It's okay to be trusting, but make sure they are worthy of your trust first! To do this, first verify that they truly do have a license to do whatever work you intend for them to do. If they are an electrician, make sure they have an electrical license. If they are a plumber, make sure they have a plumbing license. If they are a general contractor, make sure they have a general contractor's license. Next, make sure they do actually have the proper insurance and bond. As we mentioned earlier, you could ask them to bring proof, but you can also simply ask the name of their insurance agent and verify it with that agent. Either way, just make sure they have it. Remember: this protects *you*.

5. Hire Them For One Small Task

Before hiring the contractor to do a large project, hire them to do just one small task, preferably under $1,000 in cost. This will give you a good idea of what kind of work ethic they have and the quality of work that they do. If the work is done on time and on budget, and if it meets your quality standards, consider hiring them for more tasks.

Even if the contractor has passed through the first four steps of this screening process, 75 percent of them will still likely fail at this fifth step, so don't settle with just one contractor. Hire multiple contractors for multiple small jobs and see who works out the best.

8 Tips for Managing Contractors and Handymen

1. Know When to Use Bids vs. Hourly Pay

Larger jobs tend to work better by "bid," whereas smaller jobs tend to work better by hourly pay, but there is no hard and fast rule for either. Some contractors prefer one method over another, but it's usually negotiable. Having a contractor bid a job helps you estimate exactly how much the job will cost before the contractor begins, which can help you budget and plan a rehab project. You can also compare multiple bids to see which contractor will be the best fit for the job.

For some jobs, however, a bid (or multiple bids) is just overkill. Why get multiple bids from contractors just to fix a leaky sink? Other jobs are too difficult to bid until work has begun, such as water leaks or issues behind walls. Typically, anything that will obviously be over $500 we try to get a bid for, but things that will obviously be under $500, we will usually just pay hourly. Unless you plan to flip houses or do a lot of total rehabs, 90 percent of the work you'll need done in a rental will be hourly.

2. Sign a Contract

When you finally select a contractor to do work for you, make sure you get everything in writing in the form of a contract. It doesn't matter if you are hiring by the hour or by the job—just be sure the conditions are spelled out in a contract between you and the contractor. Most good contractors should have their own contract, but if not, you can pick one up online through websites like www.uslegalforms.com.

The contract should outline what work will be done, deadlines for getting the job finished, the compensation for the work being performed, and when that compensation will be rendered. This contract will keep everyone honest and remembering exactly what was agreed upon, as well as give you legal ground to sue the contractor if the work is not performed according to the contract. Also, be sure that both you and the contractor sign the document.

3. Be Clear With Instructions

When dealing with contractors, you must be 100 percent clear about what you want done. Don't simply say "paint this room," but let them know what color, brand, and sheen, if you want the ceiling and trim painted—and even spell out that you don't want paint on the carpet. It may seem silly to spell everything for the contractor, but trust us: The more detailed you can be with your instructions, the less risk you have of something going wrong.

4. Keep the Contractor Hungry

This tip is incredibly important: Keep the contractor hungry. If you pay the contractor up front for the work, they have very little motivation to get the job done fast or right. They've already been paid. Therefore, as the landlord, it's wise to always give the contractor just enough to get by, but not so much that they aren't motivated to work. Work out payments on large jobs so that there are benchmarks to hit before payment is rendered. Also, on big rehabs it's typical to get "half down" so the contractor can pay for materials, but at least in the beginning, we'd recommend directly paying the store where they plan on buying the materials (so they don't pocket the money).

5. Ask for Invoices

Don't rely on your memory to know who to pay when. Not only is this a quick way to get taken advantage of, but it will also bring hell upon your bookkeeping. Require all contractors to give you detailed invoices for the work they do and keep an accurate record of all the money you spend.

6. Get a Lien-Release Signed

When a client doesn't pay a contractor, that contractor can place a lien on the property they were hired to do work for, making it difficult to ever sell the property until they are paid. This is known as a contractor's lien or a mechanic's lien. Therefore, when a large rehab project has been completed, always get the contractor to sign a lien release form. This form simply states that the bill has been paid in full, and the contractor releases their right to file a lien on the house.

7. Verify All Work Before Paying

After a job has been finished, always check to make sure the work was done correctly. You'd be surprised at the number of times we've received a phone call that the work was "done," only to find out the contractor had left a lot of loose ends not yet tied up. At times the work hadn't even been started! Therefore, always verify that the work is done and meets your expectations before you hand over the final bit of payment.

8. Reward Great Contractors

Finally, when you find a good contractor, do everything you can to hang onto them. Perhaps the best compliment you can give a contractor is fast payment. Many property management companies wait 30 days or longer to pay a bill, so stand out from the crowd by paying immediately. Also, don't be afraid of doing other small things to make the contractor feel valued, such as the occasional thank you note or small gift card after a big project. Good contractors never need to fight for work, so make sure you are their favorite client, and you'll never need to fight for *them*.

Wrapping it Up

Dealing with contractors may not be the most glamorous part of your real estate business, but it is one of the most vital. Working with the wrong contractor will not only cost you money, it could cost you your entire business. Finding and working with a great contractor can help you make more money, work fewer hours, and have far less stress doing it. The good news is: Dealing with contractors is a learned skill, something you will get better at if you make an effort to improve.

CHAPTER 13:
WHAT TO DO WHEN YOUR TENANT MOVES OUT

When a tenant tells you they are moving, the feeling you get is going to depend a lot on the tenant. If they were problem tenants who you never got around to "firing," getting word that they are moving is enough to make you do the happy dance! On the flip side, it's always terrible to hear that your favorite tenant, the one who's been with you for years (and paid rent on time every month, sent you Christmas cards every year, *and* kept the home in pristine condition) is leaving.

In either instance, your tenant is moving on, so now what? Throughout this chapter, keep in mind that each state has specific laws regarding the move-out procedures. Become familiar with the landlord/tenant laws where you will be conducting your rental business, and make sure your move-out procedure complies with your local laws and is specified in your lease.

Notice to Vacate

When your tenant tells you they are moving, it's important that your tenant gives you their notice *in writing*. (So be sure to include that requirement in your lease.) In addition to written notice being required by law in many states, it's also an important policy to have in place to avoid misunderstandings by both parties.

If your tenant simply calls you at the beginning of the month to tell you they are moving on such-and-such date, let them know that in compliance with their lease, you will need that information in writing. Whenever our tenants call with moving news, we always let them know that we will be sending them our "Notice to Vacate" form in the mail and ask them to complete it and return it to us as soon as possible. So why is it so gosh darn important for your tenant to give you written notice? Let's take a look at an example:

Josh is on a month-to-month rental agreement and decides he is going to move to that new apartment complex down the street that has the awesome new gym. So he picks up the phone and calls his landlord. The landlord starts making plans for his upcoming vacant unit by doing a walk-through, scheduling the unit turnover crew, advertising in the local newspaper, screening prospective applicants, eventually approving a new tenant, accepting their deposit, and scheduling their move-in date.

Meanwhile, a week before Josh is supposed to move, he changes his mind about moving into the apartment down the street because he found out the rent is $200 more than what he is currently paying. Josh feels kind of stupid for not looking into the rent cost sooner, so he pretends like none of it ever happened.

Fast forward to the end of the month, and the landlord is now stuck between a rock and a hard place. When the landlord calls Josh about when he will be returning his keys, Josh pretends like the landlord misunderstood. You see, he wasn't giving his notice when he called a few weeks ago; he was just letting the landlord know he was thinking about it, but he has since changed his mind.

Obviously, the landlord heard correctly when Josh put in his verbal notice, but he has no way to prove it or legally hold him to it. So after all of that work, the landlord is stuck with a tenant who isn't leaving and a new tenant who has put money down on his new place.

That's a sticky situation!

Written notice can help prevent situations like the above landlord ran into with Josh, but it also helps minimize other smaller misunderstandings as well—on both sides. To avoid any confusion, make sure the written notice to vacate you receive from your tenant includes the date the notice was given, as well as their name, current address, forwarding address, phone number, the date they plan on moving, the reason they are moving, and their signature on the bottom. As a reminder for the tenant when the are filling out their Notice to Vacate form, we also include a clause on the form that reiterates their vacating obligations. Feel free to use our Notice to Vacate form included in the appendix of this book or online at http://www.BiggerPockets.com/LandlordBookBonus.

Notice to Vacate Form

Please return this form to the manager when you are ready to give us notice that you will be moving. Thank you!

Today's Date: _____

Your Name: _____

Current Address: _____

Forwarding Address: _____

Phone Number: _____

Move-Out Date: _____

Reason for Moving: _____

I am aware that I must give my Notice to Vacate in writing at least _____days prior to the end of my Lease Agreement.

For Month-to-Month Tenancies: I am aware that in accordance with my Rental Agreement, if a full_____ Notice to Vacate is not given prior to the end of the month I will be responsible for rent for the following month and my lease will end the last day of the next month.

I am aware that I am legally obligated to fulfill the terms of my contract through it's entire duration.

I am aware that if keys to the Rental are not returned by the last day of the month I will be responsible for the next month's rent.

I am aware that I must leave the unit in the same condition as when I moved in by completing the entire move-out cleaning checklist. I am aware that any cleaning or repairs needed to the Rental after I have vacated will be billed at my expense and deducted from my security deposit.

Tenant Signatures:

_____   _____
Name   Date

_____   _____
Name   Date

Office Use Only: Date Received: _____

If you aren't big on paper and you have a website for your tenants, add a "Notice to Vacate" tab to your site. Rather than mailing your tenant a Notice to Vacate form, you can just direct them to your website, which saves both you and your tenant a trip to the post office.

Preparing for Your Vacancy

After you have received written notice that your tenant is vacating, you'll need to pull out their lease and review the terms of their contract. There are a few things you'll want to look for when your tenant gives their notice to vacate.

Did They Give Sufficient Notice?

Each state is different regarding how much notice the tenant is required to give their landlord, but some common requirements are 20 or 30 days' written notice before the end of the rental period (you'll want to check with your state to find out what applies to you and your tenants). Whatever minimum notice your state requires needs to be in your rental contract.

For month-to-month rental agreements (an agreement for an indefinite amount of time) in the State of Washington, tenants are required to give at least 20 days' written notice before the end of the month (or rental period) that they are moving. Our rental period runs from the first day of every month through the last day of every month. So, if one of our tenants gives their written notice on the 2nd that they will be moving on the 31st, they are golden. If they give their written notice on the 24th with plans to move on the 31st of the same month, that 20-day notice goes into the following month, meaning their rental agreement legally ends the last day of the following month. In this situation, the tenant is responsible to carry out the terms of their rental agreement through the fulfillment of the lease (the following month), including paying rent.

When a tenant doesn't give us adequate notice that they will be moving, we give them two options:

1. They can stay the extra month, or
2. They can continue with their plans to move before the end of the current month, but they will be held to their obligations.

If they choose option 2, we let them know they will still need to pay rent when it is due on the 1st, but we will market the unit as normal, and if we approve a new tenant, they will receive a prorated rent refund from the day the new tenant moves in.

Are They Breaking Their Lease?

When your tenant gives their notice that they are moving, find out when their lease expires. It will be important for you to know if they are moving out in the middle of their lease so you can make sure they understand what their obligations are. So, what are their obligations exactly?

A term lease, or a lease with a specific start and end date, has its benefits, one of which is that, as long as everyone stays in compliance, the tenant is guaranteed a home, and the landlord is guaranteed rent for the entire term of the lease.

So, when your tenant surprises you with the news that they are moving halfway through the lease, it doesn't have to be bad news. Even though the tenant is moving, they are still responsible to carry out the terms of their lease through the end date listed on the lease, most importantly paying rent until you can get the unit re-rented.

One common exception of the notice to vacate rule: If your tenant is in the military and they get reassignment or deployment orders, they may be allowed to break their rental lease without repercussions. It's a small price for us to pay for those serving in our US Military.

How Much is Their Deposit?

It's good to know how much your vacating tenant's deposit is for so you can be prepared to personally cover any overages (if there are any). Of course, you will still hold your tenant responsible for all charges associated with re-turning their unit to rent-ready condition, but let's be honest, it'll be a while before (or even if) your tenant pays for any overages above and beyond their deposit. We'll discuss later on in this chapter what to do if your tenant owes you more than what their deposit will cover.

Using the Deposit as Last Month's Rent

Lastly, when a tenant gives you their notice that they will be moving, the subject of using their deposit as their last month of rent will sometimes come up. While it's understandable why a tenant would want to do this (they are most likely saving up for their next place), **never** allow a tenant to use their deposit as the last month's rent. Make sure your lease has a clause that states that the deposit may not be applied toward rent at any time.

The deposit is held by the landlord *to encourage positive behavior by the tenant during their tenancy* and to ensure they return the home to its original move-in condition when they move. If you get lazy and let them apply it towards rent, what happens when they move out and you have damages to fix, cleaning to get the unit rent-ready for the next tenant, and a garbage bill to pay? Or even worse, what if they don't move out at the end of that month and don't pay rent the following month? Now you have no rent, no deposit, and hefty eviction costs on your hands. This is important, so we'll repeat ourselves here: *Never* allow your tenant to use their deposit for rent at any time.

The Move-Out Packet

After receiving your tenant's written notice that they will be vacating, send them a Move-Out Packet, which we've included in the appendix of this book, as well as online at http://www.BiggerPockets.com/LandlordBookBonus. The Move-Out Packet is an excellent tool to inform your tenants what the move-out process is going to look like and what you expect from them during this time. It's important for you as the landlord to set the precedent for them that they still have obligations to oblige, even though in their heads they might have already moved on to the next phase of their life.

In your Move-Out Packet, begin with a letter confirming that you have received their notice to vacate, then give an overview on what is included in the rest of the packet to make the move-out process as smooth and easy as possible for them. Here's what our Move-Out Packet looks like:

- Acknowledgment of Notice to Vacate
- Itemized List of Common Deposit Deductions
- Tenant Duty Checklist: Vacating and Cleaning Instructions
- Forwarding Address Form for Disposition of Deposit and Refund
- Copy of Move-In Condition Report
- Copy of Rental Agreement or Lease (Optional)
- The Move-Out Survey

Acknowledgement of Notice to Vacate

In the Acknowledgement of Notice to Vacate, you are simply confirming that you have received the tenant's written notice that they will be moving. Our Acknowledgement of Notice to Vacate looks like this:

Acknowledgement of Notice to Vacate

Dear _____:

On_____ 20_____ we received written notice of your intent to vacate the home you are now renting by_____, 20_____. Your tenancy will terminate on_____20_____, at _____am/pm.

Residence

Before turning in your keys, the residence will need to be returned to it's original move-in condition. This means you will need to remove all of your personal belongings and thoroughly clean all surfaces before moving. We understand moving is a busy time in a tenant's life, so we have included a checklist to help you with this process.

Security Deposit

For your convenience and to assist you during your move, we have enclosed a Tenant Duty Checklist as well as your Move-In Condition Report. Remember any cleaning or damages not completed or remedied by you will be billed at your expense. An Itemized List of Common Deductions has been enclosed for your information. Your Disposition of Deposit and refund will be returned to the forwarding address you supply on the Forwarding Address Form within 14 days after you have moved. It is our desire to return your full deposit to you.

Maintenance

Please give us a call or leave a note of any maintenance issues you are aware of that may not be noticeable when we inspect your unit after you have moved.

Moving Day

When it gets close to your moving day, please call us at _____or email us at_____ of when you will be completely moved out and the home returned to *clean*, rent-ready condition. We will conduct our final walk-thru after the home has been completely vacated.

It has been our pleasure working with you; we wish you all the best in the future.

Sincerely,

Management

Itemized List of Common Deposit Deductions

Nothing motivates a tenant more to replace their dead light bulbs than knowing that if they don't, it could cost them $5 per bulb for us to hire someone else to do it. Our Itemized List of Common Deposit Deductions is fairly generic and includes a statement that says, "This list has been prepared for your information only. Actual charges will vary." The point of this list is to simply motivate your tenant to do as much themselves as possible because, let's face it, moving is not fun. It's a lot of hard work, and by the time the tenant gets everything moved out and into their new place, the last thing they want to do is deep clean and get the home they have lived in for years returned to move-in condition. The responsible ones will buck up and do it anyway. It's those others you've got to impress the importance upon that they need to do it themselves - which is where this list comes in. In reality some things may cost more, some less, but the point is to let the tenant see with their own eyes that it will cost them, probably a lot more than they think.

Itemized List of Common Deposit Deductions
This list has been prepared for your information only. Actual charges will vary.

Cleaning

Kitchen

Clean Kitchen – Normal Cleaning	$150.00
Clean Kitchen – Deep Clean	$300.00
Oven & Stove (Inside/Outside/Underneath)	$75.00
Refrigerator (Inside/Outside/Underneath)	$75.00
Dishwasher (Inside/Outside)	$75.00
Microwave (Inside/Outside/Underneath)	$25.00
Cabinets (Wash Inside/Outside)	$200.00
Countertops	$25.00
Sweep and Mop Floors	$25.00
Dust and Wash Trim	$15.00
Wipe Down Walls	$25.00
Drip Pan Replacement	$35.00

Living Room/Dining Room/Office/Recreation Room

Normal Cleaning	$100.00
Deep Clean	$200.00
Sweep, Vacuum, Mop	$50.00
Dust and Wash Trim	$25.00
Wipe Down Walls	$25.00

Bathroom

Bathroom – Normal Cleaning	$100.00
Bathroom – Deep Clean	$200.00
Bathtub/Shower	$50.00
Sink	$25.00
Cabinet (Inside/Outside)	$25.00
Toilet	$25.00
Sweep and Mop Floors	$25.00
Dust and Wash Trim	$25.00
Wipe Down Walls	$25.00
Wipe Down Fixtures	$15.00

Bedroom

Bedroom – Normal Cleaning	$100.00
Bedroom – Deep Clean	$200.00

Sweep, Vacuum, Mop	$50.00
Dust and Wash Trim	$25.00
Wipe Down Walls	$25.00

General, Damages, Repairs and Disposal

Repair Drywall	
6" x 6"	$75.00
12" x 12"	$150.00
Wash Light Fixture (Each)	$15.00
Replace Interior Door	$100.00
Replace Exterior Door	$250.00
Clean Ceiling Fan	$25.00
Change Light Bulb (Each)	$5.00
Replace Smoke Detector Batteries	$25.00
Replace Carbon Monoxide Detector Batteries	$25.00
Replace Smoke Detector	$75.00
Replace Carbon Monoxide Detector	$75.00
Replace Window Blinds	$40.00
Replace Sliding Door Blinds	$60.00
Carpet Cleaning (Normal)	$150.00
Carpet Cleaning (Deep Clean)	$200.00
Carpet Spot Treatment (Each)	$15.00
Replace Filter	Varies
Replace Carpet (12' x 12' Room)	$500.00
Replace Wood, Vinyl, Linoleum, Etc. Flooring (12 x 12 Room)	$500.00
Repaint One Room (12' x 12')	$300.00
Repair Kitchen Cabinet	$150.00
Repair Kitchen Drawer	$150.00
Wash Window (Including Tracks) (Inside)	$20.00
Fill Nail Holes	$25.00
Replace Interior Door Knob	$25.00
Replace Exterior Door Lock	$50.00
Pest or Rodent Extermination	$150.00
Odor Removal	Varies

Exterior

Trash Removal (Per Load)	$100.00
Mow Lawn	$35 - $75
Weed Flower Beds	$35 - $100
General Labor (Cleaning, Painting, Normal Repairs, Trash Removal, Etc)	$25 - $40/hr
Specialty Labor (Electrician, Drywall Repair, Plumber, Etc)	$70 - $100/hr

Tenant Duty Checklist: Vacating and Cleaning Instructions

The Tenant Duty Checklist is the single most important part of the Move-Out Packet, as it details exactly what the tenant needs to do in order to return the home to rent-ready condition. Be as detailed as you want here. Here's a look at our Tenant Duty Checklist: Vacating and Cleaning Instructions.

Tenant Duty Checklist
Vacating and Cleaning Instructions

For your convenience we have prepared a checklist of items you will need to complete prior to moving day. Remember, all expenses related to us returning your home to rent-ready condition, as recorded in your Move-in Condition Report, will be billed at your expense and deducted from your security deposit. For this reason, it is extremely important that you allow ample time to perform every item on this checklist. Also enclosed is an Itemized List of Common Deposit Deductions for your reference. After you complete the checklist completely, your Disposition of Deposit and refund will be returned to you within 14 days. Before moving, please remember to leave your forwarding address on the enclosed Forwarding Address Form.

Kitchen
- Walls: Wipe down all wall surfaces and doors, remove all nails and fill holes with spackling. Remove excess spackling to create smooth surface.
- Trim & Misc: Dust and wipe down all trim, heaters, vents, switch covers, and door knobs.
- Light Fixtures: Wash all light fixtures and replace burnt out light bulbs.
- Windows: Clean all windows, including tracks and window sills.
- Blinds: Dust and wipe down all blinds. Replace any broken blinds.
- Cabinets: Empty all cabinets and drawers, vacuum if needed, and thoroughly wash inside and out.
- Refrigerator/Freezer: Empty contents. Remove all shelves and drawers and completely wash. Wash down all surfaces inside and outside of refrigerator. Return shelves and drawers to proper positions.
- Oven/Stove: Oven: Clean racks and inside of oven to completely remove all stains. Stove: Wash down all surfaces of stove and stove top, including the sides, knobs, door, and drawer. Replace drip pans. Clean exhaust hood, fan, and filter.
- Dishwasher: Run empty dishwasher with dishwasher liquid. Thoroughly wipe down inside and out, including the door seal.
- Microwave: Wash down inside and outside of microwave.
- Sink/Fixtures: Clean sink, drains and faucets.
- Countertops: Clean all countertops and backsplash, including edges and corners.
- Floors: Sweep, mop, and wipe down all floor surfaces, including underneath refrigerator and stove.

Living Room/Dining Room/Office/Recreation Room
- Walls: Wipe down all wall surfaces and doors to remove smudges. Remove all nails and fill holes with spackling. Remove excess spackling to create smooth surface.
- Trim & Misc: Dust and wipe down all trim, heaters, vents, switch covers, and door knobs.
- Light Fixtures: Wash all light fixtures and replace burnt out light bulbs.
- Windows: Clean all windows, including tracks and window sills.
- Blinds: Dust and wipe down all blinds. Replace any broken blinds.
- Shelves: Wipe down all shelf surfaces.
- Stove/Fireplace: Clean inside and out.
- Floors: Sweep, mop and wipe down hard floor surfaces. Vacuum all carpet surfaces.

Bathroom

- Walls: Wipe down all wall surfaces and doors, remove all nails and fill holes with spackling. Remove excess spackling to create smooth surface.
- Trim & Misc: Dust and wipe down all trim, heaters, vents, switch covers, and door knobs.
- Light Fixtures: Wash all light fixtures and replace burnt out light bulbs.
- Windows: Clean all windows, including tracks and window sills.
- Blinds: Dust and wipe down all blinds. Replace any broken blinds.
- Cabinets: Empty all cabinets and drawers, vacuum if needed, and thoroughly wash inside and out. Clean mirror.
- Sink/Fixtures: Clean sink, drains, faucets, towel racks and toilet paper holder.
- Countertops: Clean all countertops, including edges and corners.
- Bathtub/shower: Completely clean all surfaces inside and outside of bathtub/shower.
- Toilet: Completely clean all surfaces of the toilet, including inside, and outside.
- Floors: Sweep, mop and wipe down all floor surfaces. Be sure to get into the corners and behind/around the toilet.

Closets

- Walls: Wipe down all wall surfaces and doors, remove all nails and fill holes with spackling. Remove excess spackling to create smooth surface.
- Trim & Misc: Dust and wipe down all trim, heaters, vents, switch covers, and door knobs.
- Light Fixtures: Wash all light fixtures and replace burnt out light bulbs.
- Shelves: Wipe down all shelf surfaces, including rods.

Garage/Outbuildings/Landscaping

- Remove all personal belongings and trash from the property
- Sweep shelves and floor surfaces of all garages and outbuildings.
- Mow and weed eat lawn. Dispose of grass clippings.
- Remove all weeds from the flower beds.

General Make-Ready

- Ensure all smoke detectors are accounted for and have a working battery.
- Ensure carbon monoxide detector is accounted for and has a working battery.
- Ensure all damages have been repaired.
- Ensure all personal property and trash is removed from the property.
- After you have completed this checklist, do a final walk-thru to ensure all items have been properly completed.
- Please leave garage door openers in the kitchen.
- When you have completed this checklist and have done your final walk-thru of the property, please give us a call to arrange returning your keys.

Your carpets will be professionally cleaned after you have returned your keys. We have enjoyed the opportunity to have you as a tenant. Please let us know if we can assist you in any way in the future.

Thank you!

Forwarding Address Form for Disposition of Deposit and Refund

Each state is going to be different regarding the deadline by which the landlord is legally obligated to return the tenant's deposit and/or Disposition of Deposit detailing any deductions after the tenant has moved, but in the State of Washington where we operate, landlords have fourteen days. There are two important reasons why you need to get your tenant's new address:

1. If they get a refund, you'll want to make sure it reaches them.

2. If they owe you additional money for repairs, cleaning, unpaid rent, unpaid utilities, etc., you will want to know where they moved so you can try and collect the debt.

Prior to us creating the Forwarding Address form, tenants would notoriously forget to get us their new address. Whether they actually forgot or just didn't want us knowing their new address because they knew we would be coming after them with a hefty cleaning bill is another story. But regardless of previous tenant intentions, this form is worded in such a way that now we almost always get our tenants' new addresses, even the ones receiving a bill instead of a refund. We just ask them leave it on the counter as they are going out the door of their rental one last time, and we collect it when we do their move-out walk-through. Easy peasy.

If you are unsuccessful in getting your tenant's new address after sending them this form and have exhausted any other forms of communication you have for them, most states just require that you send the deposit and/or Disposition of Deposit to their last known address—in other words, the address of the rental from which they just moved. Here's a look at our Forwarding Address form.

Forwarding Address Form for Deposit Refund

Your closing statement and deposit refund will be returned to you in the form of one check made out to all tenants. Before you move, please complete this form and leave it in the kitchen. Failure to return this form may delay your receiving your deposit refund.

Today's Date: _____ Rental Address: _____

Tenant Name: _____

Forwarding Address: _____

Phone: _____ Email: _____

Tenant Name: _____

Forwarding Address: _____

Phone: _____ Email: _____

Tenant Name: _____

Forwarding Address: _____

Phone: _____ Email: _____

Tenant Name: _____

Forwarding Address: _____

Phone: _____ Email: _____

Tenant Name: _____

Forwarding Address: _____

Phone: _____ Email: _____

If there is a preference on who should be sent the deposit refund, please indicate that here:
_____(Name)

Copy of Move-In Condition Report

When your tenant moved in, you should have completed and had them sign and date a Move-in Condition Report of the exact condition of the rental at that time. It's good practice to include a copy of this form with your Move-Out Packet to refresh their minds of the actual condition of the unit when they moved in. Human brains tend to get a little foggy over time, and it's common after a tenant has lived in a place for years to falsely remember certain things about the property, such as that the hole in the wall was there when they moved in or that the garage door already had that dent. The Move-in Condition Report will help with all of that.

Copy of Rental Agreement or Lease

Since the rental contract you signed with your tenant should cover the legalities of the move-out procedure, it's not a bad idea to include a copy of it with their Move-Out Packet as well in case they misplaced their original copy they got when they moved in. It's especially a good idea if your tenant didn't give sufficient notice or in other ways displayed evidence that they wouldn't be complying with the move-out procedure in one way or another. When you show them the legal obligation *with* their signature, it makes it a lot harder to argue and will at least make them think twice!

The Move-Out Survey

Tennis professional Venus Williams once said, "The day I'm not improving is the day I hang up the racket." Therefore, the final item in our Move-Out Packet includes a survey for the tenants to fill out that asks specific questions like:

- How would you rate the service you received from us?
- How would you rate the quality of service you received while renting your home in regard to handymen and contractors?
- How would you rate your overall experience with us?
- What is your overall impression of the home you rented?
- What did you like most about the home you rented from us?
- What did you like least about the home you rented from us?
- Do you have any suggestions for improvements we could make to the home?

253

- Would you rent from us again or refer others to us in the future?

Questions like these make it easy for the tenant to answer honestly and will either validate a job well done or show you areas where you need improvement. Either way, your tenants are your "customers," and while the motto "The Customer is Always Right" definitely does not apply to tenants, their insight into the home and the way you operate your business is extremely valuable. We should always be striving to improve our business, and the survey is a good way to hold your feet to the fire. The more we can improve our business, the more efficient we become, the happier our tenants will be, and the more cash flow we can potentially produce. We'd call that a win-win-win.

Move-Out Survey
Tell Us What You Think!

Thank you for giving us the opportunity to have you as our tenant. In an effort to continually improve our rentals and our service, please consider taking this brief survey and let us know what think about us and about the home you rented!

On a Scale of 1 (Lowest) – 5 (Highest)

How would you rate the service you received from us? 1 2 3 4 5

How would you rate the quality of service you received while renting your home in regards to handymen and contractors? 1 2 3 4 5

How would you rate your overall experience with us? 1 2 3 4 5

In Your Own Words...

What is your overall impression of the home you rented?

_____

What did you like **most** about the home you rented from us?

_____

What did you like **least** about the home you rented from us?

_____

Do you have any suggestions for improvements we could make to the home?

_____

Additional Comments?

_____

Would you rent from us again or refer others to us in the future? Yes/No

Thanks for taking the time to complete this short survey! Please leave the completed form in the home when it has been completed. We value your opinion.

Remember, everything you include in the Move-Out Packet is there for a specific purpose:

1. You want the rental returned to move-in ready condition by the tenant so you can move on with as little hassle and turnover time as possible.

2. You want to reduce questions, confusion, or misunderstandings as to how the move-out process works.

3. You want to reduce the temptation for bad or lazy tenant behavior at move-out.

4. Lastly, with the survey you provide for your tenants to complete, you want to know in which areas the tenants were happy and in which areas you can improve on both the administrative side and the property side.

The Move-Out Inspection

The final walk-through is your time to inspect the premises and make sure it looks the way it did when they moved in and to document anything that does not. To do this, you will take with you a Move-Out Condition Report, possibly part of the same document as the Move-In Condition Report, both of which are included in the appendix of this book, as well as at http://www.BiggerPockets.com/LandlordBookBonus. Just like when you did the Move-In Condition Report, document everything about the condition of the property. Remember, you can never document too much. Notice a hole in the door? Write it down. Notice a stain on the carpet? Write it down.

Different landlords have different strategies for carrying out the walk-through, but one rule is necessary: Never do your sole move-out walk-through while the tenant is still living in the home, as damages can easily be hidden with furniture, and more can happen while they are moving out. We once had a tenant move out of a classic, beautifully restored duplex. While they were moving their furniture out on moving day, one of their helpers literally dragged a heavy piece of furniture through the entire house, over wood floors. When we did the move-out walk-through, everything looked great - except for the half-inch deep gouge in the beautiful wood floors that went straight from the bedroom through the middle of the dining room and living room and out through the front door! Obviously, that "helper" wasn't using the brain God gave him, and it cost the tenant a pretty penny. Not to mention the horror and disappointment of seeing a beautiful piece of history destroyed by such stupidity. Had we done the walk-through prior to the tenant moving, that damage wouldn't have happened yet, and therefore, it possibly wouldn't have been noticed or documented until too late, after the Disposition of Deposit and refund had already been returned to the tenant.

So when should you do the move-out inspection? As we said a moment ago, different landlords have different processes. Some landlords will meet the tenant at the property after all the tenant's stuff has been removed to do the walk-through with the tenant. Others like us simply perform the inspection alone at our convenience. By doing the inspection alone, we can take our time to thoroughly inspect everything without the tenant there to distract us, and it also eliminates the tenant arguing about any specific damages or problems they caused. Keep in mind, some states require that the tenant be present when doing the move-out inspection, so be aware of your local laws. Additionally, if the tenant requests to be present, we will, of course, accommodate their request. But to be honest, most tenants are relieved they don't need to be there.

How to Conduct a Move-Out Inspection

Your first impression when you pull up in front of the unit will give you a pretty good indication of how the rest of the property is going to look. If the flower beds and lawn are overgrown, you see broken blinds in the living room window, and there is a pile of garbage in the backyard, brace yourself before going through the front door. If it looks great from the get-go, then congratulations, the rest should be easy!

When doing the move-out walk-through, inspect the entire property from top to bottom, just like when your tenant moved in. Take pictures (or a video) of everything, including up-close pictures of things you need to remedy; all your visual evidence will come in handy later on if any disputes arise from the tenant regarding deductions from their security deposit. Things like dusting the trim, wiping down the walls, cleaning out the oven, washing the outside of the appliances, cleaning beneath the refrigerator, and really getting into the corners while deep-cleaning are some common areas tenants miss, so while doing your move-out walk-through, just remember to be thorough so you don't get stuck with footing the bill for your tenant's grime.

Here are few other things to look for during the move-out inspection. Some of these can be charged to the tenant—if it is damage or an expense they caused—and others are just general upkeep.

- Unapproved alterations to the unit, such as changes in paint color
- Strange odors
- Evidence of smoking or pets
- Holes behind doors (from slamming the door open)
- Holes *in* doors or walls (we will never understand this one)
- Fleas and other bug evidence
- Missing or burnt out light bulbs
- Missing smoke detectors or carbon monoxide detectors
- Missing blinds

In addition to looking for damages caused by the tenants, now is also a good time to look at the property's condition and assess what you can do to improve it for the long-haul. You probably will not be able to charge the tenants for the upgrades below, but the tenant turnover period is a great time to improve the condition of your property to keep it running in tip-top shape. Therefore, while doing your walk through, keep an eye out for the following.

- Does the caulk around the bathtub, shower, or sink need to be redone?
- Are there any signs of plumbing leaks, roof leaks, or drippy faucets?
- Are there any signs of mold?
- Do all the doors open and close easily?
- Are the carpet and other flooring in good condition, or are they at the end of their life?
- Is anything outdated that can be replaced to attract more rent and better tenants, such as overhead lights, countertops, fixtures, cabinets, or appliances?
- Is the exterior of the building in good shape? How's the paint, siding, and caulking?

Turning Over the Unit

After you have completed the walk-through of your vacant unit, it's time to make the necessary repairs and schedule the appropriate people (if you haven't already) to get the unit ready for the next tenant. This is the time you either turn the unit over yourself or send in your contractors, maintenance man, carpet cleaner, cleaner, plumber, electrician, and whoever else is needed to get the unit rent-ready.

For maximum profitability, it's important to make this as quick a process as possible. In, out, and you're done and ready for your next tenant! If the vacated tenant is monetarily responsible for any of the things you are doing to get the unit rent-ready, be sure to get bids and keep receipts to minimize disputes and cover your rear.

The Disposition of Deposit

The Disposition of Deposit form is a one-page document that spells out in detail what happens to the vacating tenant's security deposit, including an assessment of charges being held against their deposit. Preparing the Disposition of Deposit is one of the final tasks a landlord must do for their former tenant after they have vacated. Of course, our *favorite* Dispositions of Deposit to complete are the ones where the tenant gets an entire refund back minus the cost of mandatory carpet cleaning. Those are usually also the tenants who paid their rent on time, took care of their unit, didn't cause unnecessary problems or hassles, and who will receive a great reference when a rental reference is requested.

Whether your tenant has any security deposit deductions or not, you as the landlord are required to send the tenant a statement itemizing the exact refund or balance owed, which is where the Disposition of Deposit comes in. The landlord is required to send the tenant the Disposition of Deposit and corresponding refund (if they get one) within a certain amount of time, which varies from state to state, so be sure to become familiar with the specific law in your jurisdiction. In Washington State, the penalty for the landlord who doesn't send the Disposition of Deposit within 14 days after the tenant has vacated is harsh. The courts can order the landlord to repay double the amount what the original deposit was for, EVEN if the tenant owed a balance. Here's a quick example.

Linda purchased her first single-family rental house a couple of towns over last year. Her first tenants just moved out after only 12 months of occupancy. After they moved, she drove over to the property to take a look around and noticed the tenants didn't clean anything, and there were some damages as well that she didn't remember and that were also not listed on the Move-in Condition Report. Linda was disappointed the previous tenants were so negligent in caring for the *home, and she was definitely not prepared for the $600 of her own money she had to put into the house to go towards the cleaning bill and damages, in addition to the tenants' deposit of $750.*

She got it done, though, and three weeks later found a new tenant and moved on. At one point about a month after the former tenants moved, they called her to find out where their deposit was. Linda informed them that she used it towards the damages they left behind. They denied responsibility and demanded she return their full deposit to them immediately, or she would see them in court. Linda wasn't worried since she had her Move-in Condition Report and pictures of the damages they caused. She decided to call their bluff. Some time later Linda finds herself in court because the former tenants claimed she stole their deposit. Linda explains to the judge that she didn't "steal" it and had used the tenants' deposit only towards the tenants' damages and cleaning up their grime. The judge awards the former tenants $1,500 anyway because Linda didn't realize she had to send the tenants a statement detailing the deductions within 14 days.

Ouch. Ignorance is not bliss, folks. It can hurt—a lot.

The actual Disposition of Deposit doesn't need to be anything fancy and can be as simple as a one-page form, like the one we use, shown below and included in the appendix of this book as well as online at http://www.BiggerPockets.com/LandlordBookBonus.

Disposition of Deposit

Tenant Name(s) _____ Date _____
Rental Address _____
Mailing address _____

Credits (Funds Held in Deposit)

Security Deposit $_____
Other Rent $_____
Pet Deposit/Key Deposit $_____
Other Deposits $_____
Total Credits $_____

Debits (Funds Being Withheld from Your Deposit)

Nonrefundable Fees $_____
Rent for period_____ through _____ $_____
Unpaid Utilities $_____
Lock Change: $_____
Late Fees, NSF, Legal Services: $_____
Carpet Cleaning: $_____
Cleaning (See Below): $_____
Damages (See Below): $_____
Other (See Below): $_____
Total Debits: $_____

Additional Details Concerning Debits: (Any Additional Details Will Be Included on Additional Pages)

_____
_____
_____

Total Credits $_____
Total Debits $_____

TOTAL AMOUNT OF MONEY DUE TO ___TENANT ___LANDLORD: $_____

Manager Signature _____ Date_____

The final credit or debit listed on this Disposition of Deposit does not waive the Landlord's right to pursue additional claims should they become apparent.

If your tenant will not be receiving their whole deposit back, always include pictures, bids, receipts, and copies of their lease stating their responsibility for the charges. We always highlight the areas of their lease we want to draw their attention to as well. The point is to include as much information as possible to support the deductions to reduce the likelihood of a dispute that ends up in a time-consuming, stressful confrontation at best—and a visit to the courthouse at worst. Basically, you're showing the tenant what you would be showing the judge, which, if you've covered all your bases, should be enough to silence any challenges that would have been forthcoming.

Your Disposition of Deposit should include the date, the tenant's name, the address of the rental, the tenant's current (forwarding) address, followed by an itemization of all credits and debits involving the rental and the security deposit.

As you can see on our Disposition of Deposit, we begin with the tenant's credits, the total amount of money we have held in trust as their deposit. According to the tenant's lease, we record how much the tenant paid in the following areas:

- Security Deposit
- Other Rent
- Pet Deposit/Key Deposit
- Other Deposits

After the credits, we break down the deductions in these categories, leaving extra space below for additional details, if needed. Remember, be as specific as possible in your details, and if you need more room, just include additional pages:

- Non-Refundable Fees
- Rent for Period_____ Through _____
- Unpaid Utilities
- Lock Change
- Late Fees, NSF, Legal Services
- Carpet Cleaning
- Cleaning
- Damages

- Other

Finally, total it all up, subtract out the debits from the credits, and you'll arrive at your final number. At this point, either you owe your tenants or they owe you. Whichever it is, make it clear on the Disposition of Deposit and mail it within your state specific allotted timeframe to your tenant's forwarding address *or* their last known address if you were unable to obtain their new address. If you really want to cover all your bases—and this next tip is required in some states—when you send the Disposition of Deposit, mail it via Certified Mail or for a slightly cheaper option, request a Certificate of Mailing.

The purpose of either Certified Mail or Certificate of Mailing for the landlord is simple: evidence of mailing. For Certified Mail, the envelope is affixed with a "Certified" label with a unique serial number, a duplicate of which the post office will postmark and give to the purchaser. The serial number is then tracked by the post office to provide proof of where, when, or even *if* the letter was delivered. This comes in handy for the landlord if their tenant denies receiving the mailing or claims the landlord didn't meet their state requirements to issue a deposit statement and corresponding refund within the allotted timeframe. With a Certificate of Mailing, you are only given a validated receipt of the time and date of the mailing—not proof of delivery. When we mail our deposit statements to our vacated tenants, we use the Certificate of Mailing. It gives the postmark evidence we want and shows we met the requirement in Washington State to mail the Disposition of Deposit to the tenant within 14 days after they have vacated. For the record, we have never needed the evidence of mailing, but as a landlord, it never hurts to be prepared.

At some point, you may find more deductions against the security deposit that you should have charged to the tenant *after* you have already sent back their Disposition of Deposit and refund. If you send your tenant a new bill for those additional items, they may argue that because they weren't listed on their final Disposition of Deposit, they cannot be held accountable for the charges. To help combat this, you may want to add a small clause at the bottom of your Disposition of Deposit form that says, "The final credit or debit listed on this Disposition of Deposit does not waive the landlord's right to pursue additional claims should they become apparent."

What Happens if the Tenant Disputes Their Disposition of Deposit?

After your tenant receives their Disposition of Deposit, you will most likely never hear from them again unless they are looking for a rental and are in need of a reference. However, if they decide to dispute it, you have a couple choices:

1. Ignore them.

2. Let them know you have reviewed their file and have found the Disposition of Deposit to be accurate based on the documentation they were already sent.

Of course, they will still most likely be madder than a hornet, but if you followed our recommendation to adequately document everything (in writing, with pictures, video, receipts, and bids) and you have followed all your state specific laws, you have already shown them that you have a solid, legal claim. Most likely they will drop it, but in the event that they do not, you are already prepared for court due to your prior thoroughness.

If the tenant pushes a legal battle and if you wish to avoid having to go to court over a security deposit dispute, you do have the option of simply returning the disputed amount of the deposit to the tenant, as much as it would hurt. The question you need to ask yourself is, "Is it worth it?" Would you rather swallow your pride, have the matter disappear, and be out the disputed dollar amount, or would you rather face it head on and keep what you are legally entitled to? That's a choice only you can make.

What if the Tenant Owes More Money Than Their Deposit Will Cover?

Our first thought was: *There is a dead body in this refrigerator.*

Of course, upon closer inspection, there was no dead body, just rotting food, garbage, and other unknown objects. The smell was unlike anything we had ever experienced before. The unit was left with garbage covering nearly every square inch of the floor, holes in the walls, doors missing, crayon on nearly every surface, and that smell that permeated every cubic foot of space. All in all, it took nearly $4,000 to get the unit fixed up and ready to re-rent, including the costs of lost rent.

Luckily, when the tenant moved in, we had collected a double security deposit due to a minor red flag when performing her tenant screening. But as any third grader can tell you, having a deposit for $1,000 and a bill for

$4,000 means one thing: We were in the hole $3,000. So what now? We wanted to include this section because although it's unfortunate, this will happen to you.

Of course, making sure you don't get screwed over by a tenant starts at the beginning, by only accepting the best tenants, collecting the right deposit amount up front, and adequately training your tenant while they live there. But even if you have incredibly strict screening standards and give the tenant detailed instructions on how they should clean their unit when vacating, someday a tenant will end up owing you money. So let's talk about some different options you have at this point. The option you choose will depend slightly on the situation itself, the amount owed, and the kind of tenant with whom you are dealing. But let us give you five possible choices you have for collecting that debt.

1. Ignore It

If the amount owed is very small, you may simply choose not to pursue it after sending the Disposition of Deposit and just move on. If they owe you $50, it might not be worth the hassle to try and collect it, so simply send the invoice, and if it is never paid, mark that in your tenant's file for future reference. Someday you'll get a reference request for that tenant, and at that point, the tenant will wish they had paid that small bill. Of course, you are not losing everything when you choose to accept that loss. The one thing you will gain is a valuable lesson, so take it gratefully! Learn from your mistakes and put systems in place so it doesn't happen again, if possible. This might be far more valuable than the money owed to you.

2. Bill Repeatedly

If you don't want to simply ignore it, but the sum is too small to take larger action, you can also set up a system that mails out a new invoice monthly, as a constant reminder that they owe money. Perhaps someday (like after they get their tax return), they will pay the bill. It might cost you a dollar a month to do this, but someday it might pay off.

3. Negotiate With Them

Recently, another of our tenants left his apartment unit in a hurry and ended up owing about $200 to us from the cleaning and repairs needed, above what his deposit would cover. Of course, we sent the Disposition of Deposit form to the tenant in the mail, and upon receiving it, he immediately called to complain. ("Complain" is a nice way of describing the words he used on the phone. We even had to hang up on him the first few conversations due to his rage.) This tenant expected to get his entire deposit back, but luckily we had photos and documentation to prove every one of our repairs. (Which, of course, is why a well-documented Move-In/Move-Out Checklist is vital for any landlord.) Our in-house manager spent nearly a week negotiating with the angry tenant, and in the end, we agreed to accept 50 percent of what was owed. Three days later we received $100 in the mail, which we gave entirely to our manager to thank her for her efforts in collecting.

4. Send it to Collections

Collection agencies are designed to pursue individuals for their past-due payments. They use a variety of techniques to get this money, including tracking down the tenant and calling them repeatedly until the debt has been paid. For their services, collection agencies typically charge a hefty fee—oftentimes 50 percent of the debt recovered. If you are fairly certain you won't get the money from the tenant, you can send the invoice to collections and let them deal with it. Who knows? Someday down the road you might get a check in the mail. We will typically choose the collection agency route when the tenant owes between $1,000 and $4,000 and they ignore our attempts at collecting the debt on our own. In fact, this is what we did for the tenant in the previous story. You were probably hoping we had a happy ending to that story, but let's be honest: Getting screwed comes with the territory when you are a landlord. Perhaps someday we will walk out to our mailbox and find a check for several thousand dollars. Unlikely, but we can hope!

5. Take Them to Small Claims Court

If the money owed to you is substantial and you think you can get the money from the tenant if a court makes them, you could pursue a lawsuit in small claims court. This court is designed to help people sue others without the need for lawyers and a lot of money. Usually, for less than a few hundred dollars in fees, you can sue someone, and if you win, you will receive a judgment against them. This judgment could be used to garnish wages or tax returns. Plus, this judgment can follow the tenant around for years, even showing up on background checks when they apply for a rental property in the future.

Wrapping it Up

Because tenant turnover is one of the highest expenses you will ever face, it is necessary for you, the landlord, to maximize efficiency during this time. That is what our goal for this chapter has been. Additionally, you'll notice a lot of the things a landlord does when their tenant move-out happens simultaneously with other tasks. For example, while you're doing your walk-through and completing your Disposition of Deposit, you are also dealing with contractors, marketing your property, and approving a new tenant. The key is to have a specific process in place for handling vacating tenants so you'll know exactly what to do and when to do it. By having a specific process, you will be able to clearly communicate to the tenant what is expected of them and also what they can expect from you during this time. This in turn minimizes confusion, misunderstandings, and laziness, making a smooth transition for both you and the tenant.

In this book we have now come full circle, from the day your tenant moves into your property to the day your tenant moves out. But one aspect we haven't discussed is how *you* should manage this process within your own business. After all, as we discussed at length in Chapter 2, property management is a business, so the way you run it is just as important as any other aspect. In the next chapter, we're going to dive deep into the organizational structure of your landlording business and discuss your office, your bookkeeping, and more.

CHAPTER 14: BUSINESS ORGANIZATION AND BOOKKEEPING

It's time to drill down and talk about one of the most unsexy, yet vital, aspects of the landlording business: keeping everything organized. We know there is a temptation to skip this chapter and move on to something more exciting, but if you want to be an effective landlord for the long haul, this chapter might just be the most important part of this book. It doesn't matter if you haven't bought your first property yet or if you own 100 units. This chapter is vital.

The 3 Benefits of an Organized Landlording Business

In this chapter we are going to dive into the actual, physical organization of your office. Before we get there, we want to lay the groundwork for *why* organization is so important. Specifically, organization is important for three major reasons:

1. Freedom

Being organized is not about rules, it's about *freedom*. The freedom to relax when you are away from your desk. The freedom to enjoy your work, knowing it's all getting taken care of. Organization helps keep your stress level at a minimum because there is a plan and place for everything.

- You won't need to worry, "Was that bill paid yet?"

- You won't need to ask, "How much money is our rental actually bringing in?"

- You won't need to wonder, "Did that maintenance job ever get taken care of?" Or, "Did I ever call that tenant back?"

David Allen, author of the incredible productivity book *Getting Things Done* calls that concept "mind like water." It's the idea that your mind becomes still, like a calm lake, when everything is organized and out of your head. The goal of this chapter is to walk you through the process of doing just that: getting your property management system out of your head and into files, computers, spreadsheets, and software. Only then can you achieve "mind like water."

2. Legality

In addition to keeping stress to a minimum, organization is also about staying legal. The IRS requires accurate reporting about the income and expenses on your property. Therefore, we're going to spend some time showing you a few different ways you can keep records about how much is coming in and how much is going out.

3. Profitability

Finally, organization is about profitability. That's right: Being organized can actually make you more profitable in your business. By knowing where all the money is coming from and where it's all going, you will always have an accurate picture of how your rentals are performing, allowing you to take action to correct it.

As you begin to set up the organization for your business, keep these three goals in mind. Does the action you take move you closer to these goals or further away? Can you improve upon them? As we talked about in Chapter 2, one of the things that sets a business apart from a hobby is the goal of always improving. Being organized will help you do just that.

The good news is, organization is largely a "set it and forget it" event. Once you have a system in place, your business organization will become second nature to you. You'll spend less time organizing, less time working, and more time enjoying life. But first you have to set up the perfect system, and that's what we're about to do.

Let's start our discussion on organization with your office.

12 Things Your Office Should Have

As a landlord, you need an office. It doesn't matter if your office is in a separate room in your house, in a corner of your bedroom, or in the back of your garage. You need a centralized location where you can keep your rental business in order. Without it, you'll struggle to stay organized and end up overwhelmed. So take some time this weekend to build yourself a nice little office somewhere in your house. Then it's time to organize that office. The following are twelve things every rental property manager's office should have. Does yours?

1. File Cabinet

The world of real estate has a LOT of paperwork in it. Although there is a shift in American society toward a paperless office, dealing with paper will still be a major part of your job. Thus, your file cabinet will become your best friend. A file cabinet is where all the documents related to your rental properties will be organized. If you have just one or two rentals, a small, portable file holder will probably be sufficient, but as you add units, you will likely want something larger and more secure. If you are low on funds, you can typically pick up a used metal file cabinet at any thrift store for under $10 or buy something new from an office supply store for under $100. Pick up some large hanging files, as well as numerous individual colored folders, one for each of the following categories:

- Insurance Info
- Mortgage Info
- Purchase Docs
- Monthly Income Statements
- Bank Statements
- Tenant Interactions
- Rehab and Maintenance
- Tenant Files
- Receipts
- Miscellaneous Paperwork

This way, each property will have one overarching folder file, as well as several color-coded folders for easy retrieval of information. Need insurance docs for 123 Main Street? Oh, that's in the 123 Main Street file, red folder. Easy, convenient, and fast. By setting this system up at the beginning of your investment business, you are able to grow in a much more organized manner later. Don't wait to organize until it's too late. Start right, start organized, stay organized.

2. Printer/Scanner/Copier

Get yourself a high-quality printer/scanner/copier machine—because you are going to need it. Don't skimp on quality here; with printers, you truly do get what you pay for, and if you buy a cheap one designed for regular families, you will spend more time cursing at your printer than actually getting work done. You need a printer designed for businesses. We'd recommend getting a medium-grade tabletop laser printer that has scanning capabilities ($200–$400). You likely will not need a color printer (you can always print a colorful flyer at Staples), but you do want something reliable and fast. If you'll be using a laptop to manage your rentals, we'd recommend getting a printer with wireless printing capabilities, so you can print from wherever you happen to be sitting in your house or office.

3. Fax Machine

A lot of the younger folks reading this book might not even know what a fax machine is, as email is quickly eclipsing the need. However, we still send and receive documents via fax several times a week involving our rentals. The truth is, a LOT of businesses still don't know how to use email and rely on the fax machine to get things done. Because you will be interacting with those businesses, you need to be able have the capability to send and receive a fax. The printer you buy may have fax capabilities, which is great, but you'll also have to have a phone line directly to your home to operate that function, which many people no longer have. Instead, there are several online fax companies that give you a fax number, and you can send and receive faxes directly online. Check out www.MyFax.com or www.HelloFax. com for two options if you plan to go this route.

4. Inbox

We are not referring to your email inbox, but rather your office inbox. This is a box (literally, it could be a cardboard box, though we use a desk tray) that contains anything that will require your immediate attention. In our business, we typically receive 10-20 pieces of mail every day, most of which are rental-related: bills, insurance correspondence, bank correspondence, tenant correspondence, bills—did we mention bills? Besides the mail, we are also constantly receiving phone calls, emails, faxes, and whatever else, adding to the list of things we need to do. Trying to keep track of everything in our heads would be overwhelming. The inbox is designed to collect every single item in our business that needs to be dealt with in the near future, after which it will be filed away in its appropriate permanent home. For more on this inbox system, be sure to read David Allen's book *Getting Things Done*.

5. Key box/System

One of the mistakes we made early on in our business was not having a good system for keeping track of keys—and it was a disaster. Start this process today, even if you have just one rental! We'd recommend getting key tags (which you can buy at any office supply store) and labeling each key in a way that will make perfect sense to you BUT NOT a random stranger. In other words: Do not write the address on the key. If you lose the key, some stranger will know exactly where it goes. Then, create a system for keeping track of those keys. Do not throw them in a plastic bag or on your own key ring, but hang them in one central location in your office. You might also consider the idea of buying a combination "key box" from a hardware store and attaching it directly to the property. These combination key boxes are about $30 and can be installed directly on a building, ensuring you always have access to the building.

6. Bill Payment System

As you collect rentals, you'll also collect a lot of bills. Each bill has a different due date, so keeping track of what to pay and when to pay it can be tough. The easiest method we've found for keeping track of bills is placing all bills first in the "inbox," and then after we've gone through the inbox to process each item, placing the bill in our "to-pay" desk tray. Once a week we simply sit down and write out all the bills we need to pay and then stamp "paid" on the bill, along with the check number and date paid. We then put the paid bill in the "receipts to process" (for the monthly profit/loss income statement) file for that property. That said, when small contractors submit a bill to us, we will often pay it immediately, as we want to reward excellent work

271

and to be known among our private contractors as quick-paying.

7. Mileage Tracker

Keeping track of the miles you drive for business is incredibly important when tax time rolls around. Many of the miles you drive will be deductible, saving you more money than you might think. However, trying to keep track of mileage can be a pain. Although there are apps for managing this, the best system we've used is simply to keep a calendar or a notebook in our vehicle. We just record what property or business establishment we visited (for which property), and at the end of the year we can calculate the total miles driven for each property.

8. Tenant Directory

No matter how many units you are currently managing, it's important that you have all your tenants' names, addresses, phone numbers, emails, and other contract information available when you need it. The easiest way to do this is in an online spreadsheet like Google Docs. This way, you can access the tenant directory anytime, from anywhere. In addition, regularly print out your tenant directory so you have it in your office for easy phone number retrieval.

9. Phone Number

Your office is going to need a phone number. Yes, you could use your existing phone number, but having a dedicated number just for your rental business will come in handy, especially as you grow. The first tenant we ever placed into one of our rentals when we were getting started *still* calls our personal cell phone numbers, even though they have the business number, because they know it's a direct line to us. By having a dedicated phone number, you are not tied to your business phone number. If you go on vacation, you can enjoy yourself and hand off calls to someone else. If you decide you no longer want to answer phones as part of your landlording job and want to outsource that, you can easily do that without it affecting where your tenants call. Most importantly, your personal number stays your personal number.

Keep in mind: You don't necessarily need a separate p*hone* for your business, just a separate phone *line*. There are several online services that will give you a phone number, and all calls will be forwarded to whatever phone you want to ring. Our favorite and the least expensive (it's free!) is Google Voice. Google Voice allows tenants to call our business phone line, and we can designate ahead of time any phone we want to ring. For example, during the day we can have all calls go to our in-house manager's phone, and at night all calls can go to voicemail or an after-hours maintenance person. We can also check voicemail and text messages online and receive text message transcriptions of all of the voicemail messages. In addition, we can record different voicemails to be used at different times of the day (for example, during business hours and after business hours). There are other similar services you could look into as well, such as Grasshopper.com, which has more features than Google Voice but also costs more.

10. Maintenance Tracker

Finally, you need a system for keeping track of your maintenance requests. If you have just one or two tenants, it may be easy to keep track of all ongoing maintenance issues in your head, but we don't recommend it. Instead, create a maintenance tracker. You can do this in several ways, such as on a spreadsheet or in an online property management software. However, what we've found the most success with is using "work orders" with every maintenance need that we pin to our office bulletin board. Once the maintenance has been completed, verified, and paid, the work order is placed in the tenant's file. For extra organization, you could also staple a copy of the receipts for the work that was completed to the completed work order.

11. Contractor List

Always maintain a list of your current contractors, so when a maintenance call comes in, you can easily call your top guys without needing to dig up the phone number again. This list changes often. You may want to keep this list in a spreadsheet like Google Docs, so you can update it and access it at anytime. Our contractor list is divided by the type of contractor they are—general contractor, handyman, electrician, plumber, landscaper, and so on—and lists their name, contact information, hourly rate, and any special notes about them, such as if they are particularly gifted at painting, tenant turnovers, big jobs, small jobs, cleaning, etc.

12. A Website

Does your business need a website? Probably not, but it can't hurt. Websites add a degree of professionalism to your business and serve some very functional purposes as well. With a website, you can advertise your vacancies, allow tenants to print out documents (applications, rules and regulations, etc.), give tenants the ability to pay rent online or submit maintenance requests, and more. Websites can also be costly to build and annoying to maintain, unless you really know what you are doing. The less you know about how to build or operate a website, the more expensive it will be. If you do decide you want a website for your rental business, consider the following options:

WIX.com or SquareSpace.com: Wix and SquareSpace are similar web companies that allow you to build a website, even if you have very few computer skills (no coding is required). You simply need to click and drag items around a pre-made template, and you can have a website up and running in a matter of hours. Both services allow you to create the website before paying anything, which can be helpful for testing out ideas. Currently, you can have either for around $12 a month.

Wordpress: If you have some technical skills, you could build your own website using Wordpress, a content-management system. To build your own site on Wordpress, you will need buy a domain name online for around $10 per year and buy hosting on a website like GoDaddy.com or BlueHost.com, which for a basic plan costs around $5 per month. Then, you'll either use a free Wordpress theme or purchase a Wordpress theme and customize the look and feel of the site, whichever you decide.

Web Design Company: The third and most expensive option is to simply hire an individual or company to build you a website. Prices for this kind of service are all over the board, but typically start around $500 and go all the way into the thousands of dollars. If you are looking for a great site but don't want to mess with options 1 or 2, this may be your best option.

Although the size of your business could alter the above 12 items, these are the most important items we use in our office to maintain strict organization. As we are sure you noticed, the organization of our business is designed to help systematize everything into repeatable processes that anyone could follow. By having these systems and processes, we can outsource any of the tasks to an employee as we see fit, giving us more free time and less worry that things are not being done right. Remember, organization is not about rules—it's about freedom, staying legal, and making greater profits. So take some time this weekend to organize your life and see what a difference it makes for you.

Now let's move on and discuss a topic that confuses and overwhelms most new landlords: the bookkeeping. Trust us, bookkeeping is far easier than you probably fear. In fact, we predict in just a few moments you'll be a master.

Bookkeeping Basics

The goal of bookkeeping is to have an accurate record of all the money going in and out of your business. Also known as "doing the books," bookkeeping is a vital task in your rental property business and something that is not optional, but required. The same benefits to being organized that we talked about earlier (freedom, legality, and profitability) hold true for bookkeeping. When you know exactly how your business is doing at any given time, you are able to make better decisions and sleep more easily at night. But don't worry—you don't need to be a professional accountant to have accurate records. Instead, anyone can become a successful bookkeeper by following these five simple steps.

1. Keep Things Separate

The first rule of bookkeeping for your real estate business is to make sure you keep your personal expenses 100 percent separate from your business expenses. Not only does this make the bookkeeping easier, but also from a legal standpoint it's a bad idea to commingle personal and business funds, especially if you are using (or plan to use) an LLC or other legal entity. So set up a separate account for your real estate investments; this includes a separate bank account, savings account, and credit cards.

If you have multiple properties, a question that often arises is, "Should I use just one bank account for all my rental properties or one bank account per property?" Although you could do it either way, if you have fewer than five properties, we would suggest having separate bank accounts, savings accounts, and credit cards for each property. However, if you are investing in multifamily properties, all the units at one location with one loan, they are considered "one" property. So you may have 20 units, but if that is made up of five fourplexes spread across town, you only need five separate accounts.

As you gain units, you will likely want to begin using one "management" account to manage all the ins and outs of your business for simplicity. You don't want to have to deal with 40 checking accounts when you have 40 properties! However, the bookkeeping becomes a little more time-consuming, as you will still need to run the numbers separately for each property. When you use one checking account per property, this becomes a much easier process, but when you need to divide up hundreds (or thousands) of transactions into separate properties, it takes some additional work. When you get to this point, you will likely want to use a more professional bookkeeping system like Quickbooks.

2. Track Receipts

The second rule of bookkeeping is to keep every receipt and designate which rental the receipt was for (we like to handwrite the property and the purpose ON the receipt). This is not only helpful for deducting the right amount at tax time (and proving to the IRS that you are legit), but it will also help keep you organized as to where your money is going, and what bills were paid and what bills were not (because trust us, businesses will bill you for things that you already paid for, and it's up to you to catch their mistake!).

For example, when we get a bill for a carpet cleaner and pay it, we always write the check number we used to pay the bill, the date the payment was made, and the property the bill was for. Then, we place the bill in the colored folder for "receipts to process" in the file for that property. If you are using a computerized bookkeeping software, you will likely want to record this transaction immediately, maybe even using the program to print the check that goes out. If you are doing the books by hand or with a spreadsheet, you may wait until the end of the month to track these expenses properly. When you have just a few properties, doing the books by hand can be easy enough, but as you gain units, you will eventually want to upgrade to a more professional accounting software, such as QuickBooks or Xero, or you may even consider hiring a bookkeeper.

3. Itemize Income and Expenses

Every dollar that flows in or out of your business must be categorized and tracked. This is when the above-mentioned receipts come in really handy. If you are doing this with a computerized accounting software, you will likely enter this information semi-daily as income is received or bills are written. If you are using a spreadsheet, you may decide to wait until the end of the month to categorize each item, though we would caution you against waiting too long. The longer you wait to categorize the dollars going in and out of your business, the greater the chance of making a mistake or forgetting what a certain expense was. This is the benefit of itemizing your income and expenses on a regular basis, which is much easier to do with professional accounting software.

When itemizing the income and expenses, we find it best to categorize them in the same categories that the IRS lists on Schedule E, the form you'll need to fill out each year at tax time. The following is a screenshot taken directly from the 2014 Schedule E form:

Type of Property:						
1 Single Family Residence	3 Vacation/Short-Term Rental	5 Land	7 Self-Rental			
2 Multi-Family Residence	4 Commercial	6 Royalties	8 Other (describe)			
Income:		Properties:		A	B	C
3 Rents received		3				
4 Royalties received		4				
Expenses:						
5 Advertising		5				
6 Auto and travel (see instructions)		6				
7 Cleaning and maintenance		7				
8 Commissions		8				
9 Insurance		9				
10 Legal and other professional fees		10				
11 Management fees		11				
12 Mortgage interest paid to banks, etc. (see instructions)		12				
13 Other interest		13				
14 Repairs		14				
15 Supplies		15				
16 Taxes		16				
17 Utilities		17				
18 Depreciation expense or depletion		18				
19 Other (list) ▶		19				

As you can see, the expense categories that the IRS defines are:

- Advertising
- Auto and Travel Expenses
- Cleaning and Maintenance
- Commissions
- Insurance
- Legal and Other Professional Fees
- Management Fees
- Mortgage Interest Paid to Banks, etc.
- Other Interest
- Repairs
- Supplies
- Taxes
- Utilities
- Depreciation Expense or Depletion (we call this Capital

Improvements)

- Other

Therefore, we try to place every expense into one of these categories. Of course, there is the "other" category if something just doesn't seem to fit, but we seldom use this. It's just easier to make it fit within one of the other listed categories.

Typically, finances are tracked on a monthly basis, as in "January 1– January 31" and "February 1–February 28." If you are using a spreadsheet, you can simply list the above categories on the left-hand side of the screen and make one column for each month. (We've included this spreadsheet with the bonus content for this book, which you can get online at http://www.BiggerPockets.com/LandlordBookBonus.)

Basic Rental Property Income / Expense Tracker

4. Reconcile With Your Bank

Bookkeeping is somewhat of a "game" or a "puzzle." To win the game, your books should match perfectly with what your bank account shows for that property. We just talked all about tracking your income and your expenses for the property using either accounting software or a spreadsheet. Now it's time to compare what should be to what is. Again, your goal is to make the numbers line up perfectly between your bookkeeping and bank account statement, a process known as "reconciling your bank account."

The purpose of bank reconciliation is to double-check everything to make sure your books are accurate. Sometimes banks or businesses will mess up, and you'll be charged for things you were not supposed to be charged for. For example, let's say that you purchased insurance for 123 Main Street for $348.83. In your accounting software or spreadsheet, you recorded that

$348.83 and labeled it correctly as "insurance." But when you looked at your bank statement, you noticed TWO charges, each for $348.83. The insurance company double-charged you! You might think this is rare, but trust us: It's not. There is seldom a month that goes by that we don't discover some kind of mistake that some business did to overcharge us. Because of this process of bank reconciliation, we can get on the phone with whoever is at fault and straighten everything out. Bank reconciliation can help save you a lot of money, and it can also help you know when you messed up and forgot to record something correctly (but of course, we never mess up anything).

When reconciling with your bank, you should also pay attention to the starting and ending balance of your bank account, and they should match. If you started with $1,000 in your account and you received $800 in income and $700 in expenses, you should be left with $1,100 in your account at the end of the month (because you will have "made" an extra $100 during the month). Of course, this is an incredibly simple example, but the same concept applies no matter how large of an operation you are running. This is just another way of double-checking (or triple-checking) to make sure everything is correct.

As we mentioned, bank reconciliation is a bit of a game or a puzzle, and when you "win" after double and triple-checking, it feels good! We know that sounds incredibly nerdy, but trust us: When the numbers line up perfectly, you will sleep better at night.

5. Create Accurate Reports

Lastly, after entering in all this data for the property, you now will be able to generate certain reports about how well your property is running. If you are using professional accounting software, this can be as simple as clicking a button. If you are doing the books by hand, though, you will be slightly limited in the kinds of reports you can generate.

The most common report you will be looking at is often known as a "profit-loss statement," and it shows all the forms of income for the property, all of the expenses, and the cash flow that resulted. If you are doing your bookkeeping in a spreadsheet, you are essentially creating the profit-loss statement each month while entering the income and expenses. If you are using accounting software, you simply need to export the profit-loss report to see how things are going in your business.

The purpose of looking at these reports is to get an accurate snapshot of how your business is running over different perspectives and over time. For example, want to know how much cash flow your business generated in the past month? You can find that out easily. Want to see a graph of the expenses over the past three years? A report can show you that trend. Again, unless you are a pro with spreadsheets, this will be much easier using accounting software. If you are not using a professional accounting software, you can simply give the spreadsheet you have been building throughout the year to your CPA, as it contains all the information they (or if you do your own taxes, you) will need.

Bookkeeping can seem overwhelming at first, but the process quickly becomes fairly routine. If you don't feel comfortable doing it or don't have the time, consider hiring a bookkeeper to help you make sense of everything. You may also want to sit down with the CPA who will be doing your taxes at the end of the year and have them explain exactly how they want you to do the books to make their job easier (and cheaper for you). The above five steps are fairly basic, but they should help you get started on the right foot.

As you can see, there are a lot of different ways you can do the books, but the important thing is that they are done—and they are done correctly. By doing so, you will realize greater freedom in your life, less stress in your work, and the increased profitability of your operation.

Wrapping it Up

You'll never hear someone exclaim that organization and bookkeeping is their favorite aspect of business. However, it may just be the most important part so give it the time and attention it deserves, especially until you have your system operating at peak performance. Over time, this process will take just a few moments each month, and you'll enjoy more time free of worry, knowing your business is running like a well-oiled machine.

Now, let's turn to the final chapter of this book, where we'll piece together all the fragmented lessons you've learned so far to ensure you become the most successful landlord your town has ever seen.

CHAPTER 15:
13 PRINCIPLES FOR BEING AN
INCREDIBLE LANDLORD

Do yourself a favor and pat yourself on the back, as most people never make it to the end of a book. The very fact that you have tells us there is something special about you—a yearning to be better. A desire to excel. A mission for excellence. These very traits will likely make you shine in whatever field you enter, but combined with the tips and knowledge in this book, we think you'll find unbelievable success and profitability in your landlording future.

As we prepare to close up this book, we want to leave you with thirteen principles for being an incredible landlord. These principles have been inter-woven throughout this book, so this chapter should come as a bit of a review to you, but because of their importance, we feel it's necessary to hit on them now one final time.

1. Commit to Taking Your Landlording Seriously

Landlording is the business of protecting and growing a real estate invest-ment through the careful placement and oversight of tenants. All the work to acquire rental properties means nothing if you don't manage correctly—because great landlording is how you protect that investment from failure and how you help it grow to become more valuable each passing year. Land-lording is not for everyone; it's for the special few who are willing to take up the mantle of responsibility in an effort to make a brighter financial future for themselves and their family. It's for those willing to work hard, think creatively, and accomplish dozens of different, changing tasks. Does that describe you? Are you willing to do the work needed to preserve and grow your investments? Have you fully committed to the success of your landlording business?

2. Run Your Business Like a Business

Landlording success is not a mystery. Those who succeed at landlording do so because they treat their business like a business, not a hobby. But it's not enough to simply run a business; after all, most businesses fail. Successful business owners set themselves apart with their commitment to eight specific principles:

- Business owners create systems and repeatable processes that help them build a "machine" that runs smoothly.

- They continuously improve their business, looking for small and large ways to tweak their operation to make more profit while simplifying the tasks that need to be accomplished.

- They are firm but fair when dealing with their customers and clients.

- Business owners outsource and delegate tasks in their business that others can do with better results, focusing on the tasks that only they can do to grow their business.

- They maintain strict financial control over their company, knowing at all times how much money is going in and how much is going out, and they are able to document every penny.

- They focus on customer service, knowing that their business relies heavily on their reputation.

- Successful business owners maintain a solid understanding of the rules and laws that govern their industry, always seeking to work within the law to create the best business possible.

- And finally, successful business owners ask for help when needed, knowing that they don't have every answer in the book but are willing to seek knowledge from other business owners and through books, podcasts, and other educational sources.

As you read that above list, ask yourself this question: Does your landlording business look like this? Do you follow those eight principles? Are you prepared to treat your landlording business like a world-class business?

3. Prepare Your Business Before Signing Your First Lease

Before you sign your first lease, you must build a solid foundation for your landlording business. Even if you already own rentals, you can reinforce that foundation today using the tips we covered in Chapter 3. By using asset protection, buying proper insurance, and setting up a bank account, you are able to keep your investment secure no matter what life (or a tenant) throws at you. By preparing documents and creating a policy binder, you'll "get your house in order" before accepting rent and dealing with questions from tenants, leading to a more simplified landlording business.

Getting to know the neighbors can help you keep a physical eye on your investments, while great bookkeeping will help you keep a financial eye on the same. Additionally, making sure your property is in the *right* condition to rent will be key to attracting the best tenants, so don't skimp on the condition. Finally, before renting out a property, you must determine the best rent to charge to maximize your profit but minimize your vacancy. All of these steps can be done *before* you open the doors for business and will help ensure a positive experience right from the start.

4. Be Mindful of Fair Housing

An entire chapter of this book was dedicated to the concept of Fair Housing, as much of your landlording business will deal with these federal, state, and local laws. If you want to avoid fines and possible jail time, don't discriminate against any of the protected classes (race, color, religion, sex, national origin, familial status, disability, and other locally protected classes). Be careful in the language you use in your advertising, on the phone, in person, in your documents, and anywhere else in your business. And maintain good records in case someone ever wants to bring a case against you for violating the Fair Housing Laws.

5. Find Incredible Tenants Through Smart Marketing

Peaceful landlording is a result of having great tenants. But great tenants are not standing on the side of the road with a sign that says, "Great tenant!" Instead, you need to go out there and attract the best tenant using a variety of marketing techniques. Newspapers, yard signs, flyers, the internet, and other people can all be great sources. Part of your business will be finding the most effective means to reach potential tenants in the most cost-effective way. Are you prepared to go out and search for the best tenants, rather than waiting for them to approach you?

6. Pre-Screen to Eliminate Duds

Once potential tenants begin getting in touch with you, you are going to hear from a lot of bad apples. Therefore, before taking an application (and before you even show a property), it's important to put on your pre-screening goggles and try to sift through the options. Pre-screening begins during the advertising period and continues throughout every interaction. Not only are you trying to get a feel for the tenant, but you are also trying to let them get a feel for you and your company. Setting and stating your minimum qualifications are a large part of the pre-screening process, as many of the "duds" will leave before taking up your time because they know they won't qualify. When you meet the tenant in person, they'll have a lot of questions that you should be prepared to answer. But you should also have questions ready to get to know them better.

7. Use Your Application to Screen for Amazing Tenants

When a potential tenant decides that your property is going to be the best option for them, they must fill out an application. The application is designed to give you an inside look into their life and help you make a quantitative decision, not one based on your gut. The application should be thorough but not so overwhelming that it turns off the good tenants. When the prospect applies, it's important that you run a thorough screening of the tenant that looks at their criminal history, their credit history, their rental history, and their income stability. When a tenant passes all your minimum qualifications, accepting them will be a joy because you know you are placing your investment into the hands of someone well-qualified. When you deny a tenant, however, you must be careful in what you say and do, as to avoid any complaints about discrimination.

8. Sign a Solid Lease

You've done all the work to find and acquire the best tenant, so now it's time to make it official (and legal) through a lease agreement. Lease agreements should be state-specific and thorough, carefully spelling out the duties and responsibilities of the tenant and the landlord. The lease will become incredibly important should the business relationship between you and your tenant go south, which it may. So don't cut corners; instead, make sure your lease—and the signing process—are as flawless as possible.

9. Train Your Tenant From Day One

In a perfect world, tenants would read every word of the lease and abide by every statute, but this is just not the case. Tenants must be *trained* to follow the lease and become great tenants. They also must be trained to respect your office hours, pay rent correctly (and on time), and communicate effectively with you. In return, you must manage your properties efficiently and effectively through routine inspections and prompt communication, which will also keep your risk of getting sued to a minimum. As a landlord, you should always be looking for ways to increase your income and reduce your expenses, helping your business to generate more profits over time.

10. Handle Problems Carefully and Effectively

No matter how well you train your tenants, you will have problems. Tenants will pay rent late, they'll get in fights with neighbors, they'll break their lease, they will complain and make demands, and sometimes they will need to be evicted. In addition, your property will break down over time and need to be repaired, so you will need to have a system in place to deal with these issues. These situations are entirely normal for a landlord—they are simply part of the cost of doing business. You can choose to freak out, get stressed, and shut down because of these problems, or you can deal with them swiftly within your landlording system and navigate a crash landing successfully with minimal (or no) stress.

11. Have a System for Dealing With Contractors

Dealing with contractors is one of the most important - and most frustrating—parts of a landlord's job. However, by having a system in your business that deals with contractors, the process can be streamlined. This begins with finding and screening the best contractors, which is not a mystery but a process. Then, the way you manage those contractors will help you determine how well they work, so manage effectively.

12. Keep Organized

Being organized will help you achieve greater freedom, stay legal, and increase the profitability of your rentals. Organization encompasses your entire business, from the way your office is set up to the website you use to showcase your properties. Always seek to become more organized and more professional in your business, and your business will thank you with greater profits. Additionally, remember that good decisions are made when you have good data, so keeping accurate records is vital to the continued success of your business. Create a system for bookkeeping and stick with it. Not only is it helpful for knowing how your rentals are financially operating, but it will also make tax time a much less stressful event.

13. Transition Tenants Out Carefully

Your tenants will not stay forever, so you must have a system in place for dealing with the turnover of tenants. Turnover can be one of the most costly expenses for your business, so minimizing the time a unit sits vacant and maximizing the condition of that property is incredibly important. This begins with setting clear expectations for your tenants through the delivery of a Move-Out Packet, continues through the proper disposition of their security deposit, and ends when you get a new, incredible tenant to take their place.

Final Words of Wisdom

Finally, we want to address all those questions that we could not answer. That's right, we fully admit that there are topics that we could not cover within the pages of this book, despite wanting to create the most authoritative book on landlording ever written. This is because there are just too many possibilities that exist in the world of landlording to cover every single scenario. This is why we want to leave you with three final tips for helping you as you journey onward:

Don't Let Your Education Fade

Henry Ford once said, "Anyone who stops learning is old, whether at 20 or 80. Anyone who keeps learning stays young. The greatest thing in life is to keep your mind young." We find this incredibly applicable to landlords. Just because you have come to the end of this book, don't think your educational journey is over. If you are not a regular listener of the BiggerPockets Podcast, we would invite you to start there. Each week, The BiggerPockets Podcast brings you interviews with real-life real estate investors from across the country, sharing their stories and strategies for being a successful real estate investor. Many of the guests are landlords, some with hundreds of units, and the lessons you'll learn each week will blow you away. Best of all, the Podcast is free. If you have an iPhone or iPad, you can find it in iTunes, and if you have an Android phone, find it on the Stitcher app. Or if you simply want to listen on your computer, just head to http://www.BiggerPockets.com/podcast. In addition to listening to the Podcast, be sure to follow The BiggerPockets Blog at http://www.biggerpockets.com/renewsblog for new posts each day written by real-life landlords and other real estate investors. So keep learning, keep growing, and stay young.

Connect With Local Landlords

Next, connect with local landlords in your area! You can learn a lot from them (both what TO do and what NOT to do) and share ideas, contractors, and resources. Don't be an island; reach out there and start building relationships. If you are unaware of local investors, check out www.BiggerPockets.com/meet to search BiggerPockets members. With hundreds of thousands of members, chances are there are many experienced investors right there in your town.

Stick Close to the BiggerPockets Forums

Finally, when you have questions that need specific answers, ask them in the world's largest real estate question forum: the BiggerPockets Forums. Each day there are thousands of conversations taking place, with hundreds of real-life landlords volunteering their time to help guide those people who have questions. So jump on today and introduce yourself to the community in the New Member Introduction Forum, and then start asking questions when you have them. We'll all be there for you. If you don't yet have a free BiggerPockets account, sign up today at www.BiggerPockets.com and join the only social network dedicated toward making its members financially free.

Wrapping it Up

Landlording doesn't need to be a drag. It doesn't need to be stressful, complicated, or risky. However, only you can decide how your landlording business will turn out. There is no one else to blame. Perhaps that is one of the reasons we love real estate so much. When the value of our stocks drop 20 percent, we can blame the economy or the hot shots on Wall Street. But when we struggle in our real estate, we can't blame anyone but ourselves. While that might sound like a negative, it's not—because the inverse is also true. We have the power to make our business exceed our wildest expectations if we so choose. You have that same power, so use it! Your landlording business will run as well as you make it run. You will be as successful as you work to be.

Our goal in this book was to give you the tools you need to become a successful landlord. However, tools are useless if you don't pick them up and use them! So don't be that person who reads a book, puts it down, and immediately forgets what they read. Put your newfound knowledge into action! Don't settle for mediocrity. Make it your goal to run the best, most efficient landlording business in your town.

We know you can do it.

Appendix

A collection of forms and state-specific landlord-tenant law summaries to help you on your real estate journey. You can also download all this information for free by visiting www.BiggerPockets.com/LandlordBookBonus.

DISCLAIMER: The forms provided in this book are examples only and are provided for educational purposes only. The author(s) and publisher assume no responsibility or liability for, and make no representations or warranties of any kind in connection with, your use of the forms. The author(s) and publisher provide the forms "as-is" and disclaim all representations and warranties of any kind. You should not duplicate or use the forms without careful consideration of the particular situation for which it may be used. The author(s) and publisher do not intend the forms to cover each and every lease situation, nor can the forms anticipate your specific needs. **Rental forms are important legal document and you should consult a licensed attorney in your area before making any contractual commitment or signing any such agreement. If you use any of these forms, have a licensed attorney review and advise on your use of them.** State laws vary and certain provisions in these sample forms may not be enforceable in every state. You may have a specific situation not addressed by these samples, and the attorney can address that particular issue for you.

Forms Table of Contents

1

Standard Lease Agreement
Copyright by BiggerPockets Inc. All Rights Reserved.

DEFINITIONS: Wherever in this Lease the term "Landlord" is used, it shall be construed to also mean The Manager/Owner/Agent, as may be indicated by the specific context. Wherever in this Lease the term "Tenant" or "Tenants" is used, it shall also include any family, visiting friends, dependents, guests, employees, or other invitees, as may be indicated by the specific context.

NAMES: This Lease is entered into between _____, (Tenant(s)) and _____, (Landlord) on _____ (today's date.) Each Tenant is jointly and severally liable for the payment of rent and performance of all other terms of this Lease. Occupancy of the Premises shall be limited to the following individuals (children and adults) and any children born of   Tenants   listed   on   this   Lease:

_____

_____

ADDRESS: *Subject to the terms and conditions in this Lease, Landlord rents to Tenant, and Tenant rents from   Landlord,   for   residential   purposes   only,   the   premises   located   at:* _____*(Herein after referred to as the Premises).*

PHONE NUMBERS: Landlord's Current Phone Number: _____ Tenant's Current Phone Number: _____. Tenant shall notify Landlord of any change to her/his telephone number immediately upon obtaining one, if there is a change.

TERM: Tenant shall lease the Premises for the calendar period beginning_____ and ending_____. In the event that Landlord or Tenant does not elect to terminate this Lease at the ending date therein (with 30-day advanced written notice), then the term of this Lease shall continue on a month-to-month basis.

RENT: The following terms apply to the rent payment for this Lease.
   a. **AMOUNT:** The rent for the Premises will be $_____ per month. For the period from Tenant's move-in date, _____, through the end of the month, Tenant will pay a prorated amount of $_____ to Landlord. This prorated amount will be due on the first day of the second month of the Lease term, and a full month's rent will be due before Tenant can take occupancy of the Premises. Tenant shall also pay $_____ towards the last month's rent of the Lease term.
   b. **OTHER RENT DUE:** Additionally, Tenant will pay parking or other monthly fees, if any, of $_____ to cover_____.
   c. **RECEIPT OF MONEY PAID:** Tenant has paid $_____ for security deposit and has paid $_____ for _____ fee(s); Tenant has also paid $_____ in _____ for rent, receipt hereby acknowledged. Landlord initials: _____
   d. **NEXT PAYMENT:** The next payment is due on _____ in the amount of $_____.
   e. **DUE DATE/LATE FEE:** Rent (including, without limitation, any monthly parking fees or other fees) shall be due on or before the 1st day of each month in advance, without notice or demand, and without deduction or offset. Monthly rent payments must be RECEIVED no later than the end of the "grace period" which is the _____ day of the month. (Weekends or holidays occurring

Tenant's Initials: _____

2

within those days shall not be added to the grace period.) If a monthly rent payment is received after the grace period, it shall be late and Tenant shall be charged a late charge of $_____ with an additional charge of $_____ for each day the rent is not paid after the grace period until rent has been paid in full including late fee billing and eviction notice. Late fees and all other balances due with rent shall be considered rent as due. Payment must be RECEIVED no later than 5:00 on the last day of the grace period. This late charge is due with the monthly rent payment. An additional $35.00 will be charged for any dishonored check returned for any reason. Bad health, reduced hours at work, the loss of job, financial emergency or other circumstances will not excuse any late rent payments. Interest will accrue at 18% per year on any amount due and owing to Landlord from the time that any such amount became due and payable. The foregoing of late fees and charges shall not be construed as a waiver by Landlord of its right to declare a default under this Lease.

f. **EVICTION NOTICE:** Should the Tenant fail to pay rent by the due date, Landlord may serve an eviction notice, as required by applicable laws (if any), the cost which shall be paid by the Tenant in the amount of a $75.00 service fee.

g. **PAYMENT OPTIONS:** Rent must be paid by ____Check ____Cashier's Check _____Money Order _____ Online _____ Bank Debit _____ Other: _____. Unacceptable forms of payment will be returned and not credited towards any payments. Checks must be made payable to _____.

h. **PARTIAL PAYMENT:** Landlord's acceptance of any partial rent payment shall not waive Landlord's right to require immediate payment of the unpaid balance of rent, or waive or affect Landlord's rights with respect to any remaining unpaid rent.

SECURITY DEPOSIT: Contemporaneously with the execution of this Lease, Tenant shall deposit with Landlord a security deposit in the amount of $_____ as security for the return of the Premises at the expiration of the term of this Lease in as good condition as when Tenant took possession of the Premises, normal wear and tear excepted, as well as the faithful, timely and complete performance of all other terms, conditions and covenants of the Lease. Provided that Tenant has paid all amounts due and has otherwise performed all obligations hereunder, the security deposit will be returned to Tenant without interest (unless required by applicable laws) within the lesser of (i) sixty (60) days after the expiration of this Lease or (ii) the maximum time period allowed by applicable laws, further provided that Landlord may deduct from the Security Deposit prior to returning it any amounts owed by Tenant to Landlord. Except to the extent otherwise required by applicable laws, Landlord may, at its discretion, commingle the security deposit with its other funds.

FURNISHINGS AND APPLIANCES: The following appliances are supplied with the Premises: (   )Refrigerator ( )Stove, ( ) Dishwasher ( ) Other: _____. Tenant agrees to keep all such appliances clean and in good repair. Supplied appliances may not be removed. The following furnishings are supplied with the Premises _____. If any furnishings break or are damaged, they are Tenant's responsibility. Maintenance of the furnishings is Tenant's sole responsibility, and Tenant will keep all such furnishings in good repair. Tenant's use of such furnishings shall be "AS-IS", and Landlord has not made, does not make and hereby disclaims any representations or warranties (including, without limitation, any warranty of merchantability or fitness for a particular purpose) as to the existence of or physical condition of the furnishings or the suitability or usefulness of the furnishings for Tenant's intended use.

Tenant's Initials: _____

3

PREMISES USE: The Premises is to be used only as a residence by the Tenants who have signed this Lease. NO OTHER PERSONS MAY LIVE AT THE PREMISES WITHOUT THE LANDLORD'S PRIOR WRITTEN PERMISSION, which may be given or withheld in Landlord's sole and absolute discretion. Guests may only stay for up to two weeks (14 days) and must abide by all applicable terms and conditions of this Lease, including any rules and regulations applicable to the Premises. Tenant shall not use the Premises, nor any neighboring premises, for any illegal purpose, or for any other purpose than that of a residence. Tenant agrees to comply with and abide by all federal, state, county and municipal laws and ordinances in connection with Tenant's occupancy and use of the Premises. No alcoholic beverages shall be possessed or consumed by Tenant, or Tenant's family, visiting friends, dependents, guests, licensees or invitees, unless the person possessing or consuming alcohol is of legal age. No illegal drugs or controlled substances (unless specifically prescribed by a physician for a specific person residing or present on the Premises) are permitted on the Premises. Tenant agrees to refrain from using the Premises in any way that may result in an increase of the rate or cost of insurance on the Premises. No hazardous or dangerous activities are permitted on the Premises. Absolutely no excessive drinking, illegal drug use, public disturbances, physical abuse, verbal abuse, threats, or unauthorized pets, firearms, or smoking is permitted on Premises. Any violations of the foregoing paragraph shall be an immediate and incurable default of this Lease and shall be cause for eviction.

SUBLETTING: Tenant may not sublease the Premises or any portion thereof nor assign this Lease without the prior written consent of Landlord, which may be given or withheld in Landlord's sole and absolute discretion.

PEST CONTROL: Pest control, after the first thirty days of the term of this Lease, shall be the sole responsibility of the Tenant, including, without limitation, prevention and remediation. Tenant must keep the Premises free of all pests, including without limitation, rodents, fleas, ants, cockroaches, gnats, flies, and beetles. Tenant shall pay for all costs associated with remediating pests from the Premises and shall inform Landlord at first sighting of any pests in order to avoid any infestation of pests. In signing this Lease, Tenant has first inspected the Premises and certifies that it has not observed any pests in the Premises.

MOLD: It is generally understood that mold spores are present essentially everywhere and that mold can grow in most any moist location. Tenant acknowledges the necessity of housekeeping, ventilation, and moisture control (especially in kitchens, bathrooms, break rooms and around outside walls) for mold prevention. In signing this Lease, Tenant has first inspected the Premises and certifies that it has not observed mold, mildew or moisture within the Premises. Tenant agrees to immediately notify Landlord if it observes mold/mildew and/or moisture conditions (from any source, including leaks), and allow Landlord to evaluate and make recommendations and/or take appropriate corrective action. Tenant relieves Landlord from any liability for any bodily injury or damages to property caused by or associated with moisture or the growth of or occurrence of mold or mildew on the Premises. In addition, execution of this Lease constitutes acknowledgement by Tenant that control of moisture and mold prevention are Tenant's obligations under this Lease.

DEFAULT: Should Tenant default under any of the terms and conditions of this Lease, Landlord shall have any and all remedies available to Landlord under this Lease, at law or in equity, including, without limitation, (1) the right to re-enter and repossess the Premises pursuant to applicable laws, (2) the right to recover all present and future unpaid rent, damages, costs, and attorneys' fees, and (3) the right to recover all expenses of Landlord incurred in re-entering, re-renting, cleaning and repairing the Premises. Interest will begin accruing at 18% per year on any amount due and owing to Landlord from the time

Tenant's Initials: _____

4

that any such amount first became due and payable. Tenant agrees to pay Landlord's reasonable attorneys' fees and costs in connection with any default by Tenant and same will be charged to Tenant as additional rent and due immediately. If evicted, to the maximum extent permitted by law, Tenant shall be responsible for all rent due for the balance of the Lease term, even though Tenant may no longer be able to live in or use the Premises due to the eviction. Landlord may proceed against Tenant either for eviction or for a money judgment, or both, either at one time or one remedy at a time, in any order.

ABANDONMENT: The Premises will be deemed abandoned if Tenant defaults in rent payment, appears absent from the Premises, and there is reason to believe that Tenant will not be returning to the Premises, as determined by Landlord in its reasonable discretion. Should the Premises be considered abandoned, Landlord will take possession immediately, change all locks, and store Tenant's personal property items, at Tenant's expense (to the extent Landlord is required to do so by applicable laws). Landlord shall have no liability to Tenant whatsoever in connection with the storage of any of Tenant's personal property. Tenant shall indemnify, defend and hold Landlord harmless from and against any and all penalties, damages, fines, causes of action, liabilities, judgments, expenses (including, without limitation, attorneys' fees) or charges incurred in connection with or arising from Landlord's storage of Tenant's personal property.

DEATH/DISABILITY DURING LEASE: If one of the Tenants under this Lease dies before the end of the Lease term, any remaining Tenants shall continue to carry out the terms of the Lease. If the deceased Tenant is the sole Tenant under the Lease, a representative of the deceased Tenant may terminate this Lease by providing verified written documentation testifying to such Tenant's death.

UTILITIES – The following utilities are the sole financial responsibility of the Tenant:

( ) Water	( ) Gas	( ) Garbage
( ) Sewer	( ) Heat	( ) Association Fees
( ) Electricity	( ) Air Conditioning	( ) Other_____

Tenant must transfer all utilities to be paid for by Tenant into Tenant's name before moving in and maintain service throughout the duration of the tenancy. If the Premises is a single-family home, Tenant agrees to pay for all metered electrical, water and sewer service charges, the cost of which is billed by the local municipality periodically, even if said bill is sent to Landlord. Tenant must pay this bill by the due date written on the invoice and include all late fees or other charges. If payment for the electrical, water and/or sewer is not paid by the due date, the total amount will be treated as additional rent payable by Tenant and due immediately. In such cases the Tenant shall be subject to eviction for nonpayment of electrical, water and sewer service charge(s), in the same manner as any other rent. Tenant's failure to promptly pay for all utilities may result in a $35.00 service charge.

PLUMBING: Tenant shall be held responsible for all costs related to Landlord's repair or maintenance of any plumbing stoppage or slow-down caused by Tenant, whether accidental or purposeful. Tenant agrees not to place into any drain lines non-approved substances such as cooking grease, sanitary napkins, diapers, children's toys or other similar object that may cause a stoppage. Tenant shall notify Landlord of any plumbing leak or slow drainage within 24 hours to avoid additional charges. Landlord shall use all reasonable efforts to remedy the plumbing problem. Tenant shall only use a plunger to attempt to fix a slow or stopped drain, and not pour chemical or other drain cleaners into any stopped or slow drains. Tenant shall also be responsible for any plumbing system freeze-ups occasioned by Tenant's negligence.

Tenant's Initials: _____

5

LIABILITY AND RENTERS INSURANCE: Tenant understands and agrees that Landlord has no obligation to obtain insurance for Tenant including, but not limited to, liability, hazard, or contents insurance. Tenant shall, at Tenant's sole cost and expense, obtain renter's insurance covering the full value of all personal property of Tenant in the Premises, and providing liability coverage to Tenant in an amount not less than $_____, which policy shall name Landlord as an additional insured. Tenant shall maintain such renter's insurance at all times during the term of this Lease. Tenant shall provide a certificate of insurance to Landlord demonstrating that Tenant has procured the required insurance coverage, within ten (10) days after the commencement of the term of this Lease and within ten (10) after any renewal or change in such insurance coverage. If Tenant fails to procure the required insurance, allows such insurance to be cancelled or to lapse, or fails to timely provide the required certificates of insurance, the same shall be a default of this Lease. In addition to the foregoing, Tenant acknowledges that if Tenant fails to obtain and maintain renter's insurance, Tenant alone shall bear the consequences of the loss or damage to Tenant's personal property.

ACCESS AND SIGNS: Tenant agrees to allow the Landlord access to inspect the Premises at reasonable times by appointment, use of key or by force, if necessary. Landlord may enter the Premises for the purpose of emergencies, inspections, repairs, prospective purchasers, bank representatives, contractors, or other individuals as deemed necessary by Landlord, in its sole and absolute discretion. Landlord may also display "For Rent" or "For Sale" signs on the Premises, including, without limitation, in the windows of the Premises or the front yard. Tenant's request for service or maintenance shall be considered Tenant's approval for all necessary access by Landlord or Landlord's agent in connection with such service or maintenance, if no other written arrangement related to such access between Landlord and Tenant is made.

MAINTENANCE: Landlord agrees to maintain the structure, roof and foundation of the Premises, and the heating, plumbing and electrical systems of the Premises unless the repairs needed are a result of any act or omission of Tenant (excluding normal wear and tear). In such case that the damage is a result of the act or omission of Tenant, Tenant will be billed for the repair. Landlord will carry out all required repairs in as reasonable time as possible in accordance to applicable laws, but will not be liable to Tenant for any disruptions or inconvenience to Tenant or any claim that the Premises is uninhabitable (except to the extent of any non-waivable warranty of habitability provided by applicable laws).

CARE OF THE PREMISES - Tenant agrees to care for the Premises and keep it in a good, neat and sanitary condition. Tenant shall keep garages, decks, porches, and other personal areas clear of trash, rubbish, and other junk, as determined by the Landlord. Trash shall be placed in approved receptacles only and may not be left outside for any amount of time, including on decks or porches. Tenant shall report all building damage, water leaks, or other maintenance issues immediately to Landlord or will be held liable for the costs of repairing any unreported damage. If the need to repair is caused by Tenant or Tenant's family, visiting friends, dependents, guests, licensees or invitees, Landlord may make the necessary repairs and the cost of which will be treated as additional rent to be paid by the Tenant upon notification of amount. Failure to pay costs of repairs will be treated as additional rent payable by Tenant and due immediately.

Additionally, Tenant hereby agrees as follows:

Tenant's Initials: _____

6

- Tenant agrees not to affix any structures to the Premises including, but not limited to, antennas, satellite dishes, or signs, without prior written consent of Landlord, which may be granted or withheld in Landlord's sole and absolute discretion.
- Tenant agrees not to use a barbeque grill (or any other similar cooking device) inside the Premises or under any covered area (as carbon monoxide (CO) is a very poisonous combustion gas that cannot be seen or smelled, but can injure or kill individuals with little to no warning).
- Tenant will maintain water heater temperature at no more than 120 Degrees Fahrenheit.
- Tenant agrees to give immediate notice to Landlord of any fire, flood, or other damage to or within the Premises. If the Premises is damaged and the Premises rendered uninhabitable, the rent shall cease until such a time as the Premises has been repaired or Landlord shall have the option of terminating this Lease upon five (5) days' prior written notice.
- Tenant agrees not to store boats, RVs, waterbeds, firearms, equipment, hazardous materials, paints, fuel, chemicals, waste, and non-usable items, including non-operating vehicles, in or around the Premises without prior written consent of Landlord, which may be granted or withheld in Landlord's sole and absolute discretion.
- Vehicles may never be parked in the yard of the Premises. Tenant may not repair vehicles on the Premises, unless in an enclosed garage, if such repairs take longer than one day.

WINDOWS: Tenant is responsible for the expense of replacing broken glass and repairing damaged screens, windows, window frames sashes, storm windows and doors regardless of who is at fault. Landlord is not required to supply window screens, door screens, or sliding screen doors.

WINDOW COVERINGS: Tenant will not use bed sheets or any other coverings over the windows of the Premises other than materials which are solely designed to cover windows, such as blinds, mini blinds, and curtains. If window coverings are provided, and Tenant destroys or damages the coverings, Landlord will, at Tenants financial responsibility, replace them, the cost of which will be treated as additional rent payable by Tenant and due immediately.

ACCESS FOR REPAIRS: If Tenant does not allow access to the Premises when Landlord or Landlord's hired contractors agree to repair the Premises, Tenant will be assessed a $100.00 fee due with the following month's rent.

PETS: Pets are not allowed to reside in the Premises, unless written permission is granted by Landlord before the pet is moved in, which permission may be granted or withheld in Landlord's sole and absolute discretion. If allowed, pets will be subject to additional upfront and/or monthly fees, which will be non-refundable. The granting of consent for pets to others in properties under management by Landlord shall in no way be considered the granting of consent to Tenant.

SMOKING - Tenant shall not smoke on the Premises, including the use of any vapor products.

MARIJUANA AND OTHER DRUGS: Tenant shall not be permitted to, and shall not permit any family, visiting friends, dependents, guests, licensees or invitees of Tenant to grow, produce, possess, consume, use, smoke, or ingest any marijuana, cannibas or any products or ingestibles containing marijuana or cannibas in any location in, on or about the Premises; the foregoing prohibition to be absolute and without exception and shall include any growing, production, possession, use or consumption pursuant to any medical use or medical prescription, or any medical, retail or recreational marijuana activities that may otherwise be permitted under any local, state or federal laws, rules or regulations now or

Tenant's Initials: _____

7

hereafter in effect. Tenant's violation of this rule shall be an immediate and incurable default of this Lease and shall be cause for eviction.

QUIET ENJOYMENT: While paying the rental and performing its other covenants and agreements contained in this Lease, Tenant is entitled to quiet enjoyment of the Premises during the duration of the term of this Lease, subject to all the terms and conditions of this Lease. Tenant may not infringe upon the quiet enjoyment right of other tenants through disturbances including but not limited to TVs, stereos, musical instruments, other loud noises, heavy walking, or other disturbing actions.

LAWN/POOL CARE: If a pool is present on the Premises, Tenant (____is / ____ Is not) responsible for maintaining the condition of the pool. Tenant acknowledges that pools are potentially dangerous (especially to small children). Tenant assumes full responsibility for any injuries to Tenant and any family, visiting friends, dependents, guests, licensees or invitees of Tenant in connection with any pool on the Premises. Tenant shall indemnify, defend and hold Landlord harmless from and against any and all penalties, damages, fines, causes of action, liabilities, judgments, expenses (including, without limitation, attorneys' fees) or charges incurred in connection with or arising from any pool on the Premises. No trampolines, pools, satellite dishes, TV antennas, air conditioners, spas, swing sets, or other similar features shall be added to the Premises by Tenant unless express written permission is given by Landlord, which permission may be granted or withheld in Landlord's sole and absolute discretion.

Tenant (____is / ____ Is not) responsible for lawn/yard maintenance and snow removal. If Tenant is responsible for lawn/yard maintenance, such maintenance shall include, without limitation, mowing, watering, edging and pruning of trees, shrubs and bushes, and Tenant shall at all times keep the lawn/yard of the Premises sufficiently watered, well maintained and in good condition. If Tenant is responsible for snow removal, Tenant shall promptly remove snow and ice from the sidewalks and walkways serving the Premises.

PARKING: Vehicles parked at the Premises must be in working, drivable condition. Tenant may not repair Tenant's vehicles on the Premises if such repairs take longer than one day, unless in an enclosed garage. Vehicles may never, under any condition, be parked in or driven on the yard of the Premises. Tenant may not park more than one vehicle, per adult living at the home, at the Premises. Tenant has no rights in or to any particular parking spot, and Landlord does not guarantee Tenant a parking spot on the Premises or any property surrounding the Premises. If street parking is permitted by applicable laws, Tenant may be permitted to park vehicles on the street in front of the Premises in accordance with all such laws; however, Landlord does not guaranty the availability, quality or location of any street parking. In no event shall Landlord be liable for any damage or loss to Tenant's vehicles or to any personal property contained in such vehicles.

ALTERATIONS: Tenant agrees not to make any repairs, improvements, or alterations to the Premises unless prior written permission is given by Landlord, which may be given or withheld in Landlord's sole and absolute discretion. Any repairs, improvements, or alterations made by Tenant must be completed in compliance with all local, state, and federal laws. As used herein "repairs, improvements, or alterations" includes, without limitation, lock changes, painting, replacing fixtures, installing wallpaper, attaching shelves, installing curtains or shades, or other permanent or semi-permanent changes to the Premises.

Tenant's Initials: _____

8

KEYS AND LOCKOUTS: Landlord shall provide a key to the Tenant for the Premises and Landlord shall keep a duplicate key for access. If Tenant changes the lock without supplying Landlord with a key, and Landlord is prevented from entering the Premises due to the lock change, Tenant shall bear the financial cost of Landlord's effort to enter by force. If Landlord or contractor is unable to enter the Premises to perform repair or maintenance tasks due to the Tenant's unauthorized lock change, Tenant will be charged $100.00 for each violation, which will be charged to Tenant as additional rent and due immediately. If such consent to a lock change is given, Tenant will immediately provide Landlord with a key for the use of Landlord or Landlord's agent pursuant to Landlord's right of access to the Premises. Upon vacating the Premises, Tenant shall return all keys to Landlord or Tenant will be charged $50.00 per unreturned key. If Tenant is locked out of the Premises, and Landlord must unlock the door for Tenant, then Tenant will be charged a $75.00 lock-out fee.

SMOKE AND CARBON MONOXIDE DETECTORS: The Premises has been equipped with ___hard wired / ___ battery powered smoke detectors and carbon monoxide detectors. Tenant agrees these detectors are in working order and agrees to periodically test and maintain the smoke detectors and keep them in working order.

MOVE IN: All appliances and systems in the Premises, including refrigerators, stoves, microwaves, dishwashers, washers, dryers, water heaters, furnaces, etc., will be deemed to be in working condition at the commencement of the Lease term, unless Tenant notifies Landlord, in writing, of any nonfunctioning appliances and/or systems within 24 hours of Tenant's move in to the Premises. As of the commencement of the Lease, Tenant acknowledges that Tenant has examined the Premises and approves of the condition of the Premises, including all systems and appliances in the Premises. Taking possession of the Premises by Tenant is conclusive that the Premises are in good order and satisfactory condition.

MOVE OUT AND CLEANING INSTRUCTIONS: If Tenant intends to move out, Tenant must give Landlord _____-days advanced written notice, delivered to the Landlord's place of business and must supply a forwarding address to Landlord, or Tenant may forfeit the entire security deposit to Landlord as liquidated damages, in Landlord's sole and absolute discretion. Tenant agrees that Tenant will leave the Premises in the same or better condition than when Tenant moved in (ordinary wear and tear excepted), or may be charged for any repairs or cleaning needed to prepare the Premises for the next tenant. Upon receipt of Tenant's notice to vacate the Premises, Landlord will schedule a move-out inspection of the Premises. Tenant has the right, but not the obligation, to be present for this inspection, which will take place after all of Tenant's belongings have been removed from the Premises.

PREMISES RELOCATION: If Tenant desires to relocate to another unit/property owned by Landlord, and Landlord consents to such relation, in its sole and absolute discretion, a relocation fee may be charged to Tenant, plus any cleaning or damage charges attributable to the Premises being vacated. In such event, Tenant's security deposit and credit for any prepaid rent shall transfer to the new unit/property; provided, that Tenant may be required to provide additional security deposit and/or prepaid rent, as determined by Landlord, in connection with such relocation.

NOTICES: Any notices required by either law or this Lease may be hand delivered to Tenant or mailed to the Premises. If there is more than one Tenant signing this Lease, then any notice given by Landlord to any one Tenant will constitute notice to all Tenants.

Tenant's Initials: _____

9

ATTORNEY/COLLECTION FEES: In the event that legal action must be taken against Tenant to enforce any part of this Lease or applicable laws, Landlord shall be entitled to its recover costs and reasonable attorneys' fees incurred in connection therewith. If Tenant becomes delinquent on rent or fees due, Tenant agrees to pay all landlord/agent charges including 18% annual interest.

INDEMNIFICATION & LIABILITY: Landlord shall not be held liable for any acts by, or injury or damage to any persons on or about the Premises. Tenant shall indemnify, defend, and hold Landlord harmless from all injury, loss, claim or damage to any person or property while on the Premises, or arising in any way out of Tenant's use or occupancy of the Premises.

INVALID CLAUSES: Any provision of this Lease that is found unenforceable or invalid shall not affect any other term or provision contained herein and all other provisions of this Lease shall be enforceable and valid as permitted by applicable laws. If such invalid or unenforceable provisions exist, at Landlord's sole discretion, those provisions shall be (a) modified to the extent necessary to comply with such law, or (b) removed from this Lease and will cease to be a part thereof.

SUBORDINATION: The Lease is subordinate to all existing and future mortgages, deeds of trust and other security interests on the Premises.

WAIVER: The failure of the Landlord to insist, in any one or more instances, upon strict performance of any of the covenants of this Lease, or to exercise any option herein contained, shall not be construed as a waiver or a relinquishment for the future of such covenant or option, but the same shall continue and remain in full force and effect.

ATTACHMENTS TO THE AGREEMENT: Tenant hereby acknowledges they have received the following documents, as addendums to this Lease or as required by Local, State, or Federal Law:

   a.) EPA Lead Paint Advisory Pamphlet
   b.) Lead Paint Disclosure
   c.) (Other)_____
   d.) (Other)_____
   e.) (Other)_____
   f.) (Other)_____

ENTIRE LEASE: This Lease agreement and any attached addendums constitute the entire agreement between parties and can only be changed by a written instrument signed by both Landlord and Tenant. No agreement made verbally outside this Lease shall be considered valid or legally binding.

GOVERNING LAW: This Lease is governed by and construed in accordance with the laws of the State in which the Premises is located. Venue is proper in the county in which the Premises is located.

HEADINGS: Section headings or titles in this Lease are for convenience only and shall not be deemed to be part of the Lease.

PRONOUNS: Whenever the terms referred to in the Lease are singular, the same shall be deemed to mean the plural, as the context indicates, and vice versa.

WAIVER OF JURY TRIAL: TO THE MAXIMUM EXTENT PERMITTED BY LAW, LANDLORD AND TENANT EACH WAIVE ANY RIGHT TO TRIAL BY JURY IN ANY LITIGATION OR TO HAVE A JURY PARTICIPATE IN

Tenant's Initials: _____

10

RESOLVING ANY DISPUTE ARISING OUT OF OR WITH RESPECT TO THIS LEASE OR ANY OTHER INSTRUMENT, DOCUMENT OR AGREEMENT EXECUTED OR DELIVERED IN CONNECTION HEREWITH OR THE TRANSACTIONS RELATED HERETO.

NOTICE OF LANDLORD DEFAULT: In the event of any alleged default in the obligation of Landlord under this Lease, Tenant will deliver to Landlord written notice specifying the nature of Landlord's default and Landlord will have thirty (30) days following receipt of such notice to cure such alleged default or, in the event the alleged default cannot reasonably be cured within a 30-day period, to commence action and proceed diligently to cure such alleged default.

COVENANTS, CONDITIONS AND RESTRICTIONS: This Lease shall be subject to and Tenant shall comply with all recorded covenants, conditions and restrictions affecting the Premises. Tenant's failure to comply with such covenants, conditions and restrictions shall be a default of this Lease.

IN WITNESS WHEREOF, Tenant hereby acknowledges they have read this Lease, understand both the Tenant's and Landlord's rights and responsibilities, and agrees to abide by the terms set forth in this Lease and any attached addendums.

Tenant _____ Date: _____

Tenant _____ Date: _____

Landlord _____ Date: _____

Landlord _____ Date: _____

Tenant's Initials: _____

Estoppel Agreement

Tenant Name(s): _____

Tenant Address & Unit Number: _____

Do you have a written lease for this apartment? _____

    If not, did you have a verbal lease agreement? _____

When did your lease begin? _____/_____/_____(date).

When does your lease end? _____/_____/_____(date).

Are you currently on a month-to-month lease? _____

Please list the legal names of all people living in your property:

_____

_____

How much is your monthly rent? _____

When is your rent due? _____

Have you paid a security deposit? _____

    If so, how much did you pay for a deposit? _____

Did you pay for "the last month's rent" when you moved in? _____

    If so, how much did you pay for" the last month's rent?" _____

When was the last time you paid rent? _____/_____/_____(date).

    For what month? _____

    How much did you pay then? _____.

What utilities do you pay for, if any? _____

Did you pay any other deposits or prepayments when you moved in? _____
    If so, how much – and for what? _____

Do you own any of the appliances in your unit? _____
    If so, what? _____

Do you have a pet? _____
    If Yes, how many? _____
    If Yes, what breeds? _____

Do you have any other written or verbal agreements with the landlord? _____
    If yes, what are they? _____

Are there any problems related to your tenancy or any repairs needed for your
unit? _____
_____

Signature

I certify that the above answers are true and correct to the best of my knowledge.

Signed by tenant _____ Date: _____

Signed by tenant _____ Date: _____

I have reviewed the answers given above and agree with the tenant's statements
regarding their payments, agreements and deposits.

Owner: _____ Date: _____
Manager:_____Date:_____

Potential Tenant Phone Questionnaire

Date: _____Time: _____

Name: _____

Phone: _____Alternate Phone: _____Email: _____

Rent Range: $_____ - $_____   Size of Rental: _____

Location: _____   Other Interests: _____

Number of People in Household: _____   Desired Move-in Date: _____

Before completing questionnaire, let potential tenant know minimum qualification standards.

Income/Credit
Do you have a steady source of income? _____

What is your monthly household income? _____

What is your credit score? _____

Background/Past
Are you comfortable completing a background check? _____

Have you ever been evicted or been given eviction notice? _____

Are you comfortable with us obtaining references from your past landlords? _____

Will you receive great references from your past landlords? _____

General
Does anyone in your household have any pets? _____

Does anyone in your household smoke? _____

If you are approved, when will you have first months rent and the deposit available? _____

Why are you moving? _____

Additional Comments:

DISCLAIMER: The forms provided in this book are examples only and are provided for educational purposes only. The author(s) and publisher assume no responsibility or liability for, and make no representations or warranties of any kind in connection with, your use of the forms. The author(s) and publisher provide the forms "as-is" and disclaim all representations and warranties of any kind. You should not duplicate or use the forms without careful consideration of the particular situation for which it may be used. The author(s) and publisher do not intend the forms to cover each and every lease situation, nor can the forms anticipate your specific needs. Rental forms are important legal document and you should consult a licensed attorney in your area before making any contractual commitment or signing any such agreement. If you use any of these forms, have a licensed attorney review and advise on your use of them. State laws vary and certain provisions in these sample forms may not be enforceable in every state. You may have a specific situation not addressed by these samples, and the attorney can address that particular issue for you.

Application Process & Qualification Standards

Thank you for your interest in renting one of our homes! Below is a detailed explanation of our application process as well as our standards for qualification.

Application

Each person over the age of 18 who will be living in the home must complete and submit a separate application and processing fee. In order to qualify, each person must meet or exceed the minimum standards for qualification. Incomplete applications will not be processed. Applications containing false information will immediately be disqualified. Please expect 1-3 days for the application process. Processing the Application will include direct contact with employers, current landlord, previous landlords, friends, personal and professional references, law enforcement agencies, government agencies, consumer reporting agencies, public records, eviction records, and any other sources that may be deemed necessary. A consumer report will be used in the processing of all applications. Should the Applicant be denied or face other adverse action based on information received in the consumer report, the Applicant has a right to obtain a free copy of the consumer report, and to dispute the accuracy of the information it contains by contacting: Fidelis Screening Solutions, LLC, 4534 Clinton St, Suite 2, West Seneca, NY 14224. Phone: 1-888-877-8501

Deposit to Hold

After approval, if tenant will not be taking occupancy within 24 hours, a non-refundable Deposit to Hold in the amount equal to one month's rent will be required within 24 hours to hold the property until a mutually agreed upon move-in date. The maximum amount of time a rental will be held is 14 days. After all move-in requirements have been met and a lease for the property completed, the Deposit to Hold will transfer to the security deposit to be held throughout the tenant's entire tenancy. If the Prospective Tenant fails to provide the Deposit to Hold within 24 hours of approval, the home will be offered to the next qualified applicant. Should the Applicant elect to pay the Deposit to Hold with their application (prior to processing), the Deposit to Hold will be refunded in full within 14 days if they fail to qualify.

Move-in Requirements

After approval and before occupancy will be granted, Prospective Tenant must supply all the required move-in funds, including the security deposit, first month's rent, and any other additional deposits and fees, all tenant paid utilities must be transferred into Prospective Tenant's name, and a lease must be executed and signed by all parties.

Qualification Standards

Applicants who do not meet minimum screening standards will not be approved.

Applicant must have current photo identification and a valid social security number.
Applicant's monthly household income must exceed three times the rent. All income must be from a verifiable source. Unverifiable income will not be considered.
Applicants must receive positive references from all previous landlords for the previous 5 years.
Applicant may not have any evictions or unpaid judgments from previous landlords.
Applicant must exhibit a responsible financial life. Credit score must be a minimum of 600.
A background check will be conducted on all applicants over 18. Applicant's background must exhibit a pattern of responsibility.
Applicant must be a non-smoker.
Occupancy is limited to 2 people per bedroom.

At landlord's discretion, compensating factors such as an additional security deposit or co-signer (guarantor) may be required for qualification if Applicant fails to meet any one of the above requirements. In the event of multiple applicants, tenancy will be granted to the most qualified, based on the above criteria.

Appendix

Rental Application

Please return this application to _____ Application Fee _____
Address Applying for _____Desired Move-In Date _____

Important Note to Applicants Please fill this application out in full. Incomplete applications will be sent back to you to complete, causing a delay in the process and decreasing your chances of renting from us.

Personal Information Please do not leave any blanks in this section.
First Name _____MI. _____ Last Name _____
Social Security # _____Date of Birth _____ Driver's License # _____
Phone Number _____Alternate Phone _____Email _____
Who else will be living with you? _____
_____

Rental History Please include all addresses you have lived at for the previous 5 years. Use additional paper if needed.
Current Address _____City, State, Zip _____
Move-in Date _____Landlord's Name _____ Landlord's Phone _____
Monthly Rent _____Reason for Moving _____
Previous Address _____City, State, Zip _____
Move-in Date _____ Move-out Date _____ Landlord's Name _____
Landlord's Phone _____ Monthly Rent _____Reason for Moving _____
Previous Address _____City, State, Zip _____
Move-in Date _____ Move-out Date _____ Landlord's Name _____
Landlord's Phone _____ Monthly Rent _____Reason for Moving _____

Employment Information Please include all sources of income. Use additional paper if needed. Self-employed: Please supply tax returns for previous two years and two most recent banks statements.
Current Employer _____ Position _____
Employer Phone Number _____ Supervisor Name _____
Gross Wages Per Month _____ Hire Date _____
Other Sources of Income _____ Amount Per Month _____
Explain _____

Questionnaire Please answer all these questions truthfully.
How long will you live here? _____ What pets do you have? _____
How many evictions have been filed upon you? _____ How many felonies do you have? _____
Have you ever broken a lease? _____Do You Smoke? _____ How many vehicles do you own? _____
Is the total move-in amount available now? _____ When would you like to move in? _____
How did you hear about this home? _____ For what reasons could you not pay rent on
time? _____ Do you have a checking account? _____ Balance: _____
Do you have a savings account? _____ Balance: _____
Emergency Contact -Name _____ Phone _____ Relationship_____
(Including to contact regarding rent or tenancy.)
Why should we rent to you? _____

Additional Information Please use this optional space for additional information, comments, or explanations.
_____
_____

DISCLAIMER: The forms provided in this book are examples only and are provided for educational purposes only. The author(s) and publisher assume no responsibility or liability for, and make no representations or warranties of any kind in connection with, your use of the forms. The author(s) and publisher provide the forms "as-is" and disclaim all representations and warranties of any kind. You should not duplicate or use the forms without careful consideration of the particular situation for which it may be used. The author(s) and publisher do not intend the forms to cover each and every lease situation, nor can the forms anticipate your specific needs. Rental forms are important legal document and you should consult a licensed attorney in your area before making any contractual commitment or signing any such agreement. If you use any of these forms, have a licensed attorney review and advise on your use of them. State laws vary and certain provisions in these sample forms may not be enforceable in every state. You may have a specific situation not addressed by these samples, and the attorney can address that particular issue for you.

Please read carefully and sign and date below if you agree. Applicant certifies that the information contained in this application is true and correct. Applicant understands that false or misleading information is grounds for immediate disqualification. Applicant shall pay to the Landlord a nonrefundable fee to accompany this application to cover the Landlord's administrative costs and expense to verify the information submitted by the Applicant.

Authorization
Applicant authorizes the Landlord or Landlord's representatives to make any inquires deemed necessary to verify Applicant is the most qualified based on the below stated qualification standards. This verification includes, but is not limited to, direct contact with Applicant's employers, current landlord, previous landlords, friends, personal and professional references, law enforcement agencies, government agencies, consumer reporting agencies, public records, eviction records, and any other sources of information which the Landlord or Landlord's representative may deem necessary. Applicant verifies that the Landlord and Landlord's representatives shall not be held liable for damages of any kind that result from the verification of the information provided. This authorization shall extend through Applicant's tenancy to ensure continued compliance to the terms of tenancy or to recover any financial obligations relating to Applicant's tenancy, and beyond the expiration of Applicant's tenancy for recovery of any financial obligations, or for any other acceptable purpose. Should the Applicant be denied or face other adverse action based on information received in a consumer report, the Applicant has a right to obtain a free copy of the consumer report, and to dispute the accuracy of the information it contains by contacting the Consumer Reporting Agency: Address:_____. Phone:_____

Holding Fee
Upon the verbal or written approval of the Applicant's tenancy, if tenant will not be taking occupancy immediately, a Deposit to Hold Agreement will be executed and signed by all parties and a **non-refundable** holding fee shall be required within 24 hours, hereinafter referred to as "Deposit to Hold" in the amount equal to one month's rent to hold the property until a mutually agreed upon move-in date. Applicant understands that no rental will be held for more than 14 days. The Deposit to Hold removes the property from public offering and holds the home exclusively for the Applicant until all other requirements have been met. After all requirements have been met and a lease for the property completed, the Deposit to Hold will transfer to the security deposit to be held throughout the tenant's entire tenancy. If the Applicant fails to provide the Deposit to Hold within 24 hours of approval, the Applicant may be disqualified and the home will be offered to the next qualified applicant. After approval and before occupancy will be granted, Applicant must supply all the required move-in funds, including the security deposit, first month's rent, and any other additional deposits and fees, all tenant paid utilities must be transferred into Applicant's name, and a lease must be executed and signed by all parties. If for any reason, the Applicant fails to complete all move-in requirements the landlord will return the property to public offering and the entire Deposit to Hold will be forfeited to the Landlord for expenses including, but not limited to, lost rent, holding costs, advertising costs, and marketing costs.

Qualification Standards *Your Application will be denied if you do not meet the below standards for qualification.*
Applicant must have current photo identification and a valid social security number.
Applicant's monthly household income must exceed three times the rent. All income must be from a verifiable source. Unverifiable income will not be considered.
Applicants must receive positive references from all previous landlords for the previous 5 years.
Applicant may not have any evictions or unpaid judgments from previous landlords.
Applicant must exhibit a responsible financial life. Credit score must be a minimum of 600.
A background check will be conducted on all applicants over 18. Applicant's background must exhibit a pattern of responsibility.
Applicant must be a non-smoker.
Occupancy is limited to 2 people per bedroom.

At landlord's discretion, compensating factors such as an additional security deposit or co-signer (guarantor) may be required for qualification if Applicant fails to meet any one of the above requirements. In the event of multiple applicants, tenancy will be granted to the most qualified, based on the above criteria.

Applicant authorizes release of all information to Landlord and agrees that the information provided in this rental application is true and correct. This authorization extends beyond the end of Applicant's tenancy.

Applicant _____Date _____

Rental Application Response
Adverse Action Notice

Date _____

Dear _____:

Thank you for your recent application to rent one of our homes. We are pleased to inform you that your application has been approved, provided you meet the following conditions:

o   Co-signer

o   Additional deposit in the amount of $_____

o   Additional monthly rent in the amount of $_____

o   Other _____

_____

Please let us know by ___/___/___, _____AM/PM if these conditions will work for you.

o   These conditions are based in whole, or in part, on information received in a Consumer Report from the following Consumer Reporting Agency:

Reporting Agency: _____

Address: _____, City_____, State _____, Zip_____

Phone Number: _____

The Consumer Reporting Agency listed above did not make the decision to take adverse action and cannot give you any information regarding the adverse action. It is your legal right to request a free copy of the report within 60 days of receipt of this notice from the above named Consumer Reporting Agency or to dispute the accuracy of the report with the above named Consumer Reporting Agency. We regret we are unable to provide any further information.

Manager:_____ Address: _____ Phone:_____

Rental Application Response
Adverse Action Notice

Date _____

Dear _____:

Thank you for your recent application to rent one of our homes. We regret to inform you that the application you submitted has been denied for the following reason(s):

- o   Your application was incomplete, inaccurate, falsified, or we were unable to verify the information you provided.

- o   You did not submit the required screening fee.

- o   The rental was already committed to another individual(s) at the time we received your application.

- o   The rental was given to an individual(s) who was more qualified based on our screening standards.

- o   You did not meet our minimum screening standards for income, references, history, credit score, credit history, smoking, pets, occupancy, use, or other.

- o   You were conditionally approved, but you did not meet our conditions for deposit, rent, co-signer, or other conditions.

- o   We could not hold the unit for you until your desired date, or until you could meet our move-in requirements.

- o   Other: _____

- o   Your application was denied based in whole, or in part, on information received in a Consumer Report from the following Consumer Reporting Agency:

Reporting Agency: _____

Address: _____, City_____, State _____, Zip_____

Phone Number: _____

The Consumer Reporting Agency listed above did not make the decision to deny your application and cannot give you any information regarding your denial. It is your legal right to request a free copy of the report within 60 days of receipt of this notice from the above named Consumer Reporting Agency or to dispute the accuracy of the report with the above named Consumer Reporting Agency. We regret we are unable to provide any further information.

Manager:_____ Address: _____ Phone:_____

DISCLAIMER: The forms provided in this book are examples only and are provided for educational purposes only. The author(s) and publisher assume no responsibility or liability for, and make no representations or warranties of any kind in connection with, your use of the forms. The author(s) and publisher provide the forms "as-is" and disclaim all representations and warranties of any kind. You should not duplicate or use the forms without careful consideration of the particular situation for which it may be used. The author(s) and publisher do not intend the forms to cover each and every lease situation, nor can the forms anticipate your specific needs. Rental forms are important legal document and you should consult a licensed attorney in your area before making any contractual commitment or signing any such agreement. If you use any of these forms, have a licensed attorney review and advise on your use of them. State laws vary and certain provisions in these sample forms may not be enforceable in every state. You may have a specific situation not addressed by these samples, and the attorney can address that particular issue for you.

Appendix

Employment Verification Form

The individual listed below has applied to rent one of our homes. In order to complete the processing of their application, we must verify their employment and income. We sincerely appreciate your taking a moment in completing this form and returning it to us at your earliest convenience. Thank you!

Date: _____

Place of Employment: _____

Attention: _____

Name of Applicant: _____
(Release of Information Signature Attached)

_____

Please complete the sections below and return this form at your earliest convenience.

Applicant's Position: _____

Applicant's Hourly Wage: _____

Applicant's Average Hours Worked Each Week: _____

Applicant's Date of Hire: _____

Is the Applicant's Position Considered Temporary? _____

Additional Comments: _____
_____
_____

Name and title of person completing this form: _____

Please return completed form to: _____

as soon as possible or by_____. Thank you!

DISCLAIMER: The forms provided in this book are examples only and are provided for educational purposes only. The author(s) and publisher assume no responsibility or liability for, and make no representations or warranties of any kind in connection with, your use of the forms. The author(s) and publisher provide the forms "as-is" and disclaim all representations and warranties of any kind. You should not duplicate or use the forms without careful consideration of the particular situation for which it may be used. The author(s) and publisher do not intend the forms to cover each and every lease situation, nor can the forms anticipate your specific needs. Rental forms are important legal document and you should consult a licensed attorney in your area before making any contractual commitment or signing any such agreement. If you use any of these forms, have a licensed attorney review and advise on your use of them. State laws vary and certain provisions in these sample forms may not be enforceable in every state. You may have a specific situation not addressed by these samples, and the attorney can address that particular issue for you.

Previous Landlord Reference Form

The Applicant named below has listed you as a previous landlord. We would sincerely appreciate your taking a moment to complete this form and returning it to us at your earliest convenience. The details of your reference will not be discussed with the Applicant. Thank you for your time!

Name of Applicant(s): _____

Previous Landlord: _____

Previous Address: _____

Dates of Tenancy: _____ - _____

To be completed by previous landlord:

Did tenant stay for stated period? Yes/No If not, what period? _____

What was the monthly rent? $_____

How much of the rent did the tenant normally pay? _____

Did the tenant always pay rent on time? Yes/No If not, how many times was the tenant late? _____

Did the tenant keep utilities on and paid in full at all times? Yes/No

Did anyone else live with the tenant(s)? Yes/No If yes, who?_____

Did the tenant(s) ever receive any legal notices (late rent, noise, unauthorized occupants, notice to

vacate, etc)? Yes/No Please describe: _____

Did the tenant have any pets? Yes/No

Did the tenant maintain the home in good condition (housekeeping, lawn, etc.)? Yes/No If no, please

describe: _____

Did the tenant give proper notice before vacating? Yes/No

Did the tenant receive their entire deposit back after vacating? Yes/No Please explain: _____

_____

Would you rent to the tenant again? Yes/No

Other Comments: _____

Name and Number of Person Completing this Form: _____

Thank you!

Co-Signer Agreement Addendum

This addendum is a part of the Lease Agreement dated: _____

Between (LANDLORD): _____

And (TENANT): _____

And (CO-SIGNER): _____

For the property located at_____

_____ (COSIGNER) understands and agrees to be jointly and
severely liable to the Lease Agreement listed above for the property located at_____
_____, guaranteeing performance of the Lease Agreement for it's entire
duration.

Co-signer agrees to pay a performance guarantee fee in the amount of $_____ (refundable at the
end of the lease, less any amounts not covered by the security deposit).

**ALL OTHER TERMS AND CONDITIONS OF THE ABOVE REFERENCED LEASE AGREEMENT SHALL REMAIN
THE SAME.**

Dated as of the _____**day** of _____, 20_____

_____   _____
Landlord/Manager   Tenant Signature

                                            _____
                                            Cosigner Signature

                                            _____
                                            Cosigner Social Security Number

                                            _____
                                            Cosigner Physical Address

                                            _____
                                            City, State, Zip

                                            _____
                                            Cosigner Phone and Email

Dear_____: Date: ____/____/____

Congratulations on your approval for _____. We are looking forward to
working with you and hope you will enjoy your new home.

We would like to make this as smooth a transition as possible for you. Below are instructions for
the next steps you will need to take before moving into your new home. **We cannot give you the
keys to your new home until all the steps have been completed.**

Step 1 - Deposit to Hold: The Deposit to Hold must be paid within 24 hours of approval and an
Intent to Rent Agreement completed. The Deposit to Hold will remove the property from public
offering to be held until a mutually determined move-in date. Note: We can only hold units for a
maximum of two weeks. Your Deposit to Hold becomes your Security Deposit after you begin your
tenancy. Your Deposit to Hold is $_____.

Step 2 - Utilities Turned On: All tenant paid utilities must be transferred into your name by moving
day. For your convenience, we have included a list of local utility providers below, along with their
contact information. The utilities you are responsible for have been highlighted.

Electricity   _____
Garbage   _____
Water/Sewer   _____
Gas   _____
Other   _____

Step 3 - All Move-in Funds Paid: Your first month of rent is $_____.
                                                        Additional Deposits $_____.
                                                        Additional Fees $_____.
                                                        Total Amount Needed: $_____.

**Please bring these funds to your New Tenant Orientation. All move-in funds must be paid by
cashiers check or money order. We cannot accept cash or personal checks.**

Step 4 - New Tenant Orientation/Lease Signing: Steps 1 - 3 must be completed by your New Tenant
Orientation where we will go through and sign your new Lease or Rental Agreement. After this
appointment you will receive keys to your new home. Please plan on this appointment taking
approximately one hour. Your New Tenant Orientation is scheduled for ___/___/___ at
_____am/pm. **All occupants over the age of 18 must be present at this appointment.**

We hope this itinerary answers any questions you may have about the move-in process. If you have
any additional questions or concerns, please do not hesitate to let us know. Once again,
congratulations on your new home!

Sincerely,

Management

New Tenant Orientation

Mission Statement

Open Door Properties strives to provide, maintain, and improve affordable homes with exceptional service.

Open Door Properties LLC is a professional property management company that takes great pride in offering clean, quality rentals at an affordable rate. We are committed to this goal long-term and seek to provide the best property management in Western Washington. At Open Door Properties, we promise to:

• Return all phone calls within 24 business hours

• Complete all maintenance issues and repairs efficiently, quickly, and courteously

• Consistently improve the aesthetic look of any property we manage

• Maintain affordability in rental rates

• Provide exceptional service and support to residents

What Is a Lease?

A lease is a legal contract between the landlord and tenant. When you lease a home from us, this is what you can expect. At the commencement of your tenancy...

The landlord (Us) will provide a home that is clean, sanitary, in good cosmetic shape, and in good working order. The landlord will continue to keep the home in good working order and abide by the terms in the lease throughout the length of your tenancy.

The tenant (You) is responsible for keeping the home in good condition by practicing good housekeeping habits, including to prevent leaks, mold growth, rodents, and pests, treating the property with care to avoid preventable damage or maintenance needs, reporting maintenance issues in a timely manner, paying rent when it is due, and abiding by the terms of the lease throughout the length of your tenancy.

Maintenance

Please call us promptly with any maintenance requests. Your home has been thoroughly cleaned and inspected for any maintenance issues prior to your taking occupancy. However, we do not live in the home and therefore will not be aware when you have a future maintenance concern **unless you tell us. It is 100% your responsibility to report maintenance issues.**

Here is a list of items we want to know about immediately:

1. Mold (within 48 hours)

2. Drippy faucets, drippy pipes, or "running" toilets (within 48 hours)

3. Moisture where there should be none (roof, under the sink, etc.)

Your Repair Responsibility

Mold (from living conditions): Mold will grow if given the opportunity. Keep your home clean and dry, with adequate ventilation and air movement. This means making sure all rooms receive heat and airflow on a consistent basis. Immediately clean up any sign of mold or mildew growth to prevent damage to the building. This includes behind furniture, in windows, in corners of walls, etc.

(Some) Leaks: You are responsible for leaks caused by misuse or neglect (such as knocking drain lines loose). Report **all** leaks immediately, as they can become a very big problem very quickly.

Faucets/knobs: Faucets and knobs can break easily if not handled properly.

Broken windows, blinds, doors, glass, locks, or any other damage caused directly/indirectly by you or your guests.

Light bulbs: These are your responsibility to replace.

Batteries: It is your responsibility to keep your smoke detector and carbon monoxide detector in working order by replacing the batteries on a regular schedule.

Clogged toilets, bathtubs, sinks, and other drains.

Unreported repair needs that lead to preventable damage, such as:

- *Mold:* Once again, mold and mildew will grow if given the opportunity. It is your responsibility to prevent mold and mildew and to clean it up at the first sign to avoid costly liability. If you do not kill mold and mildew immediately, it will continue to spread, leading to damage, damage that could have been prevented, therefore making you liable for the repair.

- *Rot/damage from leaks:* It is your responsibility to report all drippy faucets and pipe leaks within 48 hours. Non-reported leaks lead to damage that could have been prevented, therefore making you liable for the cost to repair the damage.

What is Emergency Maintenance?

An emergency maintenance problem is something that if not taken care of IMMEDIATELY will cause significant damage. Emergencies usually involve water or fire. If it involves fire, call 911.

When is Rent Due?

Rent is always due on the 1st of every month. Rent payments must be paid in full at all times to avoid a late fee. Past balances are considered rent due. For example, if you owe a balance in addition to rent, on the 1st the full amount is due, with the payment being applied first to the previous balance. To further break this down, if on June 15th you were billed $41.50 for a maintenance repair you were responsible for, and on July 1st you only paid your regular rent payment, your rent payment would be considered $41.50 short.

Paying Rent on Time is a BIG DEAL. No excuses.

Rent is due on the 1st of each month, and it is solely your responsibility to be sure your rent gets to us in time. You will need to plan ahead to be sure you pay your rent on time. We understand that sometimes you may need a little more time; therefore, we give an additional 5 days' grace period each month for instances when you cannot pay by the 1st.

If you do not pay your rent by the 5th of the month, this is what to expect:

- On the 6th, $50 will be added to your total due.
- On the 6th, you will be given Eviction Notice, at which time you have 3 days to pay your rent and late fees in full, or you will have to move.
- On the 7th, an additional $10 will begin accruing each day until your rent is paid in full.
- By the 10th, if we have still not received your rent payment and late fees, you will be evicted.

What's Going to Happen if You Are Late with Rent

- It gets expensive! Plan ahead to avoid costly late fees.
- Eviction will be filed on you immediately.
- When you are evicted, it goes on your permanent record, and it will be extremely difficult to find another home to rent.
- When you are evicted, you are billed for our attorney's costs.
- When you are evicted, you create a substantial monetary judgment against you, which if remains unpaid is sent to a collection agency and affects your credit and credibility.

Policies

Your lease outlines our policies in detail, so please be sure to become familiar with them to avoid a phone call or worse, termination of your tenancy. Below are the policies that we would especially like you to remember.

No Smoking

One of the reasons you were chosen as a tenant is because you do not smoke. We do not allow smoking in any rental or within 20 feet of our buildings. Smoke permeates and damages ceilings, carpets, walls, and floor coverings. You will be held liable for any smoke-related damage within the rental.

No Pets

Pets are not allowed without written approval from the landlord and are subject to additional fees. If you intend to hide a pet within your unit, please reconsider to avoid causing your own eviction.

Window Coverings

Bed sheets or other similar objects may not be used as curtains or window coverings. Broken blinds must be replaced immediately. If we notice your blinds are broken, we will hire a contractor to install new ones at your expense.

Decks/Balconies

Decks/balconies must remain clear of debris, garbage, bicycles, toys, furniture, tarps, and other clutter. Do not use your balcony as storage or to dry clothes. Decks/balconies are meant for your enjoyment. A barbecue, lawn furniture, and small plants are the only acceptable items. Failure to abide by this policy will result in termination of your tenancy.

Guests

Please limit your guests to 1-3 per day.

Noise Levels

Out of respect for your neighbors, please keep all noise to a minimum. Your neighbors are entitled to the quiet enjoyment of their home at all times.

Parties

Loud parties are not allowed.

Occupancy

Occupancy is limited to ONLY the people we listed on the lease agreement. If you decide to get a roommate after you move in or you have a guest staying for more than 14 consecutive days, you must notify us, and they must fill out an application and go through our approval process. All occupants must meet our screening standards. Keep in mind there is an occupancy limit for the home you rent.

Notice to Vacate

When you decide to move, remember to first take a look at the terms in your rental agreement or lease for how to proceed. If you are on a month-to-month rental agreement, you must give a minimum of 20 days' written notice before the end of the month. If you have a lease, you must give a minimum of 30 days' written notice before the expiration of your lease.

We hope this presentation has helped clarify any questions you may have had. Thank you for your tenancy and congratulations on your new home!

Pet Addendum

This addendum is a part of the Lease Agreement dated: _____

Between (LANDLORD): _____

And (TENANT): _____

For the property located at _____

Landlord/Manager agrees to permit the following animal(s), and no others, to dwell on the premises subject to the terms listed below:

Name of Animal	Breed	Description
_____	_____	_____
_____	_____	_____
_____	_____	_____

Tenant agrees to properly care for the animal at all times by providing adequate shelter, food, water, and grooming, adhere to all local laws and ordinances, and keep it current on all vaccinations and flea treatments. Tenant shall not allow the animal to cause any damage or pest infestation. Tenant will perform regular housekeeping duties, including sweeping and vacuuming, clean up all waste, and assume all responsibility and cost for any damages, cleaning, replacements or any other expense to the property that are a result of the animal. Tenant agrees to remedy any complaints regarding the animal immediately, and to return the premises undamaged and in clean condition, free of odors or pests, at the end of their tenancy, and if not, to pay for restoring the property to its original condition.

Tenant understands they are solely responsible and liable for the behavior and actions of the animal. At the Landlord/Manager's request, the Tenant agrees to remove the animal permanently from the premises should they become a threat or a nuisance. This agreement refers to only the animal(s) listed above. No other animals may be added or substituted.

Tenant agrees to:

_____ Pay the Landlord/Manager a one-time nonrefundable fee upon the execution of this agreement in the amount of $_____, and/or,

_____ Pay an additional monthly rent payment upon the execution of the agreement in the amount of $_____ which shall be paid in the same manner as rent according to the Lease Agreement, and/or,

_____ Pay an additional security deposit in the amount of $_____, which shall be refunded under the terms of the Lease Agreement at the termination of tenancy, provided all terms of this agreement are met.

Landlord/Manager reserves the right to cancel this agreement at their sole discretion. Cancellation of this agreement shall in no way nullify the Lease Agreement.

_____   _____
Landlord/Manager   Tenant

                                         _____
                                         Tenant

Rules and Regulations

The following is a part of the Lease Agreement Dated: _____

Between (LANDLORD): _____

And (TENANT): _____

The following is a list of rules and regulations that are part of the Lease Agreement. These rules and regulations are for the purpose of maintaining the aesthetic appearance and comfortable living environment of the home and insure proper use of the rental and the premises. Tenant agrees to comply with all rules and regulations and understands that they are responsible and liable for the actions and behavior of their entire household, as well as their guests and visitors. Violations of the below rules and regulations will result in termination of tenancy.

Occupancy: Occupancy is limited to those listed on the Lease Agreement. Any additional person(s) staying in the home for a period of more than 14 days must complete an application and be approved for tenancy. Unapproved occupants staying in the home for more than 14 days will result in termination of tenancy for all occupants. For emergency purposes, please inform the landlord/manager of the name and license plate number of **any** person staying in the home for any amount of time.

Contact Information: Tenant shall keep the landlord/manager informed of current contact information at all times, including phone numbers, emails, and emergency contacts.

Smoking: Smoking in the home or within 25 feet of the building is prohibited. Tenant will be held liable for any smoke-related damage, including odor or stains in the walls, ceilings, carpets, flooring, and other damage caused by smoking. Tenants are responsible and liable for the actions of their guests and visitors.

Decks/Balconies/Patios: Decks, balconies, and patios must remain clear of debris, garbage, bicycles, furniture, shoes, and other clutter. Decks, balconies, and patios may not be used to dry clothes or as storage. *Barbecues, lawn furniture, and plants are the only acceptable items allowed on decks, balconies, and patios.*

Window Coverings: Tenants may not use bed sheets, blankets, or other similar materials for window coverings. Blinds must remain in the down position. Tenant's personal curtains and window coverings cannot be visible from the outside. Damaged blinds must be replaced immediately (within 24 hours).

Satellite Dishes/Antennas: Satellite dishes and antennas may not be installed or attached to the building. Satellite dishes must be free-standing and require prior written landlord/manager approval.

Walkways: All walkways and stairs are to be kept clear and free of debris at all times. Absolutely no storage or accumulation of any items on or near walkways or interior or exterior stairs. All brooms, mops, waste receptacles, etc. must be stored inside the rental.

Tenant Initial Here _____   1

Noise: Tenants shall respect their neighbor's rights to peace and quiet and shall keep all noise to a minimum, including keeping voices, music, stereos, vehicles, and television levels to a minimum. Tenants shall use the premises in a way as to not disturb neighbors, including not slamming doors, knocking on walls, stomping on floors, honking, revving engines, or in other ways being disruptive. **Any** noise between the hours of 10pm – 8am will not be tolerated.

Housekeeping: Tenants shall keep the premises clean, sanitary, and neat by performing routine housekeeping at regular intervals, including keeping clutter to a minimum, disposing of trash and garbage in a proper manner, sweeping, vacuuming and wiping down all surfaces. Tenant may not make any permanent changes to the dwelling (including painting) without written permission from the landlord/manager. Tenant is responsible for keeping light bulbs and detectors in working order for the duration of tenancy.

Use of Driveways/Parking Lot: Driveways and parking lots shall be used solely for vehicles. No skateboarding, skating, bicycling or playing is allowed in these areas.

Parking: Vehicles shall only be parked in designated parking spaces. Parking spaces are for tenants only. Vehicles must be operational. Absolutely no obstructing other vehicles, parking on the lawn, sidewalk, or walkways. Trailers, boats, and recreational vehicles shall not be parked on the premises. Vehicles in violation may be towed without further notice.

Trash/Garbage Receptacles: All trash and garbage shall be in tied plastic bags and placed in the proper receptacles. Receptacle lids must close completely after every use. Trash and garbage shall never be placed beside or behind the receptacles. The trash and garbage receptacle is for tenant use only. Absolutely no furniture is to be placed or disposed of in or near the receptacles. The cost of disposal of such large items will be charged to the owner of the items. Recycling bins are for the proper disposal of recyclable trash only. Flatten all boxes before putting them in the recycle bin. Each Resident is responsible for keeping the area directly surrounding their home clean. Single-Family Homes: Tenants shall adhere to their city's pick-up schedule.

Lockout/Lost Key: Lockout service may be requested between 10am-4pm, Monday – Friday for a $35.00 Lockout Fee. After-hours lockouts will require the use of an independent locksmith. Tenants shall not change or add to the locks of the rental at any time. Lock changes shall be conducted only by the landlord/manager. New locks may be requested for a fee.

Laundry Facilities: Unless a single-family home, the laundry facilities shall only be used between the hours of 9am – 8pm daily. Personal belongings may not be left in the laundry rooms at any time.

Animals: No animals shall be permitted inside the rental or on the premises *at any time* unless tenant has authorization for the animal in writing from the landlord/manager.

Vehicle Maintenance: Vehicle washing and repair shall not be conducted on the premises.

Cooking: Cooking shall only be conducted in the kitchen. A barbeque outside is permitted. Tenant shall never pour cooking grease or other damaging/obstructing objects down toilets, sinks or drains.

Weapons: Tenant shall not possess, use, or store deadly weapons in the rental or elsewhere on the premises, including firearms.

Tenant Initial Here _____   2

Maintenance: Maintenance requests must be made in writing. Tenant is liable for all expenses incurred that are a result of tenant misuse or neglect, including that done by guests and visitors.

Plumbing: Tenant shall report all drips and leaks immediately to the landlord/manager. Tenant is liable for all expenses or repairs resulting from tenant stopping of waste pipes or overflow from sinks, tubs, toilets, showers, washbasins or containers.

Vandalism/Illegal Activities: Vandalism of any kind will not be tolerated. Any tenant or guest who vandalizes the rental or grounds in any way is liable for criminal prosecution. Tenant is liable for all expenses associated with returning the premises to their proper condition. Illegal activity of any sort will not be tolerated. All illegal activities will be reported to the proper authorities and will result in immediate eviction.

Common Areas: Tenant shall not keep personal belongings in common areas or obstruct halls, stairways, elevators, laundry rooms, or other common areas.

Roof: Tenant shall not be permitted on the roof of the property at any time.

Window Screens: The landlord/manager is not obligated to provide screens for windows or doors. Screens can be provided at tenant's expense.

Carpets: Carpets must be professionally cleaned. The landlord/manager will arrange for carpets to be professionally cleaned after tenant vacates at tenant's expense. If tenant would like carpets cleaned during tenancy, they must contact the landlord/manager.

Inspections: Routine inspections of the premises will be conducted with proper notice.

Tenant(s) agree that they have read, understand, and will abide by these Rules and Regulations and understands that they are personally liable for the behavior and actions of their household, guests, and visitors.

Dated as of this _____ **day** of _____, 20_____

_____
Landlord/Manager

_____
Tenant

_____
Tenant

Tenant Initial Here _____   3

Move-in/Move-Out Condition Report

This Move-in/Move-Out Condition Report is part of the Lease Agreement dated ___/___/___ between
_____ (Tenant) and _____(Landlord)
for the property located at _____.

The Landlord/Manager and Tenant have each inspected the property listed above. Tenant understands
that this Condition Report is a part of their Lease Agreement and will used to document the condition of
the dwelling upon gaining occupancy and upon vacating.

	Arrival Condition	Departure Condition
Living Room		
Floor and Floor Covering		
Walls and Ceiling		
Window(s)		
Window Covering(s)		
Lighting Fixture(s)/Fans		
Door(s)/Hardware		
Heating		
Outlets/Switches		
Smoke Alarms/CO Alarms		
Other		

	Arrival Condition	Departure Condition
Kitchen/Other_____		
Floors/Floor Coverings		
Walls and Ceiling/Caulking		
Window(s)		
Window Covering(s)		
Lighting Fixture(s)/Fans		
Door(s)/Hardware		
Heating		
Outlets/Switches		
Smoke Alarms/CO Alarms		
Cabinets/Hardware		
Refrigerator		
Stove/Oven		
Stove Vent		
Microwave		
Dishwasher		
Sink/Fixtures/Plumbing		
Counter		
Garbage Disposal		

Tenant(s) Initial _____

	Arrival Condition	Departure Condition
Washer/Dryer		
Dryer Vent		
Other		

Bathroom(s)	Arrival Condition	Departure Condition
Floors/Floor Coverings		
Walls and Ceiling/Caulking		
Window(s)		
Window Covering(s)		
Lighting Fixture(s)/Fans		
Door(s)/Hardware		
Heating		
Outlets/Switches		
Smoke Alarms/CO Alarms		
Cabinet(s)/Hardware		
Counter Surfaces		
Sink/Fixtures/Plumbing		
Bathtub/Shower/Fixtures		
Toilet		
Other		

Bedroom	Arrival Condition	Departure Condition
Floor and Floor Covering		
Walls and Ceiling		
Window(s)		
Window Covering(s)		
Lighting Fixture(s)/Fans		
Door(s)/Hardware		
Heating		
Outlets/Switches		
Smoke Alarms/CO Alarms		
Other		

Bedroom/Other_____	Arrival Condition	Departure Condition
Floor and Floor Covering		
Walls and Ceiling		
Window(s)		
Window Covering(s)		
Lighting Fixture(s)/Fans		
Door(s)/Hardware		
Heating		

Tenant(s) Initial _____

	Arrival Condition	Departure Condition
Outlets/Switches		
Smoke Alarms/CO Alarms		
Closet		
Other		

	Arrival Condition	Departure Condition
Bedroom/Other_____		
Floor and Floor Covering		
Walls and Ceiling		
Window(s)		
Window Covering(s)		
Lighting Fixture(s)/Fans		
Door(s)/Hardware		
Heating		
Outlets/Switches		
Smoke Alarms/CO Alarms		
Closet		
Other		

	Arrival Condition	Departure Condition
Other		
Exterior of Building		
Lawn/Garden		
Driveway/Walkways		
Garage		
Porch		
# of Keys Received:	Door___ Garage ___ Mailbox ___ Other___	Door___ Garage ___ Mailbox ___ Other___
Other		

Comments:

Move-in Inspection	**Move-Out Inspection**
Landlord/Manager_____	Landlord/Manager_____
Tenant _____	Tenant _____
Tenant _____	Tenant _____
Date of Move-in Inspection ___/___/___	**Date of Move-Out Inspection___/___/___**

Tenant(s) Initial _____

Disclosure of Information on Lead-Based Paint and/or Lead-Based Paint Hazards

Lead Warning Statement

Housing built before 1978 may contain lead-based paint. Lead from paint, paint chips, and dust can pose health hazards if not managed properly. Lead exposure is especially harmful to young children and pregnant women. Before renting pre-1978 housing, lessors must disclose the presence of known lead-based paint and/or lead-based paint hazards in the dwelling. Lessees must also receive a federally approved pamphlet on lead poisoning prevention.

Lessor's Disclosure

(a) Presence of lead-based paint and/or lead-based paint hazards (check (i) or (ii) below):

    (i) _____ Known lead-based paint and/or lead-based paint hazards are present in the housing (explain).

    _____

    _____

    (ii) _____ Lessor has no knowledge of lead-based paint and/or lead-based paint hazards in the housing.

(b) Records and reports available to the lessor (check (i) or (ii) below):

    (i) _____ Lessor has provided the lessee with all available records and reports pertaining to lead-based paint and/or lead-based paint hazards in the housing (list documents below).

    _____

    _____

    (ii) _____ Lessor has no reports or records pertaining to lead-based paint and/or lead-based paint hazards in the housing.

Lessee's Acknowledgment (initial)

(c) _____ Lessee has received copies of all information listed above.

(d) _____ Lessee has received the pamphlet *Protect Your Family from Lead in Your Home.*

Agent's Acknowledgment (initial)

(e) _____ Agent has informed the lessor of the lessor's obligations under 42 U.S.C. 4852d and is aware of his/her responsibility to ensure compliance.

Certification of Accuracy

The following parties have reviewed the information above and certify, to the best of their knowledge, that the information they have provided is true and accurate.

Lessor	Date	Lessor	Date
Lessee	Date	Lessee	Date
Agent	Date	Agent	Date

Roommate/Economic Unit Addendum

This addendum is a part of the Lease Agreement Dated: _____

Between (LANDLORD): _____

And (TENANTS): _____

For the property located at _____

We, _____(Tenants/Roommates) agree
that we are residing together as one economic unit. We confirm that each person is fully responsible for
all obligations of the economic unit. We understand and confirm that we are each fully responsible for
abiding by and fulfilling the terms in the Lease Agreement. We understand that this responsibility
remains until the rented dwelling has been vacated by all occupants.

Tenants/Roommates agree to make monthly rent payments to the Landlord/Manager in the form of a
single payment. The security deposit and any pre-paid funds will remain with the Landlord/Manager
until the dwelling has been vacated completely by all occupants. Any refund of the deposit will be
returned in the form of a single check within ___ days of all occupants vacating completely, will be made
payable to all persons on the Lease Agreement, and may be sent to any one of the Tenants along with
the Disposition of Deposit.

Each Tenant understands and agrees that they are jointly and severely liable to all terms and conditions
of the Lease Agreement, including the entire rent and the entire amount of any other charges incurred
under the Lease Agreement for the whole term of the Lease Agreement. Any Tenant who vacates while
this Lease Agreement is in effect continues to have financial responsibility under the Agreement as part
of the economic unit.

Dated as of this _____day of _____, 20_____

_____   _____
Landlord/Manager   Tenant/Roommate

                                                             _____
                                                             Tenant/Roommate

                                                             _____
                                                             Tenant/Roommate

                                                             _____
                                                             Tenant/Roommate

                                                             _____
                                                             Tenant/Roommate

Lease Renewal Decision Form

Date ___/___/___

Dear _____,

Thank you for your tenancy at _____! We've really appreciated having you here this past year and look forward to continuing our relationship with you. It is a privilege to be able to work with you and we thank you for your business.

According to our records, it appears that your lease-term is coming up at the end of next month and, as such, we need to discuss your future plans with you and make sure we are all on the same page. Due to naturally increasing expenses for the owner, it is necessary to gradually increase rent over time. Therefore, a slight bump in your monthly rental rate will take place soon. However, we would like your input on where to go from here.

Please choose from one of the following options for your future at your home. Simply circle the option below you would like to choose, and send this form back to us. We will prepare a new lease with the proper information and mail it to you within seven days.

Sign a new **one-year lease** at $_____ per month, which will begin on _____ and end on _____. This is an increase of $_____ per month.

Sign a new **six-month lease** at $_____ per month, which will begin on _____ and end on _____. This is an increase of $_____ per month.

Sign a **month-to-month lease** agreement at $_____ per month, which will begin on _____. This is an increase of $_____ per month.

Although we hope you'll stay with us forever, if you do not plan on renewing your lease and staying with us any longer, please let us know immediately. Our state law requires tenants to give ____ days written notice to vacate before the end of their lease. Therefore, please return this form and let us know your plans by _____ so we can make plans that work for everyone.

Once again, thank you for your residency here at [address or apartment complex name]; we look forward to many more years of working with you.

Sincerely,

Management

Rental Lease Extension Agreement

This Rental Extension Agreement ("Extension Agreement") is made this _____ day of _____, _____ between _____ ("Landlord"), and _____ ("Tenant"), whose address is _____, collectively referred to herein as "the Parties."

WHEREAS, the Parties, by previous Residential Rental Lease Agreement dated ___/___/___ ("Lease Agreement"), agreed to terms for rentals to be paid by Tenant in exchange for the tenancy located at _____ and the mutual covenants and agreements therein, the contents of said Lease Agreement is incorporated herein by this reference as though fully set forth; and

WHEREAS, the Parties desire to extend the Lease Agreement for an additional period.

NOW, THEREFORE, in consideration of the mutual promises contained herein, the Parties agree as follows:

Extension of Lease Agreement. The Parties agree that the "term" of the Lease Agreement, shall be extended to _____, _____. During said extension the Parties shall retain all of the rights, responsibilities and covenants set forth in the Lease Agreement, except as modified herein.

Rent. In connection with this renewal, the rent, payable monthly, shall be $_____ per month beginning_____.

Other. In addition to the aforementioned changes to the Lease Agreement, the parties agree to the following changes, adjustments, or modifications: _____
_____
_____
_____
_____

Incorporation of Lease Agreement. The contents of the Lease Agreement are incorporated herein as though fully set forth. In each and every other respect, except as modified by the Extension Agreement, the above-referenced Lease Agreement is hereby ratified, approved, and confirmed by the Parties hereto.

Executed by the Parties on the day and date set forth above:

_____   _____
Landlord/Manager   Tenant

                                          _____
                                          Tenant

                                          _____
                                          Tenant

Property Inspection Checklist

Address: _____ *Date:* _____ *Time:* _____

- *Smoke detectors* - Make sure there is a working smoke detector in each bedroom and one additional smoke detector elsewhere in the property per floor.

- *Carbon Monoxide Detector* – Washington State Law requires a working carbon monoxide detector in all residential rental properties, regardless of the heating source. Make sure there is at least one working on each floor.

- *Mold* - Look for any signs of mold in each room, especially in corners, behind furniture, near windows, on walls, in closets, or under cabinets. Ask tenant if they have seen any mold. Look for anything as small as a few specks, slight wall discoloration, or obvious patches of mold growing. Make note of any problem areas, take a picture and write the description of location and size of the area.

- *Leaks* – Even the smallest drip from a faucet can cause hundreds or even thousands of dollars in damage. Please make note of any leaks in the following areas:

  o *Kitchen:* Is the kitchen faucet dripping? Y/N

  o *Kitchen:* Is it dry in the cabinet beneath the kitchen sink? Y/N

  o *Kitchen:* Under the sink, are there any signs of rot or of being recently damp?

  o *Bathroom(s):* Is the bathtub faucet dripping?

  o *Bathroom(s):* Is the bathroom faucet dripping?

  o *Bathroom(s):* Is it dry in the cabinet beneath the bathroom sink?

  o *Bathroom(s):* Under the bathroom sink, are there any signs of rot or of being recently damp?

  o *Bathroom(s):* Is the toilet making a continuous sound like "running water?" If so, make a note.

- *Water Damage:* Check the ceiling throughout the property. Are there any signs of water from a roof leak (brown spots, rings, saggy drywall)? Y/N

- *Caulk* - Is the caulk around the shower/along the bottom of the tub good?

- *Interior Lighting* - Do all interior lights work? (Bedrooms, bathrooms, kitchen, etc.)

- *Exterior Lighting*: Do all exterior lights work? (Decks, porches, garages, etc.)

- *Blinds* - Are all blinds in good condition?

- *Decks/Porches* - Is the deck, porch, or other outdoor areas clear of unapproved items? (Anything that is not a BBQ, lawn furniture, or plant.)

- *General Condition* - Is the tenant keeping the unit clean and in good condition?

  Yes____ No ____

Please list any additional important details:

Inspection completed by:

Signature: _____ Date: _____

Work Order/Maintenance Request

Date: ___/___/___ Time: ___:___am/pm

Tenant Name: _____

Address: _____

Phone Number: _____

Email: _____

Description of Maintenance Requested

[ ]

Office Use Only

Maintenance Request Notes
Received ___/___/___ Time ___:___am/pm

[ ]

Date of Completion ___/___/___   Follow-up with Tenant: _____ Date: _____
Notes from Follow-up:

DISCLAIMER: The forms provided in this book are examples only and are provided for educational purposes only. The author(s) and publisher assume no responsibility or liability for, and make no representations or warranties of any kind in connection with, your use of the forms. The author(s) and publisher provide the forms "as-is" and disclaim all representations and warranties of any kind. You should not duplicate or use the forms without careful consideration of the particular situation for which it may be used. The author(s) and publisher do not intend the forms to cover each and every lease situation, nor can the forms anticipate your specific needs. Rental forms are important legal document and you should consult a licensed attorney in your area before making any contractual commitment or signing any such agreement. If you use any of these forms, have a licensed attorney review and advise on your use of them. State laws vary and certain provisions in these sample forms may not be enforceable in every state. You may have a specific situation not addressed by these samples, and the attorney can address that particular issue for you.

Courtesy Late Rent Notice

Dear Tenant: Date: ____/____/____

This is a courtesy notice that we have not yet received your rent payment for this month. As a reminder, rent is always due on the 1st of every month and considered late if not received by the 5th of the month. Please be sure your full payment is paid no later than 5:00pm today to avoid eviction proceedings.

Balances Owed

Rent for the month of _____ in the amount of $_____

Late Fee in accordance with Lease Agreement $_____

Other amounts owed for _____ $_____

Total Amount Due $_____

If you believe you have received this notice in error, or you cannot make your payment by 5:00pm today, please contact us at (___) ____-_____ as soon as possible to discuss your plans. Communication is extremely important. We are looking forward to hearing from you.

Sincerely,

Management

___-Day Notice to Pay Rent or Vacate

Name: _____ et al.
Address: _____
City: _____ State _____ Zip _____

Today's Date: _____

This form shall serve as official notice that you are hereby given __ days notice to pay the following rental amount and fees due or immediately you must vacate the premises. This __-day deadline begins the day after this notice is served.

Total Rent Due: _____

For the following rental period: _____.

Total Other Fees Due: _____

Description of Fees Due: _____.

Total Amount Due Immediately: _____

If you do not pay the above stated amount during the above stated time-frame, an unlawful detainer lawsuit will be brought against all occupants. This will result in an eviction on your record and judgment against all tenants on the lease as allowed by the law. The sheriff may also physically coordinate the removal of you and your belongings from the property.

Manager's Signature: _____
Today's Date: _____
Manager's Phone: _____
Manager's Email: _____
Posting Date: _____
Posting Time: _____

Rent must be paid to: _____

____-Day Notice to Comply with Lease Agreement

Name: _____ et al.

Address: _____

City: _____ State _____ Zip _____

Today's Date: _____

This form shall serve as official notice that you and each of you are hereby given notice to correct the following breach in your lease or rental agreement within ___ days:

_____
_____
_____
_____
_____
_____

The above breach in your lease or rental agreement must be corrected within the above stated time-frame, or an unlawful detainer lawsuit will be brought against all occupants. This will result in an eviction on your record and judgment against all tenants on the lease as allowed by the law. The sheriff may also physically coordinate the removal of you and your belongings from the property.

The landlord or manager shall inspect the above named premises for compliance on ___/___/___ at ___:___ am/pm. This shall serve as your ___ day notice to enter.

Manager's Signature: _____
Today's Date: _____
Manager's Phone: _____
Manager's Email: _____
Posting Date: _____
Posting Time: _____

___ - Day Notice to Enter

Name: _____ et al.

Address: _____

City: _____ State _____ Zip _____

Today's Date: _____

Dear Tenant: This form shall serve as advance written notice that the Landlord/Agent will be entering your rental unit on: ____/____/_____ at ____: ____am/pm for the following reason(s):

____ Inspect the premises
____ Perform necessary maintenance or repairs to the property
____ Show the property to prospective Tenants
____ Other (Listed Below)

_____
_____
_____

You are welcome to be present during this appointment, though it is not necessary. If the above date and time interferes with your schedule, please contact us immediately to make other arrangements. Unless we hear otherwise from you, we will assume your full permission to enter at the above date and time. We appreciate your understanding and cooperation and will do our best to complete the appointment with as little inconvenience to you as possible. Thank you.

Manager's Signature: _____
Today's Date: _____
Manager's Phone: _____
Manager's Email: _____
Posting Date: _____
Posting Time: _____

Change in Terms of Lease Addendum

This addendum dated ___/___/___ shall be incorporated into and made part of the Lease Agreement dated ___/___/___ between _____(Tenant) and _____(Landlord) for the property located at _____ _____.

The above named Tenant and Landlord each understand and agree to the following changes to the Lease Agreement:

_____
_____
_____
_____
_____
_____
_____

Except for the adjustments made herein, all other terms and conditions of the Lease Agreement shall remain the same and in full force.

Dated as of this _____day of _____, 20_____

_____   _____
Landlord/Manager   Tenant

                                         _____
                                         Tenant

                                         _____
                                         Tenant

                                         _____
                                         Tenant

Notice to Vacate Form

**Please return this form to the manager when you are ready to give us notice
that you will be moving. Thank you!**

Today's Date: _____

Your Name: _____

Current Address: _____

Forwarding Address: _____

Phone Number: _____

Move-Out Date: _____

Reason for Moving: _____

I am aware that I must give my Notice to Vacate in writing at least _____days prior to the end of
my Lease Agreement.

For Month-to-Month Tenancies: I am aware that in accordance with my Rental Agreement, if a
full_____ Notice to Vacate is not given prior to the end of the month I will be responsible for
rent for the following month and my lease will end the last day of the next month.

I am aware that I am legally obligated to fulfill the terms of my contract through it's entire duration.

I am aware that if keys to the Rental are not returned by the last day of the month I will be
responsible for the next month's rent.

I am aware that I must leave the unit in the same condition as when I moved in by completing the
entire move-out cleaning checklist. I am aware that any cleaning or repairs needed to the Rental
after I have vacated will be billed at my expense and deducted from my security deposit.

Tenant Signatures:

_____   _____
Name   Date

_____   _____
Name   Date

Office Use Only: Date Received: _____

Acknowledgement of Notice to Vacate

Dear _____:

On_____ 20_____ we received written notice of your intent to vacate the home you are now renting by_____, 20_____. Your tenancy will terminate on_____20_____, at _____am/pm.

Residence

Before turning in your keys, the residence will need to be returned to it's original move-in condition. This means you will need to remove all of your personal belongings and thoroughly clean all surfaces before moving. We understand moving is a busy time in a tenant's life, so we have included a checklist to help you with this process.

Security Deposit

For your convenience and to assist you during your move, we have enclosed a Tenant Duty Checklist as well as your Move-in Condition Report. Remember any cleaning or damages not completed or remedied by you will be billed at your expense. An Itemized List of Common Deductions has been enclosed for your information. Your Disposition of Deposit and refund will be returned to the forwarding address you supply on the Forwarding Address Form within 14 days after you have moved. It is our desire to return your full deposit to you.

Maintenance

Please give us a call or leave a note of any maintenance issues you are aware of that may not be noticeable when we inspect your unit after you have moved.

Moving Day

When it gets close to your moving day, please call us at _____or email us at_____ of when you will be completely moved out and the home returned to *clean*, rent-ready condition. We will conduct our final walk-thru after the home has been completely vacated.

It has been our pleasure working with you; we wish you all the best in the future.

Sincerely,

Management

Itemized List of Common Deposit Deductions
This list has been prepared for your information only. Actual charges will vary.

Cleaning

Kitchen

Clean Kitchen – Normal Cleaning	$150.00
Clean Kitchen – Deep Clean	$300.00
Oven & Stove (Inside/Outside/Underneath)	$75.00
Refrigerator (Inside/Outside/Underneath)	$75.00
Dishwasher (Inside/Outside)	$75.00
Microwave (Inside/Outside/Underneath)	$25.00
Cabinets (Wash Inside/Outside)	$200.00
Countertops	$25.00
Sweep and Mop Floors	$25.00
Dust and Wash Trim	$15.00
Wipe Down Walls	$25.00
Drip Pan Replacement	$35.00

Living Room/Dining Room/Office/Recreation Room

Normal Cleaning	$100.00
Deep Clean	$200.00
Sweep, Vacuum, Mop	$50.00
Dust and Wash Trim	$25.00
Wipe Down Walls	$25.00

Bathroom

Bathroom – Normal Cleaning	$100.00
Bathroom – Deep Clean	$200.00
Bathtub/Shower	$50.00
Sink	$25.00
Cabinet (Inside/Outside)	$25.00
Toilet	$25.00
Sweep and Mop Floors	$25.00
Dust and Wash Trim	$25.00
Wipe Down Walls	$25.00
Wipe Down Fixtures	$15.00

Bedroom

Bedroom – Normal Cleaning	$100.00
Bedroom – Deep Clean	$200.00

Sweep, Vacuum, Mop	$50.00
Dust and Wash Trim	$25.00
Wipe Down Walls	$25.00

General, Damages, Repairs and Disposal

Repair Drywall	
6" x 6"	$75.00
12" x 12"	$150.00
Wash Light Fixture (Each)	$15.00
Replace Interior Door	$100.00
Replace Exterior Door	$250.00
Clean Ceiling Fan	$25.00
Change Light Bulb (Each)	$5.00
Replace Smoke Detector Batteries	$25.00
Replace Carbon Monoxide Detector Batteries	$25.00
Replace Smoke Detector	$75.00
Replace Carbon Monoxide Detector	$75.00
Replace Window Blinds	$40.00
Replace Sliding Door Blinds	$60.00
Carpet Cleaning (Normal)	$150.00
Carpet Cleaning (Deep Clean)	$200.00
Carpet Spot Treatment (Each)	$15.00
Replace Filter	Varies
Replace Carpet (12' x 12' Room)	$500.00
Replace Wood, Vinyl, Linoleum, Etc. Flooring (12 x 12 Room)	$500.00
Repaint One Room (12' x 12')	$300.00
Repair Kitchen Cabinet	$150.00
Repair Kitchen Drawer	$150.00
Wash Window (Including Tracks) (Inside)	$20.00
Fill Nail Holes	$25.00
Replace Interior Door Knob	$25.00
Replace Exterior Door Lock	$50.00
Pest or Rodent Extermination	$150.00
Odor Removal	Varies

Exterior

Trash Removal (Per Load)	$100.00
Mow Lawn	$35 - $75
Weed Flower Beds	$35 - $100
General Labor (Cleaning, Painting, Normal Repairs, Trash Removal, Etc)	$25 - $40/hr
Specialty Labor (Electrician, Drywall Repair, Plumber, Etc)	$70 - $100/hr

Tenant Duty Checklist
Vacating and Cleaning Instructions

For your convenience we have prepared a checklist of items you will need to complete prior to moving day. Remember, all expenses related to us returning your home to rent-ready condition, as recorded in your Move-in Condition Report, will be billed at your expense and deducted from your security deposit. For this reason, it is extremely important that you allow ample time to perform every item on this checklist. Also enclosed is an Itemized List of Common Deposit Deductions for your reference. After you complete the checklist completely, your Disposition of Deposit and refund will be returned to you within 14 days. Before moving, please remember to leave your forwarding address on the enclosed Forwarding Address Form.

Kitchen

- Walls: Wipe down all wall surfaces and doors, remove all nails and fill holes with spackling. Remove excess spackling to create smooth surface.
- Trim & Misc: Dust and wipe down all trim, heaters, vents, switch covers, and door knobs.
- Light Fixtures: Wash all light fixtures and replace burnt out light bulbs.
- Windows: Clean all windows, including tracks and window sills.
- Blinds: Dust and wipe down all blinds. Replace any broken blinds.
- Cabinets: Empty all cabinets and drawers, vacuum if needed, and thoroughly wash inside and out.
- Refrigerator/Freezer: Empty contents. Remove all shelves and drawers and completely wash. Wash down all surfaces inside and outside of refrigerator. Return shelves and drawers to proper positions.
- Oven/Stove: Oven: Clean racks and inside of oven to completely remove all stains. Stove: Wash down all surfaces of stove and stove top, including the sides, knobs, door, and drawer. Replace drip pans. Clean exhaust hood, fan, and filter.
- Dishwasher: Run empty dishwasher with dishwasher liquid. Thoroughly wipe down inside and out, including the door seal.
- Microwave: Wash down inside and outside of microwave.
- Sink/Fixtures: Clean sink, drains and faucets.
- Countertops: Clean all countertops and backsplash, including edges and corners.
- Floors: Sweep, mop, and wipe down all floor surfaces, including underneath refrigerator and stove.

Living Room/Dining Room/Office/Recreation Room

- Walls: Wipe down all wall surfaces and doors to remove smudges. Remove all nails and fill holes with spackling. Remove excess spackling to create smooth surface.
- Trim & Misc: Dust and wipe down all trim, heaters, vents, switch covers, and door knobs.
- Light Fixtures: Wash all light fixtures and replace burnt out light bulbs.
- Windows: Clean all windows, including tracks and window sills.
- Blinds: Dust and wipe down all blinds. Replace any broken blinds.
- Shelves: Wipe down all shelf surfaces.
- Stove/Fireplace: Clean inside and out.
- Floors: Sweep, mop and wipe down hard floor surfaces. Vacuum all carpet surfaces.

Bathroom

- Walls: Wipe down all wall surfaces and doors, remove all nails and fill holes with spackling. Remove excess spackling to create smooth surface.
- Trim & Misc: Dust and wipe down all trim, heaters, vents, switch covers, and door knobs.
- Light Fixtures: Wash all light fixtures and replace burnt out light bulbs.
- Windows: Clean all windows, including tracks and window sills.
- Blinds: Dust and wipe down all blinds. Replace any broken blinds.
- Cabinets: Empty all cabinets and drawers, vacuum if needed, and thoroughly wash inside and out. Clean mirror.
- Sink/Fixtures: Clean sink, drains, faucets, towel racks and toilet paper holder.
- Countertops: Clean all countertops, including edges and corners.
- Bathtub/shower: Completely clean all surfaces inside and outside of bathtub/shower.
- Toilet: Completely clean all surfaces of the toilet, including inside, and outside.
- Floors: Sweep, mop and wipe down all floor surfaces. Be sure to get into the corners and behind/around the toilet.

Closets

- Walls: Wipe down all wall surfaces and doors, remove all nails and fill holes with spackling. Remove excess spackling to create smooth surface.
- Trim & Misc: Dust and wipe down all trim, heaters, vents, switch covers, and door knobs.
- Light Fixtures: Wash all light fixtures and replace burnt out light bulbs.
- Shelves: Wipe down all shelf surfaces, including rods.

Garage/Outbuildings/Landscaping

- Remove all personal belongings and trash from the property
- Sweep shelves and floor surfaces of all garages and outbuildings.
- Mow and weed eat lawn. Dispose of grass clippings.
- Remove all weeds from the flower beds.

General Make-Ready

- Ensure all smoke detectors are accounted for and have a working battery.
- Ensure carbon monoxide detector is accounted for and has a working battery.
- Ensure all damages have been repaired.
- Ensure all personal property and trash is removed from the property.
- After you have completed this checklist, do a final walk-thru to ensure all items have been properly completed.
- Please leave garage door openers in the kitchen.
- When you have completed this checklist and have done your final walk-thru of the property, please give us a call to arrange returning your keys.

Your carpets will be professionally cleaned after you have returned your keys. We have enjoyed the opportunity to have you as a tenant. Please let us know if we can assist you in any way in the future.

Thank you!

Forwarding Address Form for Deposit Refund

Your closing statement and deposit refund will be returned to you in the form of one check made out to all tenants. Before you move, please complete this form and leave it in the kitchen. Failure to return this form may delay your receiving your deposit refund.

Today's Date: _____ Rental Address: _____

Tenant Name: _____

Forwarding Address: _____

Phone: _____ Email: _____

Tenant Name: _____

Forwarding Address: _____

Phone: _____ Email: _____

Tenant Name: _____

Forwarding Address: _____

Phone: _____ Email: _____

Tenant Name: _____

Forwarding Address: _____

Phone: _____ Email: _____

Tenant Name: _____

Forwarding Address: _____

Phone: _____ Email: _____

If there is a preference on who should be sent the deposit refund, please indicate that here: _____(Name)

Move-Out Survey
Tell Us What You Think!

Thank you for giving us the opportunity to have you as our tenant. In an effort to continually improve our rentals and our service, please consider taking this brief survey and let us know what think about us and about the home you rented!

On a Scale of 1 (Lowest) – 5 (Highest)

How would you rate the service you received from us? 1 2 3 4 5

How would you rate the quality of service you received while renting your home in regards to handymen and contractors? 1 2 3 4 5

How would you rate your overall experience with us? 1 2 3 4 5

In Your Own Words...

What is your overall impression of the home you rented?

_____

What did you like **most** about the home you rented from us?

_____

What did you like **least** about the home you rented from us?

_____

Do you have any suggestions for improvements we could make to the home?

_____

Additional Comments?

_____

Would you rent from us again or refer others to us in the future? Yes/No

Thanks for taking the time to complete this short survey! Please leave the completed form in the home when it has been completed. We value your opinion.

Disposition of Deposit

Tenant Name(s) _____ Date _____
Rental Address _____
Mailing address _____

Credits (Funds Held in Deposit)

Security Deposit $_____
Other Rent $_____
Pet Deposit/Key Deposit $_____
Other Deposits $_____
Total Credits $_____

Debits (Funds Being Withheld from Your Deposit)

Nonrefundable Fees $_____
Rent for period_____ through _____ $_____
Unpaid Utilities $_____
Lock Change: $_____
Late Fees, NSF, Legal Services: $_____
Carpet Cleaning: $_____
Cleaning (See Below): $_____
Damages (See Below): $_____
Other (See Below): $_____
Total Debits: $_____

Additional Details Concerning Debits: (Any Additional Details Will Be Included on Additional Pages)

_____
_____
_____

Total Credits $_____
Total Debits $_____

TOTAL AMOUNT OF MONEY DUE TO ___TENANT ___LANDLORD: $_____

Manager Signature _____ Date_____

The final credit or debit listed on this Disposition of Deposit does not waive the Landlord's right to pursue additional claims should they become apparent.

Landlord/Tenant Resources for the 50 States

DISCLAIMER: The following pages include a very brief summary of the state-specific laws of the most common issues landlord's face on a daily basis. At the bottom of each section is a link where you can read more in-depth about your state's landlord-tenant laws. This summary for each of the 50 states is not meant to be exhaustive, nor can we guarantee that each summary is 100% accurate, as laws are often unclear and change often. These summaries are to be used for informational purposes only, are not legal advice, and are not meant to be a substitute for each person doing their own due-diligence in learning the specific landlord-tenant laws for their area.

Alabama:

Late Notice Required: 7-Day Notice to Pay or Quit

Lease Violation Notice Required: 10-Day Notice to Remedy

Late Fees: Late fee must be reasonable and mentioned in the lease

Lease Termination Timeline: 30-days for month-to-month. No mention for termination of annual

Security Deposit Laws: Maximum amount of one-month's rent. Any refunded amount must be itemized and returned within 60 days

Move-in/Move-out Document: Not required unless withholding security deposit

Notice to Enter: 48-hours, unless emergency

State Law(s): http://www.aanahq.org/Resources/Documents/lltenantact.pdf

Alaska:

Late Notice Required: 7-Day Notice to Pay or Quit

Lease Violation Notice Required: 10-Day Notice to Remedy

Late Fees: No automatic late fee unless agreed beforehand

Lease Termination Timeline: 30-days for month-to-month. No mention for termination of annual

Security Deposit Laws: Maximum deposit of two-month's rent. Any refunded amount must be itemized and returned within 14 days

Move-in/Move-out Document: Not required unless withholding Security deposit

Notice to Enter: 24-hours, unless emergency

State Law(s): http://www.law.alaska.gov/department/civil/consumer/3403010.html

Arizona:

Late Notice Required: 5-Day Notice to Pay or Quit

Lease Violation Notice Required: 10-Day Notice to Remedy

Late Fees: No Late Fee unless 5-day grace period is given

Lease Termination Timeline: 30-days for month-to-month. No mention for termination of annual

Security Deposit Laws: Maximum deposit of one and a half-month's rent (prepaid and deposit combined). Any refunded amount must be itemized and returned within 14 days.

Move-in/Move-out Document: Move-in is required. Move-out not required unless withholding security deposit

Notice to Enter: 48-hours, unless emergency

State Law(s): https://housing.az.gov/sites/default/files/documents/files/AZ%20Residential%20Landlord%20and%20Tenant%20Act%20-%20Revised%20July%203%202015.pdf

Arkansas:

Late Notice Required: 5-Day Unconditional Quit notice

Lease Violation Notice Required: 10-Day Notice to Remedy / 5-Day Notice for health & safety violations

Late Fees: Late fee must be reasonable and mentioned in the lease

Lease Termination Timeline: 30-days for month-to-month. No mention for termination of annual

Security Deposit Laws: (For Landlords with 5+ rental units only) Maximum deposit of two-month's rent. Any refunded amount must be itemized and returned within 30 days.

Move-in/Move-out Document: Not required unless withholding security deposit

Notice to Enter: 24-hours, unless emergency

State Law(s): http://www.arlegalservices.org/system/files/FS-LandlordTenant-AG.pdf

California:

Late Notice Required: 3-Day Notice to Pay or Quit

Lease Violation Notice Required: 3-Day Notice to Remedy

Late Fees: Reasonable late fees allowed and must be mentioned in the lease.

Lease Termination Timeline: 30-days for month-to-month. No mention for termination of annual Security Deposit Laws: Maximum deposit of two-month's rent (for unfurnished) and three-month's rent (for furnished). Any refunded amount must be itemized and returned within 21 days.

Move-in/Move-out Document: Not required unless withholding security deposit above $126.

Notice to Enter: 24-hours, unless emergency

State Law(s): http://www.dca.ca.gov/publications/landlordbook/index.shtml

Colorado:

Late Notice Required: 3-Day Notice to Pay or Quit

Lease Violation Notice Required: 3-Day Notice to Remedy

Late Fees: Late fee must be reasonable and mentioned in the lease

Lease Termination Timeline: 7-days for month-to-month (if less than 6 months), and 60-days for month-to-month (if more than 6 months). No mention for termination of annual if definitive, and 91-Day Notice if no fixed date.

Security Deposit Laws: Any refunded amount must be itemized and returned within 30 days, no more than 60 days

Move-in/Move-out Document: Not required unless withholding security deposit

Notice to Enter: 24-hours, unless emergency

State Law(s): https://dola.colorado.gov/app_uploads/docs/Renter_booklet_2009.pdf

Connecticut:

Late Notice Required: 3-Day Notice to Pay or Quit

Lease Violation Notice Required: 15-Day Notice to Remedy

Late Fees: Late fee must be reasonable and is not allowed to be assessed until the 10th day of due rent. Must be outlined in the lease.

Lease Termination Timeline: 3-days for month-to-month and for the termination of annual

Security Deposit Laws: Maximum deposit of two-month's rent (one month for tenant over 62). Any refunded amount must be itemized and returned within 30 days.

Move-in/Move-out Document: Not required unless withholding security deposit

Notice to Enter: Reasonable notice period, unless emergency

State Law(s): http://www.jud.ct.gov/lawlib/law/landlord.htm

Delaware:

Late Notice Required: 5-Day Notice to Pay or Quit (7-Day for manufactured homes)

Lease Violation Notice Required: 7-Day Notice to Remedy (10-Day for manufactured homes)

Late Fees: No more than 5% of the rent. May not charge until the 5th day late, if the landlord has an office within the same county. If not, then not until the 8th day late

Lease Termination Timeline: 60-days for month-to-month and 60-days for the termination of fixed term lease

Security Deposit Laws: Maximum deposit of one-month's rent. Any refunded amount must be itemized and returned within 20 days

Move-in/Move-out Document: Not required unless withholding security deposit

Notice to Enter: 48-hours, unless emergency

State Law(s): http://www.delcode.delaware.gov/title25/c053/index.shtml

Florida:

Late Notice Required: 3-Day Notice to Pay or Quit

Lease Violation Notice Required: 7-Day Notice to Remedy

Late Fees: Must be reasonable and be mentioned in the lease

Lease Termination Timeline: 15-days for month-to-month and 60-days for the termination of annual

Security Deposit Laws: No maximum. Must be returned within 15 days if getting a full refund, or within 30 days if any deductions are made

Move-in/Move-out Document: Not required unless withholding security deposit

Notice to Enter: 12-hours, unless emergency

State Law(s): http://www.leg.state.fl.us/Statutes/indexcfm?App_mode=Display_Statute&URL=0000-0099/0083/0083.html

Georgia:

Late Notice Required: 7-Day Notice to Pay or Quit

Lease Violation Notice Required: 10-Day Notice to Remedy

Late Fees: Late fee must be reasonable and be mentioned in the lease

Lease Termination Timeline: 60-days for month-to-month and 60-days for the termination of annual

Security Deposit Laws: Any refunded amount must be itemized and returned within 30 days

Move-in/Move-out Document: Move-in required to disclose any damage to the premises. Move-out not required unless withholding Security deposit

Notice to Enter: 24-hours, unless emergency

State Law(s): https://www.dca.ga.gov/housing/housingdevelopment/programs/downloads/Georgia_Landlord_Tenant_Handbook.pdf

Hawaii:

Late Notice Required: 5-Day Notice to Pay or Quit

Lease Violation Notice Required: 10-Day Notice to Remedy

Late Fees: Must be specified in rental agreement

Lease Termination Timeline: 45-days for month-to-month (by landlord) and 28-days for month-to-month (by tenant). No mention for the termination of annual

Security Deposit Laws: Maximum deposit of one-month's rent. Any refunded amount must be itemized and returned within 14 days

Move-in/Move-out Document: Not required unless withholding security deposit

Notice to Enter: 48-hours, unless emergency

State Law(s): http://cca.hawaii.gov/hfic/files/2013/03/landlord-tenant-handbook.pdf

Idaho:

Late Notice Required: 3-Day Notice to Pay or Quit

Lease Violation Notice Required: 3-Day Notice to Remedy

Late Fees: Late fee must be reasonable and specified in the lease

Lease Termination Timeline: One-month for month-to-month and annual with no end date.

Security Deposit Laws: No maximum. Must be returned within 21 days (may be adjusted if agreed by both the landlord and tenant, but may not exceed 30 days). If deductions are made it must be accompanied by a signed, itemized statement.

Move-in/Move-out Document: Not required unless withholding security deposit

Notice to Enter: No specifications, but lease must disclose landlord's rights for entry.

State Law(s): http://www.ag.idaho.gov/publications/consumer/LandlordTenant.pdf

Illinois:

Late Notice Required: 5-Day Notice to Pay or Quit

Lease Violation Notice Required: 10-Day Notice to Remedy

Late Fees: Late fee must be reasonable and mentioned in the lease

Lease Termination Timeline: 30-days for month-to-month. 60-days for termination of annual

Security Deposit Laws: No maximum, but must be returned within 30-45 days.

Move-in/Move-out Document: Not required unless withholding security deposit

Notice to Enter: Any reasonable notice, unless emergency

State Law(s): http://www.ilga.gov/legislation/ilcs/ilcs3.asp?ActID=2201&ChapterID=62

Indiana:

Late Notice Required: 10-Day Notice to Pay or Quit

Lease Violation Notice Required: No statute, though an Unconditional Quit Notice may be served in certain situations.

Late Fees: Late fee must be reasonable and mentioned in the lease

Lease Termination Timeline: 30-days for month-to-month, 3-months for termination of annual (with a fixed end-date).

Security Deposit Laws: No maximum, however, any refunded amount must be itemized and returned within 45 days

Move-in/Move-out Document: Not required unless withholding security deposit

Notice to Enter: Any reasonable notice, unless emergency

State Law(s): https://iga.in.gov/static-documents/5/2/0/b/520b05dc/TITLE32_title32.pdf

Iowa:

Late Notice Required: 3-Day Notice to Pay or Quit

Lease Violation Notice Required: 7-Day Notice to Remedy

Late Fees: Late fee may be assessed up to the limit of $60 per month ($12 per day - for rents less than $700 per month) and up to the limit of $100 per month ($20 per day - for rents more than $700 per month)

Lease Termination Timeline: 30-days for month-to-month, and 30-days for annual

Security Deposit Laws: Maximum deposit of two-month's rent. Any refunded amount must be itemized and returned within 30 days

Move-in/Move-out Document: Not required unless withholding security deposit

Notice to Enter: 24-hours, unless emergency

State Law(s): https://coolice.legis.iowa.gov/Cool-ICE/default.asp?Category=billinfo&Service=IowaCode&input=562A

Kansas:

Late Notice Required: 3-Day Notice to Pay or Quit for tenancies less than 3 months, 10-Day Notice for tenancies of more than 3 months.

Lease Violation Notice Required: 7-Day Notice to Remedy

Late Fees: Late fee must be mentioned in the lease

Lease Termination Timeline: 30-days for month-to-month, 30-day for termination of annual (with no fixed date)

Security Deposit Laws: Maximum deposit of one-month's rent (for unfurnished units) and one and a half-month's (for furnished units). Any refunded amount must be itemized and returned within 30 days

Move-in/Move-out Document: Required within 5 days of start of the lease

Notice to Enter: Any reasonable notice, unless emergency

State Law(s): http://www.kslegislature.org/li_2012/b2011_12/statute/058_000_0000_chapter/058_025_0000_article/

Kentucky:

Late Notice Required: 7-Day Notice to Pay or Quit

Lease Violation Notice Required: 15-Day Notice to Remedy

Late Fees: Late fee must be addressed in the lease

Lease Termination Timeline: 30-days for month-to-month, no mention for termination of annual

Security Deposit Laws: Any refunded amount must be itemized and returned within 30 days

Move-in/Move-out Document: Required

Notice to Enter: 48-hours, unless emergency

State Law(s): http://www.lrc.ky.gov/Statutes/chapter.aspx?id=39159

Louisiana:

Late Notice Required: 5-Day Notice to Pay or Quit

Lease Violation Notice Required: 5-Day Notice to Remedy

Late Fees: Late fee allowed if specified in the lease

Lease Termination Timeline: 10-day for month-to-month, and and 30-days for annual with no specific end date

Security Deposit Laws: Any refunded amount must be itemized and returned within 30 days

Move-in/Move-out Document: Not required unless withholding security deposit

Notice to Enter: 24-hours (recommended), unless emergency

State Law(s): https://www.ag.state.la.us/Shared/ViewDoc.aspx?Type=3&Doc=476

Maine:

Late Notice Required: 7-Day Notice to Pay or Quit

Lease Violation Notice Required: 7-Day Notice to Remedy

Late Fees: 4% late fee allowed and should be mentioned in the lease

Lease Termination Timeline: 30-days for month-to-month, 30-days for annual with no specific end-date. In some situations 7-days is allowed.

Security Deposit Laws: Maximum deposit of two-month's rent. Any refunded amount must be itemized and returned within 30 days

Move-in/Move-out Document: Not required unless withholding security deposit

Notice to Enter: Any reasonable notice, unless emergency

State Law(s): http://www.maine.gov/tools/whatsnew/attach.php?id=27933&an=1

Maryland:

Late Notice Required: 5-Day Notice to Pay or Quit

Lease Violation Notice Required: 30-Day Notice, 14-Day Notice if violation is a threat to the safety of others.

Late Fees: Maximum of 5% late fee allowed.

Lease Termination Timeline: One month for month-to-month, 7 days for weekly, 3 months for termination of annual, and 30-days for annual with definitive dates

Security Deposit Laws: Maximum deposit of two-month's rent. Any refunded amount must be itemized and returned within 45 days

Move-in/Move-out Document: Required within 15 Days

Notice to Enter: Any reasonable notice, unless emergency

State Law(s): https://www.oag.state.md.us/consumer/landlords.htm

Massachusetts:

Late Notice Required: 14 Day Notice to Pay or Quit

Lease Violation Notice Required: No mention

Late Fees: Late fee must be reasonable and addressed in the lease, but may not be collected until after rent is 30 days late.

Lease Termination Timeline: 30-days for month-to-month, no mention for termination of annual Security Deposit Laws: Maximum amount of one-month's rent. Any refunded amount must be itemized and returned within 30 days

Move-in/Move-out Document: Required within 10 days of move-in against which the tenant has 15 days to sign and return. Move-out not required unless withholding security deposit

Notice to Enter: Any reasonable notice, unless emergency

State Law(s): http://www.mass.gov/ago/docs/consumer/landlord-tenant-guide.pdf

Michigan:

Late Notice Required: 7-Day Notice to Pay or Quit

Lease Violation Notice Required: 30-Day Notice to Remedy

Late Fees: Late fee must be reasonable enough to compensate the landlord, not punish the tenant

Lease Termination Timeline: 30-days for month-to-month, no mention for termination of annual Security Deposit Laws: Maximum amount of one and a half-month's rent. Any refunded amount must be itemized and returned within 30 days

Move-in/Move-out Document: Required

Notice to Enter: Any reasonable notice, unless emergency

State Law(s): http://www.legislature.mi.gov/publications/tenantlandlord.pdf

Minnesota:

Late Notice Required: 14-Day Notice to Pay or Quit

Lease Violation Notice Required: 7-Day Notice to Remedy

Late Fees: Late fee may not more than 8% of the total rent and must be written in lease agreement

Lease Termination Timeline: 30-days for month-to-month, no mention for termination of annual Security Deposit Laws: No defined policy for maximum deposit, however interest of 1% per year is due on all deposits. Any refunded amount must be itemized and returned within 21 days

Move-in/Move-out Document: Not required unless withholding security deposit

Notice to Enter: Any reasonable notice, unless emergency

State Law(s): https://www.revisor.mn.gov/statutes/?id=504b

Mississippi:

Late Notice Required: 3-Day Notice to Pay or Quit

Lease Violation Notice Required: 30-Day Notice to Remedy

Late Fees: Late fee must be reasonable and mentioned in the lease

Lease Termination Timeline: 30-days for month-to-month, no mention for termination of annual Security Deposit Laws: Any refunded amount must be itemized and returned within 45 days

Move-in/Move-out Document: Not required unless withholding security deposit

Notice to Enter: Any reasonable notice, unless emergency

State Law(s): http://www.mslegalservices.org/resource/landlord-tenant-law-in-mississippi

Missouri:

Late Notice Required: Unconditional Pay or Quit

Lease Violation Notice Required: 10-Day Notice to Remedy

Late Fees: Late fee must be reasonable and mentioned in the lease

Lease Termination Timeline: 30-days for month-to-month, no mention for termination of annual Security Deposit Laws: Maximum amount of two-month's rent. Any refunded amount must be itemized and returned within 30 days

Move-in/Move-out Document: Not required unless withholding security deposit

Notice to Enter: Any reasonable notice, unless emergency

State Law(s): http://www.ago.mo.gov/docs/default-source/publications/landlord-tenantlaw.pdf?sfvrsn=4

Montana:

Late Notice Required: 3-Day Notice to Pay or Quit

Lease Violation Notice Required: 14-Day Notice to Remedy

Late Fees: Late fee must be reasonable and mentioned in the lease

Lease Termination Timeline: 30-days for month-to-month, no mention for termination of annual Security Deposit Laws: Any refunded amount must be itemized and returned within 30 days (10 days if no deduction from the deposit)

Move-in/Move-out Document: Move-in required. Move-out not required unless withholding security deposit

Notice to Enter: 24-hours, unless emergency

State Law(s): http://leg.mt.gov/bills/mca_toc/70_24.htm

Nebraska:

Late Notice Required: 3-Day Notice to Pay or Quit

Lease Violation Notice Required: 14-Day Notice to Remedy

Late Fees: Late fee must be reasonable and mentioned in the lease

Lease Termination Timeline: 30-days for month-to-month, no mention for termination of annual Security Deposit Laws: Maximum amount of one-month's rent. Any refunded amount must be itemized and returned within 14 days

Move-in/Move-out Document: Not required unless withholding security deposit

Notice to Enter: 24-hours, unless emergency

State Law(s): http://www.nrec.ne.gov/legal/landlordacttoc.html

Nevada:

Late Notice Required: 5-Day Notice to Pay or Quit

Lease Violation Notice Required: 5-Day Notice to Remedy

Late Fees: Late fee must be reasonable and mentioned in the lease

Lease Termination Timeline: 30-days for month-to-month, no mention for termination of annual Security Deposit Laws: Maximum amount of three-month's rent. Any refunded amount must be itemized and returned within 30 days

Move-in/Move-out Document: Not required unless withholding security deposit

Notice to Enter: 24-hours, unless emergency

State Law(s): http://www.leg.state.nv.us/nrs/nrs-118a.html

New Hampshire:

Late Notice Required: 7-Day Notice to Pay or Quit

Lease Violation Notice Required: 30-Day Notice to Remedy

Late Fees: Late fee must be reasonable and mentioned in the lease

Lease Termination Timeline: 30-days for month-to-month, no mention for termination of annual Security Deposit Laws: Maximum amount of one-month's rent or $100 - whichever is greater (only for landlords owning more than 6 units). Any refunded amount must be itemized and returned within 30 days

Move-in/Move-out Document: Move-in required within 5 days. Move-out not required unless withholding security deposit

Notice to Enter: Any reasonable notice, unless emergency

State Law(s): http://doj.nh.gov/consumer/sourcebook/renting.htm

New Jersey:

Late Notice Required: For Federally subsidized housing only: 14 Day Notice to Pay or Quit

Lease Violation Notice Required: 7-Day Notice to Remedy

Late Fees: Late fee must be reasonable enough to compensate the landlord (and must be written), not to punish the tenant. Shouldn't be assessed before 5 business days

Lease Termination Timeline: 30-days for month-to-month, no mention for termination of annual Security Deposit Laws: Maximum amount of one and a half-month's rent. Any refunded amount must be itemized and returned within 30 days

Move-in/Move-out Document: Not required unless withholding security deposit

Notice to Enter: Any reasonable notice, (preferably 24-hours), unless emergency

State Law(s): http://www.state.nj.us/dca/divisions/codes/offices/landlord_tenant_information.html

New Mexico:

Late Notice Required: 3-Day Notice to Pay or Quit

Lease Violation Notice Required: 7-Day Notice to Remedy

Late Fees: Not more than 10% of the total rent

Lease Termination Timeline: 30-days for month-to-month, no mention for termination of annual Security Deposit Laws: Maximum amount of one month's rent. Any refunded amount must be itemized and returned within 30 days

Move-in/Move-out Document: Move-in is required. Move-out not required unless withholding security deposit

Notice to Enter: 24-hours, unless emergency

State Law(s): http://www.lawhelpnewmexico.org/content/obligations-landlords-and-tenants-safety-maintenance-and-repairs

New York:

Late Notice Required: 10-Day Notice to Pay or Quit

Lease Violation Notice Required: 10-Day Notice to Remedy

Late Fees: Allowed, but not out of rent's proportion

Lease Termination Timeline: 30-days for month-to-month, 90-150 days for rent stabilized lease, and 15-30 days for non-rent stabilized lease

Security Deposit Laws: No state maximum defined

Move-in/Move-out Document: Not required unless withholding security deposit

Notice to Enter: Any reasonable notice, unless emergency

State Law(s): https://www.ag.ny.gov/sites/default/files/pdfs/publications/Tenants_Rights.pdf

North Carolina:

Late Notice Required: 10-Day Notice to Pay or Quit

Lease Violation Notice Required: Immediate Notice to Remedy

Late Fees: Maximum of 5% or $15 (whichever is greater) for monthly and 5% or $4 for weekly

Lease Termination Timeline: 7-days for month-to-month, 2-days for week-to-week, one-month for yearly with no fixed terms, and no requirement for yearly with definitive terms

Security Deposit Laws: Maximum amount of two week's rent for week-to-week, one and a half month's rent for month-to-month, and two-month's rent for longer than monthly. Any refunded amount must be itemized and returned within 30 days

Move-in/Move-out Document: Not required unless withholding security deposit

Notice to Enter: Any reasonable notice, unless emergency

State Law(s): http://www.ncleg.net/gascripts/Statutes/StatutesTOC.pl?Chapter=0042

North Dakota:

Late Notice Required: 3-Day Notice to Pay or Quit

Lease Violation Notice Required: 3-Day Notice to Remedy

Late Fees: Late fee must be reasonable and mentioned in the lease

Lease Termination Timeline: 30-days for month-to-month, no mention for termination of annual

Security Deposit Laws: Maximum amount of one month's rent. Any refunded amount must be itemized and returned within 30 days

Move-in/Move-out Document: Move-in required. Move-out not required unless withholding security deposit

Notice to Enter: Any reasonable notice, unless emergency

State Law(s): https://www.ag.nd.gov/Brochures/FactSheet/Tenant-Rights.pdf

Ohio:

Late Notice Required: 3-Day Notice to Pay or Quit

Lease Violation Notice Required: 3-Day Notice to Remedy

Late Fees: Late fee is allowed, must be reasonable, and mentioned in the lease

Lease Termination Timeline: 30-days for month-to-month, no mention for termination of annual Security Deposit Laws: No maximum security deposit. Any refunded amount must be itemized and returned within 30 days

Move-in/Move-out Document: Not required unless withholding security deposit

Notice to Enter: Any reasonable notice, unless emergency

State Law(s): http://codes.ohio.gov/orc/5321

Oklahoma:

Late Notice Required: A landlord may pursue eviction within 5 days of written notice to the tenant of the delinquent rent.

Lease Violation Notice Required: 15-Day Notice to Remedy

Late Fees: Late fee is allowed, must be reasonable, and mentioned in the lease

Lease Termination Timeline: 30-days for month-to-month, no mention for termination of annual Security Deposit Laws: No maximum security deposit. Any refunded amount must be itemized and returned within 30 days

Move-in/Move-out Document: Not required unless withholding security deposit

Notice to Enter: 24-hours, unless emergency

State Law(s): https://www.ok.gov/OREC/documents/Landlord%20 and%20Tenant%20Act%20Update.pdf

Oregon:

Late Notice Required: 72-Hour Notice to Pay or Quit

Lease Violation Notice Required: 30-Day Notice to Remedy

Late Fees: May charge reasonable flat fee after 5 days, or every day not exceeding 6% of the flat fee, or 5% of rent every 5 days

Lease Termination Timeline: 30-days for month-to-month, no mention for termination of annual with fixed terms, and 60-days for annual with no fixed terms

Security Deposit Laws: No maximum security deposit. Any refunded amount must be itemized and returned within 31 days

Move-in/Move-out Document: Not required unless withholding security deposit

Notice to Enter: 24-hours, unless emergency

State Law(s): http://www.oregonlaws.org/ors/chapter/90

Pennsylvania:

Late Notice Required: 10-Day Notice to Pay or Quit

Lease Violation Notice Required: 30-Day Notice to Remedy

Late Fees: Late fee must be reasonable and mentioned in the lease

Lease Termination Timeline: 30-days for month-to-month, no mention for termination of annual with fixed terms, and 30-days for annual with no fixed terms

Security Deposit Laws: Maximum amount of two month's rent for first year, one month's rent for subsequent years. Any refunded amount must be itemized and returned within 30 days

Move-in/Move-out Document: Not required unless withholding security deposit

Notice to Enter: Preferably 24-hours, unless emergency

State Law(s): http://www.tenant.net/Other_Areas/Penn/harris/pa-toc.html

Rhode Island:

Late Notice Required: 5-Day Notice to Pay or Quit (after 15 Day Grace Period)

Lease Violation Notice Required: 20-Day Notice to Remedy

Late Fees: Late fee must be reasonable and mentioned in the lease

Lease Termination Timeline: 30-days for month-to-month, 10-days for week-to-week, three-months for yearly with no fixed terms, and no requirement for yearly with definitive terms

Security Deposit Laws: Maximum amount of one month's rent. Any refunded amount must be itemized and returned within 20 days

Move-in/Move-out Document: Not required unless withholding security deposit

Notice to Enter: 48-hours, unless emergency

State Law(s): http://webserver.rilin.state.ri.us/Statutes/title34/34-18/index.htm

South Carolina:

Late Notice Required: 5-Day Notice to Pay or Quit

Lease Violation Notice Required: 14-Day Notice to Remedy

Late Fees: Allowed

Lease Termination Timeline: 30-days for month-to-month, no mention for termination of annual

Security Deposit Laws: No maximum security deposit. Any refunded amount must be itemized and returned within 30 days

Move-in/Move-out Document: Not required unless withholding security deposit

Notice to Enter: 24-hours, unless emergency

State Law(s): https://www.scbar.org/public/files/docs/tenantsrights.pdf

South Dakota:

Late Notice Required: 3-Day Notice to Pay or Quit

Lease Violation Notice Required: 3-Day Notice to Remedy

Late Fees: Late fee must be reasonable and mentioned in the lease

Lease Termination Timeline: 30-days for month-to-month. Termination terms for annual with no end-date must be in writing.

Security Deposit Laws: Maximum amount of one month's rent. Landlord must return any refund and an itemized list of deductions within 2 weeks. If tenant requests an itemization of damages, landlord has 45 days to supply that to the tenant.

Move-in/Move-out Document: Not required unless withholding security deposit

Notice to Enter: 24-hours, unless emergency

State Law(s): http://legis.sd.gov/Statutes/Codified_Laws/Display-Statute.aspx?Statute=43-32&Type=Statute

Tennessee:

Late Notice Required: 14-Day Notice to Remedy, 30-Days to vacate

Lease Violation Notice Required: 30-Day Notice

Late Fees: May be charged after 5-day grace period, not exceeding 10% of the rent

Lease Termination Timeline: 30-days for month-to-month, 10-days for week-to-week. No mention for termination of annual with fixed terms

Security Deposit Laws: No maximum security deposit. Any refunded amount must be itemized and returned within 30 days

Move-in/Move-out Document: Not required unless withholding security deposit

Notice to Enter: No defined law, but preferred to be 24-hours, unless emergency

State Law(s): http://www.laet.org/getattachment/993c9198-f323-49c2-981a-3ea3327df17b/Tenant_Rights_Under_The_Uniform_Residential.aspx

Texas:

Late Notice Required: 3-Day Notice to Pay or Quit

Lease Violation Notice Required: No defined law

Late Fees: Late fee must be reasonable and mentioned in the lease (1-day Grace Period is required)

Lease Termination Timeline: 30-day for month-to-month and annual

Security Deposit Laws: No maximum security deposit. Any refunded amount must be itemized and returned within 30 days

Move-in/Move-out Document: Not required unless withholding security deposit

Notice to Enter: Any reasonable notice, unless emergency

State Law(s): http://guides.sll.texas.gov/landlord-tenant-law

Utah:

Late Notice Required: 3-Day Notice to Pay or Quit

Lease Violation Notice Required: 3-Day Notice to Remedy

Late Fees: Late fee must be reasonable and mentioned in the lease

Lease Termination Timeline: 15-days for month-to-month and annual

Security Deposit Laws: No maximum security deposit. Any refunded amount must be itemized and returned within 30 days

Move-in/Move-out Document: Not required unless withholding security deposit

Notice to Enter: 24-hours, unless emergency

State Law(s): http://www.utahlegalservices.org/public/self-help-webpages/utah-renters-handbook

Vermont:

Late Notice Required: 14-Day Notice to Pay or Quit

Lease Violation Notice Required: 30-Day Notice to Remedy

Late Fees: A late fee which is not reasonably related to expenses incurred by the landlord due to the late rent is invalid and the tenant does not have to pay it. If in writing in the lease, the landlord may charge the tenant only for any expenses incurred because of the late payment.

Lease Termination Timeline: 30-days for month-to-month, 21-days for week-to-week, and 90-days for tenants who've been living for more than 2 continuous years in a property

Security Deposit Laws: No maximum security deposit. Any refunded amount must be itemized and returned within 14 days or 60 days for seasonal rentals

Move-in/Move-out Document: Not required unless withholding security deposit

Notice to Enter: 48-hours, unless emergency

State Law(s): https://www.cvoeo.org/fileLibrary/file_99.pdf

Virginia:

Late Notice Required: 5-Day Notice to Pay or Quit

Lease Violation Notice Required: 21-Day Notice to Remedy and 30-Day Notice to Quit

Late Fees: Late fee must be reasonable and mentioned in the lease

Lease Termination Timeline: 30-days for month-to-month, 90-days for termination of annual Security Deposit Laws: Maximum amount of two-month's rent. Any refunded amount must be itemized and returned within 45 days

Move-in/Move-out Document: Move-in required within 5 days. Move-out not required unless withholding security deposit

Notice to Enter: 24-hours, unless emergency

State Law(s): http://www.dhcd.virginia.gov/HomelessnesstoHomeownership/PDFs/Landlord_Tenant_Handbook.pdf

Washington:

Late Notice Required: 3-Day Notice to Pay or Quit

Lease Violation Notice Required: 10-Day Notice to Remedy or Quit

Late Fees: A reasonable late fee may be charged, but must be outlined in the lease. Late fee of 20% or $20.00, whichever is greater, is considered reasonable.

Lease Termination Timeline: 20-day for month-to-month. No mention for termination of annual with fixed terms

Security Deposit Laws: No maximum security deposit. Any refunded amount must be itemized and returned within 14 days

Move-in/Move-out Document: Move-in required. Move-out not required unless withholding security deposit

Notice to Enter: 24-hours, unless emergency

State Law(s): http://apps.leg.wa.gov/rcw/default.aspx?cite=59.18

Washington DC:

Late Notice Required: 30-Day Notice to Pay or Quit

Lease Violation Notice Required: 30-Day Notice to Remedy

Late Fees: Late fee must be reasonable and mentioned in the lease

Lease Termination Timeline: 30-days for month-to-month. No mention for termination of annual with fixed terms

Security Deposit Laws: Maximum amount of one-month's rent. Any refunded amount must be itemized and returned within 45 days

Move-in/Move-out Document: Move-in required within 3 days. Move-out not required (within 10 days, if required) unless withholding security deposit

Notice to Enter: 24-hours, unless emergency

State Law(s): http://ota.dc.gov/sites/default/files/dc/sites/ota/publication/attachments/Tenant_Survival_Guide.pdf

West Virginia:

Late Notice Required: No Notice to Pay or Quit

Lease Violation Notice Required: No Notice to Remedy

Late Fees: No limit on the late fees, but must be mentioned in the lease

Lease Termination Timeline: 30-days for month-to-month, 7-days for week-to-week, 90-days for termination of annual with no fixed terms

Security Deposit Laws: Maximum amount of one-month's rent. Any refunded amount must be itemized and returned within 14 days

Move-in/Move-out Document: Not required unless withholding security deposit

Notice to Enter: Any reasonable notice, unless emergency

State Law(s): http://www.legis.state.wv.us/wvcode/code.cfm?chap=37&art=6

Wisconsin:

Late Notice Required: 14-Day Notice for monthly or annual terms, and 30-Day Notice for terms longer than a year

Lease Violation Notice Required: Not specified

Late Fees: Late fee is allowed but must be mentioned in the lease

Lease Termination Timeline: 28-days for month-to-month

Security Deposit Laws: No maximum security deposit. Any refunded amount must be itemized and returned within 21 days

Move-in/Move-out Document: Move-in required within 7 days. Move-out not required unless withholding security deposit

Abandonment Procedure: To be mentioned in the lease

Notice to Enter: 12-hours (24-hours in Madison), unless emergency

State Law(s): http://www.legis.state.wv.us/wvcode/code.cfm?chap= 37&art=6

Wyoming:

Late Notice Required: 3-Day Notice to Pay or Quit

Lease Violation Notice Required: Not specified

Late Fees: Late fee is allowed but must be mentioned in the lease

Lease Termination Timeline: 30-days Notice

Security Deposit Laws: No maximum security deposit. Any refunded amount must be itemized and returned within 30 days

Move-in/Move-out Document: Not required unless withholding security deposit

Notice to Enter: Preferably 24-hours, unless emergency

State Law(s): http://digitalcommons.law.wne.edu/cgi/viewcontent.cg i?article=1064&context=facschol

MORE FROM BIGGERPOCKETS

If you enjoyed this book, we hope you'll take a moment to check out some of the other great material BiggerPockets offers. BiggerPockets is the real estate investing social network, marketplace, and information hub, designed to help make you a smarter real estate investor through podcasts, blog posts, videos, forums, files, and more./ Sign up today—it's free! www.BiggerPockets.com

Be sure to also read:

The Book on Rental Property Investing

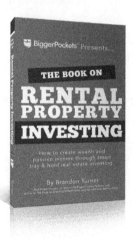

The Book on Rental Property Investing, written by real estate investor and co-host of the BiggerPockets Podcast Brandon Turner, contains nearly 400 pages of in-depth advice and strategies for building wealth through rental properties. You'll learn how to build an achievable plan, find incredible deals, pay for your rentals, and much, more more!

If you've ever thought of using rental properties to build wealth or obtain financial freedom, this book is a "must read." Pick up your copy today by visiting www.biggerpockets.com/rentalbook.

FREE: *The Ultimate Beginner's Guide to Real Estate Investing*

The Ultimate Beginner's Guide to Real Estate Investing is a free guide designed to help you build a solid foundation for your venture into real estate. In the eight chapters of this book, you'll learn how to best gain an education (for free), how to pick a real estate niche, and how to find, fund, and manage your latest real estate investment. Get it free today at www.biggerpockets.com/ubg.

The Book on Investing in Real Estate with No (and Low) Money Down

Is a lack of money holding you back from real estate success? It doesn't have to! In this groundbreaking book from Brandon Turner, author of *The Book on Rental Property Investing*, you'll discover numerous strategies a real estate investor can use to buy real estate using other people's money.

Less "hype" and more "practical strategies," you'll learn the top strategies that savvy investors are using to buy, rent, flip, wholesale properties at scale! Get it today at www.biggerpockets.com/nomoney.

The Book on Tax Strategies for the Savvy Real Estate Investor

Taxes! Boring and irritating, right?

Perhaps. But if you want to succeed in real estate, your tax strategy will play a HUGE role in how fast you grow. A great tax strategy can save you thousands of dollars a year - and a bad strategy could land you in legal trouble.

That's why BiggerPockets is excited to introduce its newest book, The Book on Tax Strategies for the Savvy Real Estate Investor! To help you deduct more, invest smarter, and pay far less to the IRS! Get it today at www.biggerpockets.com/taxbook.

The Book on Flipping Houses

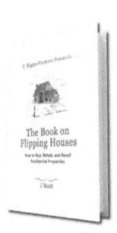

The Book on Flipping Houses, written by active real estate fix-and-flipper J Scott, contains more than 300 pages of detailed, step-by-step training perfect for both the complete newbie and the seasoned pro looking to build a killer house-flipping business.

Whatever your skill level, *The Book on Flipping Houses* will teach you everything you need to know to build a profitable, efficient house-flipping business and start living the life of your dreams. Get it at www.biggerpockets.com/flippingbook.

The Book on Estimating Rehab Costs

One of the most difficult tasks for a real estate investor is estimating repairs. To help you overcome this obstacle, J Scott and BiggerPockets pull back the curtain on the rehab process and show you not only the cost ranges and details associated with each and every aspect of a rehab, but also the framework and methodology for estimating rehab costs. You'll discover how to accurately estimate the variety of costs you will likely face while rehabbing a home as well as which upgrade options offer the biggest bang for your buck.

Whether you are an experienced home renovation specialist or still learning how to screw in a light bulb, this valuable resource will be your guide to staying on budget, managing contractor pricing, and ensuring a timely profit. Get it at www.biggerpockets.com/rehabbook.

ABOUT THE AUTHORS

This book was co-written by Brandon and Heather Turner, a husband & wife residing in Montesano, Washington with their two Yorkie dogs and two cats. Together they own Open Door Properties LLC, an investment company focused on "value-add" real estate opportunities and self-managing their investments. Brandon focuses primarily on the acquisition, while Heather focuses primarily on the management. Brandon is also the co-host of the weekly BiggerPockets Podcast, the most popular real estate podcast in the world.

For more information about The Turners, check out www. BrandonTurner.me or OpenDoorPropertiesLLC.com.

END NOTES

[i] http://www.justice.gov/usao-ndca/pr/justice-department-obtains-80000-settlement-housing-discrimination-lawsuit-against

[ii] http://portal.hud.gov/hudportal/HUD?src=/program_offices/fair_housing_equal_opp/disabilities/sect504faq

[iii] http://portal.hud.gov/hudportal/HUD?src=/program_offices/fair_housing_equal_opp/FHLaws/yourrights

[iv] http://portal.hud.gov/hudportal/HUD?src=/program_offices/fair_housing_equal_opp/FHLaws/yourrights

[v] http://www.credit.com/credit-scores/what-is-a-good-credit-score/

[vi] http://portal.hud.gov/hudportal/HUD?src=/program_offices/fair_housing_equal_opp/disabilities/sect504faq

[vii] http://portal.hud.gov/hudportal/HUD?src=/topics/housing_choice_voucher_program_section_8

[viii] http://www.hud.gov/offices/fheo/library/occupancystds.pdf

[ix] http://www.nolo.com/legal-encyclopedia/tax-rules-hiring-resident-property-managers.html

[x] https://en.wikipedia.org/wiki/Self_storage

[xi] http://www.energystar.gov/products/lighting_fans/light_bulbs

[xii] http://apps.leg.wa.gov/rcw/default.aspx?cite=59.18.070

CPSIA information can be obtained
at www.ICGtesting.com
Printed in the USA
JSHW031222300720
7014JS00002B/7